Internet-Based Workplace Communications:

Industry & Academic Applications

Kirk St.Amant
Texas Tech University, USA

Pavel Zemliansky
James Madison University, USA

 Information Science Publishing

Hershey • London • Melbourne • Singapore

Acquisition Editor:	Mehdi Khosrow-Pour
Senior Managing Editor:	Jan Travers
Managing Editor:	Amanda Appicello
Development Editor:	Michele Rossi
Copy Editor:	Maria Boyer
Typesetter:	Amanda Appicello
Cover Design:	Lisa Tosheff
Printed at:	Yurchak Printing Inc.

Published in the United States of America by
      Information Science Publishing (an imprint of Idea Group Inc.)
      701 E. Chocolate Avenue, Suite 200
      Hershey PA 17033
      Tel: 717-533-8845
      Fax: 717-533-8661
      E-mail: cust@idea-group.com
      Web site: http://www.idea-group.com

and in the United Kingdom by
      Information Science Publishing (an imprint of Idea Group Inc.)
      3 Henrietta Street
      Covent Garden
      London WC2E 8LU
      Tel: 44 20 7240 0856
      Fax: 44 20 7379 3313
      Web site: http://www.eurospan.co.uk

Library of Congress Cataloging-in-Publication Data

Internet-based workplace communications : industry & academic applications / Kirk
St.Amant, editor, Pavel Zemliansky, editor.
     p. cm.
  Includes bibliographical references and index.
  ISBN 1-59140-521-1 (h/c) -- ISBN 1-59140-522-X (s/c) -- ISBN 1-59140-523-8 (eisbn)
  1. English language--Business English--Study and teaching (Higher)--Computer
network resources. 2. English language--Rhetoric--Study and teaching--Computer
network resources. 3. Business communication--Computer-assisted instruction. 4.
Business communication--Computer network resources. 5. Business
writing--Computer-assisted instruction. 6. Business writing--Study and teaching
(Higher) 7. Internet in education. I. St.Amant, Kirk, 1970- II. Zemliansky,
Pavel.
  PE1479.B87I58 2005
  808'.06665--dc22
                              2004017924

British Cataloguing in Publication Data
A Cataloguing in Publication record for this book is available from the British Library.

All work contributed to this book is new, previously-unpublished material. The views expressed in
this book are those of the authors, but not necessarily of the publisher.

Internet-Based Workplace Communications:
Industry & Academic Applications

Table of Contents

Foreword

The essays in this collection advance the project of articulating online work-places as real and significant, as complex networks of relations that we need to take seriously. The emergent culture of networked communication poses many interesting challenges for researchers, teachers, and writers, as the essays in *Internet-Based Workplace Communications: Industry & Academic Application* make clear. In an emergent culture, even the terminologies we use to identify the subject are contested, making it difficult to agree on what we're writing about in the first place, not to mention our reasons for studying it or how we might best meet the challenges it poses.

What do we mean, for instance, by *workplace*? A workplace is simply a *place* where people *work*, right? Most will recognize that the *work* in *workplace* is a complex term with a wide range of meanings. But these days, even *place* need not be construed strictly as physical space, a geographical location in the material world. The structural metaphors of the World Wide Web already define the Internet as a place: we *travel* the information *superhighway*, visit *sites*, chat in *rooms*, manage *domains*, sit on *couches* in MOOs, and so on. Yet even though we invest digital space with the spirit of place, it's an inside joke (but with everyone on the inside). We know that virtual reality is still "unreal," an imitation with just enough difference to remind us of the "really" real. Films like those in *The Matrix* trilogy reinforce this impression that we live in two worlds: one manufactured by computers imprisoning us in an illusion (the matrix) as avatars, and another we're stuck with but that offers some hope of freedom and a better life as living beings (Zion). As Neal Stephenson wryly put it in *Snow Crash*, in this world, we're meatware, living avatars in the hardscape.

As many of the essays in this collection suggest, it may be time to rethink our conception of workplace to allow for the possibility that real work takes place in digital spaces, that the modern workplace is not simply a site, a home office, campus, a "place of employment," or a "work environment" in the desert of the real. The place of work is online, too. It is a place where real people work and communicate, where things get done, and where we spend many waking moments. This place is not an illusion. It is every bit as real as the ground we walk on, for many of the same reasons that thoughts or feelings or dreams are real.

We have naturally carried with us our familiarity with the real to digital spaces, using our metaphors to make it comfortable, but we now need to examine whether the forms of understanding that this familiarity cultivates has prevented us from seeing what's going on there. Students, teachers, and researchers need to know the lay of the land. The contexts of time and place shape our rhetorics in nuanced ways, or at least ought to in the *kairotic* moment. Inexperienced writers—regardless of the situation—usually presume that what worked elsewhere will work anywhere; they sometimes don't appreciate—or even recognize—how situations change or may be different in concrete ways. *Kairos*, the sense of what goes with what and where and when, is particularly challenging when the where and when is digital and thus capable of perpetual transformation. What's the first response to such complexity? All situations are the same, and we, inexperienced or not, can rely on the familiar terminology of material and print culture—not to mention the land and timescape—to explain and rationalize our acts in the digitized workplace.

Those of us who teach communication need to imagine the digital workplace as new territory so that we can help people communicate effectively and creatively when they work there. As John Logie notes in "Cut and Paste: Remixing Composition Pedagogy for Online Workspaces," institutional, context-based priorities shape production and practice. He reiterates James Porter and Patricia Sullivan's call in *Opening Spaces* for "reflective practices (*praxis*) that are sensitive to the rhetorical situatedness of participants and technologies that recognize themselves as a form of political and ethical action" (p. ix). Ideology exerts its influence online just as it does in bricks-and-mortar workplaces, and perhaps more obviously so. As Logie makes clear, traditional notions of authorship have regulated copyright and intellectual property law as well as composition's conception of plagiarism. When we apply reflective practices in online workplaces—to describe what people say and do there—we can see more clearly how the ideology of authorship prescribes practice and pedagogy that may no longer serve our needs or the needs of academic and corporate institutions. With such analysis, writes Logie, we learn that we can "create discursive power *without* necessarily assuming the mantle of authorship." We begin to appreciate differences manifest in space and time—context—and in other terms, not ones laced with the terminologies that reduce the unusual or different to the familiar. Essays in this collection by Mark R. Freiermuth, Stacey L. Connaughton and Brent D. Ruben, and Melody Bowdon describe how workplace simulations and virtual networks draw out these differences for students, making composition more real, but also reinforcing the principle of *kairos*. Connaughton and Ruben, for instance, note that in such settings, "Success involves creating messages that are well received by authorities, leaders, experts, and by peers, subordinates, and members of the general public. And, it is often the case that discourse that works well for one group does not resonate with others." Brian Still shows us how the Open Source community functions as a fascinating workplace even when the "work" may be unpaid or unattached to any commercial enterprise, and even when the people clearly have other identities they play out in other contexts. In fact, it is the nature of OS community as purely digital that makes it such a powerful force, one that we can learn from as we imagine new workplaces. Wendy Warren Austin, Jo Mackiewicz, Shawn McIntosh, and Rhonna J. Robbins-Sponaas and Jason Nolan, each in their distinct ways, show us how people work and write in digital spaces. All contribute to our understanding of what the nature of *work* in this new *place* looks like so that we'll know it when we see it, evaluate it, or perform it ourselves.

In "Telework: A Guide to Professional Communication Practices," Nancy A. Wiencek shows us how radically different the online workplace really may be. As I read her essay, I couldn't help but wonder why I hadn't yet imagined teleworking as a site for internships and apprenticeships. It's easy for me to understand why, in many respects, I'm a teleworker myself, even though I hold an academic position in a real place with walls around the classrooms and people strolling the campus. I am frequently approached by students at Purdue about the possibility of internships with Parlor Press, the publishing company I started last year. I would love to work with students in internships, but an internship with the Press would break the mold of internships, here or anywhere, I think.

In almost all respects, Parlor Press is a digital phenomenon. We publish "real" printed books, but almost all of that work is conducted via the Internet, with manuscripts, correspondence, and all the usual activity of a press managed electronically. There are no board or marketing meetings to observe in the hardscape. The books are printed in Tennessee, hundreds of miles to the south. I worry that the student's internship experience would be markedly different from what we might have originally intended when we created such opportunities in the curriculum. I might rarely see interns, for example, and we might meet only once or twice in-person. Then I catch myself using *seeing* and *meeting* in the senses we're all used to, but that the digital workplace challenges. Internships with Parlor Press would be *digital* internships and would almost certainly throw into question typical requirements that internships be in some setting, with the sense that *setting* does not entail the *digital*. A workplace observation for a Parlor Press intern would have to happen in that "other" place, with perhaps some assistance from hidden surveillance cameras, keyboard trackers, and some spyware. What would we need to do to our conception of internships to imagine them as teleworking?

The pace at which software systems change makes keeping up to speed extremely difficult. The production methods, distributed responsibilities, document cycling protocols, and even communication norms of professional writing, teaching, and research in the digital workplace are the forms of discursive power we need to cultivate in students. But we need to ensure we have this discursive power ourselves, too. Perhaps most perplexing about Internet-based workplace communication is that we have only begun to understand the nature of this power, and we may be even further behind the curve in wielding such power ourselves. These essays collectively suggest that we had better get started if we hope to give our work as teachers and writers the value and attention it deserves.

David Blakesley
Purdue University and Parlor Press, USA

Preface

The Internet has greatly changed how we communicate. Now, online media such as email and chat rooms allow individuals to overcome barriers of time and space to interact directly and instantly with persons located in distant regions. Additionally, online media permit users to share information easily and quickly with vast audiences. Individuals, for example, can email files to an almost unlimited number of recipients, or they can present ideas in the form of Web pages that can be viewed by an international audience. As a result, Internet-based technologies allow humans to interact on a previously unprecedented scale. The benefits of this type of communication have led to the widespread use of online media in professional settings.

Internet-based communication often relates to writing. That is, one generally uses writing, or typed text, to share information with others. The text in a Web page, for example, provides users with the information needed to understand or to navigate the related site. Moreover, media such as email, online chats, and listservs often reduce interactions to typed messages exchanged among individuals. The writing process is therefore essential to effective communication through Internet-based media.

While many organizations have recognized the benefits of online communication technologies, each can have its own perspective on what constitutes best practices for communicating through (or writing for) these media. A disconnect between the communication expectations of different groups can thus affect how successfully individuals interact when moving from one group to another. Perhaps the greatest shock in relation to this transition can be seen in students who move from an academic environment to the workplace. That is, educators may teach students the uses of specific online media and writing practices related to those media. Employers, however, might have different expectations of the communication technologies with which new employees should be familiar and the best methods for communicating through those media. For this reason, writing and communication instructors need to understand different aspects of online communication technologies so they can better prepare students for success after graduation. It is equally important that employers understand methods used to teach online communication practices so they can better anticipate the knowledge base and the skills sets new graduates bring to the workplace.

This kind of "mutual understanding" between academia and industry is particularly important at this point in time, for online communication technologies have led to major shifts in how the workplace is configured. A growing number of employees now participate in teleworking—a practice in which individuals work from home, but use online media to interact with the office or the corporate headquarters. Similarly, more individuals are participating in virtual teams in which coworkers located in different regions use online media to collaborate on the same project. Furthermore, the ability of online media to transcend borders has resulted in an increasing amount of work being done by individuals in other nations. A result of this international outsourcing is that workplace communication increasingly involves online media as a mechanism for managing international employees or for interacting with overseas colleagues.

In all of these situations, written communication is key. It facilitates the level of information sharing needed for individuals to interact successfully outside of traditional workplace environments. It is therefore important that writing and communication instructors understand discourse via online media in order to prepare students for success in their future careers. Similarly, a familiarity with uses of online media in communication instruction provides employers with insights on the abilities of prospective employees and on models for Internet-based interactions. By overviewing how online media can be integrated into educational practices, one can create a foundation for dialogue between academics and employers. Through such dialogue, these parties can work to establish the kind of education needed for success in an online age.

The purpose of this collection is to provide academics and businesspersons with the foundation for such a dialogue. To achieve this end, the collection brings together 14 essays that examine different aspects of communication via online media. These entries have been organized into six major sections, and each section focuses on concepts or approaches related to writing and online communication. In essence, the entries in a section provide examples for thinking about or applying particular technologies in different settings. Readers can use these examples to consider methods for employing online media within their related academic or industry practices. Ideally, the breadth of topics covered in these essays will create a common knowledge base for discussion related to producing good students who will also be effective employees.

The book's first section, "Computer Technology in Written Communication Instruction: A Historical Overview," provides a foundation for understanding how online communication technologies have become an important component in the teaching of communication. In this section, Mark D. Hawthorne offers a

first-hand account of this process as he experienced it during his 40-year tenure in higher education. Hawthorne begins with a story of how engineering
students in the '60s used mainframe computers to examine the stylistics of
Milton, and continues to his present experiences teaching courses in online
publications. In his account, Hawthorne overviews how changes in technologies—and attitudes toward technologies—affect educational practices. While
this chapter is not a comprehensive history of the topic, it provides readers with
important insights on the attitudes (both enthusiastic and hesitant) associated
with adopting new technologies into academia. These insights can serve as a
guide for readers considering the use of online media in their teaching practices. The chapter also draws interesting—though indirect—connections between how trends in business and technology can affect education. Such a
perspective could provide readers with ideas for how academia and industry
may form partnerships around mutual interests in online communication practices.

The book's second section, "Online Approaches to Teaching Communication,"
overviews how instructors have integrated online media into different writing
and communication classes. Ideally, this section will provide ideas for how educators can use different technologies and teaching approaches in their classes.
The essays in this section can also provide businesspersons with an overview
of the kinds of learning experiences available to students. Additionally, the information presented in these chapters could serve as a foundation for industry-
academic partnerships in which students explore the effectiveness of new methods of exchanging information online.

The objective of Wendy Warren Austin's chapter, "Hypertext Theory and Web
Writing Assignments in the Writing and Professional Communication Classroom," is to propose that writing and communication instructors focus less on
the technical aspects of Web page publication and more on teaching principles
of hypertext, visual design, and writing for online media. Austin notes that more
professional and technical communication courses incorporate assignments involving Web page creation, as do many first-year composition classes. This
convergence, Austin explains, creates interesting paradoxes for both instructors and professional website developers. To avoid such situations, Austin advocates that basic hypertext principles be taught in prerequisite courses, so
instructors can spend more time teaching the advanced hypertext theories and
the software applications used to generate such texts.

In their chapter, "Millennium Leadership Inc.: A Case Study of Computer and
Internet-Based Communication in a Simulated Organization," Stacey L.
Connaughton and Brent D. Ruben present an approach to teaching distanced
leadership and mediated communication competencies. The authors' objectives
in presenting this approach are to explain how one can use simulation as an
instructional model, to highlight the outcomes of this approach, and to discuss

how educators, students, and professionals may benefit from such a design. To achieve this end, Connaughton and Ruben focus on three key aspects:

1. Discussing the role of simulations for approximating "real-world" dynamics within the classroom.
2. Presenting a course design that allows educators to do so.
3. Giving examples of computer and Internet-based communication from this course, Leadership in Groups and Organizations, which they developed at Rutgers University.

Through this focus, readers learn how simulations help students develop "real-world" communication competencies in geographically dispersed contexts. Such a perspective could also be beneficial to individuals who participate in international teams connected by online media.

Classroom environments can benefit from asynchronous computer-mediated communication (CMC) such as online discussion groups, for they can enhance instruction in a number of ways. Shawn McIntosh explores this relationship between technology and teaching in his chapter, "Expanding the Classroom: Using Online Discussion Forums in College and Professional Development Courses." In the chapter, McIntosh examines asynchronous CMC, specifically an online discussion group, in graduate-level writing and communication classes. He also explores how the discussion groups improved the learning environment in five major ways. McIntosh then offers advice for using online discussion groups in different classes, as well as warns of pitfalls related to such media. Academics and businesspersons can use McIntosh's perspective as a guide when they consider using such technologies as a part of their organization's communication practices.

Online media often facilitate collaboration by creating communities around a particular topic or project. The book's third section, "Perspectives for Internet-Based Collaboration," examines instructional models used to facilitate such online collaboration. Educators can use the approaches in this section to plan their own online collaborative activities, as can businesspersons who use online media to create virtual work teams.

In his chapter "Creating Community in the Technical Communication Classroom," Timothy D. Giles examines how listservs can create a sense of community in technical communication classes. He begins by examining the notion of "community" through reviewing the literature related to composition and community, and then examining the concept of Psychological Sense of Community (PSC). Giles next explains how he used the Sense of Community Index (SCI) to examine community in four classes—two that used listservs and two that did not. The purpose of this comparison is to determine how online communities compare to those formed in more traditional (offline) contexts. Academics and businesspersons alike can use Giles' findings as a mechanism for creating effective online work groups (communities) around certain projects.

In her essay "Virtual Networks: Mapping Community-Based Collaboration and Professional Writing," Melody Bowdon argues that the Internet has blurred the lines between the professional writing needs of for-profit and non-profit organizations. As a result of such blurring, Bowdon claims, professional writing teachers need to train their students to work in a variety of environments. In addition to traditional training that prepares students for the workplace, Bowdon advocates exposing professional writing students to the non-profit sector.

Rhonna J. Robbins-Sponaas and Jason Nolan's chapter, "MOOs: Polysynchronous Collaborative Virtual Environments," defines, describes, and assesses the form of collaborative virtual learning environment known as MOOs. The chapter deals with understanding what a MOO is, what features make it a valuable collaborative environment, and issues of accessibility, access, and governance. The chapter considers text-based multimedia environments; general features of synchronous and asynchronous technologies; the notion of polysynchrony; tools for rapid prototyping, education, or training of users; application accessibility; costs in hardware, software, and manhours; and whether it's worth organizations getting involved in MOOs at their present state of development.

As noted earlier, online media are global in nature, for they allow individuals in different nations to interact with relative speed and ease. As a result, instructors and businesspersons could find themselves using such media to interact with students, counterparts, or managers located in different nations. Linguistic difference, however, could cause communication problems in such exchanges. The book's fourth section, "Internet Approaches to English as a Second Language Instruction," examines this situation by focusing on Internet-based approaches to teaching English as a Second Language (ESL). The essays in this section familiarize readers with methods for helping ESL students and employees improve their proficiency in English.

The section begins with Julia Lavid's chapter, "Developing a Web-Based Course for the Conventional English Grammar Classroom: Issues in Planning and Design." In her essay, Lavid presents a model for incorporating the Internet into in a traditional grammar course for non-native English speakers. Lavid hopes that her approach will encourage more ESL teachers to blend Web-based tools into traditional face-to-face courses—a perspective that could also benefit corporate training practices.

In "A Bridge to the Workplace: Using an Internet-Based Simulation in the Writing Classroom," Mark R. Freiermuth overviews an online approach to decision-making simulation in an academic writing class comprising 26 ESL students in Japan. The students in the study constructed an online glossary aimed at building sufficient background knowledge related to the simulation. Teams of students then created online documents that demonstrated their understanding of the simulation problem and offered potential solutions to situations. In this process, students received information via the Web, and all related documents were posted to student homepages. Assessment and observation revealed that the simulation motivated students by making connections between simulation activities and career choices. The results of such a study can serve as an impetus for similar simulations in academia, business, and government.

The degree of access facilitated by online media mean that they can often be a key mechanism for seeking assistance. In the case of education, this assistance could come in the form of online tutoring; in the case of industry, it is often embodied by online help activities. In both cases, it is imperative that assistance providers understand the needs and the goals of their clients in order to provide beneficial information. The book's fifth section, "Internet-Based Tutoring," presents perspectives for providing help though online media. While the essays in this section focus on tutoring practices related to writing, the ideas and approaches covered in these chapters provide insights for how businesses could provide online assistance.

In the section's first essay, "The State of Online Writing Labs: Have They Fulfilled Their Potential?," Jo Mackiewicz presents a study of 343 online writing labs (also known as OWLs). Through this presentation, Mackiewicz tries to answer the question of whether OWLs are fulfilling their potential by becoming fully interactive spaces where tutors help students become better writers through email and other media of electronic communication. The article also suggests future directions for the development of online writing labs. While such perspectives relate to educational (tutoring) practices, these results could also provide industry with insights on how to create interactive online help services.

Amy Lee Locklear's chapter, "Is This a Real Person? A Tutor's Response to Navigating Identity in the Spaces of a Synchronous Electronic Writing Center," explores some of the theoretical and pedagogical issues that emerged from a study of identity, collaboration, and discourse methods in online writing centers. The premise of this study was to advance tutor training when transitioning from traditional face-to-face to synchronous online interactions. The study reveals the complexities of online identity perception and projection, and how it affects tutoring methods in online environments.

The book's sixth and final section, "Future Trends in Computer Use for Written Communication," examines how certain business, legal, and technical trends could affect communication through online media. While the topics covered in this section are by no means comprehensive, they do provide insights on important developments that can affect online communication in both the classroom and the workplace.

The section begins with Nancy A. Wiencek's chapter, "Telework: A Guide to Professional Communication Practices." In this chapter, Wiencek discusses the need to rethink professional communication practices as a result of the growing popularity of telecommuting. According to Wiencek, telework has had a significant impact on both task-oriented and personal aspects of written communication. The author calls for a dialog between teleworkers and their managers in order to re-negotiate professional communication practices.

The section's second chapter, Brian Still's "An Open Source Primer," provides readers with an overview of Open Source Software (OSS). In this chapter, Still defines OSS and OSS movement, and explains the differences between OSS and proprietary software and the effects this difference could have on educational and workplace practices. Still believes that OSS will grow in popularity, and more and more organizations will rely on it. As a result, organizations need to know the benefits and the limitations of OSS in order to make more intelligent choices related to the kinds of software they will use.

In the section's final chapter, "Cut and Paste: Remixing Composition Pedagogy for Online Workspaces," John Logie expresses his concern with what he sees as a widening gap between traditional composition pedagogies and the realities of workplace communication. In his related discussion, Logie focuses particularly on how composition pedagogy often promotes the view of the writer as a solitary creator of the text, yet individuals in the workplace usually operate in teams. In order to address this gap, Logie offers pedagogical advice designed to promote a connection between the teaching of writing and the realities of workplace communication. Through such an approach, Logie provides readers from academia and industry with a framework from which dialogue can begin.

Online media provide academics and educators with a key point of overlap as both parties continually search for new ways to use the Internet in their activities. The readings in this collection can provide a mutual base of knowledge the two can use to explore online communication in terms of their own objectives and in terms of working with the "other." Ideally, this mutual understanding will help readers realize how perspectives on and uses of online media can contribute to the learning process and to industry practices. Such a mutual understanding can, in turn, contribute to an academia-industry dialogue that will result in the cooperation needed to help individuals make the transition from students to employees.

Kirk St.Amant, Editor
Pavel Zemliansky, Editor

Acknowledgments

The editors would like to thank all involved in the creation of this collection. We thank the expert editorial and production staff at Idea Group Publishing for their support of this book, in particular, Michele Rossi, Jan Travers, and Amanda Appicello for their assistance and professionalism throughout this project.

Our thanks also go out to all of the professionals who contributed to this collection; their expertise and commitment to teaching and to bridging the gap between academia and industry are greatly appreciated.

Finally, we wish to thank our families, colleagues, and friends for their love, friendship, and support with this project.

Kirk St.Amant, Editor
Pavel Zemliansky, Editor

Section I

Computer Technology in Written Communication Instruction:
A Historical Overview

Chapter I

Forty Years with Computer Technology:
A Personal Remembrance of Things Past

Mark D. Hawthorne
James Madison University, USA

Abstract

Technology and society are inevitably intertwined. As a result, changes in one affect the other, often in new and unexpected ways. This chapter examines how computing technology and online communication technologies have changed teaching practices in higher education. This chapter provides a first-person account of how computers and online media have changed the ways in which teachers and students approach materials.

Introduction

If three years is a generation in computer development, my experiences with computer-assisted teaching and research span almost 13 generations. Of course, the possibility of computer-assisted writing and professional communication in college was only science fiction then. Still, during the first seven generations, technology frightened academia that believed any technological intrusion would tarnish its self-proclaimed humanist facade; the last six, this same academia, sometime reluctantly and seldom enthusiastically, was forced to tolerate its proclaimed enemy and to explore how it could be accommodated without loss of face. This chapter is one person's experiences during these 13 generations. What I have learned is simple:

- Most prefer to live in ruts; they resist change.
- To grow, some must explore the unknown; they must resist the resisters.
- Usually, resistance is frustrating and can be stifling; it is easier to stay in the rut.

Living in a rut is boring.

1960s and 1970s – The Time Before Time

In the 1950s and early 1960s, most established faculty members in English departments accepted C.P. Snow's concept of two cultures. They believed that most, if not all, of the problems of their world stemmed from a breakdown of communication between the sciences and the humanities, and they fervently held that the responsibility for this breakdown lay with the scientists who lacked a proper humanistic education. Science and technology could not begin to teach the essential truths of Chaucer, Shakespeare, and Milton. After all, hadn't they recently released the atomic age along with the Cold War? Only humanists could pass on the best thoughts of the best men of the best ages.

Throughout the '60s, I proudly used a large, noisy Rheinmetall desktop type-writer that seemed to me the latest in technology, though probably made before WW2. I found the machine in a grimy pawnshop, and spent more having it cleaned and repaired than its original price. It was what any English student needed, and I became the envy of my friends. Unlike other office manuals, I could set multiple tabs accessible by tab keys, access a number of non-standard glyphs including clear diacriticals, format mathematical equations, and type on a sensitive keyboard that reacted to my slightest touch so I could type five clean carbons. In a way quite foreign to my experiences with computers, I personalized the machine as if it were an automobile or a friend; after all, "he" saw me through my graduate work and my first book. The only thing that he lacked was the ability to produce characters in the Greek alphabet.

Earning undergraduate majors in Classical Greek and English (all literature, no theory and no composition), I should have easily accepted the traditionalist line. But there were three influences that pointed me in another direction. First, I came from a family of engineers, problem solvers who lived by high ethical standards but relied on science and technology. Second, one afternoon when I had just finished mouthing off the expected diatribe against modernism, William Ruff, the Victorian specialist who directed my dissertation, silenced me by pointing out that my Rheinmetall and my new Fisher hi-fi were pieces of technology. As was his way, he sneered that no great poet or novelist—Mark Twain excepted, perhaps—ever composed on a machine, and no scratchy recording could do justice to Giulietta Simionato's voice. Third, Ants Oras, one of the kindest and most sensitive teachers in the interpretation of literature, had recently published one of the driest and most meticulous studies of prosody, *Pause Patterns in Elizabethan and Jacobean Drama: An Experiment in Prosody* (1960); he demonstrated that great poetry could be "felt along the veins" even while he introduced me to the rigorous study of prosody and the mathematical precision of great art.

So what does this have to do with my experiences with computers in higher education? As a result of these influences, I learned how to use a computer in literary and prosodic research.

My first tenure-track position was in a university primarily known for engineering programs. The majority of students, of course, interpreted this to mean that humanities departments were evil, hated because they flunked many of their classmates but tolerated because some mythological authority claimed that they needed an "exposure to art." One of my earliest teaching assignments was a required course that included *The Canterbury Tales*, *Paradise Lost*, and *Hamlet*. I was supposed to bridge the gulf between uninterested and bored engineering majors and Humanism (always spelled with a capital), and show these thickheaded scientific types that they need the lessons from great literature to live meaningful lives. My first semester was a miserable failure. Neither my students nor I believed the high-falutin rhetoric; I felt as if I were wearing a mask that concealed what I actually believed, and I realized that I wanted no part of this hypocrisy. I wrote several drafts of a resignation letter. Then, before I wrote a final draft, I found myself thinking about Bill and Ants and, after long telephone conversations with each of them, concluded that I wasn't what was wrong—the whole way the department forced literature on these kids was wrong. Maybe I needed to put literature on a basis that spoke directly to them. The notion was heresy of the first degree.

As brazen as only a first-year, idealistic teacher can be, I set out to reform the program. Without telling anyone what I planned, I skipped all of the Chaucer except the "Miller's Tale." I read the plot of *Hamlet* from *Masterplots*; then, I asked the class to pick roles and do an acted reading of the play. Amid much joking and laughter at the casting because there were no girls in the class, I described the Elizabethan theater, and the boys listened. Students who did not have acting roles became directors and "one-penny" spectators (another opportunity to sneak in a short lecture). After a couple weeks, engineering and architecture majors were actually enjoying the play and were doing homework to figure out how to interpret it. But how do you follow *Hamlet* with *Paradise Lost*? Again, I began with a plot synopsis; then, I asked the students to develop their own research projects. Smirking at what they hoped to get away with, a group of them (the "one-penny" crowd) asked if they could figure the distance between heaven and hell if measured by earthly physical laws, considering the size of the angels and the probable density of both worlds. I agreed, provided they supported all their arguments from the poem. I divided the class into five teams of five students each (with representatives of as many majors as possible on each team) and stipulated that each team needed to work in secret and be prepared to present its conclusions at a later time in the semester. They read *Paradise Lost* with more attention than the students in my first semester classes, and during their presentations defended their conclusions by offering different interpretations of the text. True, this was hardly what the required class was intended to produce; when the faculty member assigned to the new people observed my class, I received a low evaluation and many suggestions on how I should improve. But it turned me into a dedicated heretic.

For my Fall sections, I pulled out of my file a project that I had begun under Ants; I asked a class to read "Lycidas" before we started *Paradise Lost*. For homework, I asked 20 unbelieving young men to count and record the number of syllables in each line, and to determine where in the poem there were any lines that varied from the 10-syllable base pattern. Then, I asked if they could find any discernable pattern in these variations. They now read the poem for its meaning. Again, students who found usual approaches to poetry alien became interested. As in their engineering and architecture classes, they started with raw materials and advanced toward the aesthetic merging of those materials into a final product. Many were intrigued by poetry for the first time.

During one especially spirited argument about statistical variation, a discussion that I didn't understand at all, a student suggested that they use a computer to examine line length variance. As a member of the English Department, I had no access to the school's computer, and the thought of using one of them had not entered my imagination. But the class jumped on this suggestion and began to plot how they could set up a program. This I understood less than statistics, so between hatching a plot and trying to explain it to me, they set about to attempt a project when they could sneak computer time. But using a computer in the 1960s was almost impossible—why would someone want to study prosody? Why would someone even be interested? Furthermore, why would anyone financially support such an outrageous undertaking when computer time was both rare and expensive? We were in the midst of the Cold War, and computers were zealously guarded for "significant" or "real" research.

This was before the establishment of a Computer Science Department, and I don't remember who was in charge of the computers or what rules governed their use. But several students had access to a cardpunch machine and agreed to create a program to analyze line length. A mathematics or statistics student got the help of a faculty member who was amused by the project and gave them access time. I don't know how they talked him into it. With much argumentation among the students on how to write the program and what they wanted as results, they punched what ended up as a wheelbarrow of cards. The whole endeavor was clandestine because they used the cardpunch and the mainframe in the middle of the night, and like conspirators we were all sworn to secrecy. Of course, this cast a mystique over the whole endeavor. One night at about 3:00 a.m., the professor and a couple students led me into a dark basement filled with intimidating machines and a steady hum of electrical current doing something. It seemed as if I had entered Dr. Frankenstein's laboratory.

They introduced me to a machine where one of my students typed cards one by one. Whenever he finished one, it moved and another took its place. It seemed a tedious procedure, and the student agreed but pointed out that it was the necessary first step. Then, they showed me "THE COMPUTER." Flashing light bulbs seemed to mean something to everyone else; to me, they were just another reason to question why I had let myself be talked into this absurdity. I tried to follow the explanation of what was going on, but the main thing I gathered was that cards had to be "processed" and the computer had to wait until all the cards were read before it could do whatever it was supposed to do. The wait seemed interminable. But, for the first time, I understood why "Do not fold, spindle, or mutilate" was printed on all the cards we had to mess with at registration; any slightly mutilated card jammed the feeders. Finally, paper began to emerge from a noisy teleprinter; when I looked, it was almost illegible lines of numbers—completely incomprehensible. Everyone else seemed pleased.

A couple weeks later, the students made a class presentation. They concluded that while there were repeated instances of different length lines, some of which fell into repeated patterns, there was no overall pattern; that is, the project resulted in the conclusion that the irregularities were accidental. At the same time, they concluded that the project had positive results, mainly that prosodic variation could be computer analyzed but was probably too time intensive and expensive to be a valid research option. They encouraged me to continue the project during the next semester. This I did. Only this time we concentrated on *Paradise Lost*, different groups of students counting the number of syllables in each line, checking their findings against one another, trying to discover if there was any measurable variance in the different syllable counts, and suggesting creative but improbable hypotheses for their data. Unfortunately, the faculty member who had earlier gotten us into the computer room was no longer interested. We now worked with tables of handwritten numbers and slide rules.

The faculty member who evaluated my teaching took C.P. Snow literally. I received lower evaluation than the first. Even after 35 years, I still vividly remember my anger and the following meeting with the department head because I "used language unbecoming a gentleman."

At the time, I was ignorant of how others were integrating computer technology and literary studies. We worked alone or with local teams and shared information at conferences. It would be almost 20 years before I discovered that the Sedlows had coined the term "computational stylistics" or that Ted Nelson had coined the word "hypertext" to describe his Xanadu project. But about this time, my father sent me a copy of *Paul, the Man and the Myth* (1966), a statistical study of the letters of St. Paul. Here, A.Q. Morton and James McLeman analyzed word occurrence and sentence length to determine the authorship of Paul's letters. Also, I read the introduction to *The Cornell Concordance to the Poetry of Matthew Arnold* (1959) and Willard Smith's *Browning's Star-Imagery; The Study of a Detail in Poetic Design* (1965). I hoped that studies like these supported my belief that computer-based analysis would be the wave of the future.

When I met with the department head, I came armed with Morton and McLeman, but as a Sterne scholar more interested in biographical criticism than trying to merge literature and technology, he advised me to put aside such childish nonsense and continue my "significant" work on the Anglo-Irish novel and Browning's early poetry—research that was traditional and respectable. Surely, he argued, time was better spent in a "humanistic" approach to poetry than in concentrating on prosody or technique or unproductive teaching methods; besides, he concluded, what reputable journal would accept such nonsense. He refused to help me get access to computer time. This put an abrupt hiatus on any further computer-assisted research and an end to this approach to literature. During the next semester, he twice visited my classes and seemed satisfied that the students were getting a proper introduction to literature; it didn't matter that they were bored or that I was seething with resentment against the whole establishment—and myself for caving because I feared ending in Vietnam.

Surreptitiously, my work on Browning's *Sordello* kept alive an interest in repeated patterns in poetic structure, and my work on *Pauline*, his first published poem, kept alive my notion of how much computer analysis could help. At the time, I wanted to find ways to analyze the prosodic influence of Shelley on these two poems, an influence that was then much-debated and often offered as an explanation for the failure of Browning's early poems. In my opinion, Frederick Pottle's 1923 study, *Shelley and Browning: A Myth and Some Facts*, had many shortcomings. A more thorough comparison of their feminine caesurae and a statistical study of the placement of caesurae, the relation between masculine and feminine caesurae, and the relation between masculine and feminine end rimes seemed exactly the short of project that was custom-made for computer analysis.

A couple years later, I had to shelf such research when I accepted a position at a liberal arts university. Over the next decade computers, prosody, and statistics began to seem as strange to me as it had to my colleagues.

Then, one afternoon in the early '70s, two events rekindle my interest in using the technology. First, my brother showed me his "miniature" calculator: it was large, filling the better part of a briefcase, and very pricey (if I remember correctly, well over a hundred 1970 dollars). I think it was a TI Datamath and quite impressive. It was definitely the first time I saw an LED display. When I had played with it for a short time, I wanted to drag my earlier research out of the closet because this offered a fast and accurate way to calculate statistics. Second, while rereading Milton's preface to *Paradise Lost*, I recalled the "Lycidas" project. I began wondering if what Milton was telling us was that the matrix line in the epic was modeled on the syllabic prosody of the continent; that is, could it be a hybrid mixture of decasyllabic and iambic pentameter lines? Could this explain his reference to "apt numbers" in the 1674 edition?

In the midst of asking such questions, I returned to the tedious task of identifying the caesurae of each line in Browning's early poems. I figured that sooner or later, I could use a calculator like my brother's to crunch the numbers and reach reliable conclusions. When I found time, I got out my texts, marked caesurae, and recorded my figures in a notebook. But partly because the first and last lines of *Sordello* are the same, I became conscious of repeated words and phrases; I worked out a color code to mark these repetitions and hypothesized that they may operate sort of like Wagner's *leitmotifs*. Here was a topic ready made for computer analysis. Again, there was interest neither in technological studies or in the possibilities that computing could offer. Even more limiting were budgets; I could scarcely convince a dean that he should allocate a couple hundred dollars for equipment when my own salary was under $10,000. I finally completed all my figuring by color codes, paper charts, and a borrowed calculator; I wrote my article without technical or mathematical jargon so it could be published.

Soon afterwards, I was "promoted" to an administrative post and then moved as a department head to another university, taking on a much larger faculty with many classes and, of course, more students. The new position threw a new light on using technology. I had trashed my Rheinmetall for the newest technology: my secretary and I used an IBM Correcting Selectric II. I finally owned my own calculator (the price had fallen to about $100), had installed an open-reel tape player in my office, and unsuccessfully nagged the dean to let me purchase a Phillips laserdisc playback-only deck to use in classes. On the surface, everyone seemed comfortable with how technology was changing the workplace. The business world—at least the larger corporations and banks—had found main-frames (though I don't think we called them "mainframes" at the time). Even the university conducted more and more of its business on computers—although students still registered in the gym, we now distributed punch cards instead of keeping handwritten lists of whoever wanted to enroll in each class. We still scheduled over a hundred sections of Freshman English by pencil on large sheets of paper and had to produce four and five carbon copies of important letters, a procedure that usually left me with dirty hands. Class materials were either dittoed or mimeographed because the only copy machines on campus belonged to people like the president and vice-presidents. We trained student assistants to type mimeograph stencils, wax papers that were cut by the typewriter so that ink could run through them, and to hand crank the machine, a process that required the operator to keep an even flow of the thick ink. As time went on, we upgraded to an electric mimeograph machine and, even more advanced, a spirit duplicator that was cheaper but could produce enough copies for a couple classes (though the copies became increasingly unreadable toward the end).

Since I was now in a position where I could introduce new courses, I got back to exploring ways that poetic data could be statistically validated. On both undergraduate and graduate levels, I introduced courses in prosody. But these students were not my engineering students from the '60s; they were liberal arts students with little desire to acquire the precise discipline required in prosodic studies. Each semester one or two caught the bug, and each year at least one student published in a referred journal. But either the years after my first experience had romanticized it, or I had lost most of whatever it was that had earlier inspired me. Maybe, being a department head was just too exhausting.

The 1980s – The Medieval Era

In 1981, I made two career changes—I stepped down from administration to return to full-time teaching, and I bought my first computer, an Apple II+. There were no local computer stores, so I had to drive an hour-and-a-half to purchase it. The computer store was small and hidden behind an industrial complex, as if to emphasize that such an effort should be clandestine. But my new computer was an engineering marvel; it had 48K RAM on the motherboard and a 15-inch green phosphor monitor that displayed 40 columns of text, all in capital letters.

A floppy controller card let me attach two external disk drives, each of which could read and write 40 tracks to one side of a 5.25-inch floppy disk that held 360 kilobytes (I had been warned not to buy the cassette drive that came with the original Apple). The disks were fragile and expensive ($5 or $6 each). I also purchased an Epson MX-80, a ninepin printer that used continuous-feed paper. Altogether, the computer and printer cost about $5,200. I got the equipment home, unpacked it, put all the cables in the right places, then sat in front of it, afraid to switch it on. I had brought Frankenstein's laboratory into my home. Finally, I put an operating disk in one drive and *Asteroids* in the other and got down to work.

Inputting text required new skills. My first word processing program used the ESC key to shift for capitals; on the screen, caps were displayed in inverse video; *Apple Writer* assumed that all the other characters were lower case. Typographical features—indents, italics, bold—I marked in the text with XML-like codes, for example, my bold words. It was slow, but the results printed correctly in 80 columns. I could not imagine that I could use it to teach composition.

After I learned to use the equipment, the first major challenge was to learn the program and print my first letter to a colleague. My letter was returned with a handwritten note that said it was an insult—it was printed in ugly, unreadable type (the letters lacked descenders) and was fit only for "technicians," a pejorative noun. Despite heated arguments, this was the consensus of the English Department—no one would accept papers printed on ninepin printers. Aesthetics defeated technology. Officially, the department recommended that students who wanted to show off their technology must limit themselves to dedicated word-processors that produced papers with a "proper" appearance. These dedicated word-processors usually let the user type and correct one or two lines on a tiny screen before the lines were set, but they allowed no other computer function. One student had a machine that used an eight-inch floppy, the only such floppy I ever saw. Still, they produced papers that had the proper appearance.

Although this opposition began to melt with the advent of 14-pin printers, some faculty would still not accept papers that did not *feel* like typed papers. Almost unbelievable today, these actually wanted to feel the impressions that type made on paper! Eventually, the offices of higher administrators acquired daisy-wheel printers, clumsy machines in which a hammer struck a letter molded on a plastic disk so that the letter could strike an inked ribbon to leave an impression on the paper. They were slow—the plastic disk had to turn so that each letter was properly positioned before being struck—and they were noisy. Most secretaries insisted on having them placed in large sound-insulating boxes so they could talk on the phone. BUT they left impressions on the paper that you could feel, and the colleague who claimed that ninepin printing was insulting was happy.

It didn't take long before I exchanged *Apple Writer* for *Superscribe II,* a more sophisticated application. At about the same time, using an alligator clamp and a chip that I installed on the motherboard, I attached a wire between one pin of the chip and somewhere else (I don't remember, but I think it was to a contact under the shift key). This operation gave me 80 columns of upper and lower case. Although I still needed to type special codes for formatting a paper, I could see what I was trying to accomplish.

Curiosity—maybe too much time on my hands—resulted in my writing my own programs. This was not an extremely rare undertaking for Apple owners of the time because if you wanted your computer to do something, you usually had to provide the code yourself. After programming in AppleSoft Basic, I learned Borland's Turbo Pascal, 6502 Assembly Language, and later Turbo C. I became obsessed with mastering my computer—a goal much easier achieved in 1982 than in 2003. Programming in Pascal and assembly language was especially challenging in 1982 because of the low RAM and the limited storage space on the floppy: part of writing a good program was to condense code as much as possible, an art that often required much ingenuity.

After I started programming, I seriously began to think of the computer as something to introduce into my teaching; I was spending so much time learning the languages that my scholarly research had slowed to a trickle. Besides, I wanted to be able to justify claiming it as a tax deduction. My first strictly academic program was a simple database in which I could track students' performances (a grade book), attendance (a roll book), and record comments about individual progress or behavior. I had seen a demonstration of *VisiCalc*, but there was no way I could afford something like that.

The Sixth International Conference on Computers and the Humanities in Raleigh determined my direction during the next few years. First, I shared my ideas at one of the sessions and found that others had actually written programs that would help with the grading of essays. Second, I joined the discussion on word processing in college composition and learned that others were already using computers with their students. Although word processing was still awkward (by our present standards), I agreed that computers could be great tools for invention and pre-writing by combining automatic writing and editing. In the early '80s, composition was viewed primarily as a product: most compositions were graded more on grammar and mechanics than on content, and very few instructors allowed revision. I had struggled to convince high school teachers in Continuing Ed that there was inherent value in revision, and it was an even greater struggle to get my college colleagues to consider editing part of the learning process.

With the ideas from Raleigh still percolating, I talked with my department head; he did not see the value in what I was doing, so I began to research what had been published on computer-assisted instruction. Between my excitement and the research, I gathered enough support and information to make two presentations, which were somewhat like science fiction but did begin to give a scholarly aura to farfetched notions; these presentations—"Computers and the Teaching of English" presented to the English in-service in Charlottesville, and "CAI in the Composition Classroom" presented to the Virginia Association of Teachers of English—made my department head grant that, although I probably had a screw loose, others were equally demented. In this atmosphere, I began politicking for a computer lab for composition, using the argument that our students needed to have basic computing skills to compete in the new workplace. Only the School of Education had a student lab—but it was little respected. Most of the work in the lab seemed directed to introducing grade 1-6 students to reading and computation, but this was before graphical monitors, and the programs, though promising, were clumsy and often crashed.

Also in 1983, despite the growing popularity of IBM PCs in business, the college dean, for some reason known only to him, decided to purchase SuperBrains for all departmental offices. These SuperBrains had CP/M operating systems and were built as a single unit. No one liked them. Somehow, probably because no one else was willing, I got the job of teaching the secretaries in Arts and Sciences how to use *WordStar*, the word-processing program installed on the machines. My first program for the CP/M machine was a database for the English Department. Originally written in DBASE and later translated to DBASE III+, this was a basic database for keeping track of faculty data and scheduling. Where my arguments about computers and composition fell on deaf ears, the department head saw value in using a computer in the office. But he still wasn't convinced that an English Computer Lab was worthwhile. Computers were okay for business, not for education.

This drastically changed in 1985-1986. First, the university library began its transition from the traditional card catalog to an online database. When the transition was announced, consternation seized the traditionalists. One faculty meeting was given over entirely to considering the ways that librarians could be convinced that their decision was tantamount to ruining education, but the decision was immutable. It wasn't long before computers were available to the public in the Reference Area. Second, the college got a new dean, a chemist who wanted to prove that his college was on the cutting edge of technology and who had often listened to my arguments before his appointment. He replaced the SuperBrains with IBMs. Then, in October 1985, after getting approval and funding for the renovation of the English building, he unexpectedly arranged for several of us to visit a university where freshmen already used computers in composition. There, my department head saw how freshman writing could be enhanced by computer revision and watched the sharing of documents among small groups of peer editors. On the trip home, he agreed to let a classroom be turned into a 20-station lab equipped with IBMs. The renovation would not be completed until 1987, but now whenever there was grumbling from colleagues, the department head took my side.

Such changes demanded that I change. Though I seriously loved my Apple, I purchased an IBM-PC with 64 KB RAM and a monochrome display. Now, I had an 84-key keyboard and an 8088 processor running at 4.77mhz! It was strange. I taught at least two sections of Advanced Composition every term, so I had time to prepare for the lab. I used these sections to develop a program I was writing. In this program, a student could get a printout listing the grammatical and mechanical "errors" that the program found and analyzing the paper's readability scale. So far as I could, I translated Harbrace into rules and wrote code to apply those rules; for example, it looked for such grammatical units such as the passive voice, split infinitives, and comma splices, and mechanical conventions like the placement of commas in relation to closing quotation marks and opening introductory clauses. It was crude. Still, it produced a printout to guide a student through a revision while I had time to work with rhetorical structure, tone, style, and effectiveness. According to student evaluations, it was successful, and soon word of mouth publicized it in the department so that other faculty members asked to see what I was doing.

Before we could move into our new lab in Fall 1987, I wrote teaching manuals so that students and the faculty who would be using the lab would have somewhere to start. There were two of these manuals. One intended to teach the uninitiated how to handle an IBM PC, its floppies, and work within DOS; the other, how to boot *Word Perfect 4.0*, prepare a data disk, and begin using the computer to write a paper.

Then, in May with the opening of the lab looming over us, my department head and I attended the Conference on Computers and Writing at the University of Pittsburgh. Here we learned more about the physical opening of a lab, the procedures for using a lab to its maximum benefit, and the possible difficulties or problems that we might encounter. We found that many of our worries, especially those dealing with initial opening of a lab, were common and that teaching a course that included literature, the term paper, and composition could take on the addition of an introduction to word processing. We also found confirmation of our choice of *WordPerfect*, the program then used in the majority of universities that had labs. Where we had been working in the dark, mostly on our own, we learned that others shared our problems, and we got insight into how to overcome them.

But we also found that other departments got into the lab business more cautiously than we had. They seemed to have undergone an evolution that began, in most cases, with one faculty member who acted as a crusader and one or two computers; when the program reached the size of incorporating more than one or two instructors, other schools offered released time and paid workshops to train the faculty. Other schools tended to approach computers in composition by using adjunct faculty; none of the others seemed to be using the computers in literature classes. Our differences made me more apprehensive than I had been. As much as I had argued for a lab, I began to fear that I couldn't pull it off. In an ironic twist, my department head, who had originally been so opposed to technology, now became its staunch proponent; in our talking during the drive home, he revealed a newly kindled excitement—and tried his best to boost my morale. Later, he insisted that I attend a workshop on using computers in humanities courses at Poughkeepsie later in the summer. It was great to talk with people who had similar apprehensions, but, in more ways, it increased my anxiety when I discovered just how provincial all our planning had been. It seemed as if the world had passed us, and we were just finding how backward we were.

When the rest of the department moved back into our building, the lab was not complete—the floor and wall were there, but no furniture and no computers—but it had been scheduled for classes. Neither faculty nor students could follow the syllabus we had carefully planned, and we were not sure when we could definitely meet in the room. Luckily, the departmental secretary had foreseen the problem and found alternative classrooms, scattered all over campus. In short, the first weeks were confusing, frustrating, and frightening—my nightmares coming true.

Then, as if construction delays were not enough, I walked into lab the day the IBMs were delivered. The dean had cooked up some deal with the School of Business and traded my IBMs for computers made by some company I had never heard of. There was nothing I could do. The weekend before we planned to move classes into the lab, I finally got my hands on one of the IDSs and quickly rewrote the IBM manual, now "Care and Feeding of an IDS Computer." We finally moved in October, but because the department head was afraid of theft and had given no one keys, some faculty had not even looked into the room until they stepped in it to meet their first class, and few knew how the room was configured. Only after we had all met our first classes was there a free period when we could get together and learn about the teacher's console.

In the months that followed, it turned out that the delays in getting into the lab fed distrust. The most frequent comment was, "We've lost a badly needed classroom." No one wanted to teach using the computers, so we scheduled my classes and those of two graduate students and two part timers. This group, already marginalized from the literature people, met during the next term and through trial and error, mutual support, and a good sense of humor began to shape an approach to composition. Using what articles and reports we could locate through ERIC and through the then primitive BRS (conducted by librarians because of its cost), we found ways to group students, to work with peer editing, and to practice early versions of such techniques as automatic writing and question-answer brainstorming.

But to many students, the computer was so alien that what should have been a tool became the end-all of their focus; for many, these classes were the first time that they actually touched a computer. Although word processing had developed to WYSIWYG with *WordPerfect,* students needed to learn MSDOS commands to perform some of the simplest acts. For example, while our library was making its transition to a wholly online catalog, so were many others. When students in the lab began learning how to access library catalogs at other institutions, we found that slowly (and surreptitiously at first) some of the lab opponents began to "look in" to see what we were doing. The first library they wanted to access was UVA, where many sent graduate students to find resources. The Interlibrary Loan staff had a telnet link to a couple of the Virginia libraries called "Vanilla," but it was available only at certain times of the day and clunky, seeming to have a mind of its own. In the lab, however, we could access UVA's library, but it was a cumbersome process, as indicated in the following directions from one of our syllabuses:

> First type *Telnet UBLAN3.ACC.VIRGINIA.EDU* at your $ prompt (or you may prefer to use the machine address 128.143.70.101). When you have connected to UBLAN3, hit <ENTER> once or twice to get a network prompt; then type *c virgo*. Enter *V* (for VT100 access) then *Y* to confirm your choice. Sometimes when you have accessed Virgo, you will find that your cursor is frozen at the top of the screen. To move it to the correct location, press the up-arrow. This mislocated cursor can become quite annoying if you work for any time on Virgo, but you will grow accustomed to the inconvenience. When you have finished your session, you can log off with Ctrl-shift-6.

Students could also access CARL (the Colorado Alliance of Research Libraries) and Dartmouth College Library, and we were beginning to find full text documents through laborious online searches. Through we used Lynx (a character-oriented client) to access Bitnet, links mostly were 9600bps when lucky; normally, information crawled at an exasperating 1444bps. As I recall, JMU had a surface link to UVA, which, in turn, had a surface link to Virginia Tech, which had access to the satellites. If any of these links failed (which was frequent), we lost our connection altogether. I think that name servers were already being developed, but most of our links were through exact IP addresses (e.g., 192.17.5.100) that we passed from one to another through word-of-mouth or listservs. With these listservs, students and later faculty discovered email. Most listserv moderators were tolerant and let students join, so long as they followed the rules.

Separate from my school work, I taught programs to local business people. At first, I did a small workshop (three people) on *VisiCalc*. Soon, programs like *WordPerfect*, *Lotus 1-2-3*, and *dBase* were beginning to transform the way business was done, and local businesses clamored for training. The business community was convinced that computing was the way to go, but academia still dragged its feet. For example, I wrote "Spanish Business Letters," a long, comprehensive program, with Howard and Esther Cohen, but even though the program was a commercial success, Howard received no credit from his department head. This sort of discouragement ran through the university. To counter it, the president mandated that a course on computer literacy must be added to each major. After a bit of grumbling, a new course, "Computers in Literature," appeared in the course offerings, and the department further justified its compliance by letting me revise two existing courses, "Advanced Composition" on the undergraduate level and "Bibliography and Research Methods" on the graduate level.

At this time, there were few programs for textual analysis. I first used John Abercrombie's *Computer Programs for Literary Analysis* because I had met him at a conference, but it didn't get quite the results I wanted. Using his programs as guides, I wrote ANATEXT, a series of interconnected Pascal programs, for my graduate class. To use them, students needed to locate a suitable text and ftp it to their desktop; then they could analyze its linguistic structure. On *Humanist*, one of the listservs, I read about a program that analyzed the same sorts of data that interested me—and it cost only $15 with unlimited license. In November 1989, I obtained a copy of TACT (*Textual Analysis Computing Tools*) and MTAS (*Microcomputer Text-Analysis System*) from the Center for Computing in the Humanities at the University of Toronto. Students in the bibliography course used these programs through the '90s.

There was growing talk about hypertext. For the undergraduate class, I used a program called *Houdini MaxThink* to code *Computers in English: A Hypertext Textbook* and a manual for *WordPerfect 5.0,* based on the texts I had written several years earlier. I don't think either book was used very often, and the exercise seemed futile except that I learned the limitations of such texts, mainly that no one would use such packages if they could avoid them. With this insight, I set out to code a book that I could actually use in a class. I was teaching an upper-level undergraduate class on *Finnegans Wake,* so I decided that I would code an intertextual version of Chapter 1 for a first-time reader. This user would be able to work through the text, find explanatory screens when needed, and get immediate glosses on words that presented problems; the book would also give general notes on sources, background, symbolism, and narration. Finding the scholarly material was relatively easy because I had taught the course several times; getting an electronic version of the text was another matter. Ignoring problems with copyright (I figured that no one outside my class would every use it), I set out to scan it.

Scanning and OCR in 1989 were primitive. At first, I used a hand-held scanner then ran the result through a crude OCR program. It was a disaster; if my hand shook or I did not move the scanner at exactly the same speed, my only reward was gibberish. Finally, The Center for Instructional Technology (I don't remember what it was called then) purchased a scanner and an OCR program. It read only flat, single sheets that had to be fed manually; if I wanted to scan from a book, I needed first to copy it and then cut the copy so that only one column of text was on a sheet. After the machine gobbled up the paper, it took at least 10 minutes to generate the electronic text. Many fonts were damaged or faintly printed in the original, and the OCR program had a mind of its own. The electronic text resembled something a monkey could have typed! Correcting the text probably took more time than all the rest of the project together. I concluded that if I ever did something like this again, I would find a text already translated and edited. The students liked the hypertext book, and their comprehension of the following chapters seemed much improved because they had learned to read the text.

The 1990s – The Renaissance

In the early '90s, the number of listservs greatly increased; students joined discussions on almost everything from *Shaksper* to *SF-lovers* and linked into any number of bulletin boards. Available material was being organized and cataloged so that access became easier; now assignments sounded more like the following:

> Look up a program listed in one of the catalogs in NET in the local network or on one of the nodes listed in BITINFO on the VAX. Using ftp, download this file to your VAX account. Examine the JUMINFO BB on the VAX and write a paragraph telling me what information you can find here. Join a student BBS at another university. Look up a specific area that interests you, and every two weeks (included in the assignment for 1/25) write a brief report on the activity of that area.

Now, students entered the university with more computer experience, and even the traditionalists in the English Department were beginning to come around. Part of this last change resulted from updating the lab.

The dean recognized that the IDS computers were breaking down too frequently under the amount of use and that repairing them was becoming increasingly expensive. By joining the English lab with the Foreign Language lab, he finagled enough funds to buy new IBMs for us. At first, he planned to junk the old IDS machines, so I asked if I could have them. Shocked by my request since I had made such a to-do about how bad they were, he agreed. It was summer, and most of the faculty was gone. With the help of the departmental secretary, I placed a CPU, a monitor, and a nine-pin printer on 21 faculty members' desks. "Placed" because I neither plugged them in nor attached the cables. In September, several of the faculty who had been more amenable to the idea of computing asked me to connect their machines; a couple others figured out on their own how to attach all the cables; a few others were staunch opponents and left the machines in a corner of their offices to gather dust. In October, the department head scheduled a workshop on *WordPerfect* for them and insisted that all the computers be networked into the school's LAN. By November, only three faculty members were still unconnected; the rest were already using the local BBs to reach students, to conduct university committee meetings, and to search the library's online catalog.

Of course, the machines, which were already falling part, began to breakdown. Now, the same faculty members who had opposed the lab clamored for new equipment and updated software. The department budget, which had not planned for any new equipment, was suddenly strapped. It was the only year that I can remember when supplies ran so low that paper was rationed.

With the help of graduate students, I coded *Prosody: A Hypertext Handbook,* a software package that, like the *Finnegans Wake* book, was interactive. A student could look up terms to find examples, pick particular poems to see how they could be parsed, compare different ways of parsing the same poem, and take quizzes to check on his or her progress. It was a tremendous success with my classes. Meanwhile, I retrieved my prosodic studies, returning to Shelley's and Browning's placement of caesurae. I needed reliable texts—preferably texts that reflected the poets' usage rather than editors' emendations. This proved difficult. In fact, it shifted my interest from caesurae to text editing, and led me to explore how computers and editing older texts could be combined. Though we already analyzed texts with ANATEXT, MTAS, and TACT, these programs seemed to tell us little about traditional prosody and nothing about editing. I downloaded "Andrea del Sarto" and "Fra Lippo Lippi," and ran them through the grammar analysis. I was looking primarily for stylistic variations and, despite the primitiveness of the effort, did come up with enough information to put in a paper, "Analyzing Literature Through Computer Programs." This paper convinced a couple of the traditionalists that maybe computers could have some use for "grunt" work. Still, it did not address textual editing. I was stymied by my lack of accurate texts and in my research found that most literary scholars seemed to ignore that there was even a problem.

I tried to address this "problem" in my computer classes.

Looking back at my 1992 and 1993 syllabuses, I see that during the first few weeks of "Computers and Literature," I spent most class time teaching basic DOS commands like format, copy, and dir and basic VAX commands for logging on, checking and sending email, accessing the university library, and connecting to Bitnet. Early in the semester, students also had to learn how to ftp files from a remote site and unarc them using PKXARC. With these skills mastered, students had to complete a sort of online treasure hunt; they had to find such information as what the Koran says about divorce, when Spring Break begins at another university, what the current climate is in a particular city, and what novels by a certain author are in a nearby library. I then lectured on text variation and editing and on Elizabethan printing, orthography, and grammar before I assigned each student an act of *Hamlet*. Students were required to make a modern edition of their act using the Folio version as their base and the Second Quarto to help with editorial decisions. They used several programs to help such as Michael Mefford's *Compare 1.0* and David Trafton's *Lookfor 3.3*. Completing this introduction to editing, we turned to MTAS to study elisions in Donne's "First Anniversary," prepare a concordance of the first 10 of Shakespeare's sonnets, and graph the word distribution of the lemmatizations of two groups of six nouns that invoke or describe opposite states or emotions in *In Memoriam*. Finally, they used TACT to gather specific instances of word combinations that could be used to generate a scholarly paper: for example, after collecting all nouns that directly refer to animals, a student asked what animals were specifically associated with each character; with these data at hand, the student then found material on the Internet about Medieval and Renaissance bestiaries and wrote a paper on what the information could reveal about the characters.

I seemed to have been trying to make students rewrite the canon.

Brazenly I thought I was on the cutting edge; I was wrong. In 1992 the whole computing business seemed to change. Microsoft brought out Windows 3.1, and overnight all my DOS programs were archaic. Even my new computer was old-fashioned because in my great wisdom I had convinced myself that buying a color monitor was an expensive luxury that I didn't need. I guess I had become a new sort of traditionalist. Though we heard rumors about the graphical future of the World Wide Web, we used our collection of text-only programs, search engines, and servers with exotic names like Lynx, Gopher, Archie, WAIS (Wide Area Information Servers), and VERONICA (Very Easy Rodent-Oriented Net-Wide Index of Computerized Archives), and for the most part we were satisfied with the 80-column screens so long as we made (and didn't inexplicably lose) connection to the distant database. Even after NCSA Mosaic was made public in 1994, we remained in the text-only age. When I first saw a graphical interface at a computer club meeting in Philadelphia, I knew how provincial I was. It was disillusioning to say the least.

I had my third computer built according to my specifications so that I could upgrade piecemeal. I had delayed moving from DOS to Windows 3.1 as long I could, because I knew my way around MSDOS and had used it for years. Windows presented a formidable learning curve, and I wasn't prepared at this stage to give it the time. Instead of coding, new programs that came onto the market faster than anyone could have imagined absorbed my time. The luxury of being able to purchase a ready-made program instead of having to write one made us light-headed. But the new programs required graphic interfaces. I surrendered and purchased a video card and an EGA color monitor. Along with many other amateur programmers, I decided that I would spend my time learning new programs instead of trying to write them.

By 1994, I had an Internet connection at home and could access the university. Because of the way the telephone companies divided the state, it would have been long distance earlier. But I finally connected to CompuServe through a local vender. This meant that I could use email to correspond with students. It also meant that, connecting through a series of password-protected portals, I could access my VAX account and the library catalog. Looking back, it's hard to remember how frustrating and slow all this procedure was. Not only did the different password portals take their time to verify the passwords, but also my first modem transferred only 1447bps; to download a single email message sometimes took over a minute. Also, because to ftp a graphic involved translating it into ASCII before uploading it and then translating it back into binary before it could be viewed, we only rarely sent or received any images. But, despite such limitations, it seemed as if a new world of possibilities was unfolding. From the newsgroups and listservs that I had joined, I was painfully aware of how far I had fallen behind. Yet, when I was working with students, it seemed as if I were light-years in the future.

Reacting to this frustration, I tried to resurrect my familiarity with the databases and spreadsheets I taught in the mid-1980s, but they had either passed out of fashion or drastically changed. Then, for some reason that now completely escapes my memory, I got a used copy of *Xerox Ventura 3.0 Gold* at a computer show; actually it was quite inexpensive because the program had already been bought by Corel and there was a newer version on the market. Without a manual and without decent help built in, it was frustrating, almost leading to my punching a fist through the monitor, but it was enough to introduce me to desktop publishing—and to realize the need to teach computer documentation. Having some design training in my background made me appalled at how limited this tool was. Through help and patience from people on a forum and in a couple of newsgroups, I slowly learned how to accomplish on a computer what seemed easy on a layout board. Actually, this experience rekindled my faith in what I had been doing. We were before the commercialization of the Web, and it seemed that the online community was eager and willing to share and help one another in ways that now seem unreal. After all, this was a time when the word "hacker" had no pejorative connotations; we used it to praise people who had broken a barrier and shared their knowledge with others. We thought that open sourcing was the future of the Internet.

Then, Microsoft released Windows 95. We updated the lab before the opening of the 1996-1997 academic year, and with the update we installed Internet Explorer 1.0. This opened new horizons. Because the library catalog was now fully online, and more and more searchable databases were being added to the reference room, the teaching of Freshman English needed to be seriously overhauled. At first, students were on their own, and only the most savvy experimented with the new systems. A few faculty members attended work-shops to learn, but most of the entrenched upper-division and graduate faculty still distrusted the new systems and insisted that their students learn to conduct bibliographicals the old way. It was only after the library purchased the MLA bibliography on CD that some of these faculty members wavered. To teach students how to use the new tools, Lynn Cameron, a librarian, took it on herself to write a workbook. Though she also instructed faculty on the library tools, her workbook, *Go for the Gold*, was the way most students learned their ways around the collection. Later, she developed the workbook into its present online form (http://www.lib.jmu.edu/library/gold/modules.htm). In 1996, however, the English lab could not directly access the library, but through the World Wide Web and Internet Explorer 1.0, they no longer needed the cumbersome entry through the VAX and Lynx. The graduate bibliography course began to use the Web as a primary research tool. This created some havoc in the department. Tradition-alists feared that students would forget how to use the standard tools in the reference room, and some feared that students would plagiarize documents from the Web and increasingly suspected their students of buying packaged term papers.

It was obvious from reading any newspaper that the WWW was here to stay and that it would impact on everyone's teaching whether they liked it or not. After a student in the ROTC program created the first departmental homepage at the university, the powers that be had him present a workshop to interested faculty to share what he had done. It was at this workshop that I first learned of HTML, and at the student's recommendation, I downloaded "The Bare Bones Guide to HTML" and began to design a site for the English Department. Some faculty insisted that I not put their names on the site and especially that I not put any personal information such as an email address. Rumors about Web predators spread, and many refused to put course syllabuses or outlines because these predators would not only harass the innocent, they would steal their ideas. Meanwhile, the university installed Webboard so that faculty could use computers in their teaching and turned one of its mainframes into a server for student homepages. Now, rumors about piracy added to those about predators. Despite this hostile reaction to the Web, my undergraduates enthusiastically designed their own homepages. During 1997 and 1998, the university moved from *WordPerfect* to *Word*, and I moved from *Xerox Ventura* to *PageMaker* and a little later learned *Photoshop 3*. I had a newer computer and VGA monitor; working with students on Web pages had turned my interests to design and layout. While my graduate students continued in textual analysis and bibliography, my undergraduate class evolved into a course on HTML.

Only one other faculty member continued to use the lab, but she had her students use it strictly for word processing. This made it an extremely expensive drain on department resources. Finally, we could no longer afford to keep it running and worked out an arrangement with the Foreign Language Department to share it. Foreign Languages had just won a grant to modernize their own lab and had something like $200,000 they could put into our lab. They replaced the hardware with state-of-the-art equipment, and installed a laser printer and a technical command center. Still, the lab was usually empty. Only two of us met all our classes in it and used it for more than word processing. We thought the Foreign Language people would want to use it, but only occasionally did they bring a class into it. They preferred their own lab; it was set up less like a classroom than a lounge, and stored their computer and audio-visual materials. After the first year of operation, they closed the old English lab except when a class was scheduled there. The lab I had been so proud of a decade before now was now empty most of the time; only a couple adjunct faculty members and I unlocked it and turned on the lights when our classes met.

As if the browser wars and the reluctance to accept computerization were not enough change, the university administration decided to create a separate Writing Program by removing the Freshman courses from the English Department, and the Virginia Council on Higher Education allowed the Institute of Technical and Scientific Communication to be established as a separate department. My undergraduate course moved along with the rest of the courses that had anything to do with technical writing. Although I remained in the English Department for a couple more years, I taught my most interesting classes to this new group of students. Here was a department head and faculty with goals and interests like my own. Also along with its creation, ITSC built a new lab, and the new director purchased the programs I wanted—*QuarkXpress*, *PageMaker*, *FrameMaker*, *Photoshop*, *Illustrator*, and *CorelDraw*—and included courses on online publication based in part on what "Computers and Literature" had become.

Finally, after 40 years in English departments, I joined ITSC as a full faculty member—a move that was interpreted as betrayal by old colleagues. I have learned that anyone entering the field of online communication has a continuous learning curve. The last five years have demanded that I learn new programs (*Dreamweaver, Flash, FrontPage, Fireworks, Freehand*) and new languages (JavaScript, XML, VML, WML) just to stay current. And still I am behind.

As I wrote at the beginning, most people resist change, but that choice results in boredom. Better by far is to accept the frustration of knowing that you can never reach your goal. It has been an exciting 40 years.

Section II

Online Approaches to Teaching Communication

Chapter II

Hypertext Theory and Web Writing Assignments in the Writing and Professional Communication Classroom

Wendy Warren Austin
Edinboro University of Pennsylvania, USA

Abstract

This chapter proposes that composition instructors focus less on the technical aspects of having students get Web pages published and more on teaching them basic hypertext principles, visual design principles, and writing strategies for presenting arguments in hypertext form. More and more professional and technical communication courses are incorporating Web page creation and/or website design into their pool of required assignments, while at the same time a growing number of first-year composition instructors are also beginning to incorporate Web pages into their repertoire of genres. This convergence is creating interesting paradoxes for instructors of both types and for website developers in the workplace. If basic hypertext principles are taught in earlier prerequisite courses, technical communication instructors could spend more time teaching more advanced hypertext theories and instructing students in the more technical aspects of the software they are using.

Introduction

The college composition course is a staple of college life. Everyone who goes to college either has to place out of or take English composition, a requirement which frequently has as its goal the ability to write for academic audiences. The typical assignments students expect to encounter are research papers and opinion essays. However, with more and more frequency, composition instructors are exploring and incorporating different kinds of writing within their classrooms. The most recent composition textbooks and handbooks often include a chapter on online writing or even website development. However, despite the new coverage in textbooks, far fewer students *expect* to develop a website as one of their course assignments. Yet with the unrelenting and unavoidable emphasis on technological literacy the government is imposing on education even from the earliest years (Selfe, 1999), composition specialists would be short-sighted if we ignored writing for the Web as one of the sites for writing that college students are likely to encounter and produce. For the most part, "web development" classes are most frequently housed in computer science departments; it is where one would more immediately think students would learn how to create websites. The average person—or even the average English professor—is less likely to expect students to learn about hypertext theory, visual design principles, or spatial metaphors in the required composition course. On the other hand, the expectations we have of technical writers are intertwined with the world of high technology. For example, it would not be at all uncommon if the reaction at a social gathering were, upon discovering one's occupation is technical writer, "Oh, so you must develop the firm's website."

Whether or not technical/professional writers actually develop or contribute to their firm's website is irrelevant; the association between technical writing and website development remains. In fact, developing a Web page is often among the course requirements for a technical writing course, and the further into a professional writing program one progresses, the more advanced his or her tools, techniques, and knowledge become. It is not unheard of for a technical communication major to take a theory course as an upper-level or graduate class. Hart-Davidson (2001), in an article about incorporating a historical theory course in the master's degree program in Rhetoric and Technical Communication at Rensselaer Polytechnic Institute, maintains that "there is little doubt that theory—understood as critical reflection upon the various issues, conditions, and processes grounding technical communication—is valuable" (p. 2). However, it would seem even more helpful to become acquainted with basic theoretical principles of hypertext early on, in addition to the writing theory that frequently inhabits the content of writing courses. Let's face it—whether implicit or explicit, theory grounds every writing course, but writing teachers need to ground their practice in the most appropriate theory for the kinds of writing that 21st century college students need to know. The objective of this chapter is to propose that first-year composition include among its course objectives basic principles in hypertext theory, especially considering the trend in all disciplines to view the Web not only as a key source of information, but as a public forum for (and non-paper, non-academic form of) relatively easy publication and dissemination.

Background

As an instructor of both first-year composition and technical communication courses for nearly 17 years, and having witnessed a dramatic change in the way we see writing over that time, I have seen the needs of both composition and technical writing courses change rapidly, while the evolution of each course's content and assignments has been decidedly slower in reflecting these dramatic changes than we might like to admit.

Scholars writing about the history of writing instruction in American colleges (for example, Berlin, 1987; Brereton, 1995; Kitzhaber, 1990; Miller, 1993) have observed that what is taught in college writing classes, as well as how it is taught, has always been a point at issue in English Studies. For example, in the last 20 years, two recent controversies that have risen to the surface include: 1) whether to focus writing instruction strictly on academic writing (Bartholomae, 1995) or start with personal writing and then move into academic writing, (Elbow, 1995); and 2) whether the writing classroom should be (or can help but be) an ideological arena focusing on complex issues like racial discrimination or cultural diversity, or whether its content should or can focus solely on student writing (Hairston, 1992). At the same time these issues were occupying the discipline of rhetoric and composition, technological changes began affecting the writing classroom in a big way. Hawisher, LeBlanc, Moran, and Selfe came out with their book *Computers and the Teaching of Writing in American Higher Education,*

1979-1994: A History, which chronicled the beginnings of the subfield of computers and writing within rhetoric and composition. The first Computers and Writing Conference was held in 1983, and although it skipped three years between its fourth and fifth conference, conferences have been held continuously every year since 1989.

Hypertext was an exciting concept in these early conferences, particularly starting around 1992 when at Brown University, scholars like Michael Joyce and Jay Bolter were experimenting with Storyspace and constructing literary hypertexts. This was a doubly exciting time for the Computers and Writing community because of the birth and exponential growth of the World Wide Web, and widespread use of graphical browsing software. Although it seems hard to imagine now what life was like before the Web, we have to remember that barely more than 10 years have passed since the World Wide Web made its entrance before the general public and into the world of commerce, much less into the world of writing classrooms. Yet, writing scholars, as well as everyone else, are racing to keep up with this monumental shift in business, academic, and public discourse modes. In *Nostalgic Angels: Rearticulating Hypertext Writing,* Johnson-Eilola (1997) argues for a critical literacy of technology, particularly of hypertext, and a need to move out of just talking about theoretical principles of this form of discourse with other scholars and into understanding it for and conveying it to others through our teaching of writing.

Evolving Technology, Shifting Goals

The evolution of hypertext theory and development of the Web has caused many introductory composition instructors to move further away from academic discourse and more toward public discourse by having students write for the Web. Meanwhile, technical and professional communication instructors have been compelled to focus more on writing for the Web, also. The advent of the Web and graphical browsers caused the field of technical communication to change even more dramatically than composition did, since technical writers were expected to write for computers, and when computing changed, most thought that technical writers' skills would parallel the computing world's changes. Indeed, the Society for Technical Communication's website states that STC's "growth has mirrored our growing dependence on technology" (http://www.stc.org/history.asp). Thus, the goals and assignments of these two courses have begun to converge, creating interesting dilemmas and unexpected opportunities for change and growth in both fields.

Basic Characteristics/Principles of Hypertext

As the Web is itself a mammoth hypertext, we need to look at the basic principles of what constitutes hypertext. According to Landow (1988), hypertext is a series of texts connected to other text (at least one other, but probably many other texts) by means of associations, which are primarily spatially related or visually related, as opposed to a linear or sequential order. Much like the visual prewriting technique of clustering, finished hypertext structures often take on the same shapes as in that early stage of writing. (For an example of such clustering, see Figure 1, a clustering diagram the author of this chapter created during an early draft.) Like children in a family, and the endless possibility of descendents and ancestors, hypertext is an associationally related unit of related texts. Similarly, clustering takes shape through associationally related ideas. A defining characteristic of hypertext is the tendency for "multiple digressions" (Reinking, 1997), while another important characteristic is its ability to handle large volumes of material, some of which are tangentially related to minor aspects of an entire concept or theme. Of course, hypermedia expands on the notion of what constitutes a text, including music, sound, graphics, video, or animations. Like many composition teachers, hypertext theorists may come from literary backgrounds, as do Joyce and Landow, or from classical backgrounds, as do Bolter and Lanham, where the print tradition reigns supreme. However, we also find hypertext theorists in technical fields, such as computer science or engineering (Conklin, 1987), or in the arts (digital arts, usually), but compositionists are much less likely to look in these latter fields for their interdisciplinary borrowings, at least in regard to theory. According to Booth (2002), a composition teacher who advocates putting workplace writing into the first-year writing curriculum,

> Although fields such as art and architecture have used forms of rhetoric as a way to explain how visual images impact society, their concern, along with other fields (e.g., advertising), has generally been the same as theorists in technical communication and composition studies: questions about the relationship of structures and information, and the effects or responses evoked. Concerning the structure of paper-based and hypertext writing, writing teachers can expand students' rhetorical control by using visual cues inherent in hypertext writing to enhance awareness of control. Visual rhetoric can assist students with macro structures, audience awareness, and possibly the development of stronger relationships between pieces of information (p. 44).

Figure 1. Example of clustering technique in prewriting stages

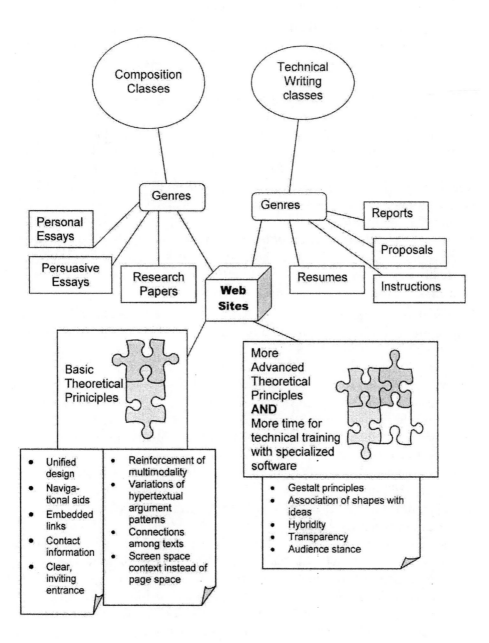

This is where technical communication teachers can help; more technical communications educators have (or gain) backgrounds in design and/or technology and guide their students in the development of these skills.

Granted, hypertext principles that would be useful (i.e., elementary enough) for composition instructors to convey to students are not laid in stone; even so, they can be gleaned from sections of handbooks that are already on the market. For instance, from a current composition handbook which has a chapter on Web design (Maimon & Peritz, 2003), we can deduce that a unified look, a consistent design, easy-to-read colors and fonts, a navigation bar, easy-load graphics, a site map, embedded links, and inclusion of the writer's name, date, and email address are critical elements to consider. Another handbook (Faigley, 2003) that has a substantial chapter called "Web Basics" also lays out the principles well: decent websites should have at least one clear and inviting entrance, a map or navigational guide of some kind, a unified, visual theme, effective focal points, not much more than 10-15 nodes, and may include "absolute" (external) and/or "relative" (internal) links. The problem with the principles of hypertext theory for composition instructors is not that there are none; it is that no one person or group has really agreed upon which ones are most important for students to learn in their first encounter with hypertext writing.

Though the wording may vary somewhat from teacher to teacher and institution to institution, the theories behind traditional first-year composition are far more established and entrenched, and have recently been codified in the text of the Writing Program Administrator's Outcomes Statement for First-Year Composition (2000). Specifically, the organization lists four general categories of expectations: in rhetorical knowledge, critical thinking, writing, reading, process, and knowledge of conventions (http://www.english.ilstu.edu/Hesse/outcomes.html). Regarding rhetorical knowledge, students should learn to "write in several genres," "respond to the needs of different audiences," and "understand how genres shape reading and writing." Regarding process, the statement says specifically that students should learn to "use a variety of technologies to address a range of audiences." Considering that the statement was written and adopted in the year 2000, it is reasonable to assume that these particular aspects of the WPA expected outcomes of first-year composition should include hypertext theory. As well, it is reasonable to assume that rhetorical knowledge includes design theory, considering that the genre of writing for the Web necessarily includes elements of design specific to writing for screen reading. Furthermore, considering that instructors spend a great deal of time teaching argumentation, and that some arguments might have occasion to be conveyed in hypertext forms as opposed to linear ones, it would be useful for instructors to have a better understanding of how arguments can best be presented in hypertext.

Hypertext theorists (Landow, 1994; Charney, 1994; Kolb, 1994; Douglas, 1998) have sometimes disagreed about the effectiveness of the form in the presentation of argument. While Douglas admits (1998) "the rhetoric of argument prefers the linear to the multiple, proof to speculation, the line to branches," she points out that philosophers like Wittgenstein and Hegel did not expect their complex philosophical arguments to fit into a simple, straight line of reasoning, but rather envisioned interdependent diagrams showing relationships between ideas or a detailed landscape crisscrossing with ideas, cases, contexts, and perspectives. Kolb (1994a, 1994b, 1998) tackles head-on the issue of whether hypertextual form supports or hinders structures of argumentative writing. He offers at least four different means by which, in the field of philosophical argumentation, hypertext could function effectively:

1) to illustrate the structure of an argument or collection of arguments;

2) to connect a related set of reference collections;

3) to support connections between thinkers' ideas which could not otherwise be accessed with normal search functions; and

4) to compose a dialogue that could allow interaction from the reader by providing multiple paths that may operate in directions the reader decided, but which the author never intended (1998, p. 324).

Commenting on the latter type of hypertextual operation, Kolb notes that, "[L]inks could embody the standard moves of argumentation—making claims, giving backing, contesting claims, raising questions, stating alternatives, and so on" (1998, p. 324).

Granted, my suggestions that more emphasis in hypertext and design theory be incorporated into composition classes might be acceptable to many composition instructors. However, one formidable obstacle to incorporating these theories into an instructor's repertoire is their own lack of knowledge about how to do so. Another obstacle might be the curricular challenge: how to fit more information/ content into an already tightly filled course within the same time frame. Indeed, faculty time is limited for such development purposes, and classroom instruction is limited by institutional policy and course objectives. One solution that might help is to use Carter's (2003) suggested writing strategies, which may include what composition instructors already use, but compress advice into five general tactics.

Carter's suggestions draw upon formal and informal logic. He declares that "argumentative hypertexts are ultimately worth writing and studying because argumentation has received a lot of attention over the past 10 years, with a new focus on argumentative writing in both the workforce and academia." Carter acknowledges that the

> still emerging field of modern argumentation recognizes three aspects to argument. The products of argument—reasons, claims, and premises—belong to the realm of logic; the procedures for conducting arguments belong to the realm of dialectic; and the processes of argumentation belong to the realm of rhetoric (p. 6).

Carter emphasizes both products and processes because his strategies relate only to "single-author hypertexts that link to themselves" (p. 6). These would be the kind that composition instructors would be most likely to employ. Although technical communication instructors might go far beyond "single-author hypertexts," it only makes sense that students learn foundation principles with a single text first, before they apply the same principles to multiple texts.

Writing Strategies in Hypertext Arguments

Carter (2003) bases his five strategies on a previous study he did several years before with his own students as he watched them try to construct arguments in hypertext.

- First, he suggests using fewer chunks in one's argument to avoid too much fragmentation.

- A second strategy he suggests is taking advantage of known starting points, ending points, and repetitive links.

- Third, he suggests relying on existing argumentative structures like the Toulmin model, classical model, or Rogerian model of argumentation, or modified variations of these.

- A fourth strategy is to rely upon two kinds of space—cognitive and graphic. Here is where knowledge about design theory and visual rhetoric will come into play in the composition classroom.

- Finally, his fifth suggestion is to "write for coherence" (p. 18), echoing advice instructors give to students already. Textual conventions must provide guides for the reader or an argument will not make sense, whether in hypertext form or print. Titles, context-providing, similar terms, and references to other links all help the reader create coherence.

Carter's article in *Computers and Composition* provides a wealth of pedagogical advice for the first-year composition instructor, even though it is not ostensibly characterized as such.

Information Literacy and the Educated Citizen

Although few authors besides Carter recommend incorporating hypertextual theory into the composition classroom, a rash of other writers are advocating hypertext writing in first-year composition. Booth's (2001) dissertation establishes a strong rationale for including hypertext writing in the composition classroom. She reminds us that the historical roots of a liberal education are to create good citizens, and to create good citizens, one must be skilled in the rhetoric of the day and be able to communicate effectively both in civic life and in the workplace. These days, effective communication skills increasingly call for an ability to write and develop an effective Web presence, so hypertext writing would be a good skill to develop. Although Booth's suggestions for including hypertext writing apply mainly to composition classes which involve research writing, they could apply to sourceless writing as well. Another reason Booth suggests for including hypertext theory in the composition classroom is because it expands students' literacy.

Incorporating more instruction in hypertext theory in the composition classroom can extend a student's information literacy. To be literate in today's society and in college means to be able to write effectively for a screen as well as a page. This is not all of what constitutes an informationally literate person, but understanding how to create as well as how to read hypertextual documents provides a stronger foundation of knowledge for any discipline. Many different definitions of information literacy now exist, but many of them focus importance on *being able to understand and evaluate* hypertext (i.e., Web) documents, as well as being able to read, write, and comprehend. While this is an extremely important skill to develop, *creating basic readable hypertext* might come in a close second, and would be crucial to learning more advanced skills in another class.

At present, quite a few composition instructors are incorporating Web writing assignments in their classes, and although many know about others who are doing so, no surveys have been done or general clearinghouses set up to collect information in one place about all of them. Stephen Krause has a variety of tips posted online for instructors who are teaching Web writing (http://

www.emunix.emich.edu/~krause/Tips/WWW.html), but they are listed under various headings such as "Student Publishing" and "Student Website Creation," and both descriptions are qualified by the prefacing statement , "depending on institutional constraints…," so it is unclear whether various institutions keep students from publishing their writing on the Web or not. Various publishers also post sections on companion websites with section headings like "Teaching Web Composition" to help instructors; often the tips posted here are technical ones, such as how to upload files, but these are helpful, nevertheless.

Sorapure's (2002) students in first-year composition used Web writing assignments in conjunction with a community service component. She states: "Assignments that combine Web writing with community service can engage students in projects that capitalize on the initial democratic promise of the Internet." Sorapure's students produced Web-based learning materials for their target community. The public nature of their writing maintained the students' motivation to do well, especially when they were representing an agency or community group. Their exigency for applying the tasks that they were given or had sought out provided a basis for the structure of their texts, and their access to the Web allowed them to work on their texts until they were satisfied with them. However, one does not need to be in a computer classroom to learn about hypertext theory. Eyman's (1996) understanding of hypertext as collaboration provides a useful underpinning for those who are in a traditional classroom, but wish to exploit the collaborative/linking qualities of hypertextual documents. Although hypertext is necessarily screen-based, hypertextuality is not, and is present in virtually all kinds of print and other media. As Eyman explains, hypertextuality is all about connections and Bakhtinian multivocality, a concept that students in a first-year composition class would be able to grasp and able to apply more technically later on, perhaps in a technical communication class.

Expanded Instruction in Visual Design Theory

A great deal of effective technical communication relies heavily on well thought-out visual design. In fact, it is certainly fair to say that the astounding growth of the World Wide Web since its inception has derived from its visual properties, its ability to display information in appealing graphical interfaces, rather than in text format. Johnson-Sheehan and Baehr (2001), writing in the journal *Technical Communication,* contend that hypertexts require users to think differently, to rely on a more subconscious gestalt level of understanding in which we are able to reunite seeing with thinking. Principles of gestalt psychology have been very helpful in giving technical communicators and instructors guidance in two-dimensional visual principles (Bernhardt, 1996; Moore & Fitz, 1993). Taking it a step further, Johnson-Sheehan and Baehr, borrowing from the three-dimensional way architects and city planners visualize concepts and plans, emphasize four principles of visual thinking from Rudolf Arnheim's book, *Visual Thinking*, that can be applied to developing effective hypertext.

- Remember that users' vision is selective, and that we pay more attention to new things on a screen.

- Be aware that focal points are helpful when they can solve a problem, so figure out what users want to do.

- Realize that, when users focus on an object in the foreground, providing context around it is less important, but when users focus on a background, providing context is more important.

- Remember that shapes create associations and users categorize shapes in certain ways.

Johnson-Sheehan and Bauehr also discuss good use of frames, navigation tools, design metaphors, icons, and dynamic interfaces.

Like Johnson-Sheehan and Bauehr, Hocks (2003) analyzes visual strategies that can be put to use in digital environments. She looks at three qualities, derived from an analysis of two scholarly hypertexts, that describe the features of visual rhetoric: audience stance, transparency, and hybridity. Audience stance refers to the way in which the author of the website creates an ethos and the extent to which the site invites interactivity. Transparency refers to the extent to which the site reflects other familiar media conventions; if it is more familiar, it is more transparent, less familiar, less transparent. Hybridity refers to the way in which the verbal and visual features interact with each other/build on each other to enhance the intended message. Hocks recommends that composition instructors not only analyze texts via this multimodality (verbal/visual rhetoricity), but teach students to create multimodal texts, maintaining that different kinds of knowledge are gained from analysis vs. creation, and that students need both types of understanding. While Hocks did not specify what kind of class the "digital environment" was like, it would be entirely possible to apply her suggestions to an electronic composition classroom.

Technical Communication Instruction

Meanwhile, technical communication instructors might find Hocks' or Carter's suggestions exceptionally useful as well, but these instructors have an even more tightly packed curriculum and expect their students to come to their classes with some basics known about writing already. Regardless of whether students are writing an argument, a report, or an informational Web page, an extremely helpful source of advice for both composition instructors and technical communication instructors is Troffer's (2000) "Writing Effectively Online: How to Compose Hypertext." She discusses how to organize hypertext documents, how to create good links, how to write for the screen, and in general, provides concepts so that instructors and students can quickly grasp them, the stated purpose of her work. It would seem reasonable for fledgling technical writers to understand how to use various writing strategies within the contexts of various writing technologies. If students come to these classes with a basic knowledge of hypertext argumentation forms, a technical communication instructor can spend a greater amount of time on conveying technical knowledge and providing more detailed help in more sophisticated visual design strategies with whatever software they are using. It would seem logical that in the first-year writing class, only generic or basic software would be used, but in reality, what happens is that instructors end up spending time showing students simply how to navigate the particular software they have. The responsibility of technical communication courses seems to be to enhance the specialized skills of their students, building on the general strategies they learned in previous classes. One way of stepping up the level of knowledge expected of students in a technical communications class is to get students to think of themselves more as designers than as writers. In fact, a detailed figure in a 1995 article from *Technical Communications Quarterly* (Kolosseus, Bauer, & Bernhardt) shows just how intricate one's knowledge of an interface needs to be; it shows 14 different layers involved in one simple screen. Teaching the more basic principles to the lower-level students makes sense because they need a smaller number of guidelines to follow to be able to absorb them efficiently. Later on in a writer's education, knowing these guidelines may help a student understand and compartmentalize those 14 different layers if one can group them by way of the principles they might have learned previously.

Private Writing, Academic Writing, Public Writing

The title of an article (Walker, 2002) published in the online journal *Kairos* echoes a sentiment that many writing program administrators and employers nationwide are asking: "yes, but can they WRITE?" (This is the actual title of the article, with upper and lower case letters exactly as it reads here.). It's all well and good if composition students can write narratives about personal experiences that are interesting, if they can pass essay exams with aplomb, but the true value of a successful education will no doubt be judged by how the world outside the academy views a person's writing. More and more now, this writing takes the form of hypertext, whether it originates that way or not; nearly everything can be viewed as a pdf file, and so the screen is the ultimate filter, the design and the structure are what register before the words do.

Setting Foundations, Looking Ahead

If composition instructors begin to focus their attention on incorporating hypertext and design theory into their curriculum, technical communication instructors can spend more time on trying to explain the intricacies of the software products they have in their labs instead of only skimming the surface or spending an excessive amount of time trying to explain the basic concepts of an effective hypertextual document. The key difference between the aspects taught would be the focus on theory in the composition course versus the focus on technology in the technical communication course. Working technical writers need to be familiar with as many types of software as possible, but without the knowledge of basic principles, all the bells and whistles won't make a bit of difference.

References

Bartholomae, D. (1995). Writing with teachers: A conversation with Peter Elbow. *College Composition and Communication, 46*(February), 62-71.

Berlin, J. (1987). *Rhetoric and reality: Writing instruction in American colleges, 1990-1985*. Carbondale, IL: Southern Illinois University Press.

Bernstein, M. (1999). Patterns of hypertext. [Online essay]. Retrieved August 22, 2000, from the World Wide Web: http://www.eastgate.com/patterns/Print.html. (Originally printed in F. Shipman, E. Mylonas, & K. Goenback (Eds.), *Proceedings of Hypertext '98*. New York: Association for Computing Machinery).

Booth, J.K. (2001). *This is not your mother's education: The need for hypertext writing in first-year composition*. Doctoral dissertation. Bowling Green State University, Bowling Green, OH. Available from Dissertation Express: http://wwwlib.umi.com (University Microform No. 3038407).

Brereton, J.C. (1995). *The origins of composition studies in the American college, 1875-1925: A documentary*. Pittsburgh: University of Pittsburgh Press.

Carter, L. (2002). Argument in hypertext: Writing strategies and the problem of order in a nonconsequential world. *Computers and Composition, 20,* 3-22.

Charney, D. (1994). The effect of hypertext on processes of reading and writing. In C. L. Selfe & S. Hilligloss (Eds.). *Literacy and computers: The complications of teaching and learning with technology*. New York: MLA.

Conklin, J. (1987). Hypertext: An introduction and survey: Computer as communication and thinking tool. *Computer, 20*(September), 17-41.

Douglas, J.Y. (1998). Will the most reflexive relativist please stand up: Hypertext, argument, and relativism. In I. Snyder (Ed.). *Page to screen: Taking literacy into the electronic era* (pp. 144-162). London: Routledge.

Elbow, P. (1995). Being a writer vs. being an academic: A conflict in goals. *College Composition and Communication, 46*(1), 72-83.

Eyman, D. (1996). Hypertext and/as collaboration in the computer-facilitated writing classroom. *Kairos, 1*(2). Retrieved July 29, 2003, from the World Wide Web: http://english.ttu.edu/kairos/1.2/binder.html?features/eyman/index.html.

Faigley, L. (2003). *The Penguin handbook*. New York: Longman.

Hairston, M. (1992). Diversity, ideology and teaching writing. *College Composition and Communication, 43*(2), 179-193.

Hart-Davidson, W. (2001). Reviewing and rebuilding technical communication theory: Considering the value of theory for informing change in practice and curriculum. *STC Proceedings*. Retrieved July 27, 2003, from the World Wide Web: http://www.stc.org/proceedings/ConfProceed/2001/PDFs/STC48-000119.pdf.

Hawisher, G., LeBlanc, P., Moran, G., & Selfe, C. (1996). *Computers and the teaching of writing in higher education, 1979-1994: A history*. Norwood, NJ: Ablex.

Hocks, M. (2003, June). Understanding visual rhetoric in digital writing environments. *College Composition and Communication, 54*(4), 629-656.

Johnson-Eilola, J. (1997). *Nostalgic angels: Rearticulating hypertext writing*. Westport, CT: Greenwood Publishing.

Johnson-Sheehan, R., & Baehr, C. (2001, Feb.). Visual-spatial thinking in hypertexts. *Technical Communication, 48*(1), 22-30. Retrieved July 31, 2001, from EBSCOhost, Academic Search Premier, Baron-Forness Library, Edinboro, PA.

Kitzhaber, A.R. (1990). *Rhetoric in American colleges: 1850-1990*. Dallas: Southern Methodist University Press.

Kolb, D. (1994). Socrates in the labyrinth. In G.P. Landow (Ed.), *Hyper/text/theory*. Baltimore: Johns Hopkins University Press.

Kolb, D. (1994). *Socrates in the labyrinth: Hypertext, argument, philosophy* [disk]. Available from Eastgate Systems. 134 Main St., Watertown, MA 02172 (http://www.eastgate.com).

Kolb, D. (1998, August 21). *Ruminations in mixed company: Literacy in print and hypertext together—Outline notes of a talk for KMI at the Open University.* July 1998. Retrieved August 17, 1999, from the World Wide Web: http://www.bates.edu/~dkolb/ou-dk.html.

Kolosseus, B., Bauer, D., & Bernhardt, S.A. (1995). From writer to designer: Modeling composing processes in a hypertext environment. *Technical Communication Quarterly, 4*(1), 79-83.

Landow, G.P. (Ed.). (1994). *Hyper/text/theory.* Baltimore: Johns Hopkins University Press.

Maimon, E.P., & Peritz, J.H. (2003). *A writer's resource: A handbook for writing and research.* New York: McGraw-Hill.

Miller, S. (1993). *Textual carnivals: The politics of composition.* Carbondale, IL: Southern Illinois University Press.

Reinking, D. (1997, May). Me and my hypertext:) A multiple digression analysis of technology and literacy (sic.). *The Reading Teacher, 50,* 626-643. Retrieved August 18, 1999 from EBSCOhost, Academic Search Premier, Baron-Forness Library, Edinboro, PA.

Selfe, C. (1999). *Technology and literacy in the twenty-first century: The importance of paying attention.* Carbondale, IL: Southern Illinois University Press.

Sorapure, M. (2002). Web writing and community service in Freshman Composition. *Kairos: A Journal of Rhetoric, Technology, and Pedagogy, 7*(3). Retrieved July 31, 2003, from the World Wide Web: http://www.ttu.edu/kairos/7.3/coverweb/sorapure/index.html.

Troffer, A. (2000). Writing effectively online: How to compose hypertext. Retrieved August 6, 2003 from the World Wide Web: http://corax.cwrl.utexas.edu/cac/online/01/troffer/htprinter.version.html (now available at: http://homepage.mac.com/alysson/httoc.html).

Walker, J. (2002). The third wave: Yes, but can they write? *Kairos: A Journal of Rhetoric, Technology, and Pedagogy, 7*(3). Retrieved July 31, 2003, from the World Wide Web: http://www.ttu.edu/kairos/7.3/coverweb/kiwi/index.html.

Chapter III

Millennium Leadership Inc.:
A Case Study of Computer and Internet-Based Communication in a Simulated Organization

Stacey L. Connaughton
Rutgers University, USA

Brent D. Ruben
Rutgers University, USA

Abstract

Technology, communication, leadership, and work processes are inextricably linked in contemporary organizations. An understanding of these topics and an ability to apply these understandings in the workplace is becoming increasingly critical for workers in all sectors. In this chapter, we discuss some of the competencies that are vital for success in the contemporary workplace, and provide a description of one approach to developing these skills: a simulated organization designed to create a dynamic classroom learning environment. We explain how simulations help students develop "real-world" competencies in effective communication and writing practices in mediated and geographically dispersed contexts, and we present how educators, students, and professionals may benefit from this approach.

Introduction

For many years, scholars and educators have investigated leadership in proximate settings—that is, in settings where leaders and subordinates are co-located with one another (e.g., Bass & Avolio, 1994; Burns, 1978; Fiedler, 1967; Mintzberg, 1994, 1973; Yukl, 1989, 1981). Contemporary organizations, however, often utilize geographically dispersed work groups. As a result, distanced leadership has become a timely and relevant issue.[1] Various degrees of geographical dispersion exist. Some organizations employ "telecommuting," a practice in which members may work at home, on the road, and/or at the office. Others have teams and operations that are globally dispersed. In these emergent organizational forms, computer and Internet-based technologies are the primary means through which organizational members and leaders communicate (Benson-Armer & Hsieh, 1997; Hymowitz, 1999; Townsend, DeMarie, & Hendrickson, 1998; Van Aken, Hop, & Post, 1998). Technology, communication, leadership, and work processes are inextricably linked in geographically dispersed organizations.

In this chapter, we present an approach to teaching and learning distanced leadership and mediated communication competencies in the classroom. Specifically, we: (1) discuss the role of simulations for approximating "real-world" dynamics within the classroom, (2) present a course design that allows educators to do so, and (3) give examples of computer and Internet-based communication from this course, *Leadership in Groups and Organizations*, developed by the authors at Rutgers University. Our approach is grounded in theory and empirical research in organizational communication, leadership in virtual teams/organizations, and written communication. The objectives of this chapter are to explain our approach to using simulation as an instructional model, highlight the outcomes of this approach, and discuss how educators, students, and professionals may benefit from such a design.

Background

Leadership and communication are central to successful distanced work relationships (Kayworth & Leidner, 2002; Wiesenfeld, Raghuram, & Garud, 1999).
And, leadership and communication are closely related phenomena (Witherspoon,
1997). For instance, *leadership is interactive and dynamic*. It constitutes an
ongoing process of interactions between leaders and followers (Connaughton,
Lawrence, & Ruben, 2003). *Leadership is also enacted through communication*. Leaders' communication competencies are critical to leadership practice.
Indeed, many of the behaviors that characterize exceptional leaders are communicative in nature (i.e., a leader may have an excellent vision for the future; but
unless he/she can articulate it to stakeholders, that vision may not become a
reality). To be an effective leader, then, one must be effective in their
communication with multiple audiences.

For educators, a critical question arises: Can leadership and communication
competencies be effectively taught in the classroom? We suggest here that they
can be taught and learned if one follows certain criteria (see Connaughton,
Lawrence, & Ruben, 2003; Prince, 2001). One criterion of leadership development programs is to provide learning opportunities for students to apply and
practice their knowledge, allowing them to experience the consequences of their
actions (Prince, 2001). In other words, in order to develop their leadership
potential, students need opportunities to lead. And, given contemporary organizational realities, students not only must have opportunities to lead others who are
co-located with them, they also must practice leading in *dispersed* organizational
and team settings.

Distanced Leadership & Communication Technologies

Distanced leadership—leading others who are not co-located with you—can be
more complicated than leadership in co-located settings (see Duarte & Snyder,
1999; Fisher & Fisher, 2001; Haywood, 1998; Lipnack & Stamps, 1997; O'Hara-
Devereaux & Johansen, 1998). Proximate settings allow organizational members and leaders to communicate frequently and spontaneously, provide opportunities for leaders and members to interact immediately if necessary, and foster
the chance for work relationships to develop and grow (Davenport & Pearlson,
1998). Leading over time and space, however, is more complex than leading co-
located teams because: (1) trust among leaders and team members may be swift
and precarious (Jarvenpaa, Knoll, & Leidner, 1998); (2) communication among
leaders and team members may be complicated by diverse cultural and organi-

zational norms (Cascio, 1999); and (3) geographically dispersed employees may feel isolated from other organizational members, from their leadership, and from "their organization" due to the physical distance (Fisher & Fisher, 2001; Lipnack & Stamps, 1997; Van Aken, Hop, & Post, 1998).

Mediated communication is central to these distanced work arrangements, and this may add another challenge to effective leadership. Distanced leaders often must use technology (e.g., email, video conferencing, computer-assisted meetings) to communicate with distanced employees. Understanding which media to use when, as well as making sure employees have access to equal media are critical to effective distanced teamwork (see Connaughton & Daly, 2004), but are not always put into practice.

Written Communication

From the perspective of leadership in the contemporary organization, written communication is a critical communication competency (Ruben & DeAngelis, 1998) and a topic of scholarly interest (Nystrand, 1982; Rafoth & Rubin, 1988; Reed, 1996). Effective written communication in the workplace is all the more critical due to the burgeoning array of options that the Internet and associated tools and technologies make possible.

There is no question that technologically mediated, text-based communication is becoming an even more primary means for conveying information in organizations than it was previously, but its importance and functionality hardly stops there. Given the increasing reliance on Internet communication and other workplace applications of information hardware and software, "writing"— broadly defined—has also become a significant activity for knowledge networking (Burtha, 2002; Drucker, 1998; McInerney, 2002; Nonaka, 1998), implementing team projects, providing formative and ongoing leadership (Connaughton, Lawrence, & Ruben, 2003), forming and maintaining relationships, and establishing and managing one's communities of practice and personal identity (Wenger, 1998).

The Traditional Paradigm in Teaching and Learning

As the previous sections have shown, Internet-based discourse is increasingly vital for dispersed organizations and individuals within today's workplace. Given this importance, a very fundamental challenge for communication instruction is: How should we prepare students with the knowledge and competencies necessary to fully comprehend and lead in a world of traditional and mediated communication, both of which define the contemporary workplace?

All too often, the process of teaching-and-learning communication has been thought of as an event in which an educator constructs and disseminates knowledge about communication concepts and skills using the accepted instructional technologies of the day—books, articles, lectures, and the Internet. The process is generally regarded as effective when there is evidence that the educator's intended message was transferred from teacher to learner—when message sent (MS) = message received (MR) (Ruben, 2004). Traditionally, educators test this process through assessments of the MS = MR correspondence. And, the more a learner is able to show that the appropriate knowledge has been acquired (through writing and speaking), the more successful the instructional effort is judged to be.

Limitations of this Paradigm

There are several potential problems with this way of thinking when it comes to teaching workplace communication competencies in the 21st century, however (Ruben, 1999; Connaughton, Lawrence, & Ruben, 2003; Connaughton & Quinlan, 2004). Perhaps the most important is that the ultimate test of a person's knowledge and skill acquisition is generally not in the knowing, per se, but rather in one's ability to use knowledge appropriately, which in many domains involves the translation of knowledge into behavior (Ruben, 1999).[2] So, for instance, while we want students to *understand* concepts, principles, and skills of mediated communication, we also want them to be able to appropriately *apply* this knowledge in their work. From the perspective of many workplace leaders, the difficulty recent graduates have effectively translating conceptual knowledge into practice application continues to be one of the primary sources of frustration (Ruben, 2004). Knowing that the Internet is important in the contemporary workplace, hearing about the types of traditional and electronic messaging used in organizations, and learning about the functions performed by organizational Internet-based communication does not ensure one's ability to perform Internet-based tasks effectively.

A second limitation of traditional approaches to teaching-and-learning as they relate to organizational and workplace communication competencies is that the traditional paradigm tends to emphasize the transmission of knowledge from an acknowledged expert to individuals in isolation, not in teams. However, teaching-and-learning about communication *outside* the classroom—and most particularly, in the workplace—is typically a collaborative enterprise. As Ruben (1999) has noted: "This leads to some very paradoxical situations. For example, what is likely to be called *cheating*—and viewed as a behavior to be extinguished—in a classroom environment, might well be called *collaborative learning* in the workplace, where it would be regarded as behavior to be idealized, reinforced and nurtured." This is certainly an issue relevant to written communication instruction. For a number of very logical reasons, writing is often taught and learned as an individual behavior. And students are evaluated on an individual basis. Yet in most organizational settings, many if not most of the writing activities one engages in are group endeavors.

A third concern with the traditional model is that the structure of classes, the physical layout of classrooms, and traditional approaches to testing convey a number of meta-messages about knowledge creation, acquisition, and use. The embedded message with the traditional teaching model is that there are a small number of informed sources (teachers) possessing the organizational and workplace knowledge that should be acquired by a large number of uninformed, passive learners (students). In the workplace, however, one's audience of evaluators for communication outcomes is generally quite diverse. In such settings, success involves creating messages that are well received by authorities, leaders, experts, *and* by peers, subordinates, and members of the general public. And, it is often the case that discourse that works well for one group does not resonate with others. The traditional classroom model may be criticized for creating dependencies on experts, and thereby doing too little to promote the acquisition of skills that assist an individual in evaluating and selecting among the wide array of competing information and information sources that one confronts outside the structured classroom environment.

Still an additional concern with the traditional teaching model is that while the workplace environment is dynamic, ever changing, and complex, the traditional classroom environment is typically quite static, syllabus-bound, and relatively simple. When compared to classical approaches to instruction in written communication, the contrast is quite striking. In the workplace, employees create messages for diverse audiences of varying sizes, composed in some instances for a single or small group of individuals they know, and others times for a large and anonymous audience of strangers. Individuals typically manage multiple writing assignments simultaneously, utilize multiple display media, and frequently engage in recursive writing—preparing multiple drafts for review and revision before the final. In the typical classroom, students create messages for one person (the instructor), manage at most a couple assignments simultaneously, typically utilize a very limited array of technologies, and generally approach written assignments as a bounded event. Students complete a test or write and submit a paper, wait for a grade, and that task is then complete. Contrarily, in the workplace it is not uncommon for a document to be rewritten a dozen times before it is disseminated. Even then, with many Internet-based documents, revision and repurposing continue, and with websites, review and updating is continual.

The contrasts between the teaching-and-learning paradigm, the kinds of instruction it provides, and the needs and realities of today's complex workplace are actually quite striking. Figure 1 captures these differences. Such contrasts prompt us to consider alternative teaching methods for communication, leadership, and writing.

Figure 1. Internet writing

Communication in the Workplace	Communication in the Typical Classroom
Complex audience dynamics	Simple audience dynamic
Variable audiences (size, familiarity)	Constant audience
Diverse audiences (gender, age, expertise, interests)	Homogeneous audience
Multiple formats (reports, resumes, emails, PowerPoint presentations, executive summaries)	Limited formats (exams, papers, presentations, email to instructor)
Multiple technologies	Limited technologies
Recursive communication (drafting and redrafting with feedback)	Single version

Experience-Based Learning: An Alternative for Teaching Communication in the Internet Age

Creating the realism of the workplace in an academic environment is a critical educational goal, when it comes to communication education. Experiential learning, and especially instructional simulations, can be a powerful vehicle for this purpose.

The theoretical foundations for experiential learning and simulations, games, and other forms of interactive, experience-based learning have been in place at least since the writings of Aristotle and the practices of Socrates. They were then reframed and popularized in the works of Dewey (1938, 1966), Bruner (1961, 1966a, 1966b), Flavell (1968), Mead (1934), Postman and Weingartner (1969), and others.

When properly designed and implemented, experience-based instruction—including simulations, games, and other structured activities—represent an attractive alternative to traditional classroom approaches.[3] Experiential models accommodate more complex and diverse instructional goals, foster interactivity, and promote collaboration and peer learning (Ruben, 1999). These approaches also allow for addressing cognitive and emotional and values-based learning, topics widely regarded as vital to workplace success. They are also of increasing importance in writing as the role of text-based communication becomes pervasive in a wide array of organizational contexts (Consortium, 2002; Goleman, 1997, 1998).

Teaching Writing for Use in Contemporary Organizations: A Pedagogical Model

Given this backdrop, we designed a teaching and learning environment to engage the complexities of communication and writing in contemporary organizational contexts. Our students in the course *Leadership in Groups and Organizations* at Rutgers University, formed *Millennium Leadership Inc.* (MLI), a start-up leadership and communication consulting organization. MLI is simultaneously a classroom activity and organizational experience. As a classroom activity, MLI is a simulated organization that seeks to engage students in organizational and leadership processes, and to foster critical inquiry and self-reflection about these processes. As an organization, MLI is a not-for-profit consulting organization that provides services to clients on internal or external communication matters.[4]

Every semester, students form various divisions (e.g., Human Resources, Public Relations, Field Operations, Research & Development), and based on students' resumes, the professors select a student "group manager" for each division. Together, divisional members write MLI's mission, vision, and goals statements; they design and execute tasks; they manage internal conflicts; they coordinate with each other; they engage in problem solving and trouble shooting; and they interface with an actual client on a project of educational, social, and civic import. With each of these responsibilities, students actively learn lessons that translate to organizational life in various ways. Specifically, the students learn how to lead and participate on project teams via communication technologies, and they learn about communication and writing via these media.

Although students have the opportunity to meet face-to-face twice per week, most of their intra-organizational and intra-team interactions take place online— through email, Instant Messenger, or Web board (Yahoo groups). Each semester, our students create different norms for communicating with one another through these mediated means, and we observe and discuss how their choices affected the organization's culture and work processes. Computer and Internet-based communication is the lifeline of MLI. Students discover firsthand how technology may enable and/or challenge communication between organizational members.

Since the course's inception, students in MLI have served one client, the Rutgers Environmental Health and Safety (REHS) department. REHS agreed to build a collaborative relationship with MLI for two reasons: (1) to gain assistance in developing and executing a communication plan that would encourage university-wide compliance with Federal Environmental Protection Agency (EPA) regulations, and (2) to support the purpose behind the collaboration—providing opportunities for experiential learning within the university (see Connaughton & Quinlan, 2004, for more details). As the next paragraphs reveal, this relationship was a fruitful one, not only for REHS but for MLI students and educators. It has led to three innovations in teaching and learning about communication, leadership, and writing:

Innovation 1: The MLI Model Complexifies the Notion of "Audience"

At MLI, students are not only writing for the "teacher"; they are continuously creating messages for multiple audiences including peers, coworkers, group managers, the CEO and President, and their client. By creating several messages with each of these audiences over the course of the semester, they learn to become attuned to individual needs and to what messages may resonate with certain audiences and not with others. They also learn that they must attend to these many stakeholder groups, particularly in making and communicating a decision.

On one occasion, the group manager of the Planning Division sent an electronic memo to all members of the other divisions reporting how the Planning Division would take over certain responsibilities. The text of that email was construed by members of other divisions as invasive and disrespectful of their abilities to execute their tasks. The email caused such disharmony that the President met with the five divisional managers and facilitated a discussion about motivations, intentions, perspective-taking, and moving forward. The session was heated at times, as meetings like this can be in professional contexts. But it concluded on a positive note, with divisional leaders expressing understanding of how others felt and why they acted the way they did. Moreover, they discussed how email was perhaps not the most appropriate channel for this sort of discussion, as recipients lacked nonverbal cues and could "read into" the textual message things that the sender did not intend. At the next class meeting, the CEO and President updated other MLI members of the meeting's process and outcomes, and they helped students make sense of why the conflict developed and how, as leaders, they can deal with similar conflicts in the future.

On another occasion, students applied their knowledge of multiple audiences to assist REHS with enhancing its website. In evaluating the website, they thought of the many stakeholders that would visit the website and how they may perceive it. When providing recommendations to their client, students learned that they should be sensitive to the fact that one REHS staff member had created the website and that he would be in the audience listening to their final presentation and ideas for its enhancement. Thus, in presenting their ideas in written and oral formats, students learned how to do so in a palatable way. They began by noting general principles of effective websites (e.g., easily accessible, consistent, adaptable to users, tested and debugged, current, documented, etc.). They then acknowledged the strengths of the REHS website before proposing general suggestions and concrete action steps, offering examples of other institutions' websites. The document that captures these ideas, presented to their client in written and mediated forms, includes clear and concise language (see Figure 2 for a sample).

Figure 2. Sample of electronic/written MLI document for enhancing REHS website

REHS Website Strengths:

Our initial task in evaluating REHS's website was to take a look at the site and pinpoint areas that work well for the site. Some strengths of the page are:

- The website provides very detailed information. For example, the BioSafety page has all valuable information.
- The site map is very organized, the color coding makes it easy to follow.
- The homepage has color and a logo, making it more friendly and less sterile.
- There is a hit meter (counter) on the page, so you can get an idea of how many people visit the site.

Suggestions for Future:

To help us better evaluate the REHS website, we found it helpful to look at other schools' environmental health Web pages. Many of our observations and suggestions stem from this examination, noting strengths and design elements REHS could use. After looking at these sites, we found that the following improvements would make REHS's website stronger and more useful for its stakeholders:

- The website itself is hard to find. Perhaps there is a way to have it listed under Rutgers' websites on the Rutgers homepage. For example, to find "REHS" a user has to go to "E" on Rutgers "A-Z". That may be difficult for users. One idea would be to list REHS under "R" for consistency.
- There is a great deal of information, but perhaps it is a little too much information. Break down information into smaller sections, so it is less intimidating.
- The wording should be easier to understand (less technical terminology). Audiences other than technically oriented ones will use the website as well.
- The website must be integrated with the other recommendations outlined in this document: include the revised Einstein logo, events REHS participates in and supports, as well as programs REHS might be running.

Innovation 2: The MLI Model Multiplies the Number of Different Media Utilized

Students engage in three genres of communication during their MLI experience: traditional written communication, mediated communication, and oral communication. Traditional written communication is practiced through periodic reflection papers in which the students are asked to critically ponder organizational experiences at MLI and write about them (e.g., "Think of a time, either at MLI or in your experience, when a leader has attempted to institute change. Assess the leader's communication strategies, using readings, lectures, and in-class presentations to support your points"). It is also practiced in their final examination in which students are asked to synthesize theory from leadership studies and organizational communication with their MLI experiences.

On a daily basis, students practice mediated communication. They use several channels such as listservs, Yahoo groups, email, and Instant Messenger to coordinate and communicate daily operations. For instance, one semester, the Planning Division (responsible for overall coordination of different divisions within MLI) decided to create and maintain an internal listserv to update all MLI members on the activities of other divisions. Students in this division learned how to implement and maintain this communication tool. They also learned how to convince group managers that such a service was critical to organizational processes so that the group managers would submit weekly updates to the Planning Division for the listserv.

Students also become frustrated when peers do not respond to their electronic messages, and they let each other know why timely responses are critical to organizational processes. One semester, the Research & Development group manager had such difficulties with her members not responding to her emails that she finally called a face-to-face team meeting to ascertain what the underlying issues were. In doing so, she learned that there were a variety of reasons for lack of response: one team member regularly checked a different email account than the one the group manager had an address for; another team member was not aware that she should be regularly checking email, thus only checked it once a week. Through these frustrating iterations, the group manager and her team members learned of the importance of setting expectations and norms for communicating via technologies.

Students also come to realize that not everyone prefers the same channel as they do for communication (e.g., some really like using Instant Messenger and others do not) and that not everyone has the same access to certain channels as they do (e.g., some students do not have Instant Messenger capabilities 24 hours a day). Both of these challenges lead to team members' lack of communication, and attributions about team members. For instance, one team member in the Creative Division was embarrassed to admit to his group manager that he did not have a computer at home; thus, he was unable to participate in Yahoo groups and Instant Messenger meetings after a certain hour every weekday and on the weekends. This unknown inequity in technology manifested in his team members initially believing that he was lazy and unwilling to contribute to work processes. In reality, he was very enthusiastic to participate and when he did so face-to-face or over the telephone, he proposed novel ideas. In this case, the MLI President and CEO (the authors) intervened by asking the student if there was something wrong that they could help with, learning of his communication obstacles, and then meeting with the group manager to brainstorm other communication ideas. His group manager worked with the student's needs and made sure to disseminate electronic memos to the team before 6:00 p.m. on weekdays and to give team members phone calls if important things came up on the weekends. That way, the student could stay in the loop.

Despite these challenges, most of the students prefer to use mediated communication for running MLI on a daily basis. Not only are most of them comfortable with using communication technologies, but the fact that they live in different parts of New Jersey and New York makes using communication technologies for everyday communication a necessity. This is one of the ways that MLI mirrors a geographically dispersed organization.

Students also practice oral communication at MLI. They do so in two ways. First, each division prepares and delivers a professional development presentation for MLI members (see Figure 3 for a description of this assignment). To do so, they research their topic (e.g., workplace diversity) and organize a 45-minute presentation that will be educating and engaging. Students also practice oral communication by delivering a final presentation to their client. With PowerPoint to enhance their talk, they create a 20-minute presentation that sells their ideas to the client. In one such presentation, students practiced integrating websites into their PowerPoint presentation so that they could show samples of websites they perceived to be effective to their client. One MLI member had previous experience in building PowerPoint presentations that visually displayed websites. As with all MLI activities, the professor (MLI CEO) asked this student to train other MLI members on how to do this. In the end, not only were the clients impressed with the presentation, but students had received training on how to integrate visual and textual data into their own future presentations.

Figure 3. Professional development presentation assignment

Presentation Length: 45 minutes–1 hour

Purpose: To teach MLI members about a topic in such a way that they can put what you are teaching them into practice immediately. Your presentation should enable members to better themselves professionally and enhance their division and organization. This assignment is designed to give you practice in developing and leading professional development presentations, for they are used regularly as methods of continuous education in many leading organizations.

Evaluation: Based on content, style, *audience involvement*, and team involvement in preparation for and/or execution of the presentation.

A successful professional development presentation will:

- Teach us things we do not know about the topic (e.g., lessons we cannot glean from our readings/lectures). If you'd like suggestions on where to look for materials, please let me know. I would also encourage you to remind us of things we already know about your topic to refresh our memories. Spend most of your time, however, teaching us new ways to look at old lessons or examining new lessons altogether.

- Apply those lessons to MLI. Why should MLI members care about your topic?

- Incorporate pertinent examples to emphasize your points.

- Involve the audience—be interactive and engaging; do not talk *to* us for 45 minutes. Include some sort of activity (activities).

- Get the audience to think critically about the topic and get us to think about the complexities of your topic.

- Have a fluid and sensible structure to the presentation (what your topic is, how it is created, its importance to organizations, etc.).

- Make the presentation appear professional.

- Have a clear handout(s) for everyone.

- Be sure to use complete citations for sources, both on PowerPoint slides and on handouts.

- Be very cognizant of the time. Presentations must be at least 45 minutes, but must not go over one hour.

- Effectively manage technology during the presentation (have back-up transparencies if we experience PowerPoint challenges).

Figure 3. Professional development presentation assignment (continued)

Things to Consider:

- Distribute an "agenda" handout—a "road map," so that the audience knows where the presentation is going. A verbal preview of main points for the day would be helpful as well.

- Consider incorporating a variety of mechanisms for learning in your presentation—I encourage you to think about the fact that people learn differently and we vary in terms of the teaching methods we prefer.

- Include your team members in the presentation—or, acknowledge their contributions in making the presentation possible. You have a choice here—all team members may participate in the actual speaking/ facilitating. Or, one or two people may lead us, as long as others contribute to making the presentation happen.

Innovation 3: The MLI Model Provides Opportunities to Practice Developing Messages

At MLI, students recognize quickly that they will be preparing different types of messages and drafting them over and over again. During the course of the semester, they gain experience writing press releases, boiler plates, executive summaries, memos to their client, survey items, interview questions, print advertisements, and internal memos (using email, Instant Messenger, Yahoo groups, etc.). The CEO and President (the professors) as well as the group managers insist that members write and re-write and re-write these documents. For example, in creating the boiler plate and press releases to be disseminated electronically to the Rutgers student newspaper and other media outlets, the Public Relations Division worked with its team and with its client, getting feedback and making several revisions before arriving at the boiler plate that they sent to REHS. All iterations of feedback are sent through electronic mail. Figure 4 shows the initial boiler plate copy submitted to the MLI CEO and President (the professors) and the first round of feedback on it. REHS will be working with a communication undergraduate intern on revising these documents even more before disseminating them to media outlets. Students also learn to plan ahead for drafting different messages. One semester, students developed a timeline to do so (see Figure 5).

Figure 4. Initial version of Boiler Plate with one round of feedback*

PR DEPARTMENT

REHS Boiler Plate:

The Rutgers Environmental Health and Safety committee (REHS) is committed to teaching Rutgers UNIVERSITY STAFF, PRINCIPAL INVESTIGATORS, AND STUDENTS ABOUT proper environmental policies. Through a continual self-auditing process, REHS plans to protect the environment, avoid monetary penalties, and implement compliance programs. Founded in 19__, REHS has put Rutgers, The State University of New Jersey, on the map as one of the first higher educational institutions to WORK ASSERTIVELY TO minimize risks in labs, dorms, and other facilities in the UNIVERSITY. At the same time, REHS has been working with the EPA to reduce environmental violations and increase training, awareness, and support FOR XXXXX at Rutgers.

*   REHS will work with a communication undergraduate intern to revise this boiler plate further before using it.

Benefits of the MLI Model

The MLI model yields several learning outcomes. Below, we have captured those related to leadership, communication technologies, and written communication:

- Leadership and Communication Competencies
  - being "other-oriented"
  - collaborating effectively with diverse team members
  - understanding the importance of reflection
  - learning how to engage in civil and constructive conflict
  - getting "buy in" from multiple stakeholders
- Communication Technology Competencies
  - heightening awareness of the need for all team members to have commonly accessible technologies to use
  - understanding the importance of "timely" communication
  - attending to team members' technological preferences

Figure 5. Timeline for developing press release

MLI
Creative Strategy Memo
Project: REHS

Objectives: To highlight the recent success of REHS in the Rutgers community, and make the public aware of the actions of the REHS in conjunction with the EPA. With special focus given to the groundbreaking relationship REHS has established with the EPA as well as tremendous amount of monetary fines REHS has allowed Rutgers to escape.

NOTE: This is an opportunity to let our client "shine" and the Rutgers community feel involved in this leadership position.

Strategy: To convince the Rutgers community of the positive attributes REHS has established within the university. Thus, gain the support of the students, professors, and researchers alike.

Execution: A final (client-approved) version of this release will then be submitted to the *Daily Targum*.

Target Audience: All Stakeholders, REHS members, MLI members, student population, and laboratory users.

Key Copy Points:

- Leadership of Rutgers within the university community in relationship with EPA

- Effectiveness/success of REHS

- Brief history/explanation of goals and functions of self-audit

- MONETARY PENALITIES AVOIDED

- Necessity of involvement and cooperation of community members

- Stress ongoing and continuous process of the self-audit and reparations

Mandatory: MLI letterhead, client approval, contact info (*Rutgers student newspaper* staff will need quotes from REHS and related parties)

Time: This press release should be submitted to [PR group manager] by 9/30 (a.m. preferred) for review. Please then be ready to receive it back with comments 11/1. Another version will be submitted to [professors] on Thursday before forwarding to the client for their feedback.

- Written Communication Competencies
  - synthesizing team members' diverse writing styles (and realizing that the process takes time)
  - writing for a specific audience…and for multiple audiences
  - writing executive summaries and briefings

Lessons for Industry

Several of the lessons our students learn during their MLI experiences are relevant to industry. One lesson that is reflected in the MLI experience is that distanced leaders must learn to select the appropriate medium to use for sending particular types of messages. This is a lesson also supported in research. Research shows that some media are better than others for sending certain kinds of messages (Daft & Lengel, 1984, 1986; Fulk & DeSanctis, 1995; Rice, 1993). Face-to-face communication, for example, is considered to be the "richest" medium because recipients can interpret multiple communication cues (e.g., nonverbals, voice inflection, and words) and give and solicit feedback immediately. This suggests that, when using Internet-based or other mediated communication tools is desirable or necessary, distanced leaders will also periodically use face-to-face communication when possible.

Another valuable lesson to include in training programs involves choices about when to use face-to-face and when to use communication technologies when trying to achieve various leadership objectives. Research suggests that managers should use rich media to communicate highly uncertain information and lean media for less ambiguous information because the latter (e.g., written messages and email) do not always allow for immediate feedback (Kiesler, Siegel, & McGuire, 1984). However, physical distance often prompts leaders to use lean (e.g., email) rather than rich media (e.g., face-to-face) (see Connaughton & Daly, 2003). And, in fact, mediated communication may be a better choice than face-to-face under certain conditions. Although we have not empirically tested this contention in MLI, in a previous study with leaders of geographically dispersed teams in global organizations, Connaughton and Daly (2003)discussed several leadership objectives which leaders perceive face-to-face and mediated communication channels to be well-suited for. Figures 6 and 7 present those data.

Another lesson that the MLI experience illustrates is that distanced leaders should make sure that distanced team members have access to equal media. For example, if two team members (one located in London and one in Caracas) have access to a particular videoconferencing system and another team member

Figure 6. Appropriate channels for achieving traditional leadership functions over distance

Channel	Give Direction	Monitor, Assess	Coordinate, Align	Review Performance	Exchange Information	Decision Making
Face-to-Face	Most Effective	Most Effective	Most Effective	Most Effective	Most Effective	Most Effective
Video-conference	Somewhat Effective	Somewhat Effective	Somewhat Effective	Somewhat Effective	Somewhat Effective	Somewhat Effective
Telephone	Effective	Effective	Effective	Effective	Effective	Effective
Email	Effective	Highly Effective	Ineffective	Ineffective	Highly Effective	Somewhat Effective

Figure 7. Appropriate channels for achieving additional leadership functions over distance

Channel	Build Trust	Maintain Trust	Inspire	Set Goals & Vision	Handle Conflict	Give Recognition
Face-to-Face	Most Effective	Most Effective	Most Effective	Most Effective	Most Effective	Most Effective
Video-conference	Ineffective	Somewhat Effective	Somewhat Effective	Somewhat Effective	Somewhat Effective	Somewhat Effective
Telephone	Ineffective	Effective	Effective	Somewhat Effective	Somewhat Effective	Effective
Email	Ineffective	Somewhat Effective	Somewhat Effective	Somewhat Effective	Ineffective	Effective

located in Hong Kong has an inferior videoconferencing system, problems may arise. Some locations may have highly sophisticated media (e.g., videoconferencing, high-speed broadband access) while other locations will have very limited equipment (e.g., telephone and 56K baud modem connections). Connaughton and Daly (2004) argue that the consequences of this disparity are grave. The "sophisticated" team members are able to communicate with one another in very different ways, and in the process, may exclude the "media poor" team members. Connaughton and Daly suggest that inequity in technology may create a perception of extreme isolation as well as an implied status hierarchy[5]. Effective distanced leaders are conscious of possible inequities in technology and find ways to deal with or correct them.

The MLI experience also offers other suggestions for training organizational leaders and employees. Not only should distanced leaders and employees be trained on which medium to use to send a particular message and on issues of access to technology, distanced leaders and employees should also be trained on

Figure 8. Communicative tactics to highlight in training programs for distanced leaders*

Distanced Leaders Should

- Engage in small talk with distanced individuals in face-to-face settings *and* in computer-mediated exchanges when appropriate.

- Regularly distribute company-wide information to remote employees (e.g., a virtual newsletter).

- Notify distanced employees of news that affects them at the same time as local employees receive the news.

- Match the appropriate communication technology to the desired leadership objective.

- Be specific and detailed with directions given over email.

- Initiate follow-up phone calls to important email messages.

- Forward email messages only to relevant parties.

Distanced Leaders Should Not

- Use email to discuss emotionally charged issues (e.g., disagreements, conflict).

- Deliver bad news over email.

- Assume that once an email message is sent, it will be read and understood.

- Relate information only one time and in only one way.

- Assume that everyone has access to the same sort of communication technology.

- Assume that meanings are shared.

- Allow email interaction to replace telephone/teleconference and face-to-face interaction entirely.

*   This checklist is adapted from original research done in global organizations. The original version of this checklist can be found in: Connaughton, S.L., & Daly, J.A. (2003). Long distance leadership: Communicative strategies for leading virtual teams. In D.J. Pauleen (Ed.), *Virtual teams: Projects, protocols, and processes* (pp. 116-144). Hershey, PA: Idea Group, Inc.

---

effective practices for communicating over distance. In some ways, communication over distance is like communication in proximate settings (e.g., writing should be clear; attention should be paid to how a message will resonate with who it is crafted for). But, in other ways, communication over distance is unique. For instance, distanced leaders must be more conscientious about finding set times to communicate with dispersed team members (see Connaughton & Daly, 2003). After all, they will not catch them in the hallway or coffee room. They must make time to communicate with them, and may choose to do so using Internet-based channels. Communication over time and space is also unique because the social or relational aspects of work must be consciously built in to mediated communication. There are not opportunities for spontaneous hallway chatter (e.g., "How are you?" "How was your daughter's soccer game?") when people are separated by physical distance. Distanced leaders must therefore use mediated communication tools (e.g., email or Instant Messenger) to send social messages to distanced employees. This requires forethought, as electronic channels are often used only to send task-related messages (e.g., to give directives or updates)[6]. Other communicative behaviors for distanced leaders that should be integrated into training workshops are included in the checklist in Figure 8.

Future Trends

As noted above, there are benefits to the MLI model. Yet educators also face challenges in facilitating a simulated organizational experience. For one, such a model is time intensive—for both students and educators. MLI is a living, breathing organization and thus, operates 24 hours a day, seven days a week. Professors and instructors leading courses like this must be prepared to live within the MLI mindset every day during the semester. Additionally, educators must find a client for students to work with and make sure that the relationship between their academic department and the client is in no way damaged by the MLI experience. Doing so requires constant oversight and coaching. Furthermore, some university colleagues may not initially "buy in" to the MLI experiential learning model, and educators may face resistance to and lack of support for such novel educational initiatives. We found that once we documented and publicized the student learning outcomes and demonstrated that external stakeholders perceive such collaborations favorably, resistance was minimized and the MLI model was championed. Still, educators should recognize that these obstacles may initially exist.

In the future, scholars and educators should work closely with organizations in various sectors to conduct longitudinal research on outcomes of leadership development programs, specifically on the impacts on writing/communication in organizations post-graduation. Currently, we have exemplary models of leadership development in higher education (e.g., U.S. Military Academy; see McNally, Gerras, & Bullis, 1996) and in the corporate arena (e.g., General Electric; see Melum, 2002). But educators and industry professionals lack a complete theory of how to develop leaders. Longitudinal studies of leadership development programs are in progress at Alverno College, Yale University, and the U.S. Military Academy (Horvath et at., 1999; Mentkowski & Associates, 2000). Such results will help educators better prepare students for leadership and communication in organizations and will assist professionals in designing workshops to enhance mediated communication and leadership in their organizations.

Scholars have often assumed that face-to-face communication is necessary when leading geographically dispersed teams and organizations. Although this is an empirical question, there is evidence to suggest that it is a perception that some distanced leaders hold. Connaughton and Daly (2003), for instance, interviewed distanced leaders in complex global organizations who were quite insistent that face-to-face is the optimal medium for communication. Email and telephone calls were regarded as necessary and helpful but not preferred for some leadership functions. None of these leaders perceived mediated technologies as optimal for personnel issues, conflicts, and relational development. Yet in interpreting these results, one must acknowledge that these responses may be tied to experience, training, and generational differences. It is quite possible that as people become more experienced with using various technologies for communication, the presumed primacy of face-to-face interactions may fade. This is an important area to explore in the future, as it will influence how organizations train distanced leaders and employees.

Conclusion

The experiences our students have had at MLI mirror many experiences that individuals working in geographically dispersed teams and organizations have had with technologies. Teachers of professional writing and composition courses, as well as students enrolled in these classes, can benefit from the MLI model because it provides an innovative framework and methodology for addressing an essential set of communication competencies. Professionals may be interested in this approach because it provides a promising model of collaboration between the workplace and the classroom, a collaboration that benefits industry and higher education. Administrators who develop writing and professional communication programs may find this instructional approach informative because it encourages increased dialogue between the academy and the marketplace, the benefits of which are many (e.g., providing students with "real-world" work-place competencies, enhancing the department/program's reputation with key constituencies and contributing to students' professional development; see Ruben, 2004). Thus, in many ways, the MLI model provides a useful approach for integrating the world of work and the world of the classroom for the benefit of all involved. Ultimately, of course, executing this model effectively involves a continuing effort to understand and analyze the changing world of work and the increasing role of mediated communication and distanced leadership, as well as working to ensure that the classroom provides the best possible preparation for our graduates relative to these evolving realities.

References

Abt, C.A. (1970). *Serious games*. New York: Viking.

Avolio, B.J., & Kahai, S.S. (2003). Adding the "E" to e-leadership: How it may impact your leadership. *Organizational Dynamics, 31*, 325-338.

Bass, B.M., & Avolio, B.J. (1994). *Improving organizational effectiveness through transformational leadership*. Thousand Oaks, CA: Sage.

Benson-Armer, R., & Hsieh, T. (1997). Teamwork across time and space. *The McKinsey Quarterly, 4*, 18-27.

Boocock, S.S., & Schild, E.O. (1968). *Simulation games in learning*. Beverly Hills, CA: Sage.

Bradford, L.P., Gibb, J.R., & Benne, K.D. (1964). *T-group theory and laboratory method*. New York: John Wiley & Sons.

Bruner, J.S. (1961). *The process of education*. Cambridge, MA: Harvard Press.

Bruner, J.S. (1966a). *Learning about learning*. Washington, DC: Government Printing Office.

Bruner, J.S. (1966b). *Toward a theory of instruction* New York: Norton.

Burns, J.M. (1978). *Leadership*. New York: Harper & Row.

Burtha, M. (2002). *Knowledge networking at Johnson & Johnson*. Presentation at the Doctoral Colloquium, Graduate School of Applied and Professional Psychology, Rutgers University, New Brunswick, New Jersey, March.

Cascio, W.F. (1999). Virtual workplaces: Implications for organizational behavior. In C.L. Cooper & D.M. Rousseau (Eds.), *Trends in organizational behavior* (pp. 1-14). Chichester: John Wiley & Sons.

Cascio, W.F., & Shurygailo, S. (2003). E-leadership and virtual teams. *Organizational Dynamics, 31*, 362-376.

Coleman, J.S. (1969). Games as vehicles for social theory. *American Behavioral Scientist, 12*, 2-6.

Connaughton, S.L., & Daly, J.A. (2003). Long distance leadership: Communicative strategies for leading virtual teams. In D.J. Pauleen (Ed.), *Virtual teams: Projects, protocols, and processes* (pp. 116-144). Hershey, PA: Idea Group Inc.

Connaughton, S.L., & Daly, J.A. (2004). Leading from afar: Strategies for effectively leading virtual teams. In S.H. Godar, & S.P. Ferris (Eds.), *Virtual & collaborative teams: Process, technologies, & practice* (pp. 49-75). Hershey, PA: Idea Group Inc.

Connaughton, S.L., & Quinlan, M. (2004). Learning leadership competencies as campus consultants. In B.D. Ruben (Ed.), *Pursuing excellence in higher education: Eight fundamental challenges* (pp. 80-87). San Francisco: Jossey-Bass.

Connaughton, S.L., Lawrence, F., & Ruben, B.D. (2003). Leadership development as a systematic and multi-disciplinary enterprise: The Student Leadership Development Institute at Rutgers University. *Journal of Educators for Business, 79*, 46-51.

Consortium for Research on Emotional Intelligence in Organizations. (2002, July). Available online at: http://www.EIConsortium.org.

Daft, R.L., & Lengel, R.H. (1984). Information richness: A new approach to managerial information processing and organization design. In B. Staw & L. Cummings (Eds.), *Research in organizational behavior* (pp. 199-233). Greenwich, CT: JAI.

Daft, R.L., & Lengel, R.H. (1986). Organizational information requirements, media richness, and structural design. *Management Science, 32*, 554-571.

Davenport, T.H., & Pearlson, K. (1998). Two cheers for the virtual office. *Sloan Management Review, 39*, 51-65.

Dewey, J. (1938). *Experience and education.* New York: Collier.

Dewey, J. (1966). *Lectures in the philosophy of education.* New York: Random House.

Drucker, P.F. (1998). The coming of the new organization. In *On Knowledge Management* (pp. 1-19). Cambridge, MA: Harvard Business School Press.

Duarte, D.L., & Snyder, N.T. (1999). *Mastering virtual teams: Strategies, tools, and techniques that succeed.* San Francisco: Jossey-Bass.

Fiedler, F.E. (1967). *A theory of leadership effectiveness.* New York: McGraw-Hill.

Fisher, K., & Fisher, M.D. (2001). *The distance manager: A hands-on guide to managing off-site employees and virtual teams.* New York: McGraw-Hill.

Flavell, J.H. (1968). *The development of role-taking and communication skills in children.* New York: John Wiley & Sons.

Fulk, J., & DeSanctis, G. (1995). Electronic communication and changing organizational forms. *Organization Science, 6,* 337-349.

Gamson, W.A. (1969). *Simulated society* New York: The Free Press.

Goleman, D. (1997). *Emotional intelligence.* New York: Bantam Books.

Goleman, D. (1998). *Working with emotional intelligence.* New York: Bantam Books.

Greenblatt, C.S., & Duke, R.D. (1975). *Gaming-simulation.* New York: John Wiley & Sons.

Haywood, M. (1998). *Managing virtual teams: Practical techniques for high-technology project managers.* Boston: Artech House.

Horvath, J.A., Forsythe, G.B., Bullis, R.C., Sweeney, P.J., Williams, W.M., McNally, J.A., Wattendorf, J.M., & Sternberg, R.J. (1999). Experience, knowledge, and military leadership. In R.J. Sternberg & J.A. Horvath (Eds.), *Tacit knowledge in professional practice: Researcher and practitioner perspectives* (pp. 39-57). Mahwah, NJ: Lawrence Erlbaum Associates.

Hymowitz, C. (1999). Remote managers find ways to narrow the distance gap. *The Wall Street Journal,* (April 6), B1.

Jarvenpaa, S., Knoll, K., & Leidner, D.E. (1998). Is anybody out there? Antecedents of trust in global virtual teams. *Journal of Management Systems, 14,* 29-64.

Kayworth, T.R., & Leidner, D.E. (2002). Leadership effectiveness in global virtual teams. *Journal of Management Information Systems, 18,* 7-40.

Kiesler, S., Siegel, J., & McGuire, T. (1984). Social psychological aspects of computer-mediated communication. *American Psychologist, 39,* 1123-1134.

Lederman, L.C. (1984). Debriefing: A critical re-examination of the post-experience analytic process with implications for its effective use. *Simulations & Games, 15,* 415-431.

Lederman, L.C., & Ruben, B.D. (1978). Construct validity in instructional communication simulations. *Simulations & Games, 9*(3), 259-274.

Lederman, L.C., & Ruben, B.D. (1984). Systematic assessment of communication games and simulations: An applied framework, *Communication Education, 13*(2), 152-159.

Lipnack, J., & Stamps, J. (1997). *Virtual teams: Reaching across space, time, and organizations with technology.* New York: John Wiley & Sons.

McInerney, C. (2002). Knowledge management and the dynamic nature of knowledge. *Journal of the American Society for Information Science and Technology, 53,* 1009-1018.

McNally, J.A., Gerras, S.J., & Bullis, R.C. (1996). Teaching leadership at the U.S. Military Academy at West Point. *The Journal of Applied Behavioral Science, 32*(2), 175-189.

Mead, G.H. (1934). *Mind, self, and society.* Chicago: University of Chicago Press.

Melum, M. (2002). Developing high-performance leaders. *Quality Management in Health Care, 11*(1), 55-68.

Mentkowski, M., & Associates (2000). *Learning that lasts: Integrating learning, development, and performance in college and beyond.* San Francisco: Jossey-Bass.

Mintzberg, H. (1973). *The nature of managerial work.* New York: Harper & Row.

Mintzberg, H. (1994, Fall). Rounding out the manager's job. *Sloan Management Review,* 11-26.

Nonaka, I. (1998). The knowledge-creating organization. In *On Knowledge Management* (pp. 19-45). Cambridge, MA: Harvard Business School Press.

Nystrand, M. (1982). *What writers know.* New York: Academic Press.

O'Hara-Devereaux, M., & Johansen, R. (1994). *Global work: Bridging distance, culture, & time.* San Francisco, CA: Jossey-Bass.

Pfeiffer, J.W., & Jones, J.E. (1969-1977). *A handbook of structured experiences for human relations training* (Volumes 1-6).

Postman, N., & Weingartner, C. (1969). *Teaching as a subversive activity.* New York: Delacorte Press.

Prince, H. (2001). Teaching leadership: A journey into the unknown. *Concepts and Connections: A Newsletter for Leadership Educators, 9,* 3.

Rafoth, B.A., & Rubin, D.L. (1988). *The social construction of written communication.* Norwood, NJ: Ablex.

Reed, W.M. (1996). Assessing the impact of computer-based writing instruction. *Journal of Research on Computing in Education, 28*(4), 418-438.

Rice, R.E. (1993). Media appropriateness: Using social presence theory to compare traditional and new organizational media. *Human Communication Research, 19*, 451-484.

Ruben, B.D. (1977). Toward a theory of experience-based instruction. *Simulations & Games, 8*(2), 211-232.

Ruben, B.D. (1978) *Human communication handbook. Simulations and games, vol. 2.* New York: Hayden.

Ruben, B.D. (1999). Simulations, games, and experience-based learning: The quest for a new paradigm for teaching-and-learning. *Simulations & Games, 30*(4), 498-505.

Ruben, B.D. (2004). *Pursuing excellence in higher education: Eight fundamental challenges.* San Francisco: Jossey-Bass.

Ruben, B.D., & Budd, R.W. (1975). *Human communication handbook: Simulations and games.* New York: Hayden.

Ruben, B.D., & DeAngelis, J.A. (1998). *Succeeding at work: Skills and competencies needed by college and university graduates in the workplace: A secondary analysis of quantitative and qualitative literature.* Report for the Conference Board, New York.

Ruben, B.D., & Lederman, L.C. (1982a) Validity, reliability, and utility in instructional simulation gaming, *Simulation & Games, 13*(2), 333-344.

Ruben, B.D., & Lederman, L.C. (1982b). Instructional simulation gaming: Validity, reliability, and utility. *Simulations & Games. 13*(2), 233-244.

Schein, E.H., & Bennis, W.G. (1965). *Personal and organizational change through group methods.* New York: John Wiley & Sons.

Tansey, P.J., & Unwin, D. (1969). *Simulation and gaming in education.* London: Methuen.

Townsend, A.M., DeMarie, S.M., & Hendrickson, A.R. (1998). Virtual teams: Technology and the workplace of the future. *Academy of Management Executive, 12,* 17-29.

Van Aken, J.E., Hop, L., & Post, G.J.J. (1998). The virtual organization: A special mode of strong interorganizational cooperation. In M.A. Hitt, J.E. Ricart, I. Costa, & R.D. Nixon (Eds.), *Managing strategically in an interconnected world* (pp. 301-320). Chichester: John Wiley & Sons.

Wenger, E. (1998). *Communities of practice.* Cambridge, England: Cambridge University Press.

Wiesenfeld, B.M., Raghuram, S., & Garud, R. (1999). Communication patterns as determinants of organizational identification in a virtual organization. *Organization Science, 10,* 777-790.

Witherspoon, P.D. (1997). *Communicating leadership: An organizational perspective*. Boston, MA: Allyn and Bacon.

Yukl, G. (1981). *Leadership in organizations*. Englewood Cliffs, NJ: Prentice-Hall.

Yukl, G. (1989). Managerial leadership: A review of theory and research. *Journal of Management, 15,* 251-289.

Zaccaro, S.J., & Bader, P. (2003). E-leadership and the challenges of leading e-teams. *Organizational Dynamics, 31,* 377-387.

Endnotes

[1]   Whereas some organizational scholars have coined the term "e-leadership" to refer to leaders who engage in many leadership behaviors primarily through electronic channels (see Avolio & Kahai, 2003; Cascio & Shurygailo, 2003; Zaccaro & Bader, 2003), we use the term "distanced leadership" to refer to leadership in dispersed contexts.

[2]   Ruben (1999) provides a broad discussion of the limitations of the traditional teaching and learning paradigm that provides a foundation for an exploration of how these issues relate to teaching and learning relative to organizational and workplace competencies in particular.

[3]   A good deal has been written about the appropriate use of experiential learning methodologies in communication. These include: Lederman (1984); Lederman and Ruben (1978, 1984); Ruben (1977); and Ruben and Lederman (1982a, 1982b). Among the contributors to the early writings on experiential learning include those addressing simulation (Boocock & Schild, 1968; Gamson, 1969; Greenblatt & Duke, 1975; Tansey & Unwin, 1969), games (Abt, 1970; Coleman, 1969; Pfeiffer & Jones, 1969-1977; Ruben & Budd, 1975; Ruben, 1978), and group learning approaches (Bradford, Gibb, & Benne, 1964; Schein & Bennis, 1965).

[4]   Although space does not permit us to include the syllabus here, please contact the first author for a copy of it.

[5]   That is, inequities in technology not only limit information sharing, but also affect people's perceptions of others and can have other unintended and long-term consequences for relationship devleopment.

[6]   It is important to note that there are also virtues of asynchronous communication such as bridging time zones, overcoming geographical distance, and responding at times that are convenient, just to name a few.

Chapter IV

Expanding the Classroom:
Using Online Discussion Forums in College and Professional Development Courses

Shawn McIntosh
Rutgers University, USA

Abstract

Traditional classroom environments can benefit from using asynchronous computer-mediated communication (CMC) such as an online discussion group (Yahoo! Groups). An online discussion group can "expand the classroom" in a number of ways, such as allowing for student and instructor interaction throughout the week at times convenient to all participants, shifting learning from a teacher-oriented to a network-oriented, collaborative learning environment, and providing rapid teacher feedback to homework that lets students immediately apply what they have learned. This chapter offers concrete advice on techniques to best use online discussion groups in a variety of class types and sizes, and warns of potential pitfalls to be aware of when using them. Evolving functions of

Yahoo! Groups and other asynchronous online formats that can further complement the learning experience outside the classroom are also examined.

Introduction

Much of the current research on information and communication technologies (ICTs) in educational settings concentrates primarily on distance learning situations or comparisons of the pedagogical effectiveness of distance learning with face-to-face (FTF), in-class learning. Although online distance learning is obviously an area of growing importance for educators, today most college students and adults taking professional development courses still attend classes, even as they use an increasing variety of ICT tools outside (and sometimes inside) the classroom. It is important for instructors in all areas to understand how best to use some of these ICT tools to create a richer, more engaging learning experience for students.

This chapter will examine asynchronous computer-mediated communication (CMC), specifically an online discussion group (Yahoo! Groups) in graduate-level writing and communication classes, and how the discussion groups improved the learning environment in five major ways. An online discussion group can "expand the classroom" in the following ways:

- participation with students and instructors can take place throughout the week and at times convenient to all participants;
- rapid feedback through the discussion group lets students apply what they have learned immediately;
- students can compare their work to that of their classmates when assignments are posted to the group;
- learning shifts from a teacher-oriented to a network-oriented, collaborative learning approach as students offer advice and information to fellow students; and
- students who are intimidated about speaking out in class have a less threatening way to participate in discussions.

Using asynchronous online discussion groups can be integrated into a variety of courses of relatively small class sizes as another tool to encourage learning. I have used these groups in graduate classes such as website publishing, organizational publications, online journalism, digital communication, and feature writing. Although online discussion groups easily lend themselves to use in communication or technology-oriented classrooms, they are also useful with more traditional subjects. Based on my experiences in using asynchronous online discussion groups, this chapter will offer concrete advice on techniques to best use them in a variety of class types and sizes, and warn of potential pitfalls to be aware of when using them. Finally, this chapter will address how some of the functions in Yahoo! Groups are evolving, and how they appear in other asynchronous online formats that have strong potential to further complement and expand learning outside of the classroom.

Background

Using ICT in educational settings has attracted growing interest in the past several years as researchers see the potential ICT has to transform the ways in which learning takes place (Littlejohn, 2002). However, educational researchers soon realized that simply using new technologies as electronic forms of traditional courses did not lead to more effective learning, although some research has shown that learning outcomes are improved with ICT at least partly because of increased student motivation (Gilliver, Randall, & Pok, 1998; Mayes, 1993). Even with such positive outcomes, however, there is a sense that in general, educators do not fully utilize ICT and CMC in distance learning environments or in classroom settings (Dehoney & Reeves, 1999; Kearsely, 1998).

The reasons for the perceived underutilization of ICT and CMC in educational settings are threefold: a lack of a comprehensive learning theory that explains the new and different learning and cognitive dynamics that ICT allows, lack of knowledge of computers and technology by educators, and unwillingness on the part of some educators to depart from passive, didactic modes of teaching (Littlejohn, 2002).

Although a thorough discussion of current learning theory regarding ICT and CMC is beyond the scope of this chapter, learning theorists have generally moved toward a constructivist pedagogy (Boyle, 1997). According to constructivists, experiencing and becoming proficient in the process of constructing knowledge is important in the overall learning process. A constructivist pedagogical framework works well within the interactive environment that Web-based and online communication tools easily foster.

As part of a more interactive approach to learning, there have been many studies in recent years that have examined Web-based or online collaborative learning (CL), also called group learning or networked learning (Joseph & Payne, 2003; McManus, 1997; Rimmershaw, 1999; Vat, 2001). Some of the studies and techniques self-consciously use various methods to foster greater interaction and collaboration between students, such as peer review and task-oriented online group projects that involve the students' own writings (Moreira & daSilva, 2003; Rimmershaw, 1999).

Educational scholars and educators have also used synchronous (i.e., chat rooms, Instant Messaging) and asynchronous (i.e., discussion groups, listservs, etc.) modes of communication for interactive online learning situations. Both synchronous and asynchronous modes can be used within a class; an educator should never feel that he or she must make an either/or decision. Each mode has strengths and weaknesses in CMC, and should be implemented when the strengths complement the specific educational task. Asynchronous communication lets students take advantage of varied schedules and time zones (in the case of distance education), and give students and educators more time to think about responses to questions or problems. Synchronous communication helps foster a sense of immediacy and closeness, even in text-based modes such as chat rooms or Instant Messaging, but forces participants to be online simultaneously and can sometimes feel slow and inefficient compared to the rate of information exchange if people were meeting in a classroom.

Social presence, or the measure of the degree of awareness of another person in a social interaction, is another important issue in online learning environments. Some researchers have claimed that social presence is the most important perception in an environment and that it is fundamental to person-to-person communication (Short, Williams, & Christie, 1976). The question for educational researchers regarding social presence has been to determine how elements of social presence such as immediacy and intimacy differ in CMC environments from FTF environments, and to determine how social relationships affect online interactions and the learning experience. The goal of course is to develop online courses that provide for a rich learning experience and that take advantage of the collaborative learning environment that often develops in classrooms as students get to know each other and help one another, with the strengths that ICT brings to learning environments.

Finding answers to the role social presence plays in online environments is not easy, however, as CMC characteristics with current technologies are mostly text-based rather than video-based. Since text-based communication does not allow for the establishing of social context cues as easily as FTF or even videoconferencing, researchers are concerned that students in online courses can feel isolated or waste time trying to establish social context cues rather than using the time on course content. Another area of concern related to a lack of social presence and social context cues is rude behavior online, such as "flaming" or verbal abuse that would normally not be practiced or tolerated in FTF situations.

Issues and Problems in Using Online Discussion Groups

With rapidly changing technologies and the theoretical, pedagogical, and practical uncertainties regarding ICT in the classroom or for distance learning, it can be difficult for educators to implement ICT in the classroom with a high degree of confidence that it will make for a better learning and teaching experience. In fact, there is a very real concern that improperly using ICT could actually hurt learning outcomes, or at least lead to negative attitudes about learning or a specific course or subject.

Even if an educator feels comfortable using ICT in the classroom, the experience may be unfamiliar to the students, causing a dual learning curve of how to use the technology as well as learning the normal coursework. Issues of computer and online access also need to be considered, although they are less important issues in most college environments than they were even a few years ago.

If technological, computer literacy, and Internet access hurdles are overcome, there can still be an issue of student attitudes toward ICT. Using a constructivist pedagogy means that ideally students are more aware of how and what they're learning, which can also lead to a perception of harder work than the traditional didactic/passive lecture mode in which students dutifully take notes, study from the notes, and take a test that they have been told will be derived from lectures and reading. One study of Australian undergraduates in a collaborative Web-based learning environment found that although the majority of students could see the value in learning from a student-centered approach, they still preferred the conventional teacher-directed form of learning experience (Oliver & Omari, 2001).

Student satisfaction with CMC courses in distance learning has been strongly linked to the social presence of the instructor, as well as instructor feedback (Moore, 2002). Issues of student loneliness, fear of failure, and lack of experience of learning in groups also contribute to feelings of dissatisfaction with online distance learning. On the other hand, CMC has given members of groups who would otherwise feel intimidated to speak out in class a chance to have a forum to discuss and participate with classmates. Some researchers have also concluded that the social interaction and social construction of knowledge that takes place in CMC (such as discussion groups) increases learning (Moore, 2002).

Important points to keep in mind when reading articles on ICT and CMC educational research are that the samples are often small, confined to a few classes of several dozen students; for experimental purposes the researchers likely put restrictions on ICT that may not apply in real-world learning environments; class assignments often draw undue attention on the use of the technology itself, rather than making the technology as transparent as possible and concentrating on learning tasks; and many of the types of classes studied tend to be technology or computer classes which likely have features that are not directly applicable for educators in other, non-technical fields.

For educators in any field who want to utilize what ICT and CMC seem to promise in terms of learning outcomes, the bad news is that computer and online technologies will continue to change rapidly, providing functionalities and modes of communication not previously available and spurring further research (and argumentation) on how such new technologies may be used in education. Likewise, the search for a solid theoretical underpinning that better explains online communication in learning environments will not end anytime soon, nor should it.

The good news is that educators can utilize currently existing, free online tools that are easy to learn that better engage students, increase attitudes toward learning and perhaps even learning itself, and allow for flexible and natural collaborative learning. With a minimum of effort and basic computer knowledge, educators can learn to use an online discussion group like Yahoo! Groups effectively to add an online, interactive component to the traditional classroom.

Solutions and Recommendations

For a class that meets regularly but that uses ICT and CMC to supplement the classroom experience, many of the most serious problems regarding distance learning, such as dissatisfaction that arises from perceived lack of social presence, are greatly mitigated or largely disappear. Problems with learning how to use the technology can also be overcome in an introductory in-class session in classrooms equipped with computers. Even without computers in classrooms, setting up a Web-based Yahoo email account and signing up to Yahoo! Groups is something most college students today can easily do.

Before explaining in detail how an online discussion group can help the classroom environment in the five ways outlined earlier, some general background information on what Yahoo! Groups is, what its functions are, and tips on setting up a group would be useful.

Group Functionality and Creation

Yahoo! Groups (first called Onelist, then called eGroups until Yahoo! bought them in 2000) is not the only online discussion group available, but it is the one

I have used and so will be the one discussed here. If a course management system such as WebCT or Blackboard allows the listserv and mailing list functionality as thoroughly as Yahoo! Groups, then it can of course be used in its place. It has been my experience, however, that sometimes accessing course management systems can be difficult for some students from computers outside the school firewalls and that they often do not have the same robustness in terms of listserv functionality.

Yahoo! Groups (http://groups.yahoo.com) is a Web-based, advertising-supported online discussion group that lets people create online groups on practically any topic. Although its primary functionality is more akin to a listserv or mailing list in that members of a group send an email to a particular email address that is broadcast to all members of the group, it has extra features that greatly enhance its value over traditional listservs or mailing lists.

Some of the features, besides a graphical user interface (GUI), include an archive of past messages up to three prior years, 20 MB of free disk space to place files, easy upload of photos, a section to add URLs of useful websites, a simple database, a chat room, a calendar, and a polling function. Although these features, or variations of them, are often found in most Web-based course management systems, what is lacking in some of the course management systems is the listserv functionality in which students receive postings to the group in their inboxes.

Some course management systems only allow instructors to broadcast email messages, not letting students post emails. This is a classic example of simply transforming the traditional instructor/student relationship to an online environment rather than taking advantage of the ease of broadcast communication for everyone in class. Most course management systems create additional barriers to the effectiveness of online discussions in that, in order to access the class discussion group, students must log into the system the school uses, then go to the Discussions area to read postings. Not all systems, especially some of the systems developed by individual schools, give students easy remote access, and even if they can access the system, there are too many steps to simply read and post messages, which discourages frequent visits. For active discussions or class sizes of two dozen students or so, even waiting a couple days to read messages means students must go through several dozen messages, which can quickly become overwhelming.

Yahoo! Groups largely avoids this problem by sending emails directly to inboxes. Group members do have the flexibility to get messages in a daily digest form of subject headings or to even get Web-only access and see posted messages only on the site. It is best to encourage students to use the email accounts they normally use so they do not have to remember to check a new account. Filtering messages from the group into a specific inbox folder can keep down inbox clutter. Students can add as many email addresses as they choose, so as work or study habits change during the semester, they can change how they access posted messages. Giving students the ability to decide how they receive messages also greatly reduces the administrative tasks of the educator, unlike many course management systems in which the instructor alone has administrative privileges.

When starting a group, there are a variety of options, including whether to be listed in the online directory (not listing makes it harder for people to find the group, which acts as a simple security measure), whether all messages should be read by the moderator or group owner before being posted (not recommended if the instructor wants to encourage free and open exchanges), whether anyone can join or has to be invited by the group owner (another useful security measure), and how much information regular group members can see. A simple, short name for the group email that will be easy to remember and type in is best, something like com440, which will become email address com440@yahoogroups. com when the group is created.

Many students in their early 20s have used CMC tools such as email, Instant Messaging, and chat rooms, so even if they are not familiar with Yahoo! Groups in particular, they will likely learn how to use it quickly. For some nontraditional students who are not confident in their computer abilities, step-by-step walkthroughs of the Yahoo! account registration process and Yahoo! Groups will help them overcome their computer anxieties.

Suggestions on Using Online Discussion Groups

I have used Yahoo! Groups both as a student in a new media technology graduate class of 30 students and as an instructor in a variety of classes with class sizes ranging from six to 20 students. Most classes have been technology-oriented (online journalism, website publishing, new media technologies, digital communications) that have some production components to them, such as developing websites. I have also used it for a feature writing class, and it worked easily in this sort of class that is not technology-oriented. Many of the same features that make it such a powerful learning enhancement tool—such as how it facilitates collaborative learning, provides an archival record of past assignments, allows for easy and informal peer review, and fosters a spirit of camaraderie and friendship among students—apply equally well to non-technology classes.

Although I have no quantitative evidence to support the following claims, they are based on my classroom and online experience. Class sizes of about 12 to 16 students seem ideal for using online discussions, although they can be used with some limitations for classes of around 30. Despite my initial assumption that an online discussion group would greatly enhance small classes of six to eight students, I found that there didn't seem to be a "critical mass" to keep discussions going among all students and the group was used less frequently and mainly to post assignments, even in proportion to larger classes in which quite often active discussions take place on topics related to lectures. Classes of more than 30 students would make reading all postings very time consuming and preclude detailed responses from the instructor. Students (and instructors) would be forced to adopt skimming or skipping strategies, thus undermining some of the usefulness of group and collaborative learning discussed later.

I use Yahoo! Groups as a place for everyone to introduce themselves, to post assignments (although graded assignments and edits are sent back or handed back privately), to post lectures or other written materials as well as hyperlinks useful to the class, and as a space to discuss relevant topics to the class or subject the students are learning about. I have learned that it is important to manage students' expectations regarding the volume of emails they will receive, to inform them what portions of online and class participation count for their grades, and to provide an example of what kind of postings regarding tone and subject matter are appropriate. There has never been a need for me to scold a student for inappropriate online comments or abuse directed toward other students, likely because of the FTF meetings at least once a week and relatively small class sizes so people quickly get to know each other.

Rather than waste the first class session having everyone introduce themselves, a tedious task at best and downright boring for a group of students who have been introducing themselves in every other class they are taking together, I spend the first class going over the syllabus and course goals, talking about some introductory content and making sure everyone is either signed up to Yahoo! Groups or can do so on their own. One of the first assignments is for people to post a brief bio of themselves online and, in some classes, post two stupid questions. Students are given extra credit if they answer someone else's stupid questions. Questions have ranged from "Why is our keyboard layout the way it is?" to "What is the difference between HTML and XML?" to "Why aren't clocks divided into 24 hours?" Many questions involve some sort of research to answer, and sometimes questions and answers have generated their own discussions.

Posting bios online serves several purposes. First, it doesn't waste a class session simply with introductions. Second, it gives the instructor a chance to post their bio first to establish the tone and sense of what is expected. Third, it gives students a chance to think more about what they want to say about themselves, and to present interesting facts about their backgrounds and experiences. Posting two stupid questions also serves a couple purposes. First, it is an easy forum for otherwise shy students to speak out. Having students ask two stupid questions (and the emphasis should be on really stupid questions, not faux-stupid questions) helps students overcome their fear of looking stupid in class and fosters an atmosphere of collaborative learning in a natural way as students answer each other's questions.

An extremely important point in this early stage of the discussion group is that the instructor provides rapid feedback to the students' postings. If the instructor posts his or her bio and then remains silent until the next class starts, the discussion group will likely be underutilized throughout the semester. Students seem to echo the energy and responses of the instructor, and if they see him or her responding to posted bios by making "small world" connections to classmates such as pointing out schools, jobs, or towns the instructor and students have in common, or commenting on similar interests, they are more likely to do the same with their peers.

It may seem that students could be overwhelmed with an avalanche of emails filled with trite, getting-to-know-you comments and quickly start looking for the drop slip, but this is not the case. Some scholars have looked at the role that observing dialogues plays in learning, and this same technique of posting most responses to the group lets others "listen in" so they can learn as well (McKendree, Stenning, Mayes, Lee, & Cox, 1998). The change from the first class of nervous, uptight strangers to the second class of students who have shared parts of their stories with each other and see each other as a group is transformative. Some students have commented in class and in evaluations that they suddenly feel like they know everyone so well that the atmosphere in the second class is similar to the spirit and atmosphere experienced at the end of semesters. Once this happens, an important hurdle has been overcome in fostering a collaborative learning environment in class and online. Other important foundations have been set as well for a successful semester that utilizes in-class learning while realizing a good part of the learning potential assumed in ICT and CMC.

Being a provocateur is another useful technique that I often use in generating discussions regarding assigned readings. Conventional wisdom has the instructor or group leader as a model of rationality and calmness among the squabbling masses, but this does not work as well as when the instructor is the one provoking students with questions or making apparently outlandish statements that students then have to successfully refute. I have made claims that print is dead—or soon will be—and challenged students to tell me why that may not be the case. This technique encourages students to think for themselves, provides a good example of how heated discussions online can take place without rancor, and again lets students learn from others' arguments and mistakes. With the "print is dead" argument, I can usually predict what the main responses will be and challenge their arguments, forcing later posters to refine their arguments and build on what's been discussed earlier.

The Seven-Day Class

As the previous example with online class introductions demonstrates, assigned postings to a discussion group work better when due dates are earlier than the next scheduled meeting. A rush of postings an hour before class begins does little to foster an atmosphere of cooperation and collaborative learning. Although some students (and instructors) would prefer to simply show up to class each week and think little about the class the rest of the week or until assignments are due, that attitude toward learning and teaching will not improve the learning experience, regardless of whether discussion groups are used or not.

Students often have questions after class or think of questions or comments during the week, and having an easy way to post questions or comments makes them more likely to do so. Again, it is best to respond as quickly as possible, usually within 24 hours, to help foster a sense of social presence online. Even a short note that an answer will come soon is better than no response at all.

An online asynchronous mode of communication of course allows students to read postings and respond according to their schedules, which further encourages participation as students can fit in short assignments and readings according to their schedules. Since a discussion group like Yahoo! Groups is Web-based, students are able to easily access the group from any Internet-connected computer, whether it be in an Internet café, at the library, from home, or even with a wireless PDA.

Conducting a "seven-day class" may appear to be less than ideal for overworked educators, but like the students it is easy to combine bursts of readings and responses into small chunks of time throughout the week, such as time between meetings. One of my professors even sent responses to postings from his Blackberry during faculty meetings, as well as when he was overseas at conferences. Responding in small bursts means less need for spending whole days and nights correcting or grading assignments that arrive en masse—unless the assignments do arrive en masse.

I try to manage student expectations on how rapidly I will respond to postings early, either by being consistent with the timing of responses or explaining to the class that responses will come within a given timeframe. I also try to be consistent in responding to students; researchers have shown that people tend to base their perceptions on whether someone likes them or not on the amount of lag time in responding to asynchronous online communications (Walther & Tidwell, 1995). An unusually long response time to a student could be perceived by them and others as a CMC equivalent of a cold shoulder.

Students can begin to expect impractically rapid responses, especially as deadlines draw near and when they themselves turn in assignments close to the deadline or late. A common, annoying question at the beginning of class is, "Did you get my assignment? I haven't heard anything back yet." It usually turns out they posted it an hour or so before class started. Explain early that posted assignments on a class-day due date, although not late, will not get immediate responses. Discussing issues or problems with earlier posts provide subtle yet powerful cues that it is in the students' best interest to turn assignments in earlier rather than later.

Rapid Feedback Speeds the Learning Cycle

In correlation with the idea of the "seven-day class," early postings of assignments and rapid feedback allow the students to apply what they have learned faster than if they had to wait a week or so for responses to assignments. In a website publishing class, for example, one of the first assignments after the bio is to pitch three website ideas and post the pitches to the group. This is typically due at least two days before the next class session, allowing time for online responses. When we meet in class, the first several minutes are devoted to going over responses, pitches, and further refining ideas or clarifying comments that were made regarding the ideas. Before the next session meets, students are expected to post a refined website idea pitch.

This technique considerably shortens what would normally be a three-week process into a class meeting once a week with weekly assignments. The end of the first week would have had students turning pitches, with no opportunity for other students to see the ideas. In the second week they would have received comments, some of which they may not fully understand, and at the end of the third week, they would turn in their refined pitch for the websites they would build the remaining weeks of the semester.

Using an online discussion group, by comparison, students are posting their ideas for everyone to see. Students are seeing responses to ideas they may well have determined are good or bad on their own, with instructor's comments that may confirm or further enlighten them as to what makes a good or bad website idea pitch. Learning from other postings and responses, they automatically refine their initial pitches, in turn getting more advanced feedback from the instructor that helps others. Class discussions help reinforce important points that were made in the discussion group and further expand the concept of social presence to online discussions. Sometimes students offer useful suggestions to others. By the time class meets the next week, students have refined their ideas and are ready to start building practical and interesting websites, although they still have a long way to go regarding practical skills and details. A whole week in the semester is saved using this system, and students have received much more feedback than the traditional method and, most importantly, have been able to learn from each other even if indirectly. Students have commented that they avidly read other pitches and the comments, and learn a lot from the process.

Group Learning

As research and the example above shows, learning from simply watching others can be effective (McKendree et al., 1998). Group learning is also effective, with some researchers even stating that learning is done best in a group situation rather than alone (Johnson & Johnson, 1991). Online discussions provide a certain economy of scale to the instructor in that comments reach all students who read the posted email, reducing redundant explanations. When there are redundancies, it further reinforces elements or mistakes that may not have been as apparent with the first response, thereby giving students the analytical skills needed to determine common factors or principles behind what otherwise may appear to be disparate issues or situations.

If students benefit by learning from the mistakes of others, it would seem that there is little incentive to be the first student to turn in an assignment, or at least turn it in earlier than others. This has not been an issue in classes I have taught so far, partly because there is a kind of event horizon in which turning something in late enough (although still on time) means they will not get a response in time for the upcoming class while others do receive responses in class. To also discourage what would seem like a natural inclination to wait to turn in assignments, I do not grade some of the early, minor assignments (such as website pitches), so students who turn in ideas early that are heavily critiqued are not penalized.

In official course evaluations, as well as evaluations I have given some classes regarding specifics of a particular class, students have repeatedly responded that for most posted assignments it was valuable for them to see what others had done and to see responses to those assignments. This type of format would work well in writing classes, for example, in which students can see edited papers or articles (sans grade) that would reinforce mistakes they may be making as well as give them a general sense of where they are in relation to others in the class. For a feature writing class, for example, by having students post their feature articles to the group, students were able to do this to some extent, and one assignment included editing each other's papers. But it would have been more useful if I had posted the actual edited papers to the group as well. Students would no doubt be comparing other comments with their comments and guessing at what other grades may be compared to theirs.

The discussion group helps make it clear quite quickly if there are points that students did not understand in the lectures or readings. One question can turn into a volley of similar questions asking for clarification on some point that was only met with silence in class. Students don't only learn as a group, even when using ITC and online communication forums—they often learn much from each other.

Collaborative Learning

As mentioned earlier, researchers have been examining ways to enhance collaborative learning in Web-based learning environments. The combination of classroom sessions with a strong online discussion group element makes fostering aspects of collaborative learning very easy to do. Best of all, online discussion groups do it in a way that does not draw attention to the pedagogical aspects of the collaborative learning experience. Rather, it stems from a natural realization that collaborating online benefits each student. An early, if unspoken example of this is the extra credit for answering a classmate's stupid question. This environment is further enhanced by any exchanges that take place between students as a result of bios that are posted—exchanges often occur between students who learn they grew up in the same state or town, share the same hobbies, or who have similar work or school experiences—all examples of the "small world" comments I mentioned earlier.

In some classes, students compliment each other on assignments that have been posted, and in the production-oriented classes, students often respond to queries on how to perform certain tasks such as making tables in HTML or adding or editing images. For classes that appear to be less reluctant to collaborate than has been my experience, continuing the offer of extra credit for sharing knowledge can be a good incentive, but usually this is not necessary as students willingly help each other.

Often "back-channel" forms of communication are created in which some students create their own small, informal online groups regarding the class. I have noticed this through references to emails that have not been sent to the group and comments from students, as well as my own experiences as a student. Discouraging such activities seems counter-productive and would at any rate be impossible to enforce. If too many students email the instructor privately with questions that would be better suited to the class as a whole, a gentle reminder to students to keep the group active would suffice.

Small sub-groups of students emailing each other would be more of a factor for group projects or assignments that by design require collaborative work. So far I have not used such consciously collaborative work, even with website projects, because assigned group projects often seem to degenerate into finger pointing and accusations of shirked responsibilities. In addition, students often assign themselves tasks that play to their skills, which lessens their potential learning experience. The individual projects and assignments I have given avoid these issues, yet take advantage of an informal collaborative working and learning environment.

Encouraging posts of relevant news articles or other online materials related to the class is another useful technique to foster collaborative learning. Students have posted useful websites on Web design techniques, interesting articles that I otherwise would not have seen, and book and other recommendations that enrich the learning experience for everyone, including the instructor.

This type of collaborative learning and practices with the discussion group help establish a more network-oriented approach to learning, in which students learn from each other as well as the instructor. That is not to say that the instructor simply fades away, as he or she still plays an important role as a kind of hub to keep all the connections together, and to oversee and direct the course. But it does change the roles of the instructor and students with each other to some extent. Some educators may find these changes threatening, but I personally find them invigorating. I continue to learn, and the students are more engaged in the learning process.

An interesting artifact of using Yahoo! Groups is that a kind of historical asynchronous collaborative learning takes place because of the archived messages. If the course number or name remains the same, there is no reason to create a new group every time a semester starts. It is much easier to remove the names of the previous semester's students (although I always ask if students want to remain on the group and contribute when they want) and add the new roster. The new students then have an accessible archive of past messages and posted assignments that they can refer to, and my students say they usually do refer to past postings on some of the more difficult or complex assignments. This is collaborative learning, with the original posters not even aware that they are collaborating with others who are learning.

Greater Participation

Online discussion groups offer students who are otherwise afraid to speak in class because of shyness, an accent, or a speech impediment a way to communicate on equal terms with more outspoken classmates. The ability to think about and craft responses also levels the playing field for those who may not be as quick with a comeback or as loud as others in spoken debate.

Greater participation plays well into the group learning and collaborative learning aspects of using discussion groups. With a twist on the well-known *New Yorker* cartoon of the dog at the computer, "On the Internet, nobody knows you're a dog," it becomes "On the Internet, nobody knows you're shy." It is especially rewarding to see students who otherwise may go unnoticed in class by the instructor and fellow classmates show that they can provide valuable contributions to class through CMC. It is interesting to consider that the lack of social presence in CMC is precisely the reason otherwise shy people can often express themselves so eloquently online—a case in which more social presence may not always be a good thing.

Future Trends

Despite changing and improving technologies, using online discussion groups such as Yahoo! Groups to enhance FTF classroom sessions can continue for some time. The principles being applied to foster collaborative, network-oriented learning, to help in group learning, and to expand the classroom to include learning in a variety of situations can be utilized with emerging technologies equally well. In some cases, current technologies are being applied and can work in conjunction with discussion groups.

For example, one weakness of Yahoo! Groups, even though it has a place to put files and another place to put URLs, is an easy-to-use knowledge base that can be coherently built on by students and used as a resource by future students. For this purpose, I used a version of a wiki, or website that can be edited by anyone with access to the site, to create a place online where students can go for production advice, links to useful website design and production websites, and instructions for signing up and using Yahoo! Groups. Best of all, students can post useful information that they have found on their own. I used swiki (a wiki with a basic GUI created by a programming language called Squeak) because of the ease of the interface (www.swiki.net). Wikis have been in use at some colleges for several years now, and there is even a wiki-based encyclopedia called wikipedia (www.wikipedia.org), which anybody can contribute to or edit entries.

In the future, it is likely that many of the functionalities that are currently separate will be combined into more seamless user interfaces, lowering the sometimes daunting hurdles in getting people to use computers and the Internet.

Although GUI interfaces may help make computers easier to use, the most profound transformations taking place are in communication patterns between students and teachers, and students with each other. The sooner educators learn how to better understand these changing patterns and to use tools that take advantage of these patterns, the better learning environments there will be.

In the meantime, education researchers should perhaps stop trying to deconstruct various minute elements of ICT and online distance learning in specific situations and try to generalize their effectiveness for learning outcomes; they should better integrate the strong points of CMC functionalities into contemporary classrooms where applicable, and study what works and doesn't work within an organic whole of FTF and CMC, just as many people encounter outside of the classroom.

Conclusion

ICT has changed many aspects of society, and academic institutions have not been spared. Despite the apparent promise of ICT and CMC to radically alter education, especially distance learning, results have largely been mixed. A lack of a coherent pedagogical theory to explain online learning behaviors and principles, combined with rapidly changing technologies and an unwillingness on the part of some educators to learn new technologies, has made implementing ICT in the classroom or in distance learning a daunting prospect even for the technophile educator. When new technologies are implemented, they have often been underutilized and then deemed failures.

However, some educators understand there is more to ICT than paperless archiving of syllabi, and that interaction among students and establishing social presence is fundamental to getting them engaged in learning and to fully realize the transformative power ICT has in education, especially in online distance learning.

Most educators today still teach in traditional classrooms however, so the question becomes how best to utilize ICT and CMC to complement classroom instruction. One simple way is to use online discussion groups for everything from posting introductory bios to assignments to discussion questions. Yahoo! Groups is one such discussion group that has mailing list or listserv functionality (an email message sent to a single address goes to everyone in the group) with additional features usually found in expensive course management programs.

An important aspect of making sure an online discussion in a course remains active is to have messages sent directly to students and not make them go through several steps to access postings. Once students are in the habit of receiving many more messages than they are probably used to, and responding to some of them, it is relatively easy to maintain an active discussion group throughout a semester.

The discussion group serves to expand learning beyond the classroom. It does this by making the entire class and instructor in some ways available all the time to answer questions or respond to postings. It allows students to work on smaller assignments or to participate in online discussions using small chunks of free time throughout the week, rather than trying to cram readings or other information in the night before class.

It also expands the learning experience from a teacher-oriented approach to a network-oriented or collaborative learning approach in which students willingly help other students and learn from posted assignments and instructor comments on those assignments. It means fewer reiterations of similar mistakes and less time spent covering the same material, which of course means more time to refine ideas and cover new ground.

By staggering assignment due dates so they are due before the next class meets, and by insisting that most if not all assignments are posted to the group, more material can also be covered if instructors are able to respond relatively quickly to assignments. This can be especially useful for short or accelerated courses.

Using CMC is likely not a new experience for most college students, and growing numbers of researchers are studying how CMC is changing social behavior and communication patterns. An online discussion group in a traditional classroom may be a different and new experience for students, but their communicative and collaborative practices during a semester are the same practices that will serve them well in today's world.

References

Boyle, T. (1997). Design for multimedia learning. In *Design for multimedia learning.* City: Prentice-Hall Europe.

Dehoney, J., & Reeves, T. (1999). Instructional and social dimensions of class Web pages. *Journal of Computing in Higher Education, 10*(2), 19-41.

Gilliver, R.S., Randall, B., & Pok, Y.M. (1998). Learning in cyberspace: Shaping the future. *Journal of Computer Assisted Learning, 14*, 212-222.

Johnson, D., & Johnson, D. (1991). *Learning together and alone.* Englewood Cliffs, NJ: Prentice-Hall.

Joseph, A., & Payne, M. (2003). *Group dynamics and collaborative group performance.* Paper presented at SIGCSE '03, Reno, Nevada, February 19-23.

Kearsely, G. (1998). Educational technology: A critique. *Educational Technology, 38*, 47-51.

Littlejohn, A.H. (2002). Improving continuing professional development in the use of ICT. *Journal of Computer Assisted Learning, 18*, 166-174.

Mayes, J.T. (1993). Commentary: Impact of cognitive theory on the practice of courseware authoring. *Journal of Computer Assisted Learning, 9*(4), 222-228.

McKendree, J., Stenning, K., Mayes, T., Lee, J., & Cox, R. (1998). Why observing a dialogue may benefit learning. *Journal of Computer Assisted Learning, 14*, 110-119.

McManus, M.M. (1997). Computer supported collaborative learning. *SIGGROUP Bulletin, 18*(1), 7-9.

Moore, M.G. (2002). (Editorial) What does research say about the learners using computer-mediated communication in distance learning? *The American Journal of Distance Education, 16*(2), 61-64.

Moreira, D., & daSilva, E.Q. (2003). A method to increase student interaction using student groups and peer review over the Internet. *Education and Information Technologies, 8*(1), 47-54.

Oliver, R., & Omari, A. (2001). Student responses to collaborating and learning in a Web-based environment. *Journal of Computer Assisted Learning, 17*, 34-47.

Rimmershaw, R. (1999). Using conferencing to support a culture of collaborative study. *Journal of Computer Assisted Learning, 15*, 189-200.

Short, J.A., Williams, E., & Christie, B. (1976). *The social psychology of telecommunications.* London: John Wiley & Sons.

Vat, K.H. (2001). Web-based asynchronous support for collaborative learning. *Journal of Computing in Small Colleges, 17*(2), 326-344.

Walther, J.B., & Tidwell, L.C. (1995). Nonverbal cues in computer-mediated communication, and the effect of chronemics on relational communication. *Journal of Organizational Computing, 5*, 355-378.

Section III

Perspectives
for Internet-Based
Collaboration

Chapter V

Creating Community in the Technical Communication Classroom

Timothy D. Giles
Georgia Southern University, USA

Abstract

A listserv can help to create a sense of community in a technical communication classroom. After reviewing relevant literature from Composition Studies, the author introduces the Psychological Sense of Community concept, which provides a research tool to direct a quantitative evaluation of the sense of community in four technical communication classes, two that use a listserv and two that do not. The author concludes that technical communication students would benefit from learning to become members of this type of discourse community because of its relevance to the working world.

Introduction

Traditionally, an Introduction to Technical Communication class drew students from engineering and scientific disciplines. As a result, students were more likely to enter the class with a better sense of community because there were more names and faces they recognized. However, as writing skills increase in value in the workplace, the technical communication classroom becomes more disciplinarily diverse, as students from education, the social sciences, and business are attracted to and often required to take the class. To foster a positive classroom atmosphere, it becomes more necessary to create a sense of community. This chapter will focus on the use of a listserv to create community in the classroom. First, relevant literature related to the composition community will be reviewed. Then, the concept of Psychological Sense of Community (PSC) as it is currently being studied in psychology will be examined. Next, the Sense of Community Index (SCI) will be applied to four classes, two that are using a listserv and two that are not using a listserv, to determine if the SCI supports the listserv as a way of increasing the sense of community in the classroom.

The Listserv in Composition Studies

The literature pertaining to listservs in technical communication classes is scant, so we must turn to the broader field of composition studies to find more discussion. Even in composition studies, however, there seems to be more focus on synchronous rather than on asynchronous communication in the classroom. Synchronous communication, which can take the shape of a chat room, MUD, MOO, or Instant Messaging, is more glamorous, perhaps even dangerous, and therefore exciting, since in this environment we read of virtual rape and banishment, middle-aged males masquerading as teenaged females, and virtual relationships turning into real-time ones that sometimes lead to face-to-face marriage. The listserv is an email medium that on the surface seems much more mundane, about as exciting as the office memo it is replacing. That in itself may be reason enough for the lack of apparent interest: since the listserv is, basically, a form of email, it is becoming as transparent as the telephone in our existence. Such transparency should not stand between it and scholarly discussion in technical communication, however, since the conventions of effective memo writing are a part of most technical writing textbooks, and some of these texts even advise students on effective telephone use. Furthermore, a variety of listservs provide people in professional fields with access to other professionals who can aid in problem solving or simply provide moral support.

Listservs have become so prevalent that it is only necessary to enter one's field in a search engine to find a relevant list. Some teachers require their students to sign on to a list relevant to their discipline, lurk for awhile, and then report on what they have discovered. Writing teachers themselves often subscribe to listservs such as the WPA-L (Writing Program Administrators) and ATTW-L (Association for Teachers of Technical Writing). Many writing teachers subscribe to one (or more) departmental or university-wide listservs, in addition to listservs for classes they are teaching. However, often these listservs may be for little more than to remind students of assignments or to circulate material for discussion in class, rather than for asynchronous discussion, which is how professionals often use a listserv.

To ignore the listserv in the technical writing classroom is a disservice to technical communication students. Hawisher and Moran (1993) have called for a rhetoric and a pedagogy of email. They support using email in the writing classroom in general because college professors use it as professionals, so we should expose our students to it because they are likely to use it in the workplace. As Hawisher and Moran conclude, "We need to build email into our discipline because in the future there will be more, not less, electronic communication. Email, we believe, deserves a place in the curriculum" (1993, p. 638). Selfe (1996) echoes their call by noting that email provides an opportunity to study the email messages themselves and the many other forms of electronic communication. She includes asynchronous communication among these. She emphasizes that in literacy studies, email represents a form of literacy that is fertile ground, which is especially important when one considers how desolate much of our culture is in terms of encouraging literacy. Email is a "participatory literacy in the form of writing, and one of the few literacy movements that has not received the formal attention of English teachers" (1996, p. 274).

Unfortunately, these calls for a rhetoric of email have been largely unheeded. Hawisher and Moran further note that, "A full rhetoric of email would consider the different rhetorical contexts for email, including in its view genres, audiences, voices, uses, and the extent to which any and all of these are influences by the properties of the medium" (1993, p. 630). Further evidence for a rhetoric of email can be found in the concept of a discourse community.

The Discourse Community

The idea of a discourse community has been prevalent in composition studies for about 20 years, and a listserv is an electronic spin on it since listservs suggest a sense of a written community, whether they are for an English Department, HTML users, scholars of fantastic literature, or molecular biology. Regardless, with a listserv, people link themselves via their email addresses, a central computer, and usually some type of moderator whose role may vary from merely overseeing the technical details of maintaining the listserv to approving messages sent to the list. Some lists are not moderated at all, however. Though it may be for as mundane a purpose as discussing TV soap operas, a listserv is nonetheless a discourse community that is created and maintained through the written word.

Students in a face-to-face class can benefit from the tools of distance education as a way of building community in the classroom. A strength of distance education for its students, especially those who engage in synchronous and asynchronous discussions, is the idea that the students write the class. Despite students' professional ambitions, these electronic discussions shape students into a discourse community. To be a part of such a class, students must write quite a bit and frequently; rather than simply attend class, hand in all required papers, and occasionally offer a comment, they must become part of a discourse community to assert their presence in such as class. Cooper and Selfe agree when they

> tacitly argue for the importance of discourse in learning, the importance of students talking and writing to one another as well as to the teacher as they attempt to come to terms with the theories and concepts raised in their courses (1990, p. 847).

Duin and Hansen support this idea as well. A strength of distance education is that students are able to extend the classroom beyond a room in a building where they meet at specific times. Instead, they can build a "peculiarly self-contained discourse community, situated literacy—limited to text-only participation and assigned class activities but nonetheless facilitating genuine meaning making, where the appropriate literacy is a situated literacy mediated by the participants" (Duin & Hansen, 1994, p. 102).

One might argue that in all disciplines, a goal is to introduce students to the discourse community. However, as Duin and Hansen have noted, "In a typical classroom situation, the discourse community is subsumed in the person of the instructor, as assessor, and arbiter" (1994, p. 96), which means that students merely observe the discourse community rather than partake of it. One purpose of writing a paper is to push the student into the discourse community, but again, these efforts in an undergraduate class usually take the shape of one or two research essays. Students in a traditional face-to-face class can benefit from electronic classroom encounters as well.

Technology in the Classroom

It is easy for teachers to become enamored with technology, especially one that is popular with their students and seems to facilitate learning. Furthermore, students are freed from the authoritative presence of the teacher. Duin and Hansen further comment: "When students examine the texts of other writers, they are often more likely to express their opinions, worry less about offending a classmate, and resist a tendency toward silence" (1994, p. 100). On the role of the teacher, Barker and Kemp (1990) note that rarely does the face-to-face classroom discussion sway from the teacher as the central arbiter. Occasions when students seize control of classroom discussions are regarded as chaotic, and after the teacher reins the class in, "It is most difficult for students to see themselves as anything but manipulated, and hardly the self-directed 'knowledge makers of real-world discourse'" (Barker & Kemp, 1990, p. 16). Selfe concurs when she notes that writing teachers must confront the problem of how to study student email without "turning the space of email into the same artificial, teacher-centered, teacher-controlled environment that the traditional classroom has become" (1996, p. 281).

Such direction supports the idea of the listserv as a site where knowledge can be socially constructed. Cooper (1999) reaches further, however, when she merges social construction with postmodern thought. Cooper expounds that:

> Postmodern theory is most often connected with nihilism: the loss of the centered self, the loss of truth and certainty, the loss of values and responsibility, the loss of the Enlightenment dream of a good society and the programs designed to achieve it. But postmodernist theory has a positive, progressive face—possibilities that open up when we jettison those things that are 'lost,' and it is those possibilities that I want to examine as they emerge in a pedagogy that employs electronic conversations. (1999, p. 140)

These losses, she notes, are part of what has pushed postmodern thought and social construction apart: As social construction builds knowledge through the group endeavor, postmodernism has been perceived as a vehicle for deconstructing social vehicles such as the traditional dominance in Western thought of Judeo-Christian Europe. In Cooper's postmodern vision, persuasion disseminates knowledge, which emphasizes knowledge as rhetorical. However, at its center, since postmodern thought depends upon persuasion, postmodernism is a social construction. Since "knowledge and the self are seen as socially constructed in language and thus multiple, contradictory, and divided, then in the classroom, the teacher is no longer the authority, so the students, along with the teacher, must socially construct the class" (Cooper, 1999, p. 144). According to Cooper, an electronic classroom discussion set up in this spirit is not an act that relinquishes control or dominates, but one that "sets up a range of possibilities set up by a face-to-face classroom discussion" (Cooper, 1999, p. 146). The teacher who creates the possibility of such an environment establishes a basis for a community where knowledge can be socially constructed.

Case Studies

There have been some attempts to study listserv interaction as it pertains to the classroom. Elias and Brown (2001) conducted a case study over four years with pre-service teachers and graduate TAs. Elias and Brown were interested in creating a space where these teachers-in-training could articulate their experiences. Elias and Brown sought to push them beyond teacher journals that tended to merely summarize activities or to complain. The listserv became a space for these teachers-in-training to share their experiences, discuss them, and work through problems. On the listserv, Elias and Brown observed conflict at times and silencing of voices over matters unresolved or unresolvable, such as how to deal with a parent who objected to a book a class was required to read.

According to Elias and Brown (2001), effective use of email requires a grasp of a system of socially distributed cognition. At its worst, email leads to a shallow treatment of issues, a hit-and-miss approach. They conclude that while not all of the interaction on the listserv was constructive, it taught the participants to read and to respond carefully.

Kinney (2001) has addressed how men tend to dominate listservs. Kinney studied the same students as Elias and Brown. In terms of gender, 80% of the list members were women, and in the beginning, their style of communication, one that builds communities and relationships, was pervasive, but as the quarter progressed, the men's style of argumentation began to dominate for both men and women, and a couple of men began to dominate the discussion. Women contributed 69% of the messages, which belied their 81% majority as listserv participants. Technology can work, then, to reinforce traditional power structures.

Kinney (2001) advocates teachers teaching respect for alternative styles of discussion. Part of the problem, according to Kinney, is Composition's reliance on traditional values of argumentation. Collaborative pedagogy asserts that what can be agreed upon is what is right. A cooperative rather than collaborative style may be the answer to some extent. The cooperative approach has feminist roots, and it suggests that relationships are built over a period of time and involve personal experience. Instructors could introduce this idea prior to discussion, or they could have the students analyze a list discussion.

Echoing Selfe's concerns about a listserv remaining student-oriented, Cubbison (1999) examines LISTSERV (Thomas 1986), a listserv software application. Few users are aware of the rhetorical limitations imposed by how the listserv is set up. This article explains how LISTERV may be configured, what subsequent decisions an administrator can make, and how those decisions shape the listserv rhetorically. If the administrator is interested in allowing voice for minority opinions without flaming, one configuration may be better than another because it influences who can and cannot speak. Decisions made for the header, for example, can control access. "Digesting" is a good example. "Digesting" refers to how messages from a list are delivered. Typically, a message is sent to the list, and then the server distributes the message to all list members. However, when a list is "digested," the messages are delivered at specific, predetermined intervals that may vary from several times a day to several times a week, depending on how busy the list is. As a result, by the time someone reads a "digest," a thread may have appeared and disappeared. Therefore, "digesting" can affect access to a list discussion.

The listserv is a place where a discourse community can be created, where students write the class. Doing so allows them to socially construct knowledge and fits in with postmodern thought, merging it with persuasion as a rhetorical act. To what extent, however, can that sense of a discourse community be measured?

Psychological Sense of Community (PSC)

The concept of a Psychological Sense of Community has been discussed for about the last 25 years, so it is reasonable to turn to this discipline to find a tool for measuring community in the classroom so that it can be used to measure the sense of community in four face-to-face classrooms, two using a listserv and the other two not using one. Sarason's *The Psychological Sense of Community: Prospects for a Community Psychology* (1974) is regarded as a seminal work. Sarason begins with an idea that resonates throughout this subfield of study, that we all know what it means to have a sense of community as much as we know what it means to lack it. Sarason also laments the sense of community we have lost in our society. Glynn provides more support for this idea of aimlessness and disaffection when he reports on a community psychologist who in 1972 began cataloging the number of books reviewed nationally with themes that expressed "loneliness, alienation, rootlessness, and not belonging—all evidence of...a declining psychological sense of community. After three months, so much material had accumulated that he stopped tallying because he saw no reason to confirm the obvious" (1981, p. 789). Today, this subfield within psychology is much more pronounced, with two journals (*Journal of Community Psychology* and *American Journal of Community Psychology*) devoted to it, as well as recognition in other journals.

Despite the fact that a PSC is accepted as a commonsense concept, psychologists who study it have had little success with a definition. Debate at a 1997 Society for Community Research (SCRA) conference ranged from "whether PSC is best conceptualized as a cognition, a behavior, an individual affective state, an environmental characteristic, or a spiritual dimension. No consensus was reached" (Chipeur & Pretty, 1999, p. 644). For the purpose of defining PSC, however, McMillan and Chavis' article, "Sense of Community: A Definition and Theory" (1986), is frequently cited. In this article, they outline what have become standard as a way of discussing PSC:

> –*membership*...the feeling of belonging or of sharing a sense of personal relatedness.
>
> –*influence*, a sense of mattering, of making a difference to a group and of the group mattering to its members.
>
> –reinforcement: *integration and fulfillment of needs*...the feeling that the members' needs will be met by the resources received through their membership in the group.
>
> –*shared emotional connection*, the commitment and belief that members have shared and will share history, common places, time together, and similar experiences. (McMillan & Chavis, 1986, p. 9)

These characteristics often guide the way a Sense of Community Index (SCI) is constructed through the intent of the chosen survey items. An example might be the Perkins et al. (1990) study of inner-city sense of community. Chipeur and Pretty (1999) recommend this study's SCI as good model because its parameters are based on the MacMillan and Chavis (1986) prototype. As a research instrument, it has been documented as "showing considerable sensitivity to detecting differences in various populations and contexts" (Chipeur & Pretty, 1999, p. 645). The actual construction of the SCI as it is generally applied and as it pertains to this study will be explained, and questions regarding its general application are discussed in the Methodology section.

A sense of community seems to be a commonsense notion in terms of its importance to a neighborhood, so a parallel might be thought to exist in the classroom. Surprisingly, given the amount of access academic psychologists have to the college classroom, little attention has been paid to it. MacMillan and Chavis (1986) have influenced Solomon et al. (1996), who evaluate the sense of community in the elementary school classroom as "when its members (a) know, care, and support one another, and (b) have the opportunity to participate actively in classroom decision-making, planning, and goal-setting" (Solomon et al., 1996, p. 722). They conclude that students "who find their school experiences to be supportive and caring are most likely to become attached and committed to school, and therefore to develop the attitudes, motives, and competencies valued by the school" (Solomon et al., 1996, p. 720). With middle school students, Goodenow designed her Psychological Sense of School Membership with the goals of measuring the extent to which students "perceived liking, personal acceptance, and inclusion...but also respect and encouragement for participation...and the perceived responses of other students...[and] teachers and other school personnel" (1993, p. 82). Though she does not cite Macmillan and Chavis (1986), her approach is quite similar, which points to the appeal of Macmillan and Chavis' objectives. She concludes that her "Psychological Sense of School Membership...may be a valuable tool both for identifying adolescent students at risk for disengaging from participation in school and for conducting research on social and contextual influences in education" (1993, p. 89). Finally, Lounsbury and DeNeui have studied the sense of community among college students. Their study compares the extent of community experienced among students at a large university (>20,000) to students at a small college (2,000<) (Lounsbury & DeNeui, 1996, p. 384). They drew upon Macmillan and Chavis (1986) for direction with creating their PSC survey. Lounsbury and DeNeui (1996) hypothesized that students at the larger university would feel a stronger sense of community, contrary to what could be surmised from previous research findings. However, they discovered that the conclusion that students at smaller colleges feel a greater sense of community was borne out by their research as well, except for a variable that accounted for extroversion as a personality trait among students, which indicated that students at a large university felt a greater sense of community if they also exhibited extroversion (Lounsbury & DeNeui, 1996).

An approach that is missing is the examination of a PSC in the college classroom. The Lounsbury and DeNeui (1996) study examines the relationship of the individual to the college as a community, not the individual classroom. As a result, some of the questions in the Lounsbury and DeNeui Collegiate Psychological Sense of Community Scale would not apply well to measuring the sense of community in the college classroom. Some examples include:

"My parents like this college."

"I someday plan to give alumni contributions to this college."

"If I am/were going to college next year, I would go here." (Lounsbury & DeNeui, 1996, p. 385)

Similarly, some questions from the Goodenow study present problems because they are gauged for the school as a whole and because they are geared to middle school students:

"Most teachers at (name of school) are interested in me."

"There's at least one teacher or other adult in this school I can talk to if I have a problem." (Goodenow, 1993, p. 84)

The Solomon et al. (1996) study published in the *American Journal of Community Psychology* does not include specific questions. However, to draw their conclusions, they utilized a questionnaire, interviews, peer nominations, and achievement and reading comprehension tests. Therefore, for measuring the PSC in the college classroom, there does not appear to be an adequate tool.

Methodology

Creating a new tool is not a drastic approach. To the contrary, it seems to be standard procedure. Chipeur and Pretty (1999) explain that researchers usually analyze existing tools, even within the SCI, and decide that for their purposes, the tools lack psychometric validity, either in general or for their particular case. Usually, the problem is that the versions of the SCI do not apply to the case in question. While Chipeur and Pretty (1999) advocate creating a consistent scale, one based on the SCI so that there will be greater consistency between studies, lending greater coherence and credibility to PSC, they agree that the "cultural and geographical influences on how people construct their notions of community" shape how it can be measured (Chipeur & Pretty, 1999, p. 645). As an example, they explain how Pretty and McCarthy (1991) constructed an SCI for their study, "Exploring Psychological Sense of Community Among Women and Men of the Corporation," by modeling theirs on McMillan and Chavis (1986); they simply substituted "workplace" and "workmates" for "block" and neighbors:

1.   I think my workplace is a good place for me to work.
2.   People in this workplace do not share the same values.

3.   My workmates and I want the same thing from this workplace.

4.   I can recognize most of the people in my workplace.

5.   I feel at home in this workplace.

6.   Very few of my workmates know me.

7.   I care about what my workmates think of my actions.

8.   I have no influence over what this workplace is like.

9.   If there is a problem in this workplace, people who work here can get it solved.

10.   It is very important to me to work in this workplace.

11.   People in this workplace generally don't get along with one another.

12.   I expect to work in this workplace for a long time. (Chipeur & Pretty , 1999, p. 652)

To study the PSC in a technical communication classroom, the Pretty and McCarthy SCI for the workplace was altered:

1.   I think my class is a good place for me to learn.

2.   People in this class do not share the same values.

3.   My classmates and I want the same thing from this class.

4.   I can recognize most of the people in this class.

5.   I feel at home in this class.

6.   Very few of my classmates know me.

7.   I care about what my classmates think of my actions.

8.   I have no influence over what this class is like.

9.   If there is a problem in this class, it can be solved.

10.   It is very important to me to learn in this class.

11.   People in this class generally do not get along with one another.

12.   I expect to apply what I learn in this class for a long time.

The questions were rated on a Mirreault scale of one to five with "one" representing "Definitely False" and "five" representing "Definitely True." To determine a better sense of the amount of group work the class engaged in, two questions were added. The first inquires if the students engaged in group work, and the second offers them a scale to indicate the amount of time spent per week on group work.

The Study

Four sections (n=58) of Rhetoric 3562, "Writing in Your Profession" at the University of Minnesota, St. Paul, were administered the survey. Two of the classes (n=29) did not use a listserv or a chat room as part of the course; the other two (n=29) used the listserv as part of their class, and for 10% of their final grade. They were required to submit at least one response each week and were told that more than one response would be considered the equivalent of class participation, which was not a quantifiable portion of the grade but definitely a factor that could determine a higher grade in borderline cases. During the semester, they were assigned to send 10 responses to the listserv. The study was set up to explore these hypotheses:

Ho: a = b

H1: a<b

with a = the control group SCI scores and b = the treatment group SCI scores.

Results

As the descriptive statistics of Table 1 reveal, there was little difference between the control and treatment groups.

Table 1. Descriptive statistics for control and treatment groups

			Statistic	Std. Error
Control	Mean		3.8508	9.223E-02
	Median		3.8333	
	Std. Deviation		.4967	
	Skewness		-.006	.434

Treatment	Mean		3.8046	7.539E-02
	Median		3.7500	
	Std. Deviation		.4060	
	Skewness		-.688	.434

However, the negative skewness differs by quite a bit, so histograms are worth examining. The histograms (Figures 1 and 2) reveal a somewhat different shape.

Figure 1. Control group

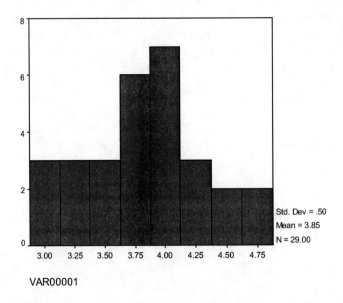

VAR00001

Figure 2. Treatment group

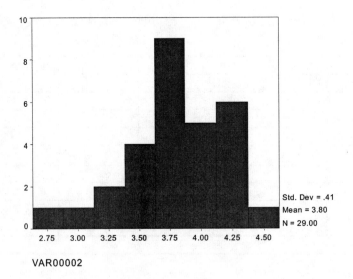

VAR00002

The histograms illustrate the more pronounced negative skewing. Therefore, examining each class individually is worthwhile.

Tables 2, 3, 4, and 5 display descriptive statistics for each of the four groups. There is a great deal of consistency between the two control groups. It is worth noting that the medians are 3.75, which is more meaningful than the means since medians are less susceptible to outliers, but they are not algebraically manipulative for the sake of correlations that describe relationships between the groups, so we will consider the means to check for correlations. At 3.8508 and 4.0109, the means for the treatment groups differ by .1601. Examining the difference of the medians, 4.0417 and 3.8333 changes these contrasts to a more significant .2084.

Table 2. Descriptive statistics for control group 1

			Statistic	Std. Error
Control 1	Mean		3.8046	7.539
	Median		3.7500	
	Std. Deviation		.4060	

Table 3. Descriptive statistics for control group 2

			Statistic	Std. Error
Control 2	Mean		3.8021	.1128
	Median		3.7500	
	Std. Deviation		.4512	

Table 4. Descriptive statistics for treatment group 1

			Statistic	Std. Error
Treatment 1	Mean		3.8508	9.223E-02
	Median		3.8333	
	Std. Deviation		.4967	

Table 5. Descriptive statistics for treatment group 2

			Statistic	Std. Error
Treatment 2	Mean		4.0109	.1261
	Median		4.0417	
	Std. Deviation		.5043	

No strong correlations exist between either the control group or the treatment group, or even between the two control groups. The strongest correlation is a negative one between the two treatment groups, and it can be characterized as moderately weak at best. Since the correlations are not strong, then the medians become more interesting in terms of their significance.

Group Work

The control and the treatment groups reveal that both groups participated in quite a bit of group work, as the average times in Table 6 below reveal.

Table 6. Average number of group work minutes per week

Group	Minutes per week
Control	47.58
Treatment	80

However, it must be remembered that these times are student estimates; 50 minutes per week would be a more realistic number for the treatment groups. However, the fact that the treatment groups perceived their group work as being greater than it was and that the treatment groups perceived themselves as participating in more group work than the control group is significant.

Discussion

While the differences between the treatment scores' medians are not as striking as they might be, it is important to note that the second treatment group's scores breach the 4.0 mark on a 5.0 scale. An overall score above the 4.0 mark is in itself remarkable.

It would have been interesting to know what type of community the students in these four classes had access to at the beginning of the semester. Future research in this area should consider testing at the beginning and at the end with the SCI to determine the extent to which the sense of community changes over a semester. A good question to add would be to ask the students to write down the first names of those they know at the beginning of the semester and then at the end. Another SCI could be varied by considering different questions in Glynn's list (1981) of over 120, so long as they conform in spirit to the guidelines set forth by McMillan and Chavis (1986).

The questions used for this version of the SCI need further refinement. For example, a student might interpret the first statement, "I think my class is a good place for me to learn," as asking for an evaluation of the teacher rather than the sense of community in the classroom. The statement can be used, but, like several others, it needs to be revised so that the focus is on the student's relationship to the other students. For example, it could be revised to, "I think my classmates create a good place for me to learn." Revisions of these questions might lead students to focus more on evaluating themselves and the group rather than the teacher.

A critical point for a longer, more comprehensive study would hinge on studying the sense of community as it relates to a listserv from the perspective of the detached observer who is not the students' classroom teacher. Hara and Kling (1999) raise this point about the findings of distance education studies in general often being questionable since, they observe, "students are likely to be polite to their instructors" (paragraph 16). On the other hand, students sometimes resist their instructors. Hara and Kling offer no evidence to support their assumption that students want to please their teachers. How often do students want to displease their teachers?

Student frustration with distance education is an issue that concerns Hara and Kling because anecdotally, they recognized the student frustration issue, but they were not reading critical, objective evaluations of it. Instead, what was being published praised distance education unilaterally. Among their findings were that students often became frustrated with the technology and the lack of access to the instructor.

Conclusion

This study demonstrates some disparity between the control groups and the treatment groups in terms of the sense of community, and it reveals directions for future research. It provides an interesting measure of community in a college classroom at an urban university.

Since the two control groups evidenced such similar scores, and disparity existed between the two experimental groups, it would be interesting to know the reasons. Qualitative research that would involve the researcher as an observer who could be a member of the listserv would allow for better observation and interaction with the listservs. More demographic information would help as well. It would be good to know information such as the students' age, class rank, work experience, and gender to try to determine a profile of the type of student who would benefit from a listserv. Such a step is supported by Thomas Russell, who has noted that "the real challenge facing educators today is identifying the student characteristics and matching them with the appropriate technologies" (1997, paragraph 5). Such a study of a listserv might make a "significant difference."

The listserv is a facet of the professional experience. Technical communication classes should introduce students to this aspect of professional communication. The technical communication classroom is an appropriate place to introduce students to the listserv so that they can learn to become members of this type of discourse community. Furthermore, a listserv is a way to introduce students to the idea of a discourse community itself. Especially as the role of technical communication expands in the workplace, students will find themselves further immersed in professional discourse communities. The technical communication class should prepare students to take their place in that discourse community, and the listserv can serve that purpose.

References

Barker, T.T., & Kemp, F. (1990). Network theory: A postmodern pedagogy for the writing classroom. In C. Handa (Ed.), *Computers and community: Teaching composition in the twenty-first century* (pp. 1-27). Portsmouth, NH: Boynton/Cook.

Chipeur, H., & Pretty, G.M.H. (1999) . A review of the sense of community index: Current uses, factor structure, reliability, and further development. *Journal of Community Psychology, 27,* 643-658.

Cooper, M.M. (1999). Postmodern possibilities in electronic conversation. In G. Hawisher & C.L. Selfe (Ed.), *Passions, pedagogies, and 21st century technologies* (pp. 140-160). Urbana, IL: NCTE.

Cooper, M.M., & Selfe, C.L. (1990). Computer conferences and learning: Authority, resistance, and internally persuasive discourse. *College English, 52,* 847-69.

Cubbison, L. (1999). Configuring LISTSERV, configuring discourse. *Computers and Composition, 16,* 371-381.

Duin, A.H., & Hansen, C. (1994). Reading and writing on computer networks as social construction and social interaction. In C.L. Selfe & S. Hilligoss (Ed.), *Literacy and Computers: The Complications of Teaching and Learning with Technology* (pp. 89-112). New York: MLA.

Elias, D., & Brown, D. (2001). Critical discourse in a student listserv: Collaboration, conflict, and electronic multivocality. *Kairos, 6*(1). Retrieved May 6, 2002, from: http://129.118.38.138/kairos/6.1/coverweb.html.

Glynn, T.J. (1981). Psychological sense of community: Measurement and application. *Human Relations, 34,* 789-818.

Goodenow, C. (1993) . The psychological sense of school membership among adolescents: Scale development and educational correlates. *Psychology in the Schools,* (January 30), 79-90.

Hara, N., & Kling, R. (1999). Students' frustrations with a Web-based distance education course. *First Monday, 4*(12). Retrieved May 1, 2001, from: http://www.firstmonday.dk/issues/issue4_12/hara/index.html#h8.

Hawisher, G., & Moran, C. (1993). Electronic mail and the writing instructor. *College English, 55,* 627-643.

Kinney, K. (2001). Online communities, self-silencing, and lost rhetorical spaces. *Kairos 6*(1). Retrieved May 6, 2002, from: http://129.118.38.138/kairos/6.1/coverweb.html.

Lounsbury, J.W., & DeNeui, D. (1996) Collegiate psychological sense of community in relation to size of college/university and extroversion. *Journal of Community Psychology, 24,* 381-394.

McMillan, D.W., & Chavis, D.M. (1986). Sense of community: A definition and theory. *Journal of Community Psychology,* (January 14), 6-23.

Perkins, D.D., Florin, R., Wandersman, A., & D.M. Chavis (1990). Participation and the social and physical environment of residential blocks: Crime and community context. *American Journal of Community Psychology, 18,* 183-213.

Pretty, G.M.H., & McCarthy, M. (1991). Exploring psychological sense of community among women and men of the corporation. *Journal of Community Psychology,* (October 19), 351-361.

Russell, T.L. (1997). Technology wars: Winners and losers. *Educom Review, 32*(23). Retrieved April 23, 2001, from: http://www.educause.edu/pub/er/review/review Articles /32244.html.

Sarason, S.B. (1974). *The psychological sense of community: Prospects for a community psychology.* San Francisco: Jossey-Bass.

Selfe, C.L. (1996). Theorizing email for the practice, instruction, and study of literacy. In P. Sullivan and J. Dautterman (Ed.), *Electronic literacies in the workplace* (pp. 255-287). Urbana, IL: NCTE.

Solomon, D., Watson, M., Battistich, V., Schaps, E., et al. (1996). Creating classrooms that students experience as communities. *American Journal of Community Psychology, 24,* 719-748.

Thomas, E. (1986). LISTSERV. [Computer software]. Landover, MD: L-Soft International Inc.

Chapter VI

Virtual Networks:
Mapping
Community-Based
Collaboration and
Professional Writing

Melody Bowdon
University of Central Florida, USA

Abstract

Today small businesses, public schools, local governments, universities, international conglomerates, and nonprofit agencies all feel the pressure to have informative and interactive presences on the Web. This new Web-based information economy has helped to significantly narrow the gap between the technical writing needs of profit and nonprofit workplaces. As local, regional, national, and international groups now compete for attention, business, and participation in the vast arena of the Internet, academic and workplace writers must develop theoretical and practical strategies for identifying and accommodating the varied needs of multiple organizations and audiences. Our technical writing students need to be cross-trained to face profit and nonprofit writing challenges, and our contact people in the community need to be aware of the benefits they can realize through working with students on major projects. In this chapter, I will offer some suggestions for making this collaboration work.

Introduction

The time in which we live in America is commonly referred to as "the era of the Internet" in political, educational, financial, and industrial communities. Virtually every product, service, organization, and concept imaginable has Web space devoted to it. The World Wide Web is a giant piece of real estate with seemingly endless space for expansion and discovery, which creates an exciting, convenient, and ethically complex reality. In this chapter, I will attempt to "map" spaces on the Internet through a model of ethical critique. I will argue that the emergence of the Internet has helped to blur the lines between the professional writing needs of profit and nonprofit groups, as every group feels the pressure to have a strong and meaningful presence on the Web. I will argue that this blurring requires that writing teachers cross-train professional communication students to work in multiple types of environments. Whereas a typical professional or technical writing course requires students to apply the skills and concepts derived from the course to hypothetical cases, rooted primarily in imagined or invoked corporate spaces, like a growing number of my colleagues, I advocate for diverse "real-world" experiences for students, including work in the nonprofit sector of the economy. I believe that an effective professional writing course should challenge students to recognize ways in which their work shapes the multiple communities in which they live. I advocate that we accomplish this objective by teaching our students to map the spaces in which they work and the ways in which language functions in those spaces. I will demonstrate the mapping principle through a description of my own Web-based graduate course in proposal writing.

Background: The Emergence and Commercialization of the Internet

Computer experts began developing the infrastructure we now call the Internet in the early 1960s. The network's purpose, at that time, was to enable researchers to share their work and to harness the power of multiple, connected computer systems. Specifically, researchers wanted to ensure their ability to communicate in the event of nuclear war. In a time when humans were facing eradication through our technologies of mass destruction, a small group of computer experts turned to this other form of technology for protection. In 30 years their secret plan for secure communication became, according to the Internet Society (2002):

"...at once a world-wide broadcasting capability, a mechanism for information dissemination, and a medium for collaboration and interaction between individuals and their computers without regard for geographic location."

Commercialization of the Internet began in the late 1970s and early 1980s when corporations saw the opportunity to make money by providing network services. During this time, users developed online communities for purposes such as research, collaboration, social connection, and increased productivity. Academics and computer experts were the primary users. When the juncture of available technology and cultural shifts made widespread access to the Internet possible, it took only a short time for the commercialization process to begin. Throughout the 1990s, all kinds of businesses saw the World Wide Web as a viable site for advertising and direct sales. As the ISOC website explains, "...it started as the creation of a small band of dedicated researchers, and has grown to be a commercial success with billions of dollars of annual investment." Clearly, in America today, commerce drives the Web.

The shift from academic and government control of the Web to the development of a vast and widely accessible space for expansion and communication has been significant for technical and professional writers. A cursory glance through important journals in technical and professional writing, including *Technical Communication Quarterly, Journal of Business and Technical Communication*, and *Technical Communication,* reveals that Web design and production of online materials, including tutorials, manuals, and so on, are staples of the work lives of technical and professional communicators. In his 1999 survey of Society of Technical Communicators (STC) members, Dayton (2003) found that 45% of 580 respondents reported that they used HTML editing/authoring programs at least occasionally and that 71% used Adobe Acrobat at least occasionally. Dayton notes that a high percentage of the documents created using Acrobat are ultimately posted on the Web, which means that even as long ago as 1999, when his data was collected, a strong majority of technical communicators were writing for the Internet on a regular basis.

Most of those surveyed in Dayton's study work in for-profit businesses, but the Internet isn't only creating a space where businesses can make money through providing Web services and selling products and services. Nonprofit organizations are also feeling the pressure and the opportunity to take advantage of this space. For purposes of clarification, in this chapter I will use the term nonprofit organization (NPO) in reference to groups that operate for religious, charitable, scientific, or educational purposes. According to the Internet Nonprofit Center (INC) website, "Once considered a dream, then a chancy bet, the Web is now widely accepted among business leaders, academics, and ordinary individuals as the next great wave of technological change in human communication." The INC encourages NPOs to develop a Web presence for at least eight purposes, including publicity, public education, fundraising, volunteer recruitment, service delivery, advocacy, research, and communication. The INC site suggests that a Web presence may be the key to long-term survival for NPOs.

In a 2000 article in *InfoWorld* magazine, Alnisa Allgood, the executive director of Nonprofit Tech, an organization that consults with nonprofits on their technology needs, echoes the concept that the Web is crucial to NPOs when she says:

> "We actually consider the nonprofit sector itself in a type of digital divide…The nonprofits who start successfully integrating technology and start reaping benefits in terms of additional grants and corporate sponsorships are the nonprofits that are going to make the transition to the Internet world."

Ethics and the Politics of Space on the Internet

The emergence of the Web as a dominant site for document production and presentation brings with it a set of ethically complex issues. Throughout human history, space has been a point of contention, the reason for wars, the architect of lives, and a motivation for movement and change. The development of this new and seemingly endless space for learning and teaching and selling and buying brings with it the same kinds of political issues that any such shift might. And our students, current and future professional communicators, stand at the edge of this space as future developers. It's crucial that writing teachers help them to recognize the politics of this space and allow them to see the importance of deliberation in making judicious use of this resource. We need to use professional writing courses to help students recognize the complexity of this space that originally was intended to support intellectual exchange and civil defense, but was soon co-opted as a place of commerce. I don't want to suggest to students that corporate influence is a necessarily negative development, but it is important to remind them that societal resources are finite and that we must use them judiciously if we hope to promote equity and diversity.

In *Justice, Nature, and the Geography of Difference*, geographer David Harvey discusses the significance of space in shaping culture and politics. Harvey underscores the point that any space is a social construction, and that in a capitalistic culture, that construction is largely tied to economic power. Even in a scene where space is relatively "free," where real estate is of relatively equal value, and where any person can register a domain for a relatively small fee, the politics of space on the Web are still complex. Harvey suggests that in order to alter or even understand spatial politics, we must learn to map the space that is in contention, and to recognize the power we hold as mappers. Harvey's historical-geographic materialism approach suggests that one key to challenging social arrangements is to challenge the maps that construct them. Harvey argues that when we knowingly engage in the process of critical mapping, we can find moments for potential change. He writes:

"The discursive activity of 'mapping space' is a fundamental prerequisite to the structuring of any kind of knowledge. Any talk about 'situatedness,' 'location,' and 'positionality' is meaningless without a mapping of the space in which those situations, locations, and positions occur. And this is equally true no matter whether the space being mapped is metaphorical or real." (p. 111-112)

Thus it is useful to help our students learn to map their activities in Web-based courses, plotting their geographic relationships and the social and economic impacts of their work. In this way we can help students to recognize their power to shape civic spaces on the Web and beyond.

Patricia Sullivan and James Porter advocate a model of postmodern mapping as a tool for inquiry in the study of writing technologies in *Opening Spaces*. Like Harvey and other postmodern geographic theorists, they suggest that such an approach can help us to understand and make use of power structures. In this case the model is proposed specifically for the development of research strategies. Sullivan and Porter write:

"For the study of writing technologies, we advocate a view of research as a set of critical and reflective practices (praxis) that are sensitive to the rhetorical situatedness of participants and technologies that recognize themselves as a form of political and ethical action." (p. ix)

These authors are hoping to bridge gaps among computers and composition, rhetoric, and professional writing as they suggest that all of these subfields can learn from each other and need to develop a more up-to-date collaborative research model. The authors invite researchers to trace relationships among entities in a rhetorical situation in order to recognize tensions, discover connections, and understand the spaces in which action takes place. I believe that this kind of mapping is an excellent tool for students, faculty members, and industry personnel who are interested in re-envisioning their relationships beyond the classroom. One key to understanding space through this model is recognition of difference.

As she critiques common models of "community" in social theory, ethicist Iris Marion Young promotes the city as a model for a culture that functions in the midst of difference. She writes:

> "As an alternative to the ideal of community, I develop in this chapter an ideal of city life as a vision of social relations affirming group difference. As a normative ideal, city life instantiates social relations of difference without exclusion. Different groups dwell in the city alongside of one another, of necessity interacting in city spaces. If city politics is to be democratic and not dominated by the point of view of one group, it must be a politics that takes account of and provides voice for the different groups that dwell together in the city without forming a community." (p. 227)

Young's vision of the city can offer a productive way of looking at the relationships between corporate and non-corporate entities on the Web and in our Web-based courses as well. We do not need to encourage students to envision these types of organizations as necessarily similar, for their differences contribute to the strength of our communities through the diversification of learning and writing models. As Young advocates that we focus on our efforts to secure justice less on distribution models and more on valuing difference, we can encourage our students to see their study and development of Web spaces for NPOs as part of this ethic of valuing difference and shaping the map of the Internet in a meaningful way through collaborating together on projects for businesses, NPOs, and other groups.

Spatial Politics of Professional Writing on the Web

In the U.S., we expect any entity whose services we might wish to use or goods we might want to purchase to have a *dot something* address. Though most consumers are not formally trained in usability studies, we know which sites we like, which sites we find easiest to navigate and access, which sites we want to share with friends. And while we likely have different standards for personal and professional websites, we expect most sites that we access in order to procure information, goods, or services to meet basic standards of professionalism and convenience. As a result, NPOs must compete for our online attention with the most expensive and professionally designed business sites on the Web.

Mega-size NPOs such as the United Way, the American Cancer Society, and the Red Cross have long had significant presences on the Web designed to provide information and to allow supporters to make donations online. Small, local, private NPOs, however, which represent the vast majority of the groups, rarely have sufficient financial resources, access to technology, or staff with appropriate expertise to be similarly present (Rogers, 2003).

But that trend is changing as Americans become more and more reliant upon Web-based information and transaction services. Smaller NPOs are feeling the pressure and seeing the benefits of strong Web presences. Despite the initial costs associated with a move to the Internet, these groups are learning that the long-term benefits outweigh the initial outlay. According to the Internet Non-profit Center: "By the end of 1995 there were over 2,500 nonprofits on the Web, over 30 million Internet users and an enormous universe of information and opportunities, all growing by leaps and bounds every day." This growth motivated more and more NPOs to move their work to the Web in the latter half of the 1990s, including groups as diverse as local domestic violence shelters, children's service providers, environmental activist groups, and so on. And this shift is changing the world of Web-based learning and Web-based working for current and future professional writing students.

In fact, businesses and other kinds of organizations have turned development of Web services for nonprofits into a kind of cottage industry. Any search engine can quickly locate hundreds of sites that offer Web services to NPOs, ranging from hosting to Web design to database construction to templates to complete "tool packages" that allow nonprofits to track and manage multiple layers of work via the Web. These businesses specialize in servicing nonprofit groups because they are a growing Web presence. In some ways nonprofits represent an unclaimed territory in Web services, a place where there is still amazing potential for growth and development. Ironically, nonprofits are becoming big business. And this is a "business" that our students need to be ready to participate in. Few students, industry representatives, or faculty members realize the economic impact that NPOs have in our nation. That impact and its relevance to the writing classroom and the workplace is the focus of the next section.

The Significance and History of Nonprofit Organizations in America

There are an estimated 1.2 million NPOs in the United States today (Salamon, 2002), and they have a major impact on our economy. In 2000, American nonprofit assets were at $2 trillion and revenues exceeded $700 billion (Bradley, Jansen, & Silverman, 2003). Lester M. Salamon, editor of *The State of Nonprofit America* explains:

> "As of 1998, these organizations employed close to 11 million paid workers, or over 7 percent of the U.S. work force, and enlisted the equivalent of another 5.7 million full-time employees as volunteers. This means that paid employment alone in nonprofit organizations is three times that in agriculture, twice that in wholesale trade, and nearly 50 percent greater than that in both construction and finance, insurance, and real estate." (p. 5)

Salamon also notes that NPOs raised more than $1.3 billion in response to the September 11 attacks, and that estimates suggest that 70% of Americans contributed to this response (p. 4).

The significance of NPOs in America is unique in the Western world, according to David C. Hammack, author of *Making the Nonprofit Sector in the United States* (1998). He writes:

> "No other nation manages its religious, cultural, social service, health care, and educational activity in this way (although in recent years Great Britain, Canada, Israel, and a few other nations have moved in this direction)...Nowhere else do nonprofits own such impressive facilities or hold such large endowments. In most of the world, governments and tax-supported religious groups continue to provide all—or nearly all—social service, higher education, health care, and opera, orchestral music, and museum exhibitions." (p. xv)

Hammack and other historians of American culture suggest that this unique relationship between business and nonprofit sectors was a logical outgrowth of the origins of American government. British rulers restricted colonists' rights to engage in activism or to form groups for the purpose of social action. As the revolutionary framers of the Constitution worked to emphasize separation of the church and state, they created a space where organizations outside the political machine could provide services to citizens largely free from governmental control. Nineteenth century institutional responses to the problems related to the industrial revolution, the civil war, and other moments of national upheaval continued this tradition.

This unique approach sparked the interest of Alex de Tocqueville, an aristocrat, survivor of the French revolution, and a student of American culture. In 1840 he observed:

"Americans of all ages, all conditions, and all dispositions constantly form associations. They have not only commercial and manufacturing compa- nies, in which all take part, but associations of a thousand other kinds, religious, moral, serious, futile, general or restricted, enormous or diminutive. The Americans make associations to give entertainments, to found seminaries, to build inns, to construct churches, to diffuse books, to send missionaries to the antipodes; in this manner they found hospitals, prisons and schools. If it is proposed to inculcate some truth or to foster some feelings by the encouragement of great example, they form a society. Wherever at the head of some new undertaking you see the government in France, or a man of rank in England, in the United States you will be sure to find an association." (p. 150)

Despite de Tocqueville's sense that these organizations were free of govern- ment control, during the late 19th century the federal government began to collaborate with nonprofit corporations that served its social service agendas. In the 20th century women and African-Americans formed nonprofit organizations to seek the right to vote and to pursue other civil rights. The expansion of science and technology in the early decades of the 20th century demanded the develop- ment of new scientific and professional societies to support growth and progress.

Later in the 20th century tax laws became a significant issue and official definitions of the term "nonprofit organization" evolved. Because of this economic connection, government organizations became more directly involved with nonprofits through regulation and collaborative projects. State and federal grants support the work of nonprofits today, and each year the lines between the government and nonprofit sectors become progressively more difficult to identify, particularly in social services, education, and health care. Hammack explains:

"The extraordinary expansion of federal spending for social and health care services brought about by Lyndon Johnson's Great Society and

Richard Nixon's New Federalism profoundly reshaped the nonprofit sector. The federal government played almost no role in funding nonprofit organizations prior to the mid-1960s." (p. 455)

But today government funding is an integral part of the nonprofit sector, and state and federal grants are a major source of support for many NPOs; in fact the current trend under President George W. Bush is to turn more responsibility for many social projects over to NPOs and corporations. Salamon summarizes the current complicated state of nonprofits in America in this way:

"In short, nonprofit America has confronted a different set of challenges over the recent past. Fiscal stress, increased competition, rapidly changing technology, and new accountability expectations have significantly expanded the pressures under which these organizations work, and this has affected the public support these organizations enjoy and their ability to attract and hold staff." (p. 22)

And as our information-driven economy changes and grows, state and federal governments are increasingly both engaging in partnerships with NPOs such as schools, hospitals, and social services organizations, and relying more on these organizations to do the social work of our communities. The threads of this economy are becoming increasingly entwined and the lines between them more difficult to identify. For this reason, too, our students must be trained to recognize the subtle differences in the audiences, purposes, and uses of discourse produced in these sectors. In order to be effective communicators and active leaders in our changing economy, students must experience diverse rhetorical situations. According to their syllabi, most professional and technical writing instructors hope to help students understand the audiences, purposes, and uses of documents they produce. A cross-training model, which exposes students to multiple writing contexts, can help to accomplish this goal.

Service-Learning and Other Models

One effective method for making these connections and diversifying students' experiences is service-learning pedagogy, which allows students to put the communication skills they are learning in their writing and document design courses to work for NPOs. This model is part of a growing national trend toward breaking down what many refer to as the "town/gown" binary. The more than 900 university and college presidents who are members of the Campus Compact recognize their institutions' responsibility to share resources with their local and regional communities and value the learning opportunities such partnerships create for students. This national organization's mission is to promote "community service that develops students' citizenship skills and values, encourages partnerships between campuses and communities, and assists faculty who seek to integrate public and community engagement into their teaching and research" (Campus Compact, 2003). To accomplish this goal, university administrators are supporting faculty interest in service-learning.

Service-learning pedagogy has been particularly significant in technical and professional writing, a field that has long recognized the value of giving students real-world opportunities to write and design documents. Through my own 10 years of experience with using a service-learning approach to teach advanced writing courses, I have found that this method allows students to develop a unique set of experiences and understandings. The service-learning model that J. Blake Scott and I advocate in our *Service-Learning in Technical and Professional Communication* encourages faculty members to make service to the community the focus of their courses. In this model, students write letters of inquiry, project proposals, progress reports, final evaluations, and many other documents throughout the course based on their service projects. Many of our colleagues around the country have had great success with this popular approach, but it is not the only option for faculty members who wish to train their students to work for nonprofit agencies, and such projects don't have to be the sole focus of a course.

Hafer (1999) argues that this kind of project can be presented to students as pro bono work, similar to that which professionals in many fields do once they are established. In the pro bono model, students could work on one discreet design or development project for an NPO as an isolated assignment for a course. Hafer describes a project in which his students designed a brochure for a youth baseball league.

Other strategies for gaining this type of experience could include paid and unpaid internships, commissioned assignments, and short-term contract work. In other words, these projects don't always have to be provided as free services to the community. They can also be paid projects that help students to recognize the economic, political, and social impact that NPOs have in our country, and they can be funded in a variety of creative ways. In a later section I'll describe an innovative method we're experimenting with at the University of Central Florida to give students an opportunity to develop this diverse background.

Writing for a Business versus an NPO

If we could give students a simple and reliable list of predictable differences between writing for the Web in businesses versus NPOs, we probably wouldn't need to provide them with extensive experiences in either setting. If a list of tips and concepts were enough to prepare students for the challenges they'll face as professionals, they wouldn't need to take our courses or buy our books. Despite the fact that a simple list of differences won't address all of these concerns, however, I would like to provide a few observations on basic differences between these two types of experiences.

- Businesses generally focus on sales; NPOs generally focus on services. For this reason, the writing for websites in each context is different. One student recently told me: "Business and professional writing allows more room for puffery: 'We're the best'; 'We're number one'; 'We beat our nearest competitor by 200%'; etc. In writing for a nonprofit, the persuasion is often more complex and subtle."

- Businesses generally have more staff members, which equals fewer responsibilities per person than in an NPO. Students find that in businesses there are more staff members available to assist them with projects, and that those staff members are available more consistently. This means that students writing for a nonprofit will likely have broader responsibilities.

- Businesses generally work from templates and models; NPOs often have few models to work from. This means that students who work in both settings gain experience in melding their work into a standardized format and style as well as in generating entirely new approaches to texts.

- Rhetorical power is not as tied to title and position in NPOs as in businesses. Because NPOs tend to be less hierarchically organized than businesses, volunteers, students, and low-level staffers can often write on behalf of the group and have significant sway over audiences from clients to potential funders.

- Business site content is often already developed; in many NPOs it must be generated. It's unusual for a business to turn a content development project over to a student worker. In most cases, students working on business sites are expected to take existing content and work on layout and design more than on language. Often NPOs have little content developed for their sites and rely on students to gather information from existing documents or to engage in original research to develop it.

- Businesses have IT coordinators; NPOs have donated computers. Few local NPOs have staff members with high-tech experience and have high-end equipment. Working in both types of environments allows students to learn about how to best take advantage of the situations they find themselves in. Many learn that they can develop effective documents that can be efficiently updated by NPO staff members after a bit of training even with fairly low-end equipment. This is an altogether different challenge from seeing how far they can push state-of-the-art computers in a business.

- Some students indicate that the actual writing process is different, largely because of the motivation associated with writing for an NPO. A response that captures this experience came from a technical writer enrolled in one of my graduate professional writing courses. She reflected on her experience of creating a brochure for an organization that provides services to families of children with cancer. She wrote, "Writing on behalf of a nonprofit has allowed me to use my voice and write with passion and emotion. The main difference between this and what I do at work is the attachment I feel to the cause that I am writing for. I feel that business writing tends to be a little more restrictive and, well…professional. I don't let my emotions come through in the tone of a business letter."

It is important to keep in mind that many other variables, including the size of the organization, its number of staff members, and its primary purpose shape the rhetorical landscape significantly. Students working with a large NPO like the United Way might find the experience similar to working at a large corporation. Students working at a small private nonprofit might find many connections to work done at a small and struggling business. The key is to give students as many diverse opportunities as possible and to help them recognize issues surrounding the profit/nonprofit divide.

Professional Writing Instruction and Practice and the Nonprofit Sector

The timely convergence of a national emphasis on partnership models in universities and the emergence of the Web-based information economy makes this an exciting time for our students. The shift to a Web-based information economy in America certainly creates new pressures and opportunities for NPOs, but these expansions in the parameters of Web-based communications will allow our students to:

- *Find diverse employment and experience.* As NPOs get more involved in providing scientific and technical advice via the Web, there is more opportunity for our students to gain real-world experience in writing for varied audiences. Students can tap these opportunities during their school years and beyond. Each year more and more NPOs, public schools, and government agencies launch and expand their Web presences. Our students can benefit from being part of this documentation boom.

- *Exercise creative license in Web design.* The many service-learning students I've worked with over the past 10 years report that working in NPOs gives them greater opportunity to apply their creative abilities than they often find in business placements. This is particularly true in the case of small, local NPOs that are self-sustained. These groups often offer students a chance to develop websites from the bottom up because they are not restricted by corporate models or by a national home office's site design plans.

- *Address civic issues of interest to them.* When I began directing the Graduate Certificate in Professional Writing at University of Central Florida, I expected that most of the students would be members of middle management from businesses in the area. What I found instead was a diverse group of people, many of whom work for NPOs, public schools, and other noncommercial enterprises. These students deeply appreciate opportunities to apply skills they are learning in class to improve their communities. This is also true for students who work in the business world. They embrace the chance to use their class work time to advance a cause that matters to them, one they might not otherwise be able to address given their busy schedules.

- *Compare types of work sites and writing practices within them to develop their writing skills.* Our students frequently report that no amount of classroom training prepares them for many of the daily challenges they will face upon entering a new work environment. Blakeslee (2002) recommends that involving students in collaborative academic and workplace research can help everyone involved to better understand the differences and similarities in our endeavors. Logically, students benefit significantly the more broad and diverse the settings in which they work and learn are. Students who work in a variety of NPO and business settings during their educations have an advantage in terms of experience with adapting to new environments and learning the ropes in a timely fashion.

- *Compare different work and management models.* Service-learning students report that nonprofit agency personnel interact with them quite differently from business personnel. NPO personnel are often quite busy and may be more difficult to contact for assistance, but they are also highly motivated to help students accomplish their tasks. Experience in both of these sectors allows students to develop strategies for dealing with a range of management models and to make some decisions about which approaches are best suited to their own strengths and career goals.

- *Gain a broader sense of the impacts of technical documentation.* Through shaping public policy and through studying the lifecycles of documents produced by NPOs for clients, volunteers, potential donors, and other stakeholders, students can recognize ways in which documents affect their communities. Students rarely see the impacts of their documents when writing for businesses because of differences in the lifecycles of documents and differences in their purposes. While students and practitioners working in businesses may have an opportunity to influence product development and other business factors for their organizations, writers working for NPOs including public schools, government organizations, and other similar groups will have opportunities to shape their communities in different ways.

- *Acquire project management experience.* Because so many nonprofit agencies are understaffed, overworked, and lacking in high-tech skills, students working for NPOs often have the opportunity to handle their Web projects from the beginning to the end. The process can involve securing hosting, designing navigation, developing content, and managing the uploading process. The management opportunity allows students to understand the full implications of taking on such a project.

- *Explore ethical issues.* Students who develop websites for NPOs have the opportunity and responsibility to consider issues such as privacy for clients and disclosure of financial information. Because they are typically involved in the processes from beginning to end, they have a greater opportunity to participate in meaningful deliberation on these issues.

- *Develop diverse portfolios.* Students who create websites for NPOs as well as businesses are able to compile a range of types of documents in their professional portfolios. This process allows them to present a well-rounded image to potential employers and to demonstrate a range of skills and abilities.

Professional Writing in the Nonprofit Sector and Web-Based Education

In order to demonstrate some of the principles and benefits I've discussed above, I will describe a course I taught recently. This Web-based class called Proposal Writing included 23 graduate students, most of whom are enrolled in the

University of Central Florida's Graduate Certificate in Professional Writing. We launched this program in 1999 largely to serve the growing high-tech sector of our region. In our four years of operation, the program has grown from an enrollment of four students in our first semester to over 40 today. The students are not exclusively the members of middle management from local businesses that many anticipated when the program was approved. Our graduates and current students are a diverse and impressive group of professionals from a wide range of fields including medicine, education, politics, engineering, law enforcement, high-tech industry, hospitality and tourism, criminal justice, sociology, human resources, and others. They work in businesses, NPOs, schools, and government agencies across the state of Florida and beyond.

Our decision to offer the option of completing the certificate entirely online as of 2000 is one of the most significant reasons for our successful recruitment of this diverse student population. We offer a minimum of two Web-based courses each semester, which allows students to complete the five-course program in under a year. Many of the students never come to our Orlando campus or to any of our 14 regional sites for courses. Yet they have developed a strong and exciting virtual community through their hard work together online. I believe that one of the keys to this successful community development is our program's emphasis on blending service-learning, commissioned project, and other real-world project-based approaches to teaching our courses. By the time they complete our three core courses, most students have developed a significant document for at least one business and one NPO.

Because our students don't have the opportunity to meet face-to-face to share their work, we rely heavily on electronic peer review processes. Through this work-intensive process, students provide each other with incredibly detailed feedback and, in most cases, find themselves quite heavily invested in a wide range of projects that impact businesses, NPOs, and government groups around their state. This work experience allows students to shape their local communities as well as those outside their own immediate geographic space. The result is a fascinating model for community development and for collaboration between businesses and NPOs.

Our emphasis on peer collaboration creates what Reither (1993) calls a scenic motivation for collaboration. Students rely on one another for feedback, for insights, for materials, and for context for their work. The model allows students to function as what Foucault (1980) calls "local" or "specific" intellectuals, while also enhancing communities beyond the local. The Web can make the world look inconceivably expansive or make it feel cozy and close, depending on the approach we take. I believe that Web-based writing courses should do both—they should allow students to sense the potential breadth of their impact on the world while encouraging them to engage in critical practice on the local level. The cross-community collaboration that emerges in programs like ours allows students to contextualize knowledge within several layers of community, across geographic strata, as well as hierarchical, political, institutional, political, and other kinds of gaps. Students can see the interactions of for-profit and not-for-profit groups and develop a sense of the rhetorical ecosystems in which all of these organizations exist.

I want to describe and "map" one course in particular to demonstrate my point. While the students in this course did not, in most cases, produce Web documents as final class projects, most of their research, writing, and interaction transpired via the Internet. The example of my proposal writing course is particularly relevant to this notion of making connections between businesses and NPOs, as many of the students were writing on behalf of NPOs to request funding from businesses. This meant that the students had to learn about the corporate ethic of the NPOs they worked with while also following the writing conventions established by the business audiences, all of which was discovered via the Web. As they participated in peer review for one another, the students were able to see documents written by and for a wide range of organizations. Their Web-based collaboration meant that a school teacher in Orlando was able to help a classmate pursue funding for a nutritional education program in rural south Georgia, for example. And the efforts didn't end within our own region. One student's project was the development of a new NPO designed to raise awareness of landmines in countries as far away as Afghanistan, Cambodia, and Croatia. Another student currently living in the Orlando suburb of Oviedo worked on a project to develop a community bookstore in her hometown in Puerto Rico. The mixture of geographic places, worksites, and Web spaces made for an exciting and productive course.

Mapping Impact Zones

To assess our efforts and their effects, my students and I mapped our projects in terms of something we called impact zones, following the lead of authors mentioned earlier in this piece, including Harvey, Sullivan, and Porter. We considered interactions among NPOs, businesses, schools, and other institutions together to keep ourselves aware of the significance of our efforts. We included my work with the NASA Explorer Schools program. I provided proposal writing training for teachers in grades 5-8 at these special schools selected by NASA to develop excellent math and science education programs. My students participated in my project by reviewing presentation materials and offering advice about grants the teachers might apply for and websites where they might get more information about the proposal writing process. In this way, the students and I connected with 21 teachers around the region.

As Figure 1 indicates, the students developed a wide range of projects in the business and nonprofit sectors. Their efforts centered throughout the state of Florida and in southern Georgia, and affected communities around the planet. Figure 2 includes the shaded "impact zones" in which their efforts will be felt. This mapping exercise helped students and me to recognize the far-reaching

Figure 1. "Mapping Student Projects" includes short descriptions of student projects in a 2003 University of Central Florida graduate-level proposal writing course (It plots the areas affected by these projects.)

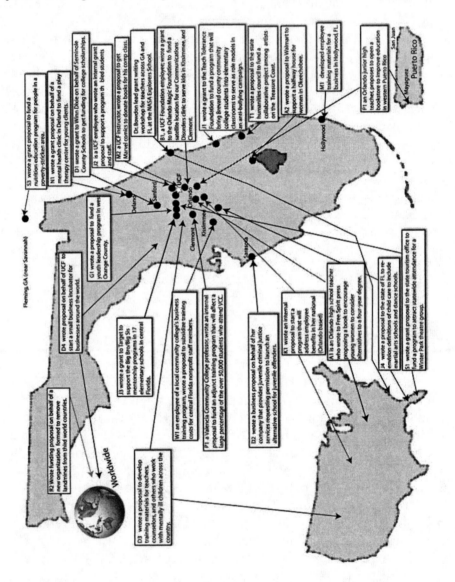

effects of our work and the intersections, interdependence, and differences among the profit and nonprofit sectors they were writing in and for. It helped students to comprehend the significance of their efforts as writers, but also as peer reviewers and as citizens, which reinforced their commitment to bringing about positive changes in their communities, defined broadly and narrowly. This

Figure 2. "Impact Zones" identifies the geographic areas in which the course projects had an impact

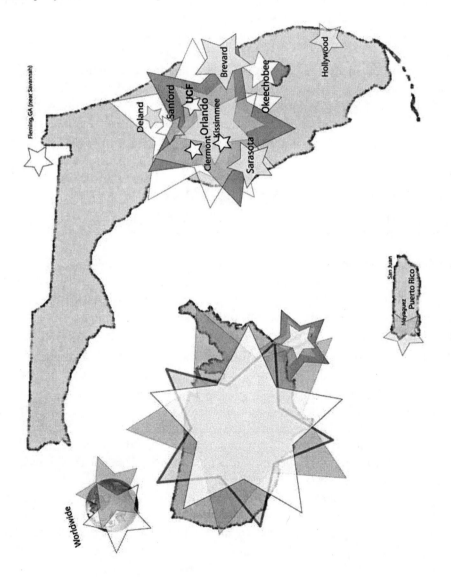

kind of recognition of their efforts encourages students to be mindful of their potential in both the profit and nonprofit sectors.

The critical function, then, of Web-based courses in professional writing for me is to allow students to participate in well-theorized mapping of the discursive spaces in which they do and will work. In order for students to get a full sense of the arena of their opportunities and challenges in Web development, such maps must include both for-profit and not-for-profit organizations and the communities which they serve and structure. Bosley (2002), Gerald Savage (1996), and others insist that technical and professional writing teachers must not only teach students to enter the workplace, but must actually be present there themselves and be willing to allow teaching practices to shape and be shaped by the "real world." This kind of interaction can happen within courses such as this one. In this case I brought my own work as a consultant into the course. My students and I were shaping the discursive practices and policy decisions of a wide range of organizations in our impact zone, and we were doing so purposefully and with the objective of learning.

A Model for Serving Diverse Groups Through Professional Writing Programs

I would like to propose one more model that universities might use to encourage the kind of cross-training and resource sharing that I've advocated in this chapter. This model moves training and service processes to an institutional level by including a formal organization to orchestrate the collaborations discussed above.

The University of Central Florida Institute for Technical Documentation came into existence in the mid-1980s to serve as a kind of clearinghouse for technical writing projects for local businesses. Because of the complexities of sharing overhead with the university research office and so forth, the institute was inactive for several years. Recently, my colleague Karla Kitalong has taken over leadership of the institute, and together we are working to make it a site for collaboration among our students, our faculty members, and local businesses and NPOs. We are in the process of creating a program that will fund a small number of graduate and undergraduate technical and professional writing students to work in the institute each semester. The institute will solicit documentation and usability study projects from local organizations and will assign students to work on a number of these projects in small teams. Students will serve as consultants for the organizations and will have the opportunity to make numerous contacts in the community and practice managing their own facsimile of a small business, while producing documents such as brochures, flyers, and Web pages for the groups. We expect that students will emerge from this experience with a heightened sense of the daily work of technical writers and project managers, as well as impressive portfolios that should help them to find employment.

We are in the process of securing grant funding for the program, which will require businesses to pay a reasonable fee for our services. We will also ask businesses that take advantage of the services to sponsor one project for an NPO for each deliverable they receive from the institute. In this way, we hope to see new partnerships grow between businesses and NPOs, in addition to cross-training our students. We hope to develop some assessment data and techniques to share with other institutions that are interested in creating similar programs that share campus resources with their communities. We believe that in the long run, collaborations between businesses and nonprofit groups will be an excellent answer to many of the questions and challenges that face both groups today. Students who are cross-trained to work in and for both types of organizations will benefit substantially, as will their employers and clients in both the profit and nonprofit sectors.

Conclusion: Future Trends

In a recent article in the *Harvard Business Review,* Bradley, Jansen, and Silverman (2003) argued that nonprofits could be increasing their revenues by billions of dollars every year if they would simply apply a few basic rules of business to their endeavors. The authors advised NPOs to reduce funding costs, to distribute holdings faster, to reduce program service costs, to trim administrative costs, and to improve sector effectiveness. Most of their suggestions involved streamlining services in communities and operating NPOs more like businesses. However, many leaders in the field of nonprofit management insist that maintaining difference from corporations is the key to balancing conflicting values systems and management models within our country. And this is where the cross-training of students is critical. Students who have studied professional writing and rhetoric and composition are able to recognize the critical distinctions among the approaches that must be taken to address varied audiences, purposes, and uses. I believe that our students are uniquely poised to lead the way in maintaining diversity on the Web, as it may be threatened by corporate models.

Harvey describes capitalism as "necessarily growth-oriented, technologically dynamic, and crisis prone" (p. 295). He suggests furthermore that, "The upshot has been to render the coercive power of competition between places for capitalist development more rather than less emphatic and so provide less leeway for projects of place construction that lie outside of capitalist norms" (p. 298). I hope that our students will find ways to fight this phenomenon and to encourage diversification of the Web and of our culture through their efforts as communicators.

As the Web grows ever more ubiquitous and the information economy ever more complex, lines between the profit and non profit organizations will continue to blur. The technical and professional writing needs of these groups will merge and diverge as our society struggles to address mounting problems through a variety of channels. Corporations will continue to diversify and to create nonprofit segments of their for-profit entities. Streamlined workforces will require that technical communicators become even more capable of multi-tasking. Our students will be in the midst of this growing and changing world, and will have opportunities to shape it. When we ask students to cross boundaries of time and space via Web-based courses, and we direct them to challenge dichotomies such as profit versus nonprofit organizations in their training for the workplace, we invite them to imagine a more dynamic world in which they can see themselves in a wider range of positions and perceive the power of language from a broader perspective. When we welcome industry and nonprofit personnel into that collaboration, we encourage connections between these two groups, and as Young suggests, through accepting and capitalizing on difference, we may be encouraging the development of more just communities.

References

Blakeslee, A.M. (2002). Research a common ground: Exploring the space where academic and work cultures meet. In B. Mirel & R. Spilka (Eds.), *Reshaping technical communication.* Mahwah, NJ: Lawrence Erlbaum.

Bosley, D.S. (2002). Jumping off the ivory tower: Changing the academic perspective. In B. Mirel & R. Spilka (Eds.), *Reshaping technical communication.* Mahwah, NJ: Lawrence Erlbaum.

Bowdon, M., & Scott, B. (2003). *Service-learning in technical and professional communication.* New York: Longman.

Bradley, B., Jansen, P., & Silverman, L. (2003). The nonprofit sector's $100 billion opportunity. *Harvard Business Review, 81*(5), 94-103.

Campus Compact. (2003). Our mission. Retrieved July 29, 2003, from: http://www.compact.org/aboutcc/mission.html.

Dayton, D. (2003). Electronic editing in technical communication: A survey of practices and attitudes. *Technical Communication, 50*(2), 192-205.

De Tocqueville, A. (1835). Political associations in the United States. In D.C. Hammack (Ed.). (1998). *Making the nonprofit sector in the United States*. Bloomington, IN: Indiana University Press.

Foucault, M. (1980). *Power/knowledge*. C. Gordon (Ed.). New York: Pantheon.

Hafer, G.R. (1999). Making the connection: Desktop publishing, professional writing, and pro bono publico. *Technical Communication Quarterly, 8*(4), 405-418.

Hammack, D.C. (1998). *Making the nonprofit sector in the United States*. Bloomington, IN: Indiana University Press.

Harvey, D. (1996). *Justice, nature, and the geography of difference*. Malden, MA: Blackwell.

Internet Society (ISOC). (2000, August 4). *A brief history of the Internet*. Retrieved July 30, 2003, from: http://www.isoc.org/internet/history/brief.shtml#Introduction.

Landesman, C. (1995). Nonprofits and the World Wide Web. *Internet Nonprofit Center*. Retrieved July 15, 2003, from: http://www.nonprofits.org/lib/website.html.

Reither, J.A. (1993). Bridging the gap: Scenic motives for collaborative writing in workplace and school. In R. Spilka (Ed.), *Writing in the workplace*. Carbondale, IL: Southern Illinois University Press.

Rogers, S. (2003). How to put the Web to work for nonprofits. In L.K. Grossman & N.N. Minow (Eds.), *The Digitalpromise Report*. Retrieved July 12, 2003, from: http://www.digitalpromise.org/report/backgroundpapers/_9.pdf.

Salamon, L.M. (Ed.). (2002). *The state of nonprofit America*. Washington, DC: Brookings Institution Press.

Sanborn, S. (2000, June 19). Nonprofits reap the rewards of the Web. *InfoWorld, 22*(25). Retrieved July 12, 2003, from: http://archive.infoworld.com/articles/hn/xml/00/06/ 19/000619hnetrend.xml.

Savage, G. (1996). Redefining the responsibilities of teachers and the social position of the technical communicator. *Technical Communications Quarterly, 5*(3), 309-327.

Sullivan, P., & Porter, J. (1997). *Opening spaces: Writing technologies and critical research practices*. Greenwich, CN: Ablex.

Young, I.M. (1990). *Justice and the politics of difference*. Princeton, NJ: Princeton University Press.

Chapter VII

MOOs:
Polysynchronous Collaborative Virtual Environments

Rhonna J. Robbins-Sponaas
Florida State University, USA

Jason Nolan
University of Toronto, Canada

Abstract

This chapter defines, describes, and assesses the form of collaborative virtual learning environment known as MOOs. MOOs offer opportunities impossible in any other actively developed online communication tool, but they have remained largely the purview of hackers, coders, and academics. This chapter deals with understanding what a MOO is, what key features make it a valuable collaborative environment, and issues of accessibility, access, and governance. Key aspects include defining and historicizing MOO, exploring the technology's current development, discussing issues that presently limit large-scale acceptance, and speculation about the possibilities and the future of MOO. The chapter considers text-based multimedia environments; general features of synchronous and asynchronous technologies; the notion of polysynchrony; tools for rapid prototyping, education, or training of users; application accessibility; costs in hardware, software, and manhours; and whether it's worth organizations getting involved in MOOs at their present state of development.

Prologue

One dark, winter evening, gathered around a Norwegian coffee table laid with strong English tea, a Mexican pear dessert, and American chocolate chip cookies, a small group of women began a discussion that generated more blank stares than a report about the United States' national budget. Seven of the 10 women were teachers representing three different levels of education from four different countries.

> *"Candice tells me you're teaching for Florida State,"* began one. *"But how in the world are you doing that from here? By email?"*
>
> *"Partly,"* the other answered. *"But I'm also using a lot of my own Web pages, blogs, Blackboard (a courseware), and a MOO."*
>
> *"Ok,"* laughed a third, *"you lost me after 'Web pages.'"*
>
> *"And I've just gotta ask...what the heck is a MOO? I'm guessing you don't mean the sound a cow makes,"* grinned another.

Most of us who teach online are familiar with the mild amazement that comes with the concept of conducting a class without ever seeing one's students, and those of us who use the virtual environments of MOOs are equally familiar with the quick bovine jokes and uncomprehending looks that surface when we happen to mention the tools we're using.

What is a MOO?

In brief, MOOs are text-based virtual environments that allow users to create representations of people, places, and things, and share them with others (Nolan, 2001). A MOO is a collaborative space where people come together for communal purposes. They construct the MOO-space according to agreed-upon criteria. They can create their own towns, buildings, rooms, objects, and personal avatars, and then interact with others in these created spaces. The spaces can be institutional—like a school or a classroom—or they can be literary, like the topology of a novel. Or they can be chaotic, like a frat house. Each MOO has its own personality, characteristics, special features, and purpose that creates cohesion and community within its boundaries.

Literally, MOOs are collaborative online virtual environments that go worlds beyond the concept of a chat room or a simulation. A simple way to visualize a

MOO is to think of a chat room, then add a room description so the chatters have some idea of a place, perhaps graphics, a character description for each user, objects that the participants can pick up, handle, and manipulate. Allow the participants the ability to create their own objects or object behaviors (e.g., an object designed as a dog may bark at irregular intervals), or to work together to create as many rooms as they would like and link them all together to create a house, office building, or village. Throw in the potential for HTML and multimedia content and tools, and you'll begin to have the idea.

Introduction

MOOs are generally perceived as being a new and breaking technology, and, perhaps in a biological evolutionary scheme of things, they are. In the fast-paced world of information technology, however, MOOs and their MUD predecessors are rather like the modern-day shark—they're constantly redefining themselves into a more effective species, but they've been around for the data equivalent of eons. Unlike the immediately recognizable silhouette of the shark, however, MOOs have inadvertently maintained such a modest profile that even within the communities which most use them, the technology is still relatively unknown and boasts virtually no recognition value with the general public. While that condition is changing with the advent of more sophisticated MOO technologies and interfaces, reactions such as those described in the anecdote above still tend to be the rule rather than the exception.

In fact, MOOs could be said to suffer from dual difficulties. The opportunities they can afford for online learning, in a conceptual and practical sense, outstrip anything presently available; they are just too much a part of the cutting edge of both learning and technology. Conversely, much of the code that makes up the bulk of MOOs—even the fancy GUI, Web-based MOOs—is moribund and requires significant redesign and coding so that its connection to the contemporary Internet is more than jury-rigged patches. Nevertheless, even with these "patches," MOOs currently offer more opportunities than most other tools presently in use.

Despite the fact that MOOs offer opportunities impossible in any other actively developed online communication tool, they have remained largely the purview of hackers, coders, and academics for a number of reasons, none of which preclude their potential value in mainstream academic and commercial environments. Rather, they offer a potential pathway for collaborative virtual learning environments (CVEs) to reach the promise only hinted at in today's offerings.

The goal of this chapter is, therefore, to define, describe, and critically assess the form of collaborative virtual learning environment known popularly as MOOs. MOOs predate the onslaught of interest in the Internet brought about by the popularity of the World Wide Web in 1994 by a number of years. Organizations such as Xerox Parc, AT&T Research Labs, and NASA's Jet Propulsion Labs (JPL) (http//spider.ipac.caltech.edu/staff/brundage/supernova.html) have devoted resources to exploring the possibilities that MOOs afford, and many commercial ventures, such as PlaceWare (now known as Microsoft Live Meeting) and Diversity University have developed as off-shoots of MOO-based technologies. Organizations and institutions such as the University of Toronto's Knowledge Media Design Institute, MIT's Media Lab, SRI International, and University of Toledo's Department of Health and Safety have hosted MOO-based projects, with research sponsored by the U.S. Department of Defense, SUN, the NSF, Industry Canada, and NASA, among others.

This chapter is organized into sections dealing with understanding what a MOO is, what key features make it a valuable collaborative environment, and issues of accessibility, access, and governance. Key aspects will include defining and historicizing MOO, exploring the technology's current development, discussing key issues that presently limit large-scale acceptance, and speculation about the possibilities and the future of MOO. In order to do this, we will consider text-based multimedia environments in general, describing the general features of synchronous and asynchronous technologies and the notion of polysynchrony, tools for rapid prototyping, the question of the education or training of users, application accessibility, and what costs—in hardware, software, and manhours—are involved, as well as whether it's worth organizations getting involved in MOOs at their present state of development.

Background

The first question that comes up when discussing MOOs is, of course, "What the heck is a MOO anyway?" MOOs are collaborative virtual environments that are generally hosted on the Internet and are accessible via a variety of programs that range from Telnet to Web browser. Their ancestors, MUDs (Multi-User Dungeons), were—as the name suggests—originally widely used by the gaming community. As technology redefined itself and grew increasingly more sophisticated, the environments gained the opportunity to be object based; that is, they could be generated by creating a series of inter-relating but relatively self-contained segments of code that in turn served as rooms, containers, features, interactive objects, player characters, and so on. This technological digression (or potential advancement) became MOOs, or M(UD)s that were object oriented. There is a certain amount of diversity in the types of MOOs currently in operation, but at the time of this writing, they tend to fall within three different categories: pure text, Web-based, and enCore. There is an ongoing debate between the two MOO camps—webbed MOOs and text-based MOOs—about which is the better forum. Users of Web-based or GUI MOOs often find text-based MOOs cumbersome and awkward, while users of text MOOs tend to find webbed MOOs cluttered and distracting. Both styles of MOOs have their particular advantages. For a beginning MOOer, the simple reality is that a GUI'd MOO is easier to learn; MOOing becomes much less intimidating when a user is able to utilize existing skills or find something familiar (suring the 'net and Web pages) on which to base her experience. Text MOOs, on the other hand, are exemplary for pure rhetoric discussion and exploration since the only available input is via the text under examination.

Pure-text MOOs are precisely what one may expect: they are MOOs which operate in a pure text environment. The user (player) must type all communications, commands, and actions, and all object and environment clues are portrayed entirely in text. There are no visuals to speak of; everything—objects, events, and other players—is portrayed and all actions are performed through the written word. From a creative perspective, the success of such environments often depends heavily on the developer's ability to use language in such a way that it is both concise and heavily visual; the more the user is able to form a concrete picture of the space and events, the stronger her experience will naturally be. On a practical level, nothing more than a bare-bones description or contextualization is necessary for the environment to function on the most basic of levels. There are a number of available software clients for both the PC and Macintosh platforms in order to avoid the ugliness of Telnet (e.g., zMUD, gMUD, WinMoose, MacMoose), but the operations and appearances are very much the same: one functions in a flat-text environment only through the power of the typed command.

As Web browsers gained respect—and sophistication and power—an increasing number of MOOs began developing their own Web-based graphic user interfaces, most often relying on Javascript and HTML in order to embed a Java Applet right into the Web page that emulates the functions of a Telnet client. In these instances, the user accesses the MOO through a browser (typically Netscape or Internet Explorer) the same way she would access any other Web page. The screen is traditionally divided into at least two parts: one segment, the Java Applet, contains all the text descriptions, conversations, events, messages, etc., while the other contains icons and images, many of which will be interactive and function as any normal Web page. In these environments, a user will still be required to perform most actions by using a typed command, but there is an increased flexibility in how information is presented and accessed. She may, for instance, be able to click on an exit icon and move to another room rather than type the text command for the same action, or click on an icon of a bulletin board to see a welcome message. Because these Web-based MOOs tend to be individually designed and built, and are heavily dependent upon their owner's programming and coding abilities—and access to outside development resources—they run the gamut in both quality and appearance. Some are clean, coherent, easy to navigate, and are even easier to conceptualize as place rather than just space, while others are cluttered, cumbersome environments that make a user feel a bit like she's walking through a construction site before the walls are up. Generally speaking, no two will either look or function alike.

With the release of graphical browsers for the World Wide Web in 1994, MOO developers started to experiment with adding graphical elements to MOOs, and by 1996 MOOkti, Tapped In, Diversity University, LinguaMOO, and others either had or were actively developing graphical interfaces. The surge of those early years offered up a number of failed efforts and a surprising number of startling successes. Unfortunately, while many of the success stories of that period would be more than competitive with later (perhaps even current) developments, they lacked the funding and promotional resources that would have made them available to the general public—or at least taken them beyond their own small and rather limited niches. Nevertheless, both the successes and failures of that period provided the building blocks and created the opportunity for something that would happen the following year.

In 1997, Cynthia Haynes of the University of Texas at Dallas, and Jan Rune Holmevik and Sindre Sorensen of the University of Bergen in Norway released the beta version of a software that was to radically change the face of MOOs— literally—for much of the educational community, and do so in very short order. The release offered MOO designers an alternative to existing resources in a two-part package: the High Wired enCore core (the heart or, in essence, the database skeleton of a MOO), and the graphic user interface, enCoreXpress. While the majority chose to use both the core and the interface, a fair percentage of builders with programming skills and resources opted instead to apply the enCoreXpress interface to their own cores. The interface is what made and continues to make this package most noteworthy; it increased the Web applications of the MOO in such a way that an inexperienced user could log onto the MOO and be able to function in a relatively short period of time by taking advantage of her already-present ability to perform basic Web browsing activities with Netscape or Internet Explorer. It provided a graphic user interface for those who wished one and lacked the skills, time, or resources to build their own, but it also offered the opportunity for some degree of uniformity and consistency between MOOs. While some functions changed from MOO to MOO depending upon the core or the MOO's programming resources and the owner's ability to fine-tune the appearance or function of the existing package, the basic appearance and general operations remained the same, allowing users to go from one MOO to another without having to negotiate a completely new environment and learning curve.

Thanks in part to enCore's funding and publicity resources—advantages most MOO developers don't generally have—enCore has become a by-word within the MOOing community. The majority of Web-based MOOs are currently using the enCoreXpress interface, and the software's popularity has spread globally, making it the dominant graphic user interface in use at this time, particularly within the educational community for which the program was first developed and introduced. Publication of Haynes and Holmevik's two texts—High Wired and MOOniversity, texts which are based on enCore's development—has created increased interest in the software and like ripples in a pond; the enCore interface has moved beyond its home court of academia and is becoming a growing presence in the world of social MOOs as well as MOOs associated with industry, science and technology, and the private sector.

The State of MOO

Just as the faces of MOOs vary according to software design and coding, so too do their scope. MOOs currently occupy the entire spectrum of online activity, but they are most heavily concentrated in the educational, social, and gaming communities. Even within their niches, however, their range is nothing short of eclectic. One educational MOO in Bergen (cmcMOO) plays host to a display of Shakespeare's "A Midsummer Night's Dream" while others, like Diversity University, replicate campus classroom spaces. ESL (English as a Second Language) and foreign language MOOs include everything from Portugese to Japanese. One social MOO is heavily "green" and builds clearly defined outdoor spaces, while yet another has created a fantasy space of imaginative and impossible proportions. Gaming MOOs cover everything from the original "Dungeons and Dragons" to more modern role-play games. Industry is gaining an increasing interest in the potential of these environments, and MOOs are now being considered for everything from virtual offices and customer support to scientific simulation. Regardless of their purpose, MOOs are very much a technology in a state of flux, and that condition of relative instability brings with it a mixed bag of both positive and negative conditions and results.

In addition to what has been mentioned already, MOOs are polysynchronous environments (Nolan, 1998, 2001). Nolan (1998) coined the term polysynchronous in order to describe the unique communicative affordances that MOOs offer.

Polysynchronous environments are defined as virtual spaces which closely approximate real-life environments. People communicating polysynchronous not only talk synchronously (in real time), but also create temporal objects such as mail messages, newsgroup messages, as well as objects that can be experienced by others. This form of virtual reality has potential as a dynamic learning environment.

This concept challenges the prevalent notion that online communication must be separated into synchronous and asynchronous activities. Most technologies only allow one activity; you can chat with your Instant Messenger or you can send an email message. Though this limitation results from limitations on the part of those who conceptualize and design technologies, it has been taken up by both academics and the general public as a rigid limitation inherent in online communication. MOOs show that this does not have the be the case. MOOs were polysynchronous environments years before most Internet users ever took their first online steps.

Almost all the information that passes back and forth across the Internet is text, usually in the form of ASCII or Hexadecimal. All our instant messages, emails, Web pages, and blogs exist as some form of alphanumeric characters. It doesn't take much of a stretch of the imagination to realize that what may start as an instant message or a conversation in a MOO (synchronous) can be saved and pasted into a Web page, email message, or a blog and become an asynchronous document. This has always been the case in MOOs. What we say (through typed text) can be recorded, archived, consulted, or displayed at a later time. Furthermore, we can asynchronously program or script objects or robots (called bots) that are able to carry on complex conversations with individuals or groups at future points in time, and even the results of those bot/human conversations can be recorded and become material for future conversations (Leonard, 1997; Turkle, 1995). Though it is only slowly being recognized as such, the Internet is inherently polysynchronous, and the synchronous/asynchronous dichotomy has been a temporary imposition by software designers.

A MOO of One's Own

When it comes to getting a MOO for an institution or company, there are a number of costs one must consider. And, as with most technologies, the hardware and software are the least important. The main costs are in development, implementation, support, and governance. MOOs run primarily on the Unix platform, along with most of the Internet. Although Microsoft may control the world's desktops, Unix is the backbone of the Internet.

Basically, any properly configured Unix computer can run a MOO without any special modifications. The easiest step would be to download a copy of enCore (at http://lingua.utdallas.edu/encore) and follow the instructions. It is possible to run a MOO on Windows computers, as well as Apple computers. Apple computers run a variant of BSD-Unix. That is the easy part.

The difficulties come in when you start to imagine what your virtual MOO space will look like, how it will be configured for users, and how it will be governed. These are creative and social issues, not technological ones. No doubt the creative issues will be resolved by personal taste or corporate profiles. Support and governance, however, are potentially both more complicated and more taxing.

Support is a question that carries its own set of thorns. If the MOO is a small operation dedicated to a limited and clearly identified group of users (e.g., a professor establishes his own MOO specifically for use with his own small group of students), support is liable to be his own responsibility. Just as he created his own MOO, he'll also be responsible for fixing his own broken code, developing the environment to meet the educational objectives, or training his own students and teaching assistants. If, however, the MOO is one that is available to a larger population of users (or even the general public), then support can quickly become a nightmare task for the MOO owner. Practically speaking, one individual can only do so much. If a public-MOO owner is responsible for his own support and user training, he's liable to find himself in a black hole of activity that swallows his time, energy, creativity, and possibly financial resources, all to the detriment of other professional and personal responsibilities, and—when he finally reaches the point where he cannot keep up with his own demand—the MOO's users and membership. Corporate MOOs have, perhaps, the advantage in this area in that they often have a more flexible budget: they can hire resources or use existing staff members. Educational and personal MOOs are more often dependent upon the goodwill and skills of its own community of users; they rarely have the necessary funding to hire programmers, developers, and trainers.

An entire chapter could be dedicated to the issue of governance, and there are many resources that discuss the governance of online environments. Nolan and Weiss (2002) go into great detail to describe the major issues surrounding the question of governing MOOs. They describe a curriculum of community that all participants must learn. This process is usually a social act of observation and modeling of acceptable practice. This curriculum is broken down into issues of access—how to connect to a MOO and use the environment, membership—how to interact with others and feel like a participant, and governance—how to keep the environment running both socially and technologically. Very few organizations, online or off, actually take these aspects of interaction into conscious consideration, but rather leave individuals to flounder and make their way on their own. For an environment to be successful, however, those who run them have to ensure that not only are they interesting places full of interesting people and interesting things to do, but they also have to govern with a light touch, so that the experience is not a restricting one.

The Good

There are a number of features that make MOOs valuable collaborative environments, and potentially the least of those is the ability to communicate in a real-time environment. While many limit their use of the technology to synchronous communications, MOOs are much more than chat rooms. The ability to converse with students, customers, teachers, and colleagues is indeed important, but MOOs go one step further than most chat technologies in that they allow a fuller mode of expression. MOOs recognize and create the required space for demonstration and performance of personality. For instance, rather than seeing a dislocated smilie or emoticon beside a user's screen name, the audience sees a sentence that makes that expression both more vivid and more coherent: Janet smiles. Or, even better: Janet smiles at you. Permanent characters (non-guest avatars) are more than anonymous screen names; rather, they offer an infinite range of options for self-description and self-definition. Depending on the software and interface, users are able not only to provide text descriptions of themselves—including their special interests, e-mail address, or home Web page information—but they also have the opportunity to add graphics, photos, video, and sound, all of which help create a sense of the user's individuality and provide depth. Likewise, places—whether designed as outdoor spaces, fantasy realms, historical re-enactment, or traditional rooms—have the opportunity for personalization. Descriptions can be tailored to the creator's personal, artistic, or professional preferences and needs; graphics can be used (or eliminated) to help develop the setting; room activities and events can be generated in order to strengthen the sense of place and grant it dimension. In short, MOOs offer the advantage of making personal interactions much more "real" and immediate.

That immediacy of experience is a large part of what makes MOOs special and helps differentiate them from the usual chat program. The user loses the sense that she's operating in something so mundane as a computer program, and feels instead that she's part of a virtual community—often one that has as much reality and life as the "real" one away from her computer.

That ability to describe oneself has opened the path for discussions of gender and identity theory in ways that are not available to the face-to-face class. In a MOO, students can choose to call themselves by non-gender-specific names, alter their descriptions, or change the avatar's settings to those of the opposing gender or gender-neutral pronouns; they can experiment with genders other than their own. Likewise, they could choose to experiment with different class, race, or cultural identities. While such experimentation does not (indeed cannot and should not) attempt to assume full understanding of the experiences of those who live the lives students are role-playing, the experiment does open the door for dialogue that cannot otherwise be generated so freely—or portrayed so vividly. Students are able to redefine themselves, and that process not only raises questions about casting of the "other," but also pokes at the means by which they go about defining themselves in their own daily lives, and the way in which they interpret themselves as well as how they present themselves to be interpreted.

Nor should it be believed that the only expression of personality and identity is that of the user. Just the opposite is true. While the MOO is a collection of code, if that code is designed properly and managed well, it becomes an interactive element of its own and performs in response to its users. While not living in the same sense as its players, their use and development of the MOO itself has the potential to turn it into a receptive and expressive environment with a personality of its own.

Personality and identity—regardless of whether it's the MOO's or the players'—is, of course, not the only advantage to a MOO. Another very large advantage is the ability to create an object that another user can pick up, look at, manipulate, or use, incorporating a "sensory" and hands-on application to an otherwise purely visual learning experience. Such applications can be invaluable when it comes to recognizing and making the most of different learning styles; it allows students to explore their own learning processes in a manner that works best for them and by which they may gain the most benefit. As part of that approach, not only can the student "handle" the object or lesson, but she can create her own in response. For instance, if the MOO-lesson guides students through the different aspects of writing dialogue for a creative writing class, she may create two objects that "talk" to one another in a demonstration of those concepts, or she may program a bot to perform an interactive dialogue with the instructor. Nor is that hands-on experience limited to a single-builder concept. MOOs are unique for their ability to not only allow but encourage collaboration. In short, a space may be developed by a group of people all working toward a given goal. For instance, a history class may recreate Civil War Gettysburg using very structured guidelines (each student creates objects and room space given a specific aspect of the assignment), or via the wonderful chaos of a free-for-all approach, allowing the class to brainstorm, create, and implement their ideas in their own unique learning process.

Another advantage is that the MOO incorporates multiple resources; one is not limited to a single medium. Aside from the opportunity for real-time discussion, information can be provided in everything from a simple note to an interactive riddle, depending on the creator's specific needs and goals. For instance, math workshop may use a series of progressive rooms or objects to teach the various steps toward solving a particular type of problem. A science class may devise a series of riddles which, only by answering correctly, allow the student to move to the next room, object, or prompt. A professional organization, business, or large lecture class may install objects that demonstrate the various qualities of a product or subject. Less complex but no less effective, a lecture or presentation may be prepared beforehand, then activated by the student or customer and received at her own pace. Likewise, external Web pages can be pulled in for a more detailed presentation, and video and audio content can be added to provide different medium support. MOOs offer their own version of email (MOOmail), allowing on online webmail tool that can, as needed, be exported and sent to an owner's regular email address.

The collaborative nature of MOOs is such an inherent feature that it is often overlooked in discussion, and it is frankly a difficult aspect to address, simply because of the sheer enormity of the possibilities. Small groups or entire communities can work together to create a representational space that combines knowledge and personalities of all the participants. For instance, a history class may create a series of rooms and objects that represent their understanding of the pre-Civil War American South, or a biology and natural science class may recreate the problems associated with a specific resource depletion. On a more limited level, a single user can create an object or space, then hand it over to another user for further development in a never-ending cycle of creation. By the same token, we must remember that the entire MOO—its programming, representation, geographic structure, and thematic construction—is the result of a collaborative effort of a MOO's community and all its users. MOOs, as with people, do not exist in isolation, but rather are designed, created, and implemented by the society which uses it.

The sheer flexibility of MOOs is part of their attraction. There is, quite literally, very little one cannot do with the proper resources and training.

The Problematic

While MOOs have an unrealized potential, there is much that is problematic in their use or current state of development.

One of those difficulties is the question of software required to access the MOO. As we touched upon earlier, different types of MOOs require different means of access. Pure-text MOOs require a Telnet-type client. While Telnet can be used, most text-MOO users prefer to use one of the currently available clients instead; Telnet is indescribably ugly and terribly cumbersome. Nor is it particularly easy for a Windows-generation user to acclimate to the program. Telnet emulators tend to be easier for users to adjust to, but here's where things can get sticky. If we're talking about putting a class of 20 distance students on a text-based MOO, then we have to assume that there will be at least half a dozen different machine configurations. Even if we were to assume the class consisted of only Windows users, we'd have consider the range of old Windows 98 machines to the most current Windows XP release, and a variety of hardware and memory configurations that may or may not allow for easy installation of our preferred client program. In real life, however, that scenario is compounded by the fact that there will be a fair percentage of Macintosh users—and not all Windows programs have Mac equivalents—and the odd Linux user for whom the situation becomes even more difficult. Things may become even more problematic if any of the students—and indeed this will be true for a certain percentage of the group—don't have their own machines and must borrow time on a friend or family member's computer, or use campus or work equipment. In those cases, it's unlikely that they'll be able to install software on a machine they don't own, particularly if they must use campus or employment hardware.

Obviously, the problem here is finding a software that's compatible for all users, and equally obviously, that's impossible. Generally speaking, the best that can be done is to recommend two different Telnet clients, one for Macs and one for PCs. At that point, one must also consider cost, then training or user orientation. In the event of a hybrid class that happens to meet in a computer lab, the lab can be set up to meet the online, and students can spend a class session learning the basics of the new software. For distance students, the necessary download and installation information must be made available (including a tutorial that explains how to install the package), and some degree of teaching the software (again, probably via Web page tutorial) must be created. For commercial applications where the MOO is used for customer or staff support, that same type of assistance must be made available, but clearly it's unlikely that a client who will be a one-time visitor will go through the extra effort to download and install a software, even assuming that the software is free. And therein lies a secondary problem: cost. Not all Telnet clients are freeware, and requiring a specific software may also mean that you impose an additional cost on the user.

As an aside, there is an ongoing debate between the two MOO camps—webbed MOOs and text-based MOOs—about which is the better forum. Users of Web-based or GUI MOOs often find text-based MOOs cumbersome and awkward, while users of text MOOs tend to find webbed MOOs cluttered and distracting. Both styles of MOOs have their particular advantages. For a beginning MOOer, the simple reality is that a GUI'd MOO is easier to learn; MOOing becomes much less intimidating when a user is able to utilize existing skills or find something familiar (surfing the 'net and Web pages) on which to base her experience. Text MOOs, on the other hand, are exemplary for pure rhetoric discussion and language exploration since the only available input is via the text under examination. The real issue, however, is how well each environment is implemented. For instance, MOOcanada has a very sophisticated text-only interface that is more interactive and dynamic than many GUI-based interfaces.

For Web-based MOOs, the standard requirement is that a user have a good browser that allows cookies and is fully Java compatible. As of this writing, that limits the field to Netscape and Internet Explorer. Opera has made long strides in recent releases, but it still fails with some Java-intensive environments, and the Linux browser is equally problematic. For almost all Web-based MOOs, AOL's browser is a recipe for disaster; AOL has not yet made its browser fully compatible with the rest of the Internet, and it tends to handle Javascript and Java applets very badly. For practical purposes, then, users are currently limited to Netscape and Internet Explorer, assuming the given stipulations of cookies and Java. While not all users understand about cookies and Java—and the reality is that sometimes we assume greater knowledge and expertise than our students or users possess—talking users through the process of changing those settings is a fairly easy task.

One additional problem that often crops up when it comes to questions of access is that of firewalls. For academic MOOs which are hosted on their own university servers and whose class load comes from within its own student body, there is generally no difficulty. If, however, the MOO resides on a server off campus and is being used by a student body which accesses via an on-campus connection, the university's firewall may well bar students from accessing the MOO. Most campus network administrators can resolve the problem easily enough if they have the proper IP and port information, but it's a question that needs to be considered early.

As with any program, MOOs need an organized system of governance. The environment is indeed a virtual one, but it still requires the same level of administration and support as any successful face-to-face program. That means that responsibilities need to be assigned to staff members, problem resolution avenues need to be prepared, operating expectations and standards established. Because of their online components, MOOs often become very personal very quickly; a sense of community can become so nearly a tangible characteristic that the MOO may well feel more like a family than a professional work environment—a family with all the egos, personality conflicts, and misunderstandings of any face-to-face family. If there is no administrative structure in place, it's far too easy for those critical elements to overwhelm the positive and the MOO to become a place of chaos, confusion, and factions.

The Controversial

One of the biggest reasons MOOing fails is because users are not properly trained and the MOO is not properly prepared. There is no faster avenue to ensure that a MOO session—or even a MOO itself—fails. Teachers create space and begin online classes without being able to function comfortably themselves, often without being able to perform the activities they're requiring of their students or audience. Students are brought online with no orientation or training; they're left to assume that a MOO is nothing more than a chat space, and that their actions have neither reactions nor repercussions.

The first difficulty is that teachers—primarily those who are relatively new to the environment—all too often neglect to coordinate their activities with the hosting MOO. If the MOO is owned and managed by the instructor or facilitator, this is obviously not a problem. If, however, the activity is happening on a MOO someone else owns, that coordination must be a part of the preparation process. While some MOOs are very limited in what support they can give, others are not only willing to do more, but prefer to provide active support. At a minimum, instructors need to follow the MOO's established procedures for planning, preparation, and notification before they ever bring their first student online. The process is no different than teaching in a face-to-face environment; instructors are expected to coordinate the necessary permissions and activities (or simple notification) just as they would to teach a face-to-face class in a space owned by another department. Just because the space is a virtual one does not mean that it requires any lesser level of professional courtesy.

There are, of course, a host of practical reasons for that coordination process. The first is that all MOOs are communities. Their level of integration varies, but one class (or even one individual) can—however unintentionally—impact the rest of the MOO's population; users do not operate in a vacuum. The second reason is a more practical one. Unless the teacher also happens to be a wizard on that MOO, it's always a good idea to be sure the MOO's staff are included in the planning process. The unexpected will always happen, and having a staff member with administrative abilities online at the time of the class can provide a safety net that would make the difference between success and failure. The other primary reason is equally pragmatic. Unless the instructor is an experienced and skilled MOOer, there will be questions along the way, and things she'll need to do but won't know how or, equally problematic, will do in such a way that it makes the task more difficult for both herself and her students. Instructors or program facilitators should spend time in a structured training and orientation program before they bring their first classes, students, or clients into a MOO. At a minimum, they should understand and be able to execute without error every task they would ask of their students. The blunt fact of the matter is that the more experience and understanding they have of the environment they're using, the more valuable they're going to be able to make their students' experiences, and therefore the more effective both the experience and the lesson.

The second typical error is no less problematic: students are improperly prepared for both the environment and the experience. Far too many instructors assume that all they have to do is get their students online and make sure they know how to talk, and that's an error of judgment that can sabotage a class—and a student—faster than anything else. If students are not properly prepared for the nature of the environment, they tend to experience the equivalent of a culture shock. They don't quite understand what the place is, how it operates, and have absolutely no sense of community. At a minimum, students should understand those things, in addition to the basic operating expectations of that particular MOO (traditionally, manners), and have a sense of how the MOO is physically laid out and thematically organized. Only after those issues have been explored should students be taught the basic commands and given activity guidelines and teacher expectations. That last item is equally critical. Just as with any other assignment, students must know what's expected of them, what performance is considered acceptable and what is not, and what the goals and objectives for the exercise are.

Once they're properly prepared, students generally acclimatize to the basic functions within the first 15 minutes of their online time. If that groundwork is not laid, however, they tend to experience higher levels of anxiety and frustration, and leave the MOO at the end of the class feeling as if they've just wasted an hour's worth of time in a pointless and confusing activity.

A Case in Point

In the spring of 2002, one small division of the Florida Department of Agriculture and Consumer Services considered using an enCore MOO in a customer support function in order to help a bemused clientele find its way through the bureaucratic maze of forms the state requires for certain functions, and which had recently been organized and made available online in an electronic format. The idea was that they could offer an electronic "support desk"—a virtual office—for those users who either couldn't afford the long-distance call to the state's capitol or, when they did call, weren't able to get through the blocked lines. They also thought that the application might prove to be very helpful to their own field agents, most of whom were scattered throughout the state and tended to find themselves in isolated locations during the bulk of their working day; providing the necessary backup materials and information in an interactive format would give them office support at a time when the office was normally closed and the phones left unanswered. A number of retailers (e.g., QVC) offer customers online help through some form of chat program; why then, thought the program instigators, shouldn't they? The division investigated the hardware and software requirements, technical support needs, and discovered that while they could easily install the software on one of their own servers, there was already an enCore MOO running in the local community which would have been more than happy to grant them space and initial training support for a nominal fee in order to subsidize operating costs. While using a local host was less than ideal as far as ownership was concerned from the local government's perspective, the division's single IT support staff member would have saved considerable time in learning the software in order to install and troubleshoot it properly and, given his existing workload, was more than happy to consider the option.

The staff members who would have manned the online desk worked out a tentative service schedule of two or three hours each work day, projected their needs in order to get such a program up and running, and organized all their requirements into a comprehensive and coherent statement. Unfortunately, the approval process was rather less coherent, and by the time the information was routed through the various offices and individuals who might have had any-thing—or nothing—to do with the project, funding and priorities had been so allocated and reallocated that the project eventually died. One major contributing factor to the problem was that upper management saw no overwhelming need for the new technology. After all, the telephones worked, didn't they?

The problem is one with which every program administrator is painfully familiar, and for which there are no easy answers. In order for a program to succeed, it must gain support from the system within which it operates, and that means that management must both understand the need for the program and—and perhaps this is the more critical point—have a solid understanding of what the program is. That can be a difficult thing to achieve, and now and again the best way to accomplish that goal is via hands-on experience; in other words, to physically sit down with management in front of the computer and see what all the ruckus is about.

Such an understanding is only beginning to solidify within small core pockets of academia, where MOOs are more commonly used, but it remains very much a grey area outside of academia. For instance, one former IT employee recently commented that, had he known about MOOs a year ago, he could have used a MOO to help coordinate the agency's international branch offices and customer support functions.

As a postscript, that division is again considering the use of a blog or a MOO to support an emergency contingency plan activity and the training events associated with it. It will be interesting indeed to see how the future develops.

Future Potentialities: MOO Quondam, MOO Futurus

Clearly, the overall state of the MOO as a concept is due for a major overhaul. Though it is presently a powerful and exciting tool, with great potential for business and learning implementations, and there are numerous projects underway using existing cores such as LambdaCore, enCore, and Jhcore (http://jhcore.sourceforge.net/) running on the LamdaMOO (http://sourceforge.net/projects/lambdamoo/) server, there are no active projects underway to develop the LambdaMOO server itself. There have been no changes to LambdaMOO since version 1.8.1 sometime before January 2000.

There is no open-source comunity dedicated to bringing MOOs in line with existing standards of development. And, until there is some concerted effort to collaboratively develop the MOO, it will languish as a powerful and useful oddity, clinging to new changes in Internet technologies by virtue of its inherent flexibility and the skills of the programmers working within the environment.

What we need is to reposition MOO as a paradigm for technology development and integration. The MOO paradigm, which is compatible with the hacker ethic and the various open source movements (REFS), is a way of looking at communication, online interactions, and programming. These three features are not seen in the MOO paradigm as separate functions, but rather integrated. Anyone who has an account on a MOO has the potential to become a programmer within the same environment. A user does not need to study programming, but rather learn how the MOO environment functions first through communication, then constructing representations of people, places, and things. Through participation in the MOO community and the sharing of skills, experiences, and stories, the user gains (or constructs) knowledge about the virtual environment. At this point, many users learn to program the aspects of the environment. Programming is one step beyond building 'things.' It is the point where the user can now delve into the very structures with which the MOO is built. She can now program dynamic interactions, create whole new classes of objects for other people to use, or develop novel tools for communication and social interaction.

There is no other online or virtual environment that allows this breadth of participation from this wide a range of users—from guest, to a participant, to a builder creating virtual spaces, to a database programmer—all within a single virtual environment. In fact, very few environments and technologies can even be developed from inside by users. It is the concept of the MOO paradigm, loosely based on Seymour Paper's notions of constructionism (Davie & Nolan, 1999), to facilitate any kind of communication, social interaction, learning experience, creating of virtual spaces, along with the capacity to develop and program new tools from within a single community, that sets MOOing apart from all other kinds of online interactions.

There is a very real potential for MOOs to finally rise to the challenge of being the concept that will finally facilitate the creation of widespread, open-source, user-extensible virtual reality. This is an ambitious statement, but as things stand, there is no available technology that has the potential that MOOs exhibit. The

MOO paradigm needs to be stripped down to its basic elements, legacy ghosts need to be exorcised, and MOOs need to return as a lean tool that will allow for the integration of what makes MOOs special with all the other elements of the Internet—present and future—that fulfill niche needs.

What a MOO Paradigm Can Offer the Future Internet

The MOO paradigm is important for two major reasons. First, it offers constructivist virtuality—the fact that anything that can be described can be created in a MOO. Likewise, there is the internal object-oriented programming language that allows users to co-develop tools and applications from within. These two features allow for the rapid prototyping of new tools, collaborative co-development of virtual spaces, users' construction/control of their own environments, and the ability to glom (stick together or integrate) almost any other technology onto itself with minimal fuss.

The ability of the MOO paradigm to glom other technologies together requires some explanation. Although most Internet tools have some rudimentary ability to communicate with each other, and there are multi-function tools—such as Web browsers—which are able to handle browsing, email, chat, Web page creation, and Usenet news reading, it is difficult to make any changes to the provided suite of tools without waiting for the software vendor to provide a new version of the software.

Even with the existing MOO tools, however, both fledgling MOO programmer or experienced user is able to unilaterally attach any Web-based multimedia tool to a MOO object. For example, in early 1996 MOOktiMOO, a precursor to Project Achieve, was live streaming realnetworks video through the MOO to viewers who were then able to communicate with each other, and post text questions to the live audience using the MOO's chat functions. It took less than a day to work out this prototype. Since that experiment, users have added shared whiteboards, audio-messaging systems, live-cams, and other tools they have found around the Net and determined to be useful. Because a user can add a useful tool with just a few lines of code, there is no requirement for a new version of MOO to come out in order to add new functionality. If a user doesn't like what is available, she can find something better and add it herself. Or, for that matter, she can create her own entirely new tool.

In order to extend the capacity of MOO at present, MOOs have built-in Web, email, newsreader, gopher servers, and clients. Keeping these sorts of built-in tools are unnecessary in today's distributed Internet. Most users already have tools that perform these functions that are more suitable to individual tastes. What the MOO should, and can, afford is the option of joining the user's selection of tools together in the MOO, along with a plethora of other tools that work best for the user. The MOO would then facilitate the communication between these tools, and those of other users, in a seamless, transparent fashion.

MOOs are bandwidth independent. High-end users can still stream audio and video, and use Web-based Java tools. But this is not a minimum requirement. Anyone can access a MOO with the most minimal tools, such as a dumb terminal (computer screen and keyboard without a computer) and the oldest of modems to connect to a server with access to the Internet. This means that the system requirements for text-MOOing are small enough that MOOs can be used in environments that have poor Internet connections or old phone lines. It also means that MOOs can be used via wireless devices. There are no limitations as to what type of tools can be used to access MOOs, and regardless of how MOOs are developed, this capacity is unlikely to disappear.

Taking into consideration these sorts of capacities and flexibilities, it is possible to put together a picture of tomorrow's MOO. Imagine, if you will, a user-configurable core tool, self-sufficient and functioning all by itself. The core would include the following: Telnet protocol-based text entry and response to handle communications to and from the MOO; hooks going from the MOO to a Web server (probably Apache, since it is ubiquitous on the Internet); hooks to PHP, Perl, and other scripting languages that are usually installed as modules in Apache servers; the MOO object-oriented programming language; all the basic MOO objects and classes for creating people, places, and things; all the MOO administration tools, help files, and tutorials; and added utilities for adding and configuring all the various multimedia communication tools that are the staple of the average user of the Internet. What we have is the equivalent of an Internet sticky tool to which a user can stick anything she or he wants in such a manner that the user can add or change any functioning element (email, chat, streaming media, file and document servers) at will or whim without requiring the intercession of a programmer or system administrator.

Conclusion

At present, MOOs on the Internet are charting two distinct paths. Projects such as enCore and TAPPED IN are providing powerful tools and environments for the creation of collaborative virtual learning environments that can be used by learners or in business situations. However, TAPPED IN, for example, has minimized the constructionist capacity of MOOs, making building and programming almost impossible. Their MOO hides all its inner workings in a metaphoric black box, not even openly acknowledging its MOOness. And enCore, while on its way to becoming the most popular MOOing platform, cedes all control to project developer Jan Holmevik. As a one-man show in terms of development, enCore does not have the robustness and development potential of open source projects where the project coordinators bring together work from a variety of programmers, and it is the highest quality work that makes it into the new releases. According to Project Achieve administrator, Michelle Levesque, EnCore—and all GUI-based MOOs—suffer from a security hole that can be exploited when using Web-based programming functions. This is an option that does not have to be allowed—the problem need not exist—and has been known to many for a couple of years.

This does not mean that MOO development is dead, but rather it is somewhat dormant. TAPPED IN and enCore are spreading the popularity of MOO, and have well-organized and easy-to-use environments. Clients such as MOOzilla (see Additional Resources) are exploring new ways of interaction that do not suffer from the inherent problems of Web-based programming. Both the academic and business community are watching MOOs, however, and no major paper or book on virtual community is complete without reference to MOOs. And with the thousands of young people learning programming skills in these social environments, a high percentage of whom are female, there is a growing body of future professionals who understand what MOOs are and what they can do to extend our experience online. Unfortunately, there are no major projects presently underway that are undertaking the renovation of MOOs, or developing a MOO paradigm that facilitates the enhancement of constructionist learning, polysynchronous communication, and internal programming capacities. At present, MOOs are just beyond the event horizon, still waiting to be the next-big-thing.

Additional Resources

MOOs

Connections
<http://web.nwe.ufl.edu/~tari/connections/>
Connections is, perhaps, one of the more active and better known pure-text educational MOOs currently in operation. Hosted out of the University of Florida and in operation since 1994, it has an active academic community and regularly serves as a hosting site for the online counterparts of educational conferences such as the Computers and Writing conference.

Diversity University
<http://www.duets.org/>
Supported by the University of Wisconsin and Marshall University, Diversity University has been around since 1994. DU does offer a limited graphic interface, but it is awkward and serves only for browsing the MOO; in order to operate in real time, the user must also run a Telnet client at the same time. DU's primary focus (and strength) is in pure-text operation. The MOO is designed to mimic a brick-and-mortar university campus and notes that it was the first educational MOO offered to the general public and designed specifically for classroom use.

Lingua MOO
<http://lingua.utdallas.edu>
Currently hosted by the University of Texas at Dallas, Lingua is home to enCore and enCore's creators. It is a good example of a pure enCore MOO. Lingua serves as a central clearinghouse for the latest information and news releases about enCore, and offers both the core and the interface for free download from its main pages.

Project Achieve
<http://projectachieve.net>
Project Achieve is one of those MOOs which opted to apply the enCoreXpress interface over its own core, and the use of their own Java-based Telnet application MOOcaJava. Because of its original affiliation with the University of Toronto in Canada and Canada's Schoolnet, it's had the benefit of a certain degree of funding in its early stages and has been able to modify the interface to meet its own needs. Many of those modifications and applications—such as the Virtual Assignment Server Environment (VASE)—are currently included in enCore's Xpress interface. Achieve differs from many MOOs in that it has historically been both a project-based MOO and active in researching and developing the MOO programming environment.

TAPPED IN
<http://ti2.sri.com/tappedin>
A research-oriented academic MOO, The Teacher Professional Development Institute (TAPPED IN) uses its own interface, a Java applet it calls "TAPestry," and which is radically different from enCore.

MOOcanada
<http://www.moo.ca/>
MOOcanada is a nine-year-old MOO for young Canadians.

cmcMOO
<http://cmc.uib.no>
cmcMOO is based out of the University of Bergen in Bergen, Norway.

Online Resources

Lost Library of MOO
<http://www.hayseed.net/MOO>
The Lost Library of MOO is the most complete collection of online MOO resources, papers, and references that was, as the name suggests, lost. The page has been restored and, despite the odd failed link, still serves as an outstanding source of historical context for MOOs and MOOing in general.

Rachel's Super MOO List
<http://moolist.yeehaw.net/>
Rachel's list has been around since 1996, and is continuously updated.

Telnet Clients and Browser Emulators

MOOzilla
<http://www.moo.ca/moozilla>
MOOzilla is probably the most innovative of all clients. MOOzilla is a cross-platform MOO client capable of rendering inline HTML directly from a MOO. MOOzilla is open source.

zMUD
<http://www.zuggsoft.com/zmud/zmudinfo.htm>
zMUD is a popular Telnet client for the PC/Windows platform.

gMUD
<http://sourceforge.net/projects/g-mud/>
gMUD is another Telnet client for the Windows platform.

WinMOOse
<http://www.cc.gatech.edu/elc/moose-crossing/winmoose/>
Amy Bruckman's WinMOOse is (currently) a freeware Telnet client alternative
for the PC. It's a small and easy-to-use program. It is a port of MacMOOse,
which incorporates Amy's $moose_utils, which facilitate moo programming.

MacMOOse
<http://www.cc.gatech.edu/fac/Amy.Bruckman/MacMOOSE/>
MacMOOse is the Macintosh counterpart for WinMOOse. This software has
not been updated for OS X, but works very well with OS versions up to 9.2.2.

Savitar
<http://www.heynow.com/Savitar/>
Savitar is a shareware Telnet client designed for Mac OS X.

Cantrip
<http://www.solidsun.com/cm/>
Yet another Telnet client for the Apple OS X operating system.

TinyFugue
<http://muq.org/~hawkeye/tf/> and <http://www.druware.com/tf/>
Probably one of the most popular MUD clients for the all platforms.

tkMOO-light
<http://www.awns.com/tkMOO-light/>
An advanced chat client, tkMOO-light runs on Unix, Windows, and Macintosh
platforms.

References

Aarseth, E. (1997). *Cybertext perspectives on ergodic literature.* Baltimore,
    MS: Johns Hopkins.

Benedikt, M. (1992). Cyberspace some proposals. In M. Benedikt (Ed.),
    Cyberspace first steps (pp. 119-224). Cambridge, MA: MIT Press.

Curtis, P. (1992). Mudding social phenomena in text-based virtual realities.
    Intertrek, 3(3), 26-34.

Curtis, P., & Nichols, D. (1993). MUDs grow up: Social virtual reality in the real world. Paper presented at the *Third International Conference on Cyberspace,* Austin, Texas.

Davie, L., & Nolan, J. (1999). *Doing learning building constructionist skills for educators, or, theatre of metaphor skills constructing for building educators.* Paper presented at the TCC, Maui, Hawaii. Accessed August 1, 2003, from: http://jasonnolan.net/papers/doing.html.

Haynes, C., & Holmevik, J.R. (Eds.). (1998). *High wired on the design, use and theory of educational MOOs.* Ann Arbor, MI: University of Michigan Press.

Haynes, C., & Holmevik, J.R. (Eds.). (1999). *MOOniversity.* New York: Allyn & Bacon.

Kolb, D. (1984). *Experiential learning.* Toronto: Prentice-Hall.

Kollock, P. (1998, 1996). Design principles for online communities. *PC Update, 15*(5), 58-60.

Leonard, A. (1997). *Bots: The origin of new species, the strange and wild saga of Cyberspace's software robots.* Toronto: Penguin.

Moore, D. (1981). Discovering the pedagogy of experience. *Harvard Educational Review, 51*(2), 286-300.

Nakamura, L. (n.d.) *Race in/for Cyberspace: Identity tourism and racial passing on the Internet.* Accessed August 1, 2003, from: http://www.humanities.uci.edu/mposter/syllabi/readings/nakamura.html.

Nolan, J. (1998). *Educators in MOOkti: A polysynchronous collaborative virtual learning environment.* Accessed April 25, 1999, from: http//noisey.oise.utoronto.ca/jason/mookti.html.

Nolan, J. (2001) *The techneducator effect colliding technology and education in the conceptualization of virtual learning environments.* Unpublished Dissertation. Accessed August 1, 2003, from: http//achieve.utoronto.ca/jason/dissertation.PDF.

Nolan, J. (Forthcoming). The influence of ASCII on the construction of Internet-based knowledge. In J. Hewitt (Ed.), *OISE-UT papers in technology education.* Toronto: Imperial Oil Centre for Science, Mathematics and Technology Education.

Nolan, J., & Weiss, J. (2002). Learning Cyberspace: An educational view of virtual community. In A. Renninger & W. Shumar (Eds.), *Building virtual communities: learning and change in Cyberspace.* Cambridge: Cambridge University Press.

Rheingold, H. (1993). *The virtual community homesteading on the electronic frontier.* Reading, MA: HarperPerennial.

Tomas, D. (1991). Old rituals for new space rites de passage and William Gibson's cultural model of Cyberspace. In M. Benedikt (Ed.), *Cyberspace first steps*. Cambridge, MA: MIT Press.

Trondstad, R. (2003). Performing the MUD adventure. In G. Liestøl, A. Morrison, & T. Rasmussen (Eds.), *Digital media revisited: Theoretical and conceptual innovations in digital domains* (pp. 215-238). Cambridge, MA: MIT Press.

Turkle, S. (1995). *Life on the screen.* New York: Shuster.

Weiss, J., Nolan, J., & Nincic, V. (In Press). Virtual communities. In P. Trifonas (Ed.), *The communities of difference.* New York: Palgrave (Global Publishing).

Wellman, B., & Gulia, M. (1996). Net surfers don't ride alone: Virtual communities as communities. In P.K.a.M. Smith (Ed.), *Communities in Cyberspace.* Berkeley: University of California Press.

Section IV

Internet Approaches to English as a Second Language Instruction

Chapter VIII

Developing a Web-Based Course for the Conventional English Grammar Classroom:
Issues in Planning and Design

Julia Lavid
Universidad Complutense de Madrid, Spain

Abstract

Currently, there are three possible teaching scenarios: conventional, lecture-based teaching; Web-managed teaching where lectures have been removed altogether and all learning is online; and supplemental (Web-based) teaching, which combines the previous two. This chapter describes the first phase of a project on the integration of Web-based technologies into the conventional lecture-based scenario of English grammar teaching at a large public university in Spain. It focuses on issues of planning and design of Web-based tools and materials which can potentially support the

Seven Good Teaching Principles. It also describes a tentative plan to introduce the Web-based tools progressively into the lecture-based classroom so that both students and instructors become familiar with the new learning environment as the course proceeds. The author hopes that the work reported here will encourage instructors to keep abreast of innovative methods that extend the students' learning environment beyond the traditional face-to-face meetings.

Introduction

The use of Web-based technologies is gradually changing the face of education. In many universities and other institutions of higher education all over the world, the educational model is shifting towards the networked learning model, a Web-based approach that encourages a high degree of collaborative learning and knowledge integration and creation. This networked learning model is the result of the new learning paradigm that characterizes the information society, a learner-centered model where students can learn at their own pace using online materials and tools, and in a non-linear manner. This change is evolutionary rather than revolutionary and requires new skills on the part of the teacher to satisfy the growing demands of learners. Figure 1 summarizes the main characteristics of what Reinhardt (1995) calls the old and the new educational model.

While the old educational model was teacher-oriented (the instructor was in charge of conveying stable content, and the student was a passive recipient of that content), in the new educational model—inspired in the proposals of Piaget,

Figure 1. The old and the new educational models (Reinhardt, 1995)

OLD MODEL	NEW MODEL	TECHNOLOGY IMPLICATIONS
Classroom lectures	Individual exploration	Networked Pcs with access to information
Passive absorption	Apprenticeship	Requires skill development and simulations
Individual work	Team learning	Benefits from collaborative tools and e-mail
Omniscient teacher	Teacher as guide	Relies on access to experts over network
Stable content	Fast-changing content	Requires networks and publishing tools
Homogeneity	Diversity	Requires a variety of access tools and methods

Paert, and Vygotsky—the student learns by exploring changing contents, and the teacher is his/her guide through the content.

Information technologies play an essential role in this new learning paradigm, as explained by IT scholars such as Chang (1995), who is in favor of the non-linear learning offered by the Web, hypertext navigation, and collaborative learning:

> "What about non-linear learning where people can learn things in different disciplines and varied complexity in a path not predetermined? ... In fact, changes are coming. Internet and hypertext provide people with a tremendous technology to learn in a non-linear manner."

Chua, Debreceny, & Ellis (1995) express the same idea in their project of virtual learning of the Southern Cross University (Australia):

> "The model moves the focus of education from strongly teacher centered to strongly student centered and from low technological inputs to high. The traditional linear presentation and teaching model moves to a 'hypertext' model where students can seek out knowledge from a richer and more extensive environment from both within and outside the educational institution. Students can navigate through the course material at a pace which suits their educational styles. The Networked Learning model can be used to encourage a high degree of collaborative learning and knowledge integration and creation."

However, as pointed out by Reinhardt (1995), we must not consider technology as the single solution or the panacea that will renew the old educational model. Technology by itself is not the answer; other changes are necessary, such as the creation of new teaching scenarios, new curriculum materials, and new teaching methods. Currently, there are three possible teaching scenarios: conventional, lecture-based teaching; Web-managed teaching where lectures have been removed altogether and all learning is online; and supplemental (Web-based) teaching, which combines the previous two. Only Web-managed teaching and supplemental Web-based teaching can be considered as new teaching scenarios, but the latter has important advantages over pure online teaching (Goldberg, n.d.).

At a large public university, and probably one of the largest in Europe, such as the Universidad Complutense of Madrid, where teaching is basically lecture based, a pilot project is being organized to introduce Web-based tools as a supplement to conventional teaching in different faculties. As part of this pilot project, and as a lecturer in the area of English grammar, I have developed a series of online materials for enhancing interaction and student-centered learning using the WebCT platform as Web-based software. My intention is to gradually introduce these online tools as a supplement to lectures over several course offerings so that both instructors and students become familiar with this new learning environment. The project has two main phases: on the first phase the work focuses on course planning and design issues, such as the selection of the platform, the selection of tools provided by the platform, the selection of materials, and of self-tests and quizzes to be implemented. The aim of this first phase is exploratory, examining the potential of the developed tools to support the Seven Good Teaching Principles (Chickering & Gamson, 1987). On the second phase, the developed software will be integrated within the lecture-based scenario of English grammar teaching, and its effectiveness will be measured over several course offerings.

The purpose of this chapter is to describe the first phase of this project, that is, how and why the courseware was developed. This implied making a series of logistic and pedagogical decisions: the logistic decisions concerned aspects such as the selection of the platform and the selection of tools provided by the platform; pedagogical decisions concerned aspects such as the selection of materials, the selection of activities, and the selection of self-tests and quizzes to be used by students.

The chapter is organized as follows: The next section presents some background discussion on the development of the Web-based course, while the discussion then concentrates on planning and design issues. Next is presentation of a tentative integration plan of the developed tools into the conventional lecture-based scenario described above. General recommendations on planning and design issues, and an outline of some avenues for future research follow. Finally, the main points of the chapter are summarized and concluding remarks are offered.

Background Issues

As explained above, the Universidad Complutense, one of the largest universities in Europe and probably the largest public university in Spain, is a higher education institution where both graduate and postgraduate teaching is lecture based. However, following the recommendations of the European declarations of Bologna and Sorbonne on harmonization of the architecture of the European higher education system, an effort is being made to promote the ability to use new information technologies as an extended learning environment. Also, in order to increase the international competitiveness of the European system of higher education, teachers are encouraged to introduce new teaching methodologies, comparable to the ones already used worldwide.

In this context, a pilot project is being organized to introduce Web-based tools as a supplement to conventional teaching in different faculties. As a lecturer in the area of English language and linguistics, I participate in this project with the creation of a Web-based course on English grammar which could be used over several course offerings within the studies plan of English philology.

Among the reasons that encouraged me to create the course was the possibility to renew my teaching methodology and reevaluate my own teaching by experimenting with pedagogy that did not exist before. I was basically attracted by the enormous opportunities for interaction offered by Web-based technologies, and by the possibility to extend the students' learning environment beyond the traditional face-to-face meetings. In addition, I hoped the Web-based course would offer students the opportunity to get actively engaged with the course content and to become knowledge builders. Also, although the course did not focus specifically on writing, I expected that it would give students the opportunity to practice their writing skills as part of the activities of a series of units in the syllabus. Finally, I was interested in checking whether the use of Web-based technologies would support the so-called "Seven Good Teaching Principles" (Chickering & Gamson, 1987).[1] This is clearly a long-term objective that would require actual testing with students. However, as a first approximation it was necessary to examine whether the features of a platform such as WebCT could potentially support these principles. These seven principles are based on 50 years of research on the way teachers teach and students learn, how students work and play with one another, and how students and faculty talk to each other. They are basically intended as guidelines for faculty members, students, and administrators to improve teaching and learning. The seven principles are the following:

1.   *Good practice encourages contacts between students and faculty.*

     According to Chickering and Gamson (1987), the most important factor in student motivation and involvement is frequent student-faculty contact in and out of classes. When a student knows a few faculty members well, he/she feels encouraged to keep on working and to get through rough times.

2.   *Good practice encourages cooperation among students.*

     Good learning is "collaborative and social, not competitive and isolated," explain Chickering and Gamson. Working with other students, sharing one's ideas increases involvement in learning, sharpens thinking, and deepens understanding.

3. *Good practice encourages active learning.*

Learning is not a passive activity, or a spectator sport, as explained by Chickering and Gamson. Students must make what they learn part of themselves by talking about it, writing about it, relating it to past experiences, and applying it to their daily lives.

4. *Good practice gives prompt feedback.*

Students need to receive feedback on their performance to benefit from courses, and they also need chances to reflect on what they have learned, what they still do not know, and what they need to know in order to be able to focus their learning.

5. *Good practice emphasizes time on task.*

Learning does not happen in a vacuum. It is critical that students learn to use their time well as part of their training. Therefore, institutions and trainers should allocate realistic amounts of time to ensure effective learning for students and effective teaching for faculty.

6. *Good practice communicates high expectations.*

"Expect more and you will get more," explain Chickering and Gamson. Communicating high expectations to students and helping them to do their best stimulates their cognitive skills significantly.

7. *Good practice respects diverse talents and ways of learning.*

There are many different learning styles and talents. Some students are more analytical and reflexive while others are more practically oriented. Therefore, all types of students should be given the chance to show their talents and learn in ways that work for them.

Planning the Supplemental Web-Based Course

As explained in the previous section, the English grammar course described in this chapter has been planned as a supplement to lecture-based teaching, not as a substitute for it. This feature allows a greater degree of flexibility in course design than in a pure online teaching scenario, where all the contents and tools must be ready from the beginning and there is little room for modification. In a supplemental Web-based course, it is possible for the instructor to modify contents and the use of tools on the basis of feedback from the students, to add more exercises of a specific type to satisfy the students' needs, or to create new Web-based activities that were not considered at the beginning of the course.

From the teacher's perspective, a supplemental Web-based course gives the teacher the opportunity to implement the online tools gradually, thus becoming familiar with the new learning environment. One can start modestly with some online syllabuses, online discussions, online image repository, online glossary + self-tests, online practice quizzes, etc., and then proceed with more challenging activities. In the following section I will describe the decisions that were taken for the creation of some of these online tools.

Course Design: Logistic and Pedagogical Decisions

The creation of a supplemental Web-based course that could be integrated into conventional lecture-based teaching required a series of decisions that can be grouped into two main blocks:

1. Logistic decisions, concerning aspects such as the selection of the platform, and the selection of tools provided by the platform.
2. Pedagogical decisions, concerning aspects such as the selection of materials, the selection of activities, and the selection of self-tests and quizzes to be used by students. The following sections concentrate on each of these aspects in turn.

Selection of Platform

The platform selected was WebCT (Web Course Tools), a commercially available tool to create entire courses online or to complement a classroom-based course. This tool was built in Canada and is used in more than 70 institutions around the world—North America and Canada, Australia, Finland, The Netherlands, and Spain, to mention some countries. In the higher education area, WebCT and Blackboard are considered to be the leaders of the market.[2] This, together with the perception of its long-term stability in the market and the fact that it has been adopted by other Spanish universities, such as the UNED (the Spanish Distance Education University), motivated its selection. Some of its more important features are the following:

*   It allows the user to provide course materials that include text, images, video, and audio.

- It allows the user to evaluate students with quizzes and assignments.

- It facilitates learning using searchable indexes, glossaries, and image databases.

- It allows the user to integrate Web resources into one's courses.

- It encourages student interaction by using hyperlinks to websites, student Web pages, and a note-taking tool.

- It allows the user to communicate with students via discussions, email, real-time chat sessions, and an interactive whiteboard.

- It allows the user to manage grades.

- It supplies student feedback via an online grade book, self tests, and progress tracking.

Another important motivation for choosing WebCT was its potential to support the Seven Good Teaching Principles presented above.[3] This is discussed in the following sections.

Selection of Tools

WebCT includes a series of tools for the creation of Web-based courses. Some of these tools were exploited in the supplemental Web-based course described in this chapter. The course welcome page is shown in Figure 2[4].

As Figure 2 shows, the course is accessible by clicking on *login*. This will immediately request a password, and the student will then access the course main page, shown in Figure 3.

Figure 2. Course welcome page

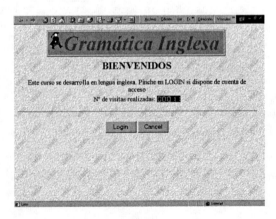

Figure 3. Course main page

Figure 3 also shows the tools available to manage the course. I used a Spanish version of WebCT to create the course, so the names of the tools are in Spanish. These tools are the Calendar ("Calendario" in Spanish), the Contents Tools ("Materiales"), the Communication Tools ("Comunicación"), the Assessment Tools ("Evaluación"), the Student Tools ("Seguimiento"), and the Information Tool ("Information"). As explained in the previous section, in creating this Web-based course, I wanted to check whether the tools provided by WebCT could potentially support the Seven Good Teaching Principles. In the following paragraphs, therefore, the selected tools will be described together with their potential for supporting those principles.

The *Calendar* allows us to visualize the course events. All types of announcements relevant to the students can be published through this tool, presented in Figure 4.

Figure 4. Calendar of example course

The proper use of this tool could potentially support the fifth good teaching principle, as it sets time-achievement expectation at the beginning of the course. If students consult the calendar at regular intervals during the course, they will learn how to use their time well as part of their training.

Another selected tool for the Web-based course was the *Content Tools*, which allowed the creation of the course syllabus, organization of the contents of the course, and creation of a glossary for the students. These tools also include a search facility so that students can search for specific content. Figure 5 illustrates the *Content Tools* page of the Web-based course.

The *Contents Tool* can potentially support the fifth and the seventh teaching principles as follows: By having access to highly structured and organized material and references to external information in the Content Tools, students can save time that would otherwise be wasted trudging to the library, scanning microfilm and microfiche, or scrounging the reference room (fifth good teaching principle). Also, by having course materials, the syllabus, an online search tool, and a glossary, students can learn at their own pace and find their most effective learning strategy (seventh good teaching principle). Thus, bright students can move quickly through materials they master easily and go on to more difficult tasks; slower students can take more time, and get more feedback and direct help from teachers and fellow students.

Through the *Communication Tools*, presented in Figure 6, students can consult a bulletin board with news from the course, manage their email, chat with other students, etc.

Clearly this group of tools encourages interaction both between the instructor and the students, and among the students themselves, thus supporting several good teaching principles (the first, the second, the third, and the fourth). More specifically, through Chat the instructor can schedule virtual office hours to provide feedback to students (fourth good teaching principle), and the students

Figure 5. Course content tools of example course

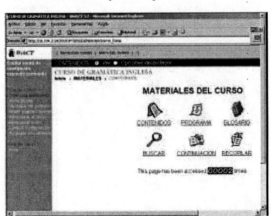

Figure 6. Communication tools of example course

can contact each other (first good teaching principle); through email it is possible to establish one-to-one private discussion, work on group projects, and solve problems in groups (first and second good teaching principles); through the Discussion forum or Bulletin Board, it is possible to provide one-to-many public discussions (first good teaching principle). Also, students can introduce themselves to the rest of the group, thus providing specific opportunities to interact with other students (second teaching principle). Through the Discussion forum or the Chat, formal debates online can take place between students and experts, and virtual guest speakers can be invited to participate in debates (third good teaching principle). Also, students can evaluate each other's postings.

Another group of tools selected for this course were the *Assessment Tools*, which allow the instructor to evaluate the student's progress through quizzes, tests, and assignments. Students can also self-test their progress through a specific self-test tool, as illustrated in Figure 7.

Figure 7. Assessment tools for example course

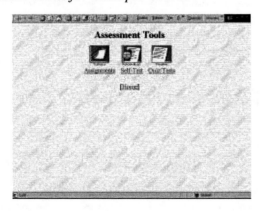

The *Assessment Tools* can also support several good teaching principles. For example, students can present their assignments carried out in small teams or groups that interact via email. These assignments can be made available online so that other students can critique each other's work (second good teaching principle). Through Quizzes, "paragraph" type essay questions can be posted to students so that they submit their regular observation/reflection writings. Tools such as Self-Quizzes support active learning on the part of the student, and through the Notes tool students can take electronic notes while reading the Content pages (third good teaching principle). The fifth good teaching principle can also be supported through the use of Student Tools. With this tool students can track their record, check their grades, and even create their own Web pages, as shown in Figure 8.

In addition to the above-mentioned tools, an Information section was created so that students could have access to the course guidelines. These include general

Figure 8. Students' tools

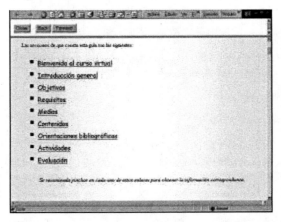

Figure 9. Course guidelines

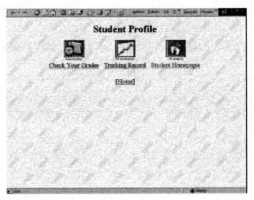

Figure 10. Course objectives

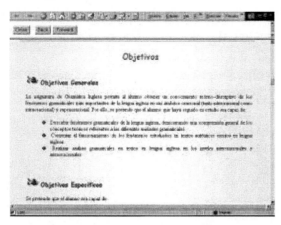

information about the course, such as its *objectives, requirements, syllabus, bibliography, activities,* and *evaluation.* Figure 9 shows the page for the course guidelines including these sections, and Figure 10 shows the page including the general and the specific objectives of the course.

Selection of Materials

The materials selected for the Web-based course are distributed along 10 units, with an emphasis on the communicative and functional aspects of English grammar. The list of units is illustrated in Figure 11.

Figure 11. Course syllabus and partial view of Unit 9

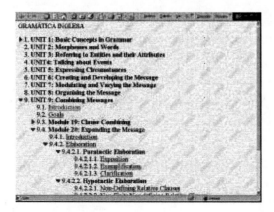

The units that make up the syllabus are the following:

1. Basic Concepts in Grammar
2. Morphemes and Words
3. Referring to Entities and Their Attributes
4. Talking About Events
5. Expressing Circumstances
6. Creating and Developing the Message
7. Modulating and Varying the Message
8. Organizing the Message
9. Combining Messages
10. Making Texts

Each of these units includes a series of sections such as: *introduction, objectives, content structure, content development, summary, bibliography, activities, and self-test exercises.* This type of organization stimulates self-learning and guides the student through the content presented in each unit. Units 6 to 10 make a connection between grammar and discourse, with specific tasks related to writing. For example, Unit 9 is devoted to sentence-combining skills, as shown in Figure 12.

In this introduction to Unit 9, students are presented with a text where all clauses are brief and of equal length. The following text is an example of such a text:

Figure 12. Introduction to Unit 9

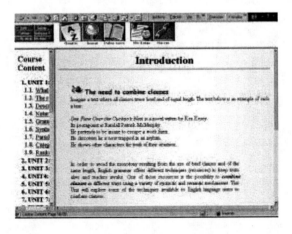

One Flew Over the Cuckoo's Nest is a novel written by Ken Kesey.
Its protagonist is Randall Patrick McMurphy.
He pretends to be insane to escape a work farm.
He discovers he is now trapped in an asylum.
He shows other characters the truth of their situation.

In order to avoid the monotony resulting from the use of brief clauses and of the same length, English grammar offers different techniques (resources) to keep text alive and readers awake. One of those resources is the possibility to combine clauses in different ways using a variety of syntactic and semantic mechanisms. In this way, the Unit is presented as an exploration into some of the techniques available to English language writers to combine clauses. The Unit is divided into three modules: Module 19 is an introduction to the issue of clause combining and to the main types of relationships between clauses: syntactic and logico-semantic. The possible syntactic relationships holding between clauses are Hypotaxis, Parataxis, and Embedding. The logico-semantic relationships can be of two kinds: Expansion and Projection. Module 20 concentrates on the logico-semantic relation of Expansion and its main subtypes: Elaboration, Extension, Embedded Expansions and Acts. Module 21 studies the relation of Projection and its main subtypes: Quoting ('direct speech') and Reporting ('indirect speech'). It also studies the projection of speech acts such as offers, suggestions, and commands, and the notions of free direct and indirect speech. In each of these modules, students will find different activities which will help them learn the functions of these clause-combining relationships in texts and to use them adequately in writing. For example, students will have to complete unfinished clauses, or will have a text online to be filled with appropriate connectors, or will have to rephrase a given text extract using different clause combinations. Figure 13 illustrates different activities for Modules 19, 20, and 21.

Figure 13. Activities for different modules of Unit 9

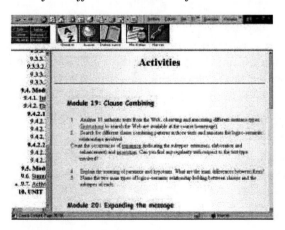

Figure 14. Summary of key points for Unit 9

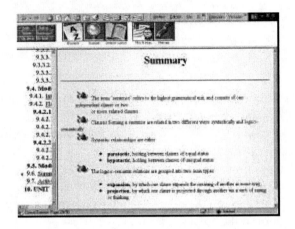

Each unit includes a summary so that the student can easily find the key points presented in the different modules, as illustrated in Figure 14.

Selection of Tests, Self-Tests, and Exercises

As part of the course design, some assessment activities have been planned, such as multiple-choice tests, self-tests, and other types of exercises. The purpose is that students can test their own performance, thus promoting active learning. These tests are supposed to be supplemental to other ways of assessment which instructors may decide to use in the lecture-based course. Therefore the exercises shown in Figures 15 and 16 are purely illustrative to give the reader an idea of the type of tests that can be created with the WebCT package. Figures 15 and 16 are two parts of a test on sentence-combining skills.

As the figures illustrate, a specific type of writing skill, such as sentence-combining, is assessed by means of an exercise where the student is supposed to combine a group of sentences into one effective sentence containing only one independent clause. The student is then given an example containing an effective sentence, and he/she is supposed to provide his own clause combination. He/she is also given the chance to send email to the instructor suggesting other possible combinations different from the one suggested.

Figures 17 and 18 illustrate a multiple-choice test on sentence types. If the student provides the wrong answer, the system responds with a red-cross. If the student provides the right answer, the system responds with a green tick.

Figure 15. Self-test on sentence-combining skills (question 1)

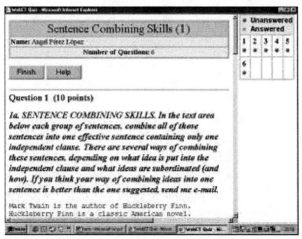

Figure 16. Self-test exercise on sentence-combining skills (question 2)

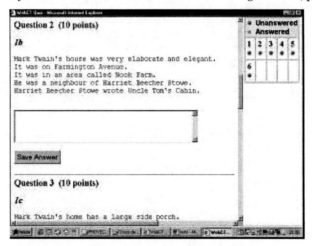

Figure 17. Multiple-choice test on sentence types (wrong answer)

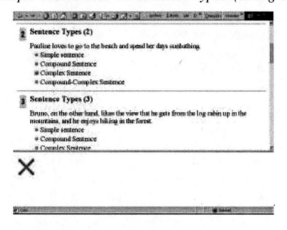

Figure 18. Multiple-choice test on sentence types (right answer)

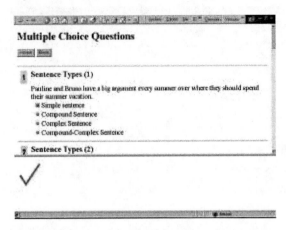

Planned Integration into the Lecture-Based Classroom

As explained at the beginning of this chapter, the English grammar classroom for which the Web-based tools are being developed is currently planned within a lecture-based teaching scenario. Instructor and students meet three hours a week over a four-month period to complete a total of six credits in each course offering, four of which are devoted to lectures and two to students' project work and exam preparation. The integration of the Web-based tools within the lecture-based teaching scenario is being planned as a gradual process, so that both students and instructors become familiar with the new learning environment. This integration is tentatively planned as follows:

1. During the first week of class, the instructor will distribute the official course syllabus on paper and will also introduce students to the supplemental Web-based course. An online syllabus (subject to changes and modifications) will be made available online so that all students, including those absent when a change is presented, can have access to the syllabus.

2. Students will be given a password to access the course and a private email account to communicate with their group instructor and among themselves. The Communications Tools of WebCT will be introduced and the students will visit the computer lab to test their password and their email account. Their first assignment will consist of providing a personal introduction to the rest of the group by email. They will also have access to the Student tools through which they will be able to "publish" their personal page.

3.   Traditional lecture-based teaching will take place in the following week until the first topic of the course syllabus is completed. At that point students will visit the computer lab again and will be introduced to the Content Tools. Using the search facility, they will read the topic presented in the lecture and will read the summary with the main key points of the unit. They will also be asked to carry out the activities corresponding to that unit. If the activities are Web-based, it will give them the chance to surf the Web and become familiar with the online environment.

4.   The next face-to-face session should allow for discussion about how the technology worked, what students liked and disliked, and what may require additional assistance. Also students should hand in the activity tasks presented online. These can be done in groups, thus promoting collaborative learning.

5.   Each time a course unit is finished, the student will be introduced to the Assessment tools so that the students can test their own learning throughout the different course units. Self-tests can be done individually or in groups. Monitoring their own progress gives students a sense of control over their own learning and is a constant source of stimulus.

6.   Each new tool added to the online course should repeat this process. The discussion regarding the new tool could occur in the online discussion board. This will extend the students' learning experience.

This integration plan is exploratory and can certainly be subject to changes and modifications through the implementation process. Above all, it is important that both the instructor and the students feel confident with the online tools and do not pretend to master all of them from the beginning. In this sense, the Communication Tools should be available and extensively used from the beginning of the course, as they have the greatest impact on the educational experience, not the online content.

Recommendations and Opportunities for Future Research

The advantage of the proposed mixed scenario presented in this chapter is that course content can be made initially available through lectures and be progressively put up on the Web in different course offerings. It is a mistake to think that one needs a complete online course, containing all course content, before introducing online tools in the lecture-based scenario. As online course developers know well, one of the main difficulties one has to face when implementing a Web-based course is the amount of time required to either create the course material, or to bring one's existing course material into a form worthy of public exposure. Asynchronous instruction takes 200% to 300% more development time than traditional classroom instruction. Such a time-consuming task should therefore be carried out stepwise and throughout different offerings of the same course. Students can also participate in this task by taking notes during lectures which may later serve as a good starting point for online lecture notes. Also, during the first course offerings, it will be possible to learn more and more of the course management software, experiment with online quizzes or questionnaires, and gain comfort with the course, with the tools, and with the process of using online technologies.

The second part of the project will concentrate on testing the developed software both with students and through a process of internal evaluation. Testing with users is a fundamental part of any computational system. In our case it is necessary to get feedback from students on how this supplemental Web-based course extends their learning experience. One way of testing the effectiveness of the proposed mixed teaching scenario would be to check with the students how the Seven Good Teaching Principles outlined above are better supported through the use of the proposed combined design rather than with purely lecture-based or totally online teaching. This could be done by means of questionnaires and surveys to measure student satisfaction with the integration of the online tools in the conventional lecture-based scenario.

Internal evaluation will be carried out jointly with the course creator(s) and the instructor(s), with the purpose of improving the effectiveness of the implemented tools in the proposed mixed teaching scenario, making as many changes as necessary on the course contents, the tests and exercises, the activity tasks, etc., and deciding on how to handle—given the time limits available for the course offering—the communication channels between faculty staff and students in an efficient way.

Many research opportunities open up for the future both within the implementation and the testing phases. Within the implementation phase, issues regarding the development of course contents and the associated activity tasks will give the instructor the opportunity to reevaluate both the content of his/her teaching and the way in which it is taught. Pedagogical goals can be examined and the teaching methodology can realigned to meet those goals. This process is highly beneficial both for instructors and for students. However, it is a labor-intensive task that consumes a lot of time and energy on the part of the instructor. One way of saving time is enlisting the help of students. They can take notes of the lectures in a Web-ready format. These notes can then be collected, edited as necessary, and posted online. Although this method is not work-free, it does save work and it benefits students.

Within the testing phase, it will be interesting to examine the students' perception of the Web as a viable environment for grammar learning along the lines suggested by Felix (2001) for a Web-based language learning environment. That study did not investigate the effectiveness of Web-based learning in terms of achievement, a topic that lacks research and scholarly rigor (Windschitl, 1998; McIssac & Gunawardana, 1996), but concentrated on aspects related to the students' experience of Web-based learning, such as how comfortable students felt about working in a Web-based environment, how enjoyable they found such an environment, whether students found it useful to work with Web-based materials, or how they perceived the advantages and disadvantages of Web-based learning over conventional learning, among others.

A future avenue of research for the experimental course outlined in this chapter will be to investigate similar aspects to the ones analyzed by Felix, but in the context of the combined teaching scenario proposed here. It will also be interesting to check whether the students who will take the supplemental Web-based course presented in this chapter together with the lectures prefer this combined scenario to the traditional lecture-based one. The results of Felix's study indicate that students preferred to use the Web as an addition to face-to-face teaching. Reported advantages fell into the broad categories of time flexibility, reinforced learning, privacy, and wealth of information; disadvantages fell into the categories of distraction, absence of teacher, and personal interaction and lack of speaking practice.

In another study by Goldberg (n.d.) at the University of British Columbia, three groups were formed; the study concluded that the students who performed the best overall were those with access to both lectures and the online course.[5] Goldberg also found that the happiest students overall were those in the combined section having access to both the Web and lectures. Moreover, the students in that study said there was a need for lectures, but that its number should be reduced to half of the currently planned ones. Therefore, students felt there was a need for lectures, but a reduced schedule of lectures. I share Goldberg's opinion that it is not a question of replacing lectures with the Web, as lectures clearly contribute to the learning process, but reducing their number could be highly beneficial to faculty and students alike. The precise reduction rate in the proposed supplemental Web-based course presented in this chapter remains an interesting topic for future research.

Summary and Concluding Remarks

The changes brought into education by Web-based technologies are not a matter of the future, but are already here to stay. In this sense, Web-based technologies offer an immense potential for education that attracts teachers, administrators, and students in different ways. In this chapter I have described the first phase of a project on the integration of Web-based technologies into the conventional lecture-based scenario of English grammar teaching. This first phase has focused on issues of planning and design of Web-based tools which can potentially support the Seven Good Teaching Principles. As described, interactive tools—such as the ones included in the Communication group—clearly encourage interaction both between the instructor and the students, and among the students themselves, thus supporting several good teaching principles (the first, the second, the third, and the fourth). The rest of the tools are also promising in this respect, although their effectiveness should be tested with students in the second phase of this project.

Although incomplete, the type of developmental work reported in this chapter is a useful phase which, in my experience, gives instructors a unique opportunity to reevaluate their teaching methodology and to keep abreast of innovative methods that may impact positively in their teaching. The development of the described tools and materials is not a trivial matter, but requires hours of development time. Fortunately, the combined scenario for which the tools were developed allows a progressive introduction so that students and instructors become familiar with the new learning environment as the course proceeds. The second phase of this project will focus on testing the developed tools with students and on carrying out an internal evaluation of their effectiveness. This remains, however, the matter for future research.

References

Aggarval, A. (Ed.) (2000). *Web-based learning and teaching technologies: Opportunities and challenges*. Hershey, PA: Idea Group Publishing.

Chickering, A., & Ehrmann, S.T. (1996). Implementing the Seven Principles: Technology as lever. *AAHE Bulletin*, (October, 3-6). Retrieved July 2003 from: http://www.tltgroup.org/programs/seven.html.

Chickering, A.W., & Gamson, Z.F. (1987). Seven principles for good practice in undergraduate education. *AAHE Bulletin*, *39*(7), 3-7.

Chong, N.G.S.T. (2001). Internet technologies: Towards advanced infrastructure and learning applications. In F.T. Tschang & T.D. Senta (Eds.), *Access to knowledge. New information technologies and the emergence of the virtual university* (pp. 129-166). Amsterdam: Elsevier.

Chua, K., Debreceny, R., & Ellis, A. (1995). Networked learning: Some issues in implementation at Southern Cross University. In J.M. Pearce & A. Ellis

(Eds.), *Proceedings of the 12th Annual Conference of the Australian Society for Computers and Learning in Tertiary Education* (ASCILITE95) (pp. 63-71). Melbourne: University of Melbourne Press.

Felix, U. (2001). A multivariate analysis of students' experience of Web-based learning. *Australian Journal of Educational Technology, 17*(1), 21-36.

Goldberg, M. (n.d.). *To lecture or not to lecture.* Retrieved June 2003 from: http://distancelearning.dbcc.cc.fl.us/faculty/DLArticles/lecture.htm.

McIssac, M.S., & Gunawardana, C.N. (1996). Distance education. In D. Johanssen (Ed.), *Handbook of research for educational communications and technology* (pp. 403-437). New York: MacMillan.

Reinhardt, A. (1995, March). New ways to learn. *BYTE.* Retrieved June 2003 from: http://www.byte.com/art/9503/sec7/art1.htm#paradigm.

Windschitl, M. (1998). The WWW and classroom research: What path should we take? *Educational Researcher, 27*(1), 28-33.

Endnotes

[1]   The Principles, created by Art Chickering and Zelda Gamson with help from higher education colleagues, AAHE, and the Education Commission of the States, with support from the Johnson Foundation, distilled findings from decades of research on the undergraduate experience. Several hundred thousand copies of the Principles and Inventories have been distributed on two- and four-year campuses in the United States and Canada.

[2]   More information on its availability and new features can be obtained from its homepage at http://www.webct.com.

[3]   Chickering and Ehrmann (1996) describe some of the most cost-effective and appropriate ways to use communication technologies to advance the Seven Principles. My purpose here is simply to check whether the features of the WebCT platform could potentially support those principles.

[4]   Some of the implemented tools described in this section were originally developed as part of a pilot study for the Spanish Distance Education University (UNED). However, as most of those materials and online tools are up-to-date, some of them are being reused in the context described in this chapter.

[5]   The three groups were: one taught totally online, a second one taught by traditional lecture-based methods, and a third one combining access both to the regular lecture schedule and access to the full online course.

Chapter IX

A Bridge to the Workplace:

Using an Internet-Based Simulation in the Writing Classroom

Mark R. Freiermuth
University of Aizu, Japan

Abstract

In this chapter, we examine the ways in which the Internet was used to run a case study-based, decision-making simulation in an academic writing class of 26 Japanese students studying English at a computer science university. The students had to construct an online glossary aimed at building sufficient background knowledge related to the simulation and then, in teams, create online documents demonstrating an understanding of the simulation problem and offer potential solutions. Information was delivered to students via the Web, and all documents produced by students were posted to their homepages. Assessment and observation revealed that the objectives of the simulation were achieved and that students were quite motivated throughout the simulation because they were able to make connections between the simulation activities and their chosen career. It is hoped that this study will act as an impetus for additional online simulation experiments in academia, business, and government.

Introduction

Simulations have been used in a variety of settings dependent upon the goals of the organizers or sponsors. In business, company executives have found simulations to be a viable training tool for employees; in education, simulations have been found to be an interesting and motivating way to teach a variety of concepts and ideas. For many, the word simulation is associated with aerospace or business. In the aerospace realm, we think of astronauts training in a simulated space pod, so that decision-makers can see how they will perform when under stressful and perhaps even dangerous conditions. Business simulations are often used within business courses at the university level. A common backdrop in a business-oriented simulation is for students to run a mock company. Written communication in such simulations is often times a vital aspect of the simulation, and might include such items as business letters to customers, memos from bosses, and reports about the "bottom-line" (Jones, 1985; Gredler, 1994). In education, simulations have been used to expose cultural biases, develop teamwork, make difficult decisions affecting many people, reveal how various social systems function, and probably most importantly, they have become a tool whereby participants can reflect upon experiences gained from the simulated tasks that help them draw parallels to real-world activities that affect humans in everyday situations (Crookall et al., 1988).

Here we are concerned with the incorporation of simulations that take advantage of technology but are for the purposes of language learning. Recently tried simulations addressing both of these areas simultaneously provide some good examples how technology and simulations have been integrated for language learning purposes. The always-innovative Coleman (2002) used SIM-software that effectively taught the skill of providing directions. Students had to pilot a helicopter through a virtual environment by giving accurate directions in English. Additionally, Freiermuth (2002a) developed a simulation that was run using Internet chat as the forum of communication. It was found that English language learning students were more effective communicating and solving problems in English online than they were in face-to-face environments. Also, recently a number of commercially designed software titles have been developed that incorporate the use of simulations (whether they are called by this name or not), coupled with language learning activities (see Li & Topelewski, 2002).

In our case, we wanted to design a simulation that incorporated the use of the Internet while maintaining an EST (English for science and technology) focus. From the outset, our goal was to design activities that helped foster decision-making processes that mimic processes that students might encounter in a professional setting (Freiermuth, 2002b). This concept runs parallel to one of the cornerstone ideals of language learning in an EST setting—the classroom should act as bridge to the professional world. Students generally start at a place where they have limited (or almost no) knowledge of the language, activities, and genres of the discourse community and slowly move in a direction towards greater understanding. However, this concept of learning is not merely valid for language learners; professionals (and students aiming at the goal of becoming professionals) must be aware of the discourse domains associated with their chosen field and often must become accustomed to flourishing within the parameters of those domains (Swales, 1990; Bhatia, 1993). Hence, simulations such as the one proposed in this chapter can be adapted to fit practically any situation and any group of students, dependent upon the objectives that the teacher/professional has in mind. The beauty (and the curse) of simulations is that they need to be custom-tailored to fit the needs of the students. What this means in practical terms is that a teacher who wishes to employ a simulation with clearly defined guidelines may have to jettison some parts and add others to make it work effectively.

We have mentioned the importance of activities that mimic professional activities, so it is wise to think about what kinds of tasks can be incorporated into a simulation that might engender such activities. The simulation used in this study was designed to incorporate the Internet; the principle being that computer science students are constantly online for any number of reasons—some personal and some academic. Thus, applying this principle to include Internet use in an English language academic writing course seemed an appropriate and logical choice. Taking this one step further, the Internet seemed a suitable vehicle because the tasks developed needed to incorporate content from the students' area of specialization, and/or require students to use skills that are consistent with skills that they might encounter in either their specialized university courses or upon their entrance into the workforce (Bhatia, 1993).

Of course, if students are not engaged in writing that provides the potential for knowledge gain, any efforts would be wasted. Thus, one goal in using a simulation approach was to move students away from tasks focusing on prescriptive grammar tasks and towards tasks where content was the central issue. It is upon this concept that the idea of forming a bridge between the academic and the professional rests.

A second goal was to assess the simulation from the viewpoint of the students, because the simulation obviously could not be considered a success if students failed to see the value in it. A third goal was to add the technical aspect to the equation in consideration of the students' professional proclivities. The objective here was to simply integrate Internet use into all aspects of the course.

The Simulation

A classroom simulation, such as the one developed for this course, should consist of a number of phases. We considered the following elements to be of importance when developing this simulation:

- Preparation of the materials
- Preparation of the students
- Role cards (briefing)
- Running the simulation activities
- Production
- Student assessment (debriefing)
- Teacher assessment

Preparation of Materials

First and foremost, a simulation must have a structure; that is the simulation must be conceived and implemented with a clear notion in mind of the processes and tasks that are likely to unfold (Jones, 1982). This involves incorporating the initial idea into a workable activity. It would be folly to fall prey to the idea that this can be done the hour before a class starts. The majority of work involving simulations occurs well before the first attempts at implementation. After a thorough analysis and concluding that the chosen idea constitutes a reasonable basis for a simulation (which may involve a trial run with other students or teachers), the framework must be developed. The following items must be considered (Freiermuth, 2003, pp. 230-231):

- What are the tasks to be implemented?
- How many class sessions will be needed to complete the entire simulation? How much time will each task consume? What is an alternative plan if a task finishes early? Can the next task be started immediately? What is an alternative plan if a task takes longer than intended? What if one student or group of students finishes a task early?
- Does the simulation have multiple sections (e.g., Part "A," Part "B," etc.)? Are the sections interconnected? If so, what happens if the results from the initial section are unexpected? Will this render the second section useless?

- How does this simulation address the linguistic needs of EST students? What linguistic elements are going to be addressed? How are they going to be assessed?

- Will there be group work? (In many simulations this is an essential element.) What are the consequences (if any) if one member from a particular group is absent? Can the parameters of the simulation be easily adapted to counter such problems?

- What roles will students have? Will each student have the same role as his/her peers, or will each student have a specific role within a group or classroom (e.g., engineer, consultant, designer, etc.)?

- Is there some type of debriefing where students can either discuss their experiences or write down them down?

- How will the Internet be incorporated?

Once we had addressed these questions and designed the simulation, the simulation was ready to be put into practice. Since our primary goal was to incorporate a simulation that could be linked to the probable career of the majority of the students, we developed a simulation based upon a court case involving two software game companies, Sega and Accolade. Students, acting as engineers working for one of the two software companies, made decisions within small groups that they thought would be most beneficial to their company. In the subsequent sections, we will describe the simulation in more detail.

Preparation of Students

Sometimes simulations will need to include some preparatory activities for students which are pre-emptive measures to improve the chances of successful implementation. For simulations involving technology, this is often the case. In our simulation, considering that all of the students' work was to be posted on the Web, students had to develop a Web page linked to their main homepage and to the teacher's course homepage. Also, students had to create login codes on the *Nicenet* database and then familiarize themselves with its functions, since *Nicenet* was to act as the interface between the teacher and the students.

The second part of preparation was tied to the necessity that students have appropriate background knowledge in the target language (English) to success-fully navigate the simulation. Accordingly, they needed to define the following words over a three-week period: *hardware platform, proprietary, compatible, free competition, console, source code, software licensing fee, reverse engineering, interface standard, reverse compiler, "peeling a chip,"* and *copyright protection.* All of the words were posted in *Nicenet* using *Nicenet*-created documents (these were produced in *MS Word* and then pasted into the appropriate *Nicenet* form); the definition rating matrices were also posted there. Students were required to write a five-sentence definition that incorporated a clear understanding of each concept (these were graded for content and grammar). These definitions needed to be linked to the students' homepages, which in turn were linked to the teacher's homepage. Examples of the best definitions were posted on the teacher's homepage each week to encourage students to give their best effort, to provide examples of what constituted exemplary work, and to form an online glossary for the other parts of the simulation.

Role Cards

One aspect of simulations that should never be overlooked by teachers is the preparation of role cards. Whether students are homogenously "engineers," or if each person in a group or class has a different role, role cards must be provided to students. The foundation of most simulations rests upon the ability of students to clearly understand their roles and what they need to accomplish during each phase of the simulation. The goals the teacher has for the students should be inherent in the various roles assigned to students. A failure to adequately define roles by the teacher will doom the simulation. An additional caveat along these same lines is that students must assume their roles. In other words, they are not play-acting that they are engineers—they ARE engineers! Just like in any workplace setting, they must accept the duties and responsibilities that are assigned to them via the information provided on their role cards (Jones, 1982, 1985; Gredler, 1994).

In this simulation, before handing out the role cards, the students were put in groups consisting of three to four members based upon in-class performance up to that point (mixing students with higher and lower proficiencies in English together). Half of the groups were given role cards informing students they were engineers working for Sega, while the other groups received cards informing them that they were engineers working for Accolade. In reality, Sega and Accolade are competitors because they both make software games. Smaller software companies, such as Accolade, had long been in the business of making games for larger companies' consoles. Accolade had in fact produced games to run on Sega's game consoles in the past and was not punished for this practice. Nevertheless, Sega wanted a little more proprietary protection for their hard work and consequently developed complex security code for their "newest" console (called *Genesis*). The problem occurred when Accolade decided to reverse engineer the complex security code; they of course were successful and so began producing games to run on the console. Sega subsequently sued Accolade in northern California on the basis of copyright violation (see Spinello, 1997).

The tenets of our simulation did not follow the case exactly. This is common simulation practice (Jones, 1982). The students employed at Sega were under the impression that Accolade had just successfully reversed engineered their Genesis console. Under a directive from the president, the engineers were to decide what action was best for the company. They were provided three potential solutions (but could devise their own as well):

- Allow Accolade to develop the software, which Sega had done in the past.
- Demand that Accolade pay a software licensing fee (made especially hefty for the purposes of the simulation—$200,000,000 per software title).
- Take legal action against Accolade in a U.S. court for violating copyright.

The group of engineers from Accolade faced a different problem. Their role card stated that Sega's Genesis console had just been developed. The company president asked the engineers from Accolade what should be done about this latest development. The options were as follows (Freiermuth, 2003, p. 24):

- Not develop any games for the new console.
- Pay Sega's licensing fee.
- Use reverse engineering to discover the source code of the console, and continue to develop the new games that are being worked on.

Of course, engineers at either company could develop their own solutions (a strategy encouraged by the teacher), so long as the core information on the role cards was not distorted. A fundamental principle of simulations is that outcomes should not be predetermined by the teacher. The role of the teacher is not that of controller; the teacher should only act as a facilitator to help students travel down the path. Based upon information that is provided (if it is sufficient) or that they have gathered, the students should be able to draw their own conclusions. This is one reason why Jones (1982, 1985) believes that simulations are motivating to students. If role cards are slanted towards a specific outcome, then it is not a real simulation; students have not determined anything, and most likely perceptive students will see through the veiled attempts to guide them and the pseudo-simulation will fail. That is why one of the foundational principles associated with decision-making simulations is that decisions to be rendered have both negative and positive consequences (Gredler, 1994).

Running the Simulation

Running a simulation involves varying degrees of complexity. Our simulation was quite easy to get up and running since the role cards explained virtually all of the information the students needed to know. During the first day of the simulation, students discussed the simulation within their groups and decided the appropriate actions based upon group consensus. They continued to discuss their decisions even into the production phase.

Production

For language learning simulations, students should be given the opportunity to produce something in the target language. In our simulation, teams using Unix-based *Star Office* wrote up their decisions as teams. "Good" writing was to incorporate the discourse elements common to problem-solutions documents, including background information, clear identification of the problem and any negative consequences associated with the problem, proposed solutions, and the finalized solution based upon reasoning. The teams were then to post these documents on their Web pages so that the teacher could access them.

Debriefing

Decision-making simulations need to incorporate some kind of debriefing segment once the activities of the simulation have been completed (Jones, 1985). This will help the teacher identify whether or not the simulation had the desired outcome, and if not, what it did actually achieve. The debriefing can take the form of a class discussion, small-group discussions, online interaction, or the completion of a debriefing handout. The teacher should ask enough questions to be able to determine whether or not the simulation was implemented successfully and also what feelings the students had during the activities. Obviously, if students have a negative experience, the simulation might need to be altered or even abandoned (dependent of course on the goals of the simulation).

In this simulation, we provided the students with online questionnaires, which were administered via the *Nicenet* interface to give students a chance to reflect upon the simulation. The questions on the questionnaire included items about the ability to work and write in teams, the value of writing definitions, the value of using *Nicenet,* and general assessment questions concerning the simulation.

Subjects

The students involved in this simulation curriculum were 26 (22 male and four female) second-year Japanese university students enrolled in Academic Writing II at a Japanese university where computer science is the sole major. They are required to take a number of English language courses throughout their four years at the university. Academic Writing II acts as a preparatory course for Technical Writing I. The bulk of the remaining courses they take are core courses offered from either the hardware department or the software department. Students need to write a senior thesis in English, so many of the students are motivated to improve their English writing ability. Most of the students had studied English for seven or eight years; unfortunately, for the most part, English writing instruction in Japanese high schools consists primarily of translation from English to Japanese and vice versa. In general, there is little essay-length writing done in English during high school. Due to their lack of essay-writing experiences, students tend to have difficulty using content effectively in topic-specific writing as this sample emphasizes (Freiermuth, 2003, p. 222).

> I find that to help someone to understand is very hard and difficult. And that, I have to take (a matter) into consideration about individual personality. In the other hand, I must teach by individual fitting study style.
>
> When student's result of test is bad, I feel…, but heartbreaking thing is not all. At the same time, I get many many things! What is more, I ,maybe do same things towards you, I'm sorry. So no matter how hard, I am satisfaction, because I get many many things in exchange for bitterness.

There are a number of grammatical errors in the text above; however, what is much more troubling is the writer's inability to inform. The piece is written solely for the teacher's consumption and so is completely decontextualized (the piece was an explanation about the student's part-time job as a tutor). Of course, this type of problem is not exclusive to language learners; many university teachers must deal with this kind of inward-looking writing, even when teaching communication skills to native speakers. Nevertheless, the prevalence of this kind of writing by our Japanese students was one of the principal reasons that a simulation was employed; it was our contention that students could move beyond the student-teacher relationship and write more effectively for a boss who had hundreds of ongoing projects to attend to and so needed concise information that would clearly identify all of the necessary details.

From the perspective of technical writing, the aforementioned writing problems are compounded in two ways. First, the students are inexperienced writing about problems and solutions in English (as well as in Japanese for that matter). Most of their writing instruction is strongly grammar focused, especially in high school. In their first academic writing course at the university, students again spend a great deal of their time focused on grammar exercises and developing their writing. For example, they spend time writing a number of one-paragraph texts about different topics.

Second, although they are fledgling computer scientists, they are novices in communicating using subject-specific English. In fact, this was one of the major reasons that one of the simulation tasks was a requirement of students to define key vocabulary. The goal was that the students would build sufficient background knowledge to be able to handle the content portion of the simulation tasks.

To sum up, students' writing problems can be attributed to both language disorientation and an inability to write (in any language) in a conventionalized (genre-based, logical) manner or for a specific context. Again, clearly these problems are not restricted to English language learners. Teachers who have taught freshman composition in U.S. universities to native-speakers of English can attest to the fact that many students produce texts that are difficult to read because students are unfamiliar with writing in a rhetorically logical style, and these problems are magnified if they must produce writings bound by a specific context. In addition, technical writing teachers are well aware that the problems associated with writing under the constraints of specific contexts do not necessarily vanish once the students have conquered their freshman writing courses.

Technology

Although simulations have been used in the past in writing courses in a variety of settings, Internet applications present new adventures to simulation lovers (and potential lovers). In our case, save one handout, the entire simulation process was intricately tied to Internet activities.

Justification

The importance of implementation of activities that allow learners to use the Internet goes beyond the simple view that we should use the Internet because of its prevalence in the modern world. Rather, it is related more to the fact that the subjects in this study are fledgling computer scientists, learning about computer science in a computer-enriched environment. To be sure, the students in this study are language learners of English, and as language teachers, it is imperative that we not lose sight of this fact. (In fact, there is the ever-present danger to bow to technology at the expense of providing opportunities for students to improve their writing.) Nevertheless, to be tied to the more traditional forms of production, such as writing with pencil and paper (which is still the prevalent writing method for many Japanese university students) would be to show indifference to the reality that the students are using computers constantly in all of their core subjects.

Closely related to the issue of using computers with computer science students is the issue of using computers with prospective employees whose source of income will be tied to computer knowledge, because these students are going to be working (for the most part) in computer science arenas once they leave the confines of the university. Thus, it is important to allow a classroom culture that encourages using computers, and using them in a way that emulates a workplace setting. The Internet becomes the research tool, the means to communicate with peers and teachers (coworkers and managers), as well as the venue of publication—all of which will become important elements in the lives of a great many of these students once they find themselves entrenched in the work environment. From a practical perspective, this means that students used the Web to check for task specifications and task objectives that had been posted by the teacher; they communicated with one another face-to-face, but also used email (electronic bulletin boards are certainly an option); they produced texts using word processing software or text editors; they posted their work on the Web; they also checked the posted scoring matrices that the teacher used to evaluate them (which also acted as a guide to students because they had the opportunity to develop and evaluate their productions based upon grading criteria identified in each matrix); and finally, they received and read emails from the teacher evaluating their online productions.

The *Nicenet* Interface

To make the coursework truly tied to the Internet, an online database was used as an interface between the teacher and the students. For this application, the database available from *Nicenet* (http://www.nicenet.org/) was chosen because it appeared to have the needed features. Basically all activities were conducted using the *Nicenet* classroom.

The initial interface for *Nicenet* appears like this (webshots used with permission from *Nicenet.org*) (see following page):

Nicenet's Internet Classroom Assistant

NEW ICA USERS START HERE

For Everyone:

For Students: **For Teachers:**   Learn More About the

Join a Class   Create a Class   ICA

CURRENT ICA USERS

Username: **Password:**

| | | Log In to the ICA |

[Forgot Your Password?]

Students login to the system using provided "dialogue boxes" (we advised students to use their student ID numbers). Once students are logged into the Internet classroom, they can access posted documents, get assignment updates, send email messages (to the teacher, an individual in the class, or even the whole class), and make postings at the teacher's behest. The menu is on the left-hand side of the screen. Here is a webshot of the *Nicenet* classroom interface (see following page):

NICENET Internet Classroom Assistant

Mark R. Freiermuth   Tuesday, July 8, 2003 12:44AM CST

AW II Wed

Conferencing

Link Sharing

Documents

Class Schedule

Class Members

Personal Messages :

View | Send

Classes :

Join | Create | Drop |

Delete

Class Administration

Edit User Profile

ICA FAQ

Enter New Class:

AW II Wed ▼

Change Class

PROTECT YOUR

PRIVACY:

LOG OUT

Home - AW II Wed

Since you last logged in on Tuesday, July 08 :

- No new personal messages have been sent to you.

  [View Messages | Send a Message]

Conferencing

- No new comments have been posted under any

  topics.

  [View Topics | New Topic | New Message]

Link Sharing

- No new links have been posted.

  [View Links | New Link]

Assignments

- No new assignments have been turned in.

Documents

- No new documents have been posted

WEEK AT A GLANCE

[View Schedule | New Event | New Assignment]

The *Nicenet* database allows the teacher to post all assignments, give due dates, send email messages to students (or to the class or all students in every section), and even set up automatically emailed homework reminders. Documents allow HTML code to be used and links can also be added to the website (although in our case, we wanted students to do searches without any assistance from the teachers, so we did not provide links to the appropriate sites).

Internet Searching

Of course, the other online tool that students needed to use in this simulation was a Web browser. Students used *Netscape* as their Web browser to conduct all of their searches (since this university employs Unix-based workstations, *Netscape* is used exclusively). Although students were never specifically instructed to search the World Wide Web, it was clear from the start that they would retrieve any relevant information exclusively using the Web, both to define terms and to investigate the two companies involved in the simulation.

Production

Recall that students needed to post all of their work on their homepages, which had been previously linked to the teacher's homepage. This included the online definition glossary and the team writings.

Definitions

One of the goals of this simulation was to have students write about issues that were closely linked to computer science. In this way, they could incorporate language common to computer science; however, it was necessary to make sure students understood concepts related to computer science prior to the simulation; otherwise, the simulation was bound to fail. Quality definitions, then, needed to demonstrate an understanding of the concept being defined. Here is an example of a quality definition produced by a student:

> Reverse engineering is the technology which makes the product that has compatibility with a certain product. In other words, reverse engineering is a process which analyzes an existing system or product, recognizes composition elements and those relations, and clarifies a basic design.

Moreover, reverse engineering is focused on the challenging task of understanding legacy program code without having suitable documentation. For example, Seiko Epson developed the compatible personal computer of PC-9800 series of NEC with reverse engineering. It may be useful in respect of system maintenance or security strengthening, such as leading to discovery of a security hole or a bug by reverse engineer.

What makes this definition exemplary is that the student demonstrated a clear understanding of the concept by providing an example. Students whose definitions were poor were given an additional chance to rewrite them because the ultimate goal of the exercise was to make sure that students understood enough of the background information associated with the tenets of the case to be able to write about the concepts in an intelligent and logical manner in their problem-solution paper.

Team Writing

After the simulation was run, students produced their group writings. Here is a rather typical example of what was produced.

Accolade's Position

Accolade was established by the founders with an advanced idea and creative soul in 1999. We, *Engineer A*, *Engineer B*, and *Engineer C*, working as an engineer of this company, are deeply concerned with development of much software, and since having had many excellent actual results, we are greatly trusted by the president. We are developing many software towards various hardware consoles. Especially, "Ishido: Way of Stones" has been a big seller out of our products. Although this game looks simple apparently, since its back is too deep, in fact, there are 4 million or more sales in all over the world surprisingly, and it gained the 1st place in the world game ranking. However, since we do not consider that this game is the highest masterpiece, we are tackling the development of new software which has an novel idea every day to exceed it with might and main. Our purpose is developing software and contributing to the profits of this company, and now, some software which run on console of Sega is under development.

However, the report that Sega developed Genesis of new console yesterday went into our company. As a result of investigation, since Genesis was incompatible with the present console, we cannot operate the software that under present development on Genesis. Therefore, our company will be pressed for judgment whether the development of software for the present console is continued or software is redeveloped to Genesis. Moreover, in case software is redeveloping to Genesis, we have to decide whether we use reverse engineering or pay licensing fee and acquire the details of the source code of Genesis from Sega.

After an intense argument, when development is continued by the present console, even if the software under present development hits, since a consumer having shifted to Genesis is considered (that is to say, a thing without possibilities), profit's decrement will be mentioned. For the game industry, possibilities are the most important. The next problem is whether licensing fee is paid to Sega and software is developed or not paid, licensing fee of $200 million which Sega presents are too high. Even if the software under development hits, it seems difficult to obtain the profits beyond $200 million. Furthermore, even if our under developing software hits, it is hard to acquire more than $200 million, much less the loss in case of not selling will become big. If the price of one software is set to $50, we have to sell at least 4 million or more software to pay licensing fee of $200 million. This number is considered not to be realistic when we considered the sales of "FINAL FANTASY 7" which is the game made by SQUARESOFT was 3.7 million. Since $200 million are not the amount of money which a small game company can pay, software development is considered to impossible for small game companies. Our company thought that this was contrary to the principle of free market. Therefore, we resulted in the conclusion of analyzing the source code of Genesis by using reverse engineering. Genesis has passed only for one month from release, at a present stage, it can not predict whether how much market share is occupied in a game machine market hereafter. However, Genesis has epoch-making functions which were not in old console, such as a DVD reproduction function and a hard disk loading function, and hide a possibility of hitting explosively. Therefore, under such situation as we cannot foresee the future, we thought it the most important to take always flexible correspondence (i.e., to always get ahead). It is important to acquire the technology which manufactures the software for Genesis by using reverse engineering and get ready to shift to console of Genesis at any time. Since it was such, we thought that the best action which should be taken now was analyzing Genesis of Sega and developing the software corresponding to it.

This piece of writing is not an exception. Here is an example from one group of engineers at Sega:

Sega's Position

1. Background Information

We are computer engineers for Sega Enterprise, Ltd. in Tokyo, Japan. Sega has developed as manufacture of amusement machines since establishment in 1960, and it has made game machines for home use since 1983. Now, Sega gets high evaluation as manufacture with globally soft property.

Sega made the software games running on the originally developed console, but other companies have developed software games to run on Sega's console. This means that Sega suffers damage, but we allowed their software in the past. This time, Accolade use reverse engineering to get the source code of the Sega's new Genesis console, and they were able to obtain the source code for the new console. That's a very big problem. We express the best opinion which we considered about this problem.

2. Problem of Solutions

2-1. Explaining of problem.

Case a: *allow Accolade to develop the software; Sega has done this in the past.*

This "Case a" is the most easy idea, and it had been doing in the past. This case needn't spend time and money, but we miss a chance to get potential money because this may encourage other companies to reverse engineer the Genesis console and it has dangerous possibility to do breakdown the hardware source code. If our Genesis console is done breakdown by other companies, they must be made a new console more ability has than it, so many time and money to develop complicated security are wasted. Therefor this case's problem is possibility to be wasted time and money to develop.

Case b: *demand that Accolade pay the software licensing fee for each piece of software they develop (about $200,000,000 for each game) or threaten legal action (taking Accolade to court).*

This "Case b" is official idea. If Accolade pay the software licensing fee, this case is very good, but it is doubtful for them to pay the fee because they have decide to reverse engineer the console. Also it has been bad not to do that we still have not prevented other software game companies from copying Sega's software. Therefor this case's problem is not to know Accolade pay the fee.

Case c: *take legal action against Accolade in court (in the U.S.) and sue them for copyright violation; after all Accolade had to designed to keep them from making games to run on the system.*

This "Case c" isn't good idea because this case must be spent many time and money. Also it has possibility to separate each other's relations. Even if we win in court, Accolade will probably appeal the decision, so the cost must be become higher cost. Also if we lose in court, we need to allow to continue. Therefor this case's problem is time and money and each other's relations.

2-2. Decision to do.

We recommend "Case b" but Accolade has high probability not to pay the fee, so we recommend "Case a" too but we don't recommend "Case c".

3. The Best of Solution and Reason

We thought about three method of solutions (a,b,c). So we decided the best of solution.

At first, we should demand that Accolade pay the software licensing fee for each piece of software they develop (about $200,000,000 for each game) or threaten legal action (taking Accolade to court). It is doubtful that Accolade will pay the fee. However if Accolade pays the fee, we can get much money. When Accolade suffer from payment, we should negotiate with Accolade about reducing the price of licensing fee. Sega's licensing fee is much higher than other company. So, Accolade will agree to the proposal because Accolade may not have a lot of money. Also, Accolade will reject that Sega takes legal action because it is expensive and wasted time for both Accolade and Sega. Even if Accolade disagree the negotiation that reduce the price of licensing fee, we should not take legal action because the rate that Accolade will win in the judgment is higher. In this case, we must allow Accolade to develop the software. Sega has done this in the past. Though we gets no profit, we have no risk. Finally, even if we get licensing fee or not get it, we should make new game software in popular series made by Sega because there are great profit to create a popular game in the game market. Therefore, we will get much profit if the game is sold on other popular console because there are more user on the famous console than Sega's console.

Assessment

This section looks at an assessment of the students' writings, the simulation and the technology employed.

Assessing the Writing

What becomes immediately apparent about the students' writing abilities is the knowledge that they are able to provide to the reader. Generally speaking, students in the second year at this university have problems with context and are quite shortsighted (as was apparent from the fairly typical example that was provided in an earlier part of this work). Here the writings show that they are able to clearly identify a problem, and offer an appropriate solution based upon logical reasoning, while rejecting other "solutions" that are deemed as less effective. In this regard, the writing produced by the students more closely mimicked the workplace because students were able to address problems in a standardized professional manner (Kennedy & Montgomery, 2001). What is also clear is that the writers have not constructed this piece of prose solely for the teacher's consumption; the documents are publicly readable. And although the visual representation of the student-produced prose is not particularly attractive, the simulation achieved one of the goals presented at the outset, which posed the question, "Could novice Japanese writers express the notions of problems and solutions in a manner that would demonstrate their understanding?" In other words, from a genre-analysis perspective, the students were successful.

In addition, students were able to effectively use language related to situations that would only occur in the context of computer science. Some of the terms may have been easy for the students to use (such as *software*), but others would have been very difficult (such as *reverse engineering*). In any case, it is interesting to note that more than 10% of the words in the essay (no less than 71 words out of the 651 words) can be directly tied to this particular computer science context. Moreover, settings in computer science where such terminology would be used are not hard to imagine. In other words, from an EST perspective the students were also successful, demonstrating effective uses of computer-science-related vocabulary.

Assessing the Definitions

Recall that one objective of using a simulation in this course was to examine students' opinions about a number of issues. The first three items from the questionnaire addressed the value of the definitions. Table 1 indicates students' responses.

In general, the students found the definitions *helpful* or *extremely helpful*. Actually, no students found the writing of the definitions useless (i.e., *not helpful*). Students who mentioned that the definitions were not helpful to them while "discussing the issues," indicated that they found the definitions *helpful* or *extremely helpful* while "writing the paper." Only one student indicated that the

Table 1. Definitions: Student assessment

How helpful were definitions toward:	Extremely Helpful	Helpful	Not Very Helpful	Not Helpful
1) Discussing the issues	11	12	1	2
2) Writing the paper	7	17	1	1

definitions were *not very helpful* toward "discussing the issues" as well as "writing the paper." This notion is accentuated by the graph in Figure 1, showing how often the students accessed their own Web definitions while writing the group paper.

According to this poll, only two students disregarded their definitions during the writing stage of the group paper. The Web page definitions students created proved to be their own effective resource, which was a goal of the activity and certainly contributed to extending students' background knowledge.

Additionally, we wanted to see if students thought that writing the definitions helped their overall English writing ability. Table 2 illustrates the usefulness according to students.

Figure 1. Graph of student access frequency to self-created Web definitions

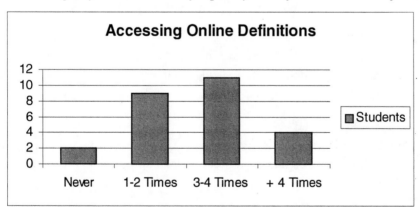

Table 2. Definition application

Usefulness to English writing ability:	Extremely Helpful	Helpful	Not Very Helpful	Not Helpful
Rating	7	17	2	0

These data support the numbers from Table 1 and Figure 1. It appears that from a psychological perspective (at least) that the definitions were useful toward improving students' English writing ability in computer science. Whether or not students' perceptions were realized, the task was valuable, nevertheless, from a motivational standpoint (Crookes & Schmidt, 1991). And, even if this point is debatable, what is not in doubt is that students understood the content and how to integrate it effectively into their writing, so gains were made.

Assessing Teamwork

The next part of the debriefing survey looked at the group experience. We wanted to examine the difficulties and benefits experienced by group members as they tried to resolve their problems and subsequently write the paper as a team. Here a list of a few of the more poignant difficulties that were mentioned:

- It was difficult for us to take time to work together. Each member is so busy that we seldom can gather. If the team member is close friend, this prbrem finds the ??? to solve. Under the situasion of this time, we couldn't work together.
- We had many idea so my team had difficult to make decision.
- Searching background information.
- We rarely had difficulties during the working.
- Not all member didn't do his work properly.
- We didn't communicate by email well. We can't talk each other because we don't know each other. I speak from any aspect. I can't make one.
- We didn't match time each other.
- It is difficult to express my opinion.
- We have few time to discuss and write. The reason is, we have different time table. So we couldn't contact togethe enough. So, I feel difficulties on this work.

The vast majority of students expressed that their greatest difficulties were caused by time constraints. However, it is important that tasks of this nature have some realistic properties. Working in groups in the work-a-day-world is fraught with similar types of problems, such as getting group members together at an appropriate moment when everyone can devote their full attention to a task, getting everyone to contribute the same amount to a task, compromising with others, effectively expressing an opinion, and effectively clarifying a point of view. Despite this, if the group assignment did not produce any positive counter-effect, it could not be considered a valuable tool simply because of the lack of a motivational aspect. Hence, it was important that the debriefing handouts also asked the students to consider any benefits from working in groups. The following are some of the students' comments:

- We could discuss and write like a real Sega engineer.

- I could know many opinions in my team's members.

- We could know other members opinion. It is interesting for me. Contrastly, unifying members opinion is difficult.

- I could be to write what we discuss in Japanese.

- I can derive some information from this working. For example, definitions of computer terminology, about community, etc.

- I could learn the different way of writing expression from mine. Every member has their own expression. Moreover, in reflecting every member's expression, we could review the grammer.

- One of the benefits is saving time, and helping each other for advice.

- It becames benefit for my future, because group working is had frequently in company. We need to get along with others in this situations.

- We divided the role each section, like comany, and presentor introduction, showing strategy and reason. We didn't know about Accolade before this project. So the amount of research task were distributed, then we finished this report before a week of deadline.

- In the future, I'll do these things. Thinking these, this working was good for us. I could learn many words that I didn't know.

These comments speak volumes concerning the value of the experiences of working with others, which was certainly an aim of the simulation. The students realized that significant rewards could be gained while working with others, especially the notion of learning from one another. Moreover, obviously a number of students realized that this kind of groupwork was a microcosm of what they might face beyond the ivied walls outside the university. These comments alone make a strong case for using case-based simulations in any classroom that is trying to bridge the academic world with the professional world. The question-naire also asked students to rate their group experience. Table 3 illustrates the findings.

Table 3. Group experience student assessment

Experience working in a team:	Really Enjoyable	Enjoyable	Not Very Enjoyable	Not Enjoyable
Rating	0	21	5	0

Interestingly, students claimed that they generally enjoyed working in teams, but no one claimed that the experience was *really enjoyable*, nor did anyone say that the task was completely devoid of enjoyment. Upon reflection, it is probably what can be expected. Group members saw the benefits of working in groups, such as hearing others' opinions and learning from peers, but they also struggled with compromise and finding time getting together. This student comment reflects this very point.

- I enjoyed writing because it was easier than to write all by myself. However, working as a team produced another kind of problem. Sometimes two people's sentences are similar to each other, and we had to revise many times. Thus, I feel the working was not *really enjoyable* but *enjoyable*.

The following comments are related to the enjoyment level of working together (or lack thereof):

- Because I got new knowledge, and I talked with classmate whom I usually talk a little.
- There are almost no time to meet together. So, the partition of role is not done well. Consequently, I have to do the translation of Japanese to English alone.
- Working for big company is very enjoyable. I'm thinking so by this simulation.
- It is *enjoyable* because I read others' paper and discussed about our (virtual) company. To work together is hard but important.
- We couldn't choose the members of the team. That is the worst point. If we could choose, we had much more time to take it in and enjoyed it.
- Some member did work properly in the other hand, the other members didn't do at all! I can't allow them to get some grade with us.
- It is team play. I like it because it is like a company.
- We could discuss seriously.

Here again comments reflect the realities of working in groups. It is interesting to note that many students looked beyond their difficulties to realize that there was much value, even when group members held opposing opinions, and decisions were difficult to achieve due to disagreement and time constraints.

Assessing the Simulation

In the final section of the debriefing questionnaire, the students were asked if they thought the simulation was useful or not, under the auspices that the simulation would be used in future courses. Table 4 indicates how useful students thought the simulation was (Freiermuth, 2003):

It is unusual, but certainly encouraging to find activities that corral a 96% positive assessment from students. Their comments generally reflected their beliefs.

- I think that there are nothing which will not be useful in the future.

- I think it's important to work together, and teammates check my English, and communicate each other. I think another simulation maybe agree.

- Through this simulation, I understood that I must not think only income and must think the near future economy.

- It's important to think for company's and make a decision.

- At first, we thought that not to develop any games for the new console because it seemed to be the safest decision. However, we realized that to run a risk produces better result in some cases through this working.

- I reflected this problem seriously. Perhaps, I never reflect such a thing like this if I don't face such a problem. It was a good experience. ·

- This simulation makes our more thinking deeply.

- This simulation was study for not only English but economy as well.

- When I start working, I need to have and speak my opinion about my company.

Table 4. Simulation 1 student assessment

Simulation's usefulness (future implementation):	Extremely Useful	Useful	Not Very Useful	Not Useful
Rating	9	17	1	0

- I didn't know this issue. We will get a job related to computer, so we had better know this information.

- Like this simulation is possible in the future in fact, so we can simulate and think about "what is copyright" seriously. This experience will be utilize a lot.

- I think this experience is the most important, so I think this simulation is very useful. I have to gain experience by practical use.

Students took this simulation seriously, and these comments indicate that they tended to place high value on working in a group under simulated conditions. If one of the goals of writing courses is actually to prepare students for the workplace, simulations, such as the one used in this EST study, offer the well-prepared teacher substantial opportunity toward this end. Even the negative comments related to the problems of groupwork can be looked at in a positive light—these students studying hardware and software faced lifelike problems that are common to in-company working groups, and the problem they needed to resolve (based upon a real court case) is potentially similar to one that they could actually encounter once they become professionals in the workplace. Students seemed to realize this, and so valued the experience despite the difficulties working with their peers.

With that said, from a teacher's viewpoint, it would still be pointless to recommend using simulations in an online environment if students were not particularly motivated by the activities (see Leppner, 1988; Leppner & Cordova, 1992). That is why the debriefing aspect is vital to understanding whether or the not a simulation is effective. And, although classroom activity that occurred during this simulation was not formally measured, mere observation provided evidence that the students were highly motivated and their actions reflected this motivation. And this in turn was reflected in the quality of the writing they produced.

Assessing the Technology

Observation of the students by the teacher also provided sufficient evidence that students used the World Wide Web extensively to search for information. Specifically, they used the Web to help them discover important background information for the two companies, which they needed to include in the document. This was followed by the students integrating this information into their texts and developing publicly readable Web-based documents. And, as previously mentioned, the students used their online definitions as an integral tool to help them write their proposals. Since this was the desired outcome from the implementation of the simulation, it was successful inasmuch as students spent the vast majority of the time in the computer lab searching for information needed for the definitions and the team writings.

The students also commented about using the online activities that took place during the simulation. Here are some of their comments:

- At this work, we must search some page wrote in English. Usualy we don't brows English page. So, this is very important experience to brows English page.

- The simulation was useful because I read many Web page in English to search.

Not all of the comments were positive, however, as these comments reflect:

- We didn't communicate by email well. We can't talk each other because we don't know each other.

- If the Accolade's website never die during our projects, I would give the rate "A."

Again, despite the frustration indicated by the students, these kinds of communication troubles reflect real-world problems that will naturally be encountered in the workplace. Regarding the former comment, it is clear that students need to be engaged more often in groupwork in the university since many of them will need to work in teams once they are employed in the computer science field. This kind of information is also valuable to teachers because it illustrates that communication does not automatically occur within student peer groups; we must become aware that students need practice, even when learning to communicate online.

The other online tool, *Nicenet*, proved to be an invaluable resource for a number of reasons. First, *Nicenet* is free and user-friendly. Certainly such a database could have been designed within the university; however, the time and cost of developing such a database would have been hardly worth the time and effort.

Second, *Nicenet* had more than enough "options" to satisfy the requirements of the simulation. The week-by-week schedule was put in the "Class Schedule" page. Also, since all of the class members provided email information upon initial login, on the "Class Members" page, the teacher and the students were able to simply click on any student's email address to create a quick message. From the teacher's perspective this proved to be a very nice feature since all of the evaluations could be quickly and easily sent via the *Nicenet* interface. Moreover, messages are archived on *Nicenet*, so teachers have the option of going back to check messages sent and received from students (this is one of the options provided exclusively to teachers). Additionally, (although not employed in this simulation), the bulletin board feature, which can be found on the "Conferencing" page, makes for a nice communication tool for online discussions.

What is particularly convenient about using an online class organizer like *Nicenet* is that it eliminates the need to process so much paperwork, which benefits both students and teachers; this equates to fewer papers piled up on the teacher's desk and fewer office visits by students who are mysteriously missing handout "x" for some reason. Additionally, if assessments are emailed via the *Nicenet* interface, the teacher can go back into the archived email messages to see what suggestions were made to students in the past and if those suggestions had any positive effect on students' writing. One of the most useful features that also reduces paperwork is the automatic email function. This provided a quick and easy way to let the students know of any updated information that had been posted concerning the simulation and also was used to remind students a few days in advance that a particular assignment was due.

Finally, *Nicenet* simply performed very well. It was stable and secure, and the students had very little trouble with the system. In general, they were very happy with the system, as these comments reflect:

- I agree to this system. This system was very useful.
- It is very useful to understand the information and easy to use.
- We can easily see Document, Class Schedule and etc.
- Nicenet is very useful! We must continue to use Nicenet!
- It is easy to look.

These comments from the students mimic those of the teacher in this instance. *Nicenet* really was quite nice to use, and some of us here have stated for the record that we are planning to keep on using *Nicenet* to teach writing because of all of the aforementioned conveniences.

To briefly sum up, Internet technology was employed from the start to the finish of the simulation. This allowed computer science students to create Web pages and search Web pages in the target language. And, *Nicenet* acted as the perfect teacher's resource, where students could go to refresh their memories concerning what was due, see what documents were posted, send email messages to their peers, and retrieve email messages as well.

Future Simulations

Using simulations in the classroom is certainly not a new idea; however, technology has pried the door of possibilities wide open. For writing professionals, a promising area of interest is simulations that engage students and/or professionals who must produce collaborative works but from different locations—even across oceans (Wilson, 2002a, 2002b). This goes beyond simulations aimed at language learners. With the recent globalization of business English through organizations such as the World Trade Organization, the desire to reach some consensus as to how we should communicate on an international scale has become an issue. Communication activities that engender the actual participation of students and/or businesses located distantly or overseas are a great place to begin. Simulations can be used to help piece together the international communication puzzle, and this will undoubtedly entail more advanced applications of technology. Indisputably, the paradigms of international communication are being formed and reformed every day. Resources, including simulations, to help shape these paradigms should be considered as invaluable tools because they can help provide the kinds of certainties and best practices that are needed to make international business function more effectively.

Another technological domain ripe for simulations is the application of *MOOS*, *MUDS,* and other forums that allow for online synchronous communication. Although this has been tried here and there, the possibilities to connect such venues to professional writing are nearly endless (Freiermuth, 2001). Communication continues to demand faster and faster responses, which means more and more opportunities for synchronous means of communication (other than telephone). Business has already begun to move in that direction, so academic activities ought to follow this lead.

Concluding Remarks

We conclude by saying that using Internet technology as the information engine of a simulation designed for fledgling computer scientists was a success. *Nicenet* provided the Internet classroom that allowed students easy access to the important assignment information, schedules, and email. They did not have to rely on their own "notebook" database, which often times proves to be deficient. They also used the Internet to access vital information to both understand basic terminology and background information, which were the keys to writing about the case successfully. They also posted all of their writings on the Web. From the teacher's side, *Nicenet* provided an excellent interface, and allowed quick and easy access to the students. In fact, all of the handouts (save one) were provided in an online manner, even lecture notes. Because of this, there certainly is nothing to prevent the running of such a simulation in a remote location or as coursework in an online class.

The Internet acted as the liaison for the elements of the simulation between the teacher and the students; however, the tenets of the simulation fit the concept of operating in an online environment exceedingly well. This was verified by the responses of the students to the debriefing questionnaire. The students found the simulation to be useful and also enjoyed it. More importantly, they could see how such a simulation could be tied to an actual workplace setting. The simulation really did get students thinking about writing in the workplace and all that this idea entails (such as working in a team, negotiating, compromising, etc.).

Finally, students demonstrated their ability to write for the appropriate audience. The students were able to give sufficient background information, clearly identify the problem, offer possible solutions, and give appropriate reasons for choosing one option over another. They produced writing with the rhetorical style and content that really exceeded our expectations.

This simulation represented a simple idea of integrating the Internet into the fabric of a simulation, and as such really only scratches the surface as to how technology can be applied to simulations. Whatever the future holds for simulations, undoubtedly, the Internet will continue to play an ever-increasing role as a facilitation vehicle and as a valuable simulation tool.

References

Bhatia, V. (1993). *Analyzing genre: Language used in professional settings.* New York: Addison Wesley Longman.

Coleman, D. (2002). On foot in SIM CITY: Using SIM COPTER as the basis for an ESL writing assignment. *Simulation and Gaming Journal, 33*(2), 217-230.

Crookall, D., Klabber, J., Coote, A., Saunders, D., Cecchini, A., & Delle Piane, A. (Eds.). (1988). *Simulation-gaming in education and training.* Oxford: Pergamon Press.

Crookes, G., & Schmidt, R. (1991). Motivation: Reopening the research agenda. *Language Learning, 41*(4), 469-512.

Freiermuth, M. (2001). Native speakers or non-native speakers: Who has the floor? Online and face-to-face interaction in culturally mixed small groups. *Computer Assisted Language Learning, 14*(2), 169-199.

Freiermuth, M. (2002a). Online chatting: An alternative approach to simulations. *Simulation and Gaming Journal, 33*(2), 187-195.

Freiermuth, M. (2002b). Connecting with computer science students by building bridges. *Simulation and Gaming Journal, 33*(3), 299-315.

Freiermuth. M. (2003). Case-based simulations in the EST classroom. *IEEE Transactions on Professional Communication.*

Gredler, M. (1992). *Designing and evaluating games and simulations: A process approach.* London: Gulf Publishing.

Jones, K. (1982). *Simulations in language teaching.* Cambridge: Cambridge University Press.

Jones, K. (1985). *Designing your own simulations.* New York: Methuen.

Kennedy, G., & Montgomery, T. (2001). *Professional and technical writing: Solving problems at work.* Upper Saddle River, NJ: Prentice-Hall.

Leppner, M. (1988) Motivational considerations in the study of instruction. *Cognition and Instruction, 5*, 289-309.

Leppner, M., & Cordova, D. (1992). A desire to be taught: Instructional consequences of intrinsic motivation. *Motivation and Emotion, 16*, 187-208.

Li, R., & Topolewski, D. (2002). ZIP & TERRY: A new attempt at designing a language learning simulation. *Simulation and Gaming Journal, 33*(2), 181-186.

Spinello, R. (1997). *Case studies in information and computer ethics.* Upper Saddle River, NJ: Prentice-Hall.

Swales, J. (1990). *Genre analysis: English in academic and research settings.* Cambridge: Cambridge University Press.

Wilson, L. (2002a). International Internet simulations for language learning. In E. Borgmann (Ed.), *Intercultural, interactive, interpersonal* (pp. 8-16). Frankfurt: Verlag für Akademische Schriften.

Wilson, L. (2002b). Communication and collaborative writing: The way forward. In E. Borgmann (Ed.), *Intercultural, interactive, interpersonal* (pp. 22-41). Frankfurt: Verlag für Akademische Schriften.

Section V

Internet-Based Tutoring

Chapter X

The State of Online Writing Labs:
Have They Fulfilled Their Potential?

Jo Mackiewicz
University of Minnesota Duluth, USA

Abstract

This chapter analyzes the "state of the art" of OWLs, or online writing labs. It reports the results of a study of 343 OWLs that examined the extent to which OWLs have emerged into what Crump calls "true OWLs"—fully-interactive OWLs where tutors provide individualized help to students via computer-mediated communication like email. This chapter also examines what the literature and research on online tutoring say about the advantages and disadvantages of online tutoring in comparison with face-to-face tutoring. It is hoped that this chapter can illuminate the extent to which OWLs have fulfilled their promise to be places where students and tutors can freely exchange ideas and texts. It is also hoped that this chapter can suggest the extent to which OWL services can be expanded and improved.

Introduction

The online writing labs and centers of universities and colleges (commonly called "OWLs") once garnered an incredible amount of praise for their potential to be "places" where writers, especially student writers, could interact with tutors, freely exchanging ideas and texts. Although time has moderated initial optimism surrounding OWLs to some degree, it is clear that OWLs have emerged as an important means of delivering writing assistance to students both physically near and distant (as well as to university faculty and staff and, sometimes, community members).

This chapter offers an analysis of the "state of the art" of OWLs. First, I report the results of a study of 343 OWLs. In this study, I investigated the extent to which OWLs have emerged into what Crump (2000, p. 225) calls "true OWLs"—interactive OWLs where tutors provide individualized help to students on their papers via computer-mediated communication like email and MOOs. I also explore what the literature and research on online tutoring suggest about its disadvantages and advantages when compared with face-to-face tutoring. I explore these issues in terms of tutoring professional (such as business, technical, and science) writing online. I also discuss some of the resources and services related to professional writing that are available through OWLs, and I discuss how these offerings might be expanded and improved.

Background on OWLs

Since the early days of OWL development, those who work in and research OWL environments have claimed that the benefits of OWLs are evident at both theoretical and practical levels. Monroe (1998), for example, claims that tutoring via email is more dynamic than face-to-face (F2F) tutoring and challenges "ideologies of print and academic literacy" (Monroe, 1998, p. 23). Coogan (1995) claims that email tutoring "invigorates the tutoring process" by "channeling the social energy of reading a person into the reading of a text" (p. 179).

The more practical benefits of OWLs, according to OWL administrators, include increased opportunities for distance learning (e.g., Beebe & Boneville, 2000, p. 46) and for outreach (Brown, 2000, p. 27). An example of successful collaboration via an OWL is that between graduate student tutors at the University of Arkansas at Little Rock and community college students at Roane State Community College in Tennessee (described in Jordan-Henley & Maid, 1995). This project is often cited as an example of how online tutoring can broaden the "spatial and temporal dynamics" of a writing center (Leander, 2000, p. 667).

Early optimism about the potential for OWLs to create new opportunities for learning has since been mitigated somewhat. For example, Russell (1999) presents a rather pessimistic view of OWLs, saying that they embody a move "toward less and less contact with those whom they serve" and a greater emphasis on "numbers served and money generated" (p. 71). Even those not so pessimistic question the consequences of online interactions about writing, asking, as Shadle (2000) does, "Are we an increasingly collaborative society via the World Wide Web or a nation of lonely electronic individuals?" (p. 14).

Besides theoretical questions like Shadle's, researchers have also wondered about the extent to which OWLs are actually interactive, noting that many seem to be "clearinghouses" of handouts about the writing process and grammar rather than sites for interactions between individual tutors and writers (Colpo, Fullmer, & Lucas, 2000, p. 77). Hobson (1998), in his introduction to *Wiring the Writing Center,* for example, observes that "many OWLs consist primarily of the contents of old filing cabinets and handbooks—worksheets, drill activities, guides to form—pulled out of the mothballs, dusted off, and digitized" (p. xvii). Such OWLs provide writing tips and style guides online but do not offer interactive, online tutoring. Leander (2000) notes that the materials OWLs provide often focus on academic writing and less experienced writers, as opposed to the professional writing that upper-division students, as well as faculty and staff, practice: "Across the vast array of online writing centers, one generally finds that they are primarily engaged with the relatively narrow line of generic practices associated with academic literacies: argumentation and re-search, a regular but small stream of personal essays, resumes, cover letters, and the like..." (Leander, 2000, p. 665). This study examines the extent to which Leander's observation, made in 2000, still holds true.

A Quantitative Analysis of OWLs

Methodology of the OWL Study

I attempted to analyze the total of 361 OWLs listed on the websites of the International Writing Centers Association (http://writingcenters.org, formerly http://iwca.syr.edu/IWCA/IWCAOWLS.html) and of the Purdue University OWL (http://owl.english.purdue. edu/internet/owls/writing-labs.html). Of the 361 hypertext links to these OWLs, 88 were broken (mainly on the IWCA website), leading to "404" or "page not found" error messages. However, with varying amounts of searching through universities' websites, I was able to access 70 of these 88 OWLs.

The search process through these 88 OWLs demonstrated to me how important it is for writing center administrators to argue strenuously for a link on (at least) a second-tier Web page on their college or university website. I found that links to some OWLs are buried at the fourth-tier level, substantially decreasing those OWLs' accessibility and prominence.

All totaled, I analyzed 343 OWLs. My quantitative analysis, at least at the beginning of my analysis, was grounded in Lasarenko's (1996) classification of OWLs. In 1996, she observed that OWLs tended to fall into three categories:

1.   OWLs that simply advertise an on-site (i.e., traditional) writing center.

2.   OWLs that advertise an on-site writing center and that provide writing tips, style guides, and links to other resources online.

3.   OWLs that are either asynchronously or synchronously interactive, offering individualized feedback via (for example) email or MOOs, that advertise an on-site writing center, and that provide tips, style guides, and links to other resources.

My analysis soon made clear that Lasarenko's first two categories should now be counted together, unlike in 1996, and categorized as **non-interactive**. Very few of the OWLs fell into Lasarenko's first category; that is to say, few simply advertised an on-site writing center, listing that center's hours and services. Most OWLs offered at least some grammar guidelines and some links to other resources, such as documentation style resources (particularly for MLA and APA style), as well as links to other OWLs. None of these OWLs, however, allowed for individualized feedback from tutors to writers.

Within the realm of **interactive** OWLs, my categorization again diverged from Lasarenko's. My analysis made clear a category of OWLs that Lasarenko did not identify: OWLs that offer a grammar "hotline" via email. These OWLs, in addition to listing an on-site center's hours and services and offering writing guidelines and links, are interactive in that they allow users to email questions that can be answered quickly. However, they do not accept submissions of students' papers. Therefore, I call them **narrowly interactive**. I separated these OWLs from other interactive OWLs, since their narrowly interactive service was qualitatively different in that it was far more limited than the service offered by OWLs that offered individualized feedback on users' writing submissions.

I counted what I call **fully interactive** OWLs as well, OWLs that provided feedback on individual submissions of writing, usually entire papers. These OWLs, which Crump (2000, p. 225) calls "true OWLs," used either **asynchronous** (e.g., email) or **synchronous** (e.g., MOOs) communication. Besides accepting submissions of writing, these OWLs also advertised an on-site center,

Figure 1. Types of OWLs

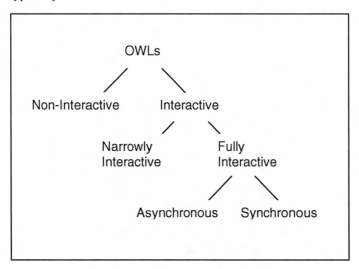

provided writing guidelines and links to other resources, and answered quick questions about writing. Figure 1 diagrams my categorization of the OWL types found in this study.

Results of the OWL Study

Table 1 shows the frequency and percentages of the 343 OWLs across the categories described above and diagrammed in Figure 1. It is important to note that these classifications are not mutually exclusive; OWLs that offered fully interactive (asynchronous and synchronous) tutoring also offered non-interactive and narrowly interactive services as well.

Quantitative analysis of the 343 OWLs shows that 223 OWLs (65%) are non-interactive. That is to say, they fall into Lasarenko's (1996) first two categories: they advertise their college or university's on-site writing center, and they also link to resources about writing. Closer analysis of these 223 websites reveals that little has changed since Leander's 2000 assessment that "the proliferation of online writing centers should not be necessarily taken as an indication of a vast degree of diversity among them" (Leander, 2000, p. 663). Mainly, these 223 OWLs provide the hours and location of the physical writing center on campus, some information about the types of services the writing center offers, and perhaps some information about individual tutors or the history of that university's writing center (characteristics of Lasarenko's first category).

Table 1. Frequencies and percentages of OWL types

Types of OWLs	Descriptions of OWL	Frequency	Percent
Non-interactive	• Advertises an on-site writing center • Provides writing tips, style guides, and links to other resources	223	65
Interactive: Narrowly interactive	• Advertises an on-site writing center • Provides writing tips, style guides, and links to other resources • Provides an email "hotline," answering questions about grammar, documentation, and punctuation	19	6
Interactive: Fully Interactive-Asynchronous	• Advertises an on-site writing center • Provides writing tips, style guides, and links to other resources • Provides individualized feedback on papers, often via email	79	23
Interactive: Fully Interactive-Synchronous	• Advertises an on-site writing center • Provides writing tips, style guides, and links to other resources • Provides individualized feedback on papers, often via a MOO	22	6
Total		343	100

In addition, most of these 223 OWLs provide links to other resources, such as the handouts of other OWLs. As Leander (2000) notes, "As a high value is often placed on writing centers with the largest number of student handouts…, these centers and their handouts become constructed as more central centers to other more peripheral centers that develop in (linked) relation to them" (p. 664). A few of the "more central centers" include the OWLs of Purdue University, the University of Illinois at Urbana-Champaign, and Brigham Young University. These OWLs provide writers a myriad of handouts on topics ranging from writing cover letters to literary analysis. These and other "more central centers" also provide interactive tutorials, as well as audio and video files that can be downloaded. Table 2 lists some of these popular OWLs.

OWLs like that of Purdue University provide so much information that, it seems, they put into question the worth of constructing a new OWL. About implementing an OWL, Colpo, Fullmer, and Lucas write that they were "unsure what information to provide, considering that so many other OWLs had developed such rich resources. We were reluctant to reinvent the wheel" (2000, p. 77).

Table 2. Popular OWLs

University	URL	Examples of OWL Content
Brigham Young University	http://english.byu.edu/writingcenter	writing process, research, literary theory, punctuation
Purdue University	http://owl.english.purdue.edu	handouts and information writing process, research, documentation, report writing, ESL writing
University of Illinois-Urbana Champaign	http://www.english.uiuc.edu/cws/wworkshop/index.htm	ESL resources, tips for writing essay exams, personal statements, and proposals
University of Madison	http://www.wisc.edu/writing	handouts on writing process, common genres, grammar and style, documentation
University of Missouri	http://www.missouri.edu/~writery	handouts on writing process, research, documentation, creative writing

As noted above, some interactive OWLs were narrowly interactive rather than fully interactive in that they provided an email "hotline." The 19 OWLs (6%) that provided email hotlines promised to answer questions about such topics as "grammar, mechanics (punctuation, quotations marks, capitalization, etc.), style, word choice, documentation" (Dickinson College Writing Center), but did not accept submissions of student papers.

Of the 343 OWLs surveyed in this study, 101 (29%) were fully interactive, offering individualized feedback on writers' papers. More specifically, 79 (23%) offered asynchronous tutoring, allowing writers to send their papers to the writing center via email or through the website itself. Despite the growing number of articles that have discussed the implications of tutoring via MUDs and MOOs (e.g., Crump, 1998; English, 2000), just 22 (6%) of the OWLs offered synchronous tutoring. This finding calls into question English's (2000) claim that "in the past six years, many writing centers have found MOOs to be viable and valuable environments for writing conferences" (p. 171). The veracity of English's claim clearly depends upon how the determiner "many" is defined.

Finally, it should also be pointed out that most of the OWLs that offered either asynchronous or synchronous tutoring offered these services only to their respective university's students, faculty, and staff, explaining that they must exclude others because their staff could not possibly meet the demand. This finding reinforces what Shadle (2000) found in his survey of 67 writing centers: most OWLs, 88% in Shadle's survey, target students as their audience. Shadle also found that 75% see faculty as a target audience and 50% see staff and distance learners as target audiences (p. 5). These findings suggest that professional writers who are interested in using OWLs as another means of getting feedback on their writing may have difficulty finding an OWL that will accommodate them. Few OWLs offer their services to people outside their university community.

Slow Movement Toward Fully Interactive OWLs

The results reported above show that most OWLs are non-interactive, suggesting that little has changed since Crump (2000) surveyed the OWLs listed on the NWCA (now IWCA) site in 1998. At that time, he found that most writing centers had "not yet opted to apply serious resources to creating online learning environments" (Crump, 2000, p. 225). However, it is important to keep in mind, as Hobson (1998) and Selfe (1989) note, that the services OWLs offer should be dictated by their missions and who they have been designed to serve. That is, the impetus behind an OWL should not be, for example, some unwarranted quest to keep pace with other writing centers or use up fleeting technology dollars. It is also important to keep in mind that writing centers are limited by the resources available to them (Hobson, 1998, p. xv).

These findings suggest that despite the growing number of articles and book chapters devoted to the theoretical and practical implications of asynchronous and synchronous tutoring and their differences from F2F tutoring, discussions of fully interactive OWLs remain academic and abstract for most writing center administrators. As Crump (2000) writes: "For the most part we are not on the open road yet, I am afraid, and our wheels, in fact, are mostly spinning" (p. 224). Crump is especially disappointed by the slow emergence of fully interactive tutoring because he sees the potential for OWLs to lead the way toward a new and exciting learning environment: the "interversity" (p. 230). Crump writes that OWLs could create a space where a university's stability converges with the Internet's potential for community and "productive chaos" (p. 230). This study suggests that most OWLs have yet to play a role in Crump's dream of the interversity.

The Problems and Potential of Fully Interactive OWLs

One question that arises from the results of this study of OWLs is this: What might be gained if more OWLs offered fully interactive tutoring, either asynchronously or synchronously? That is, what are the advantages of fully interactive tutoring done online, especially when compared to F2F tutoring? Also, what are the disadvantages? These questions need to be explored before we make the claim that more OWLs should offer fully interactive tutoring. This section explores what the literature and research on OWLs have said about the disadvantages and advantages of online tutoring.

The Lack of Nonverbal Cues

Although writing center administrators and researchers were quick to see the potential benefits of both asynchronous and synchronous online tutoring, many worried about whether such tutoring could be as effective as F2F tutoring. Writing in a 1994 issue of the *Writing Lab Newsletter,* Spooner, for example, voiced a concern others after him would echo, namely that online tutoring, lacking the nonverbal cues so important to F2F tutoring interactions, is much more "impersonal," and therefore, unlikely to be as effective as F2F tutoring. Spooner worried that online interactions "simply cannot accommodate the nuance of eye-contact, gesture, or thoughtful silence that are so deeply a part of the discourse in a face-to-face writing conference" (p. 7).

It is difficult to argue that nonverbal communication is not central to tutoring. Coogan (2001), ordinarily enthusiastic about asynchronous and synchronous tutoring, acknowledges that tutoring done online lacks the "silences, tone of voice, body language, and so on"—that are "half the job [of] reading the person" (p. 558).

Recent research has confirmed Spooner's concern. Enders (2000), describing his writing center's use of Microsoft's NetMeeting for synchronous tutoring, observed that tutors' need for nonverbal communication when tutoring was so strong that they actually performed the nonverbal communication they intended, even though the tutee could not see it: "As Tory and the other consultants responded to clients' questions and demands, they would often sit and think, sometimes out loud using hand gestures and facial expressions, before typing their responses" (p. 15).

In addition, recent research suggests that nonverbal communication may play a large role in how non-native speakers construct meaning during consultations about writing. Liu and Sadler, in their study of computer-mediated peer review, state that a lack of nonverbal cues is especially detrimental for ESL students: "Given that the ESL students come from diverse cultural backgrounds, taking the nonverbal communication away from communication can create potential problems for meaning negotiation" (Liu & Sadler, 2003, p. 221). They write that students needed to perform more conversation maintenance in MOO communication than in F2F communication in order to compensate for the loss of nonverbal communication.

On a brighter note, though, it seems as though students no longer are as likely to view computer-mediated communication (CMC) as "impersonal," as their familiarity with it has grown. They frequently than ever communicate with family and friends through the Internet and email (Liu & Sadler, 2003, p. 218). In fact, Liu and Sadler report that students "considered their experience using the MOO to be 'fun'" (p. 218). Moreover, research on CMC suggests that people work to overcome the limitations of CMC in order to build acquaintanceships: "CMC interactants work to overcome limitations of the channel as they get to know one another" (Tidwell & Walther, 2002, p. 342).

It may be, then, as Kastman Breuch and Racine (2000) argue, that it is helpful to "focus on what virtual environments have to offer rather than on what they lack when compared to face-to-face centers" (p. 247). For example, because asynchronous and synchronous tutoring consist of written communication (at least for now), they can prompt careful word choice by students and, consequently, increase their meta-analysis of their writing. Increased meta-analysis seems especially likely in the case of asynchronous tutoring, where fewer conversational "turns" could drive participants to pick their words carefully. Shewmake and Lambert (2000) confirm this advantage: "Instead of the communication being verbal and nonverbal, ideas and comments are presented in written form, thus enhancing the students' writing and critical thinking skills" (p. 168).

There may be other advantages to OWLs' lack of nonverbal communication. Carlson and Apperson-Williams (2000) claim that because tutoring done online increases the likelihood that writers will feel distanced from tutors, writers may be more likely to raise questions that they wouldn't raise in F2F communication. The ability to communicate more freely, according to Carlson and Apperson-Williams, stems from online communication's ability to flatten "[s]ome aspects of the power dynamic between tutors and students" (p. 135).

Indeed, as Nipper (1989) notes and Kaye (1989) underscores, CMC shifts control, making the teacher or tutor into a "facilitator of learning" rather than one who "tries to be the sole arbiter of learning and dispenser of knowledge" (Kaye 1989, p. 16). Similarly, Kastman Breuch and Racine (2000) note that tutoring done via an OWL highlights the tutor's role as a peer reviewer. They argue that peer review is important because it models what occurs in professions: "In the spirit of Bruffee's declaration that students attempt to join the conversation of their peers, we can also advocate that students practice the forms of online conversation that we ourselves practice regularly" (p. 257). Thus, it may be that students studying professional writing may benefit even more than other students of writing from their online interactions; they not only obtain feedback on their writing, but they also get to practice the sorts of collaborative interactions about writing that they are likely to encounter later in their careers.

Sustained Dialogue and "One-Round" Consultations

One of the most troubling disadvantages to tutoring done via OWLs has been observed in asynchronous tutoring: "one-round" consultations. These are tutoring interactions that consist of a writer's submission of his/her paper and a tutor's emailed comments in response, i.e., they are consultations that lack sustained dialogue. As Coogan (1994) notes, tutoring via email "lavishes a lot of time on a student's text," but it does not "guarantee" that anything [like a follow-up response or a question from the student] will happen" (p. 558).

Whether "one-round" email tutorials are the norm is not at all clear, as little empirical research has investigated the matter. One study, Castner's (2000) analysis of 554 email consultations at Texas Tech University, found that only 12 of the 554 consultations (2%) resulted in a sustained dialogue, i.e., a consultation that amounted to more than the student submitting the paper and the tutor reading and returning comments about it. Castner investigated whether students did in fact have questions about the tutor responses they received. She found that 16 of 29 students *did* have questions, a finding that suggests these students would have benefited from extended dialogue (p. 121). She also investigated why students who had questions about the tutor responses did not pose those questions to the tutors. Time constraints were the main problem; 41% of students said they did not ask follow-up questions because they had to turn their writing in and couldn't wait another 24-48 hours for a response (p. 123). The results of Castner's study are troubling, given that dialogue and collaboration are guiding principles of the writing center and that engaging in "one-round" tutorials "promotes the wrong idea about the goal of the writing process itself" (p. 120).

However, anecdotal evidence, at least, suggests that students are more likely to ask follow-up questions, moving the interaction beyond one-round, as they and tutors become familiar with CMC. Jackson (2000), for example, writes that "as our [Purdue University OWL] online tutorials became more organized…'one-round' tutorials decreased dramatically, while 'multi-round' dialogues have increased" (p. 6). While Jackson doesn't provide any specific evidence to support his claim, his advice to tutors to take the initiative, inviting a dialogue with writers, makes sense. In addition, Jackson's claim is corroborated by Kastman Breuch and Racine's (2000) experience with the University of Minnesota's Online Writing Center (OWC). They write that "students can (and in our experience, have) emailed tutors for further clarification" (p. 248).

Kastman Breuch and Racine's (2000) discussion of sustained dialogues via email is especially heartening in terms of tutoring professional writing, given that the University of Minnesota's OWC is specifically geared toward professional, science, and technical writing. Kastman Breuch and Racine's experience is just one example. However, their OWC may indicate that students seeking help with professional writing, perhaps because they tend to be more experienced writers, may be more inclined to engage in extended dialogues. Consequently, such writers may be more likely to improve their writing skills as well as an individual piece of writing.

Yet another characteristic of asynchronous tutoring that is sometimes identified as a disadvantage is the potential for a "slow" turn-around time between the submission of a writer's paper and the tutor's response. My analysis of the 79 OWLs that offered asynchronous tutoring suggests that OWLs, in general, require 24-72 hours to respond with comments. It should be pointed out that OWLS offering synchronous tutoring may also require writers to wait for a response. Some of these OWLs require writers to submit their papers in advance, so that tutors can be prepared for the online discussions.

Waiting for tutor comments, however, may not be as disadvantageous as it first seems. Coogan (1999), for example, questions the extent to which writing centers should buy into the idea of a short turn-around time. Responding to pressure to be quick in responding may indulge student writers' view of writing as "emergency" (1999, p. 55), a view writing center philosophies certainly contradict. In addition, Kastman Breuch and Racine (2000) note that there are advantages to responses that are not immediate; time delays, they write, "may actually facilitate [the] writing process as we know it to be: recursive and ongoing, allowing for time between drafts" (p. 248). Finally, research on CMC suggests that time limits and pressure generate more confrontation and less social orientation (Reid, Ball, Morley, & Evans, 1997; Reid, Malinek, Stott, & Evans, 1996; Walther, Anderson, & Park, 1994). Thus, a response lag may actually benefit student writers, even though they—especially the busy upper-division students doing professional writing—would probably rather have their papers read and returned to them within an hour.

The Retrievability of Tutors' Comments

In asynchronous tutoring, tutors' comments are written and permanently available to writers. In synchronous tutoring, students have access to transcripts of their consultations, in addition to any comments tutors attach to the writing. New ethical considerations arise from the retrievability of OWL tutoring's written communication. According to Baker: "The generation of text or writing raises an essentially ethical question as to how much the tutor can respond without feeling that she is writing the student's paper for her" (Baker, 1994, p. 6). Although Pemberton and Harris (1995) note that transcripts help ensure that student writers will not forget what was discussed in the tutorial, they acknowledge that transcripts make it possible for students to "appropriate tutor's words as their own" (1995, p. 154). Spooner (1994) seems more certain that plagiarism will, indeed, occur, claiming that transcripts and written comments "will tempt the student to insert helpful language from the tutor into the text uncritically—or worse, intentionally" (p. 7).

Most researchers, however, seem to believe that the benefits of retrievability outweigh the risk that a student writer may appropriate a tutor's words. Kaye (1989), for instance, writes that "[t]he psychological significance of such retrievability should not be underestimated: gone is the pressure many students feel at face-to-face seminars to note down every word the tutor says; it is all there..." (p. 12; see also Crump, 1998, pp. 182-183; Shewmake & Lambert, 2000, p. 165).

Mabrito (1992, 2001) points out other benefits. He says that retrievability allows students to view the writing process more closely and, thus, demystifies it (1992, p. 29). He writes that "[b]y reviewing transcripts...writers can see the evolution of their texts," underscoring the idea of writing-as-process (2001, p. 147). According to English (2000), transcripts facilitate metacognition, helping students "describe how and what they have learned about their writing processes and allows them to generalize and apply the process to future writing situations" (English, 2000, p. 172). Finally, as Kastman Breuch and Racine (2000) note, more detailed and thorough feedback from tutors is possible and worthwhile because the comments have permanence. In terms of helping students with professional writing, tutors may, for example, have time to help not only with how the writing communicates verbally, but also how it communicates visually through graphics and layout.

In sum, researchers have pointed out several potential disadvantages to fully interactive tutoring that is carried out online, but these disadvantages seem to be outweighed by the benefits of increased meta-analysis of writing and the benefits of retrievability of comments and interaction transcripts. The written nature of students' interactions with tutors may be especially beneficial for students of professional writing who can practice collaborative interactions like those that they will engage in when on the job, engage in sustained dialogue about their writing, and also practice meta-analysis that will help them consider more carefully the audience of their writing.

OWLs and Professional Writing

OWL administrators who responded to Shadle's (2000) survey of OWLs said that they planned to revise their OWLs to meet the needs of multiple audiences, including adding other materials, such as resources for professional writing (p. 12). My qualitative analysis examined the extent to which the OWLs reflected this planned change. That is, I analyzed OWLs to gauge the extent to which they offered resources and tutoring services that were specifically geared toward professional writing, such as business, technical, and science writing. Like Leander (2000, p. 665), I found that OWLs remain largely concerned with academic writing, like essay writing. In other words, this study suggests that the resources about professional writing are not as extensive as might be expected, given what OWL administrators reported to Shadle and given the growing number of OWLs.

Still, some OWLs provide professional writing resources, especially resources for business writing, such as letters of complaint and proposals. A few others focus on technical or science writing, describing genres like instructions and lab reports. Table 3 lists some of the best OWLs in regard to professional writing resources.

Table 3. OWLs with professional writing resources

University	URL	Contents
Colorado State University	http://writing.colostate.edu/ references/index.cfm	descriptions of policy statements, review papers, technical reports, lab reports and examples of student writing with instructor comments
Iowa State University	http://www.engl.iastate.edu/ OWL	descriptions of user manuals, lab reports, catalogs, Web design, proposals, a few examples, articles about the process of creating different documents
Purdue University	http://owl.english.purdue.edu	descriptions and examples of business letters, memos, cover letters, abstracts
Rensselaer Polytechnic University	http://www.rpi.edu/web/writingcenter/ wc_web/school/index.htm	descriptions of lab reports, proposals
University of Minnesota	http://www.owc.umn.edu	online tutoring in professional writing
University of Toronto	http://www.ecf.utoronto.ca/~writing	descriptions and analysis of reports, interactive tutorials, resources on oral communication
Texas A&M University	http://uwc.tamu.edu/handouts/tech	descriptions of memos, business letters, abstracts and a few examples

However, even the best OWLs for professional writing, such as Colorado State University's OWL, could be improved with the addition of more writing samples. "Writing Guidelines for Engineering and Science Students," a website developed by the engineering departments of Virginia Tech, Georgia Tech, the University of Illinois at Urbana-Champaign, and the University of Texas (and, apparently, not affiliated with their writing centers), provides examples of students' writing, as well as examples of workplace documents (see Table 4). An OWL that offered both kinds of examples would help writers see that they too can be successful and would give them some insight into the genres that are produced daily in their field of study.

OWLs might also expand their resources to include both successful and unsuccessful examples of professional writing. They could also provide meta-analysis of writing examples so that students could better understand why individual samples succeeded or failed. Students could then model their own writing on successful examples and learn to avoid the mistakes pointed out in less successful examples. OWLs might model such examples on David McMurray's online textbook, *Online Technical Writing,* which demonstrates excellent meta-analysis of professional writing by students.

Besides the need for more examples of professional writing and more meta-analysis of those examples, there seems to be little need for more OWLs to reinvent the wheel by adding more of the same materials, like descriptions of business letters, proposals, and lab reports. Instead, OWLs might consider offering specialized tutoring, as the University of Minnesota's OWC has done by specializing in science and technical writing.

Table 4. Other online resources for professional writing

Professional Writing Resource	URL	Contents
Online Technical Writing	http://www.io.com/~hcexres/tcm1603/acchtml/acctoc.html	Examples and meta-analyses of numerous genres, including business letters, proposals, and feasibility reports
"Writing Guidelines for Engineering and Science Students"	http://writing.eng.vt.edu/	Analysis and examples of numerous genres, such as lab reports, proposals, and instructions

Conclusion

This study of 343 OWLs has revealed that 65% of OWLs are non-interactive, i.e., many OWLs do not offer individualized feedback. Rather, they consist of websites that provide information about an on-site writing center, materials like handouts about grammar, and links to other OWLs and other writing resources. Just 6% of OWLs were classified as narrowly interactive. These OWLs offer an email "hotline" for writers in addition to the services provided by the non-interactive OWLs. Finally, only 29% of OWLs are fully interactive, providing individualized feedback on students' papers through asynchronous or synchronous tutoring.

This study also examined what the literature on OWLs has said about the disadvantages and advantages of tutoring conducted online. It seems that the advantages of such tutoring outweigh possible disadvantages, like its inability to convey nonverbal communication and its potential to stifle sustained dialogue. The potential advantages of tutoring via OWLs, such as the ability to facilitate students' meta-analysis and increased opportunities for collaboration, are especially important in relation to students of professional writing, who must pay close attention to audience analysis and who need to practice the writing situations that they are likely to encounter in the workplace.

What remains to be seen, however, is how *effective* asynchronous and synchronous tutoring are, especially in comparison with F2F tutoring. If tutoring done via OWLs is not as effective as F2F tutoring, some OWLs might consider saving a vast amount of effort by simply quitting the business of providing fully interactive tutoring. This option might be especially attractive for OWLs that primarily serve clients with easy access to an on-site writing center. Right now, it is unclear just how many geographically distant writers OWLs are serving. That is, what Hobson noted in 1998 remains true today: We know little about OWL audience demographics (1998, p. xxii).

One study of tutoring attempted to compare the effectiveness of synchronous (technology-enhanced) tutoring with traditional, F2F tutoring. Liu and Sadler (2003) compared ESL peer reviewers' comments in two modes: 1) on paper with F2F meetings to explain those comments; and 2) in Microsoft Word, with synchronous online meetings via a MOO. They found that although the overall number and the percentage of revision-oriented comments were larger for the technology-enhanced group, the percentage of revisions actually made based on revision-oriented comments was much higher for the traditional group. The researchers conclude that "even though the technology-enhanced group did have a larger number of revisions, the comments made do appear to be less effective overall" (p. 218).

While this study, at first glance, seems to add to arguments *against* fully interactive OWLs, it must be noted that this study measured effectiveness by the number of changes students made based on their peers' comments. However, operationalizing the effectiveness of students' comments in this way may be problematic—students who did not act on their peers' comments may actually have been making *good* decisions if the advice they were getting from their peers was faulty. What is needed, then, is research on interactions that involve tutors, who have some writing expertise, working via CMC with writers. The effectiveness of these interactions might be better operationalized with a writing assessment that is checked for inter-rater reliability. Such research will tell us whether pushing for more fully interactive OWLs is worth the effort.

References

Baker, J. (1994). An ethical question about on-line tutoring in the writing lab. *The Writing Lab Newsletter, 18*(5), 6-7.

Beebe, R.L., & Boneville, M.J. (2000). The culture of technology in the writing center: Reinvigorating the theory-practice debate. In J.A. Inman & D.N. Sewell (Eds.), *Taking flight with OWLs: Examining electronic writing center work* (pp. 41-51). Mahwah, NJ: Lawrence Erlbaum Associates.

Brown, L.F. (2000). OWLs in theory and practice: A director's perspective. In J.A. Inman & D.N. Sewell (Eds.), *Taking flight with OWLs: Examining electronic writing center work* (pp. 17-28). Mahwah, NJ: Lawrence Erlbaum Associates.

Carlson, D.A., & Apperson-Williams, E. (2000). The anxieties of distance: Online tutors reflect. In J.A. Inman & D.N. Sewell (Eds.), *Taking flight with OWLs: Examining electronic writing center work* (pp. 129-139). Mahwah, NJ: Lawrence Erlbaum Associates.

Castner, J. (2000). The asynchronous, online writing session: A two-way stab in the dark? In J.A. Inman & D.N. Sewell (Eds.), *Taking flight with OWLs: Examining electronic writing center work* (pp. 119-128). Mahwah, NJ: Lawrence Erlbaum Associates.

Colpo, M., Fullmer, S., & Lucas, B.E. (2000). Emerging (web)sites for writing centers: Practicality, usage, and multiple voices under construction. In J.A. Inman & D.N. Sewell (Eds.), *Taking flight with OWLs: Examining electronic writing center work* (pp. 75-84). Mahwah, NJ: Lawrence Erlbaum Associates.

Coogan, D. (1995). E-mail tutoring, a new way to do new work. *Computers and Composition, 12,* 171-181.

Coogan, D. (1999). *Electronic writing centers: Computing the field of composition.* Greenwich, CT: Ablex.

Coogan, D. (2001). Towards a rhetoric of online tutoring. In R.W. Barnett & J.S. Blumner (Eds.), *The Allyn and Bacon guide to writing center theory* (pp. 555-560). Boston: Allyn and Bacon.

Crump, E. (1998). At home in the MUD: Writing centers learn to wallow. In C. Haynes & J.R. Holmevik (Eds.), *High wired* (pp. 177-191). Ann Arbor, MI: University of Michigan Press.

Crump, E. (2000). How many technoprovocateurs does it take to create interversity? In J.A. Inman & D.N. Sewell (Eds.), *Taking flight with OWLs: Examining electronic writing center work* (pp. 223-233). Mahwah, NJ: Lawrence Erlbaum Associates.

Dickinson College Writing Center. Retrieved July 24, 2003, from: http://www.dickinson.edu/departments/engl/writingcenter.

Enders, D. (2000). Virtual success: Using Microsoft NetMeeting in synchronous, online tutorials. *The Writing Lab Newsletter, 24*(6), 12-16.

English, J.A. (2000). Putting the OO in MOO: Employing environmental interaction. In J.A. Inman & D.N. Sewell (Eds.), *Taking flight with OWLs: Examining electronic writing center work* (pp. 171-179). Mahwah, NJ: Lawrence Erlbaum Associates.

Harris, M., & Pemberton, M. (1995). Online writing labs (OWLS): A taxonomy of options and issues. *Computers and Composition, 12,* 145-159.

Hobson, E.H. (1998). *Wiring the writing center.* Logan, UT: Utah State University Press.

Jackson, J.A. (2000). Interfacing the faceless: Maximizing the advantages of online tutoring. *The Writing Lab Newsletter, 25*(2), 1-6.

Jordan-Henley, J., & Maid, B.M. (1995). Tutoring in cyberspace: Student impact and college/university collaboration. *Computers and Composition, 12,* 211-218.

Kastman Breuch, L.M., & Racine, S. (2000). Developing sound tutor training for online writing centers: Creating productive peer reviewers. *Computers and Composition, 17,* 245-263.

Kaye, A. (1989). Computer-mediated communication and distance education. In R. Mason & A. Kaye (Eds.), *Mindweave: Communication, computers, and distance education* (pp. 3-21). Oxford, England: Pergamon Press.

Lasarenko, J. (1996). Pr(OWL)ing around: An OWL by any other name. *KAIROS 1.1*. Retrieved July 14, 2003, from: http://english.ttu.edu/kairos/1.1/binder2.html?owls/lasarenko/prowl.html.

Leander, K.M. (2000). Laboratories for writing. *Journal of Adolescent and Adult Literacy, 43*(7), 662-668.

Liu, J., & Sadler, R.W. (2003). The effect and affect of peer review in electronic versus traditional modes on L2 writing. *Journal of English for Academic Purposes, 2,* 193-227.

Mabrito, M. (1992). Computer-mediated communication and high-apprehensive writers: Rethinking the collaborative process. *Bulletin of the Association for Business Communication, 55,* 26-30.

Mabrito, M. (2000). E-mail tutoring and apprehensive writers: What research tells us. In J.A. Inman & D.N. Sewell (Eds.), *Taking flight with OWLs: Examining electronic writing center work* (pp. 141-147). Mahwah, NJ: Lawrence Erlbaum Associates.

Monroe, B.(1998). The look and feel of the OWL conference. In E.H. Hobson (Ed.), *Wiring the writing center* (pp. 3-24). Logan, UT: Utah State University Press.

Nipper, S. (1989). Third-generation distance learning and computer conferencing. In R. Mason & A. Kaye (Eds.), *Mindweave: Communication, computers, and distance education* (pp. 63-73). Oxford, England: Pergamon Press.

Reid, F.J.M., Ball, L.J., Morley, A.M., & Evans, J.S.B.T. (1997). Styles of group discussion in computer-mediated decision making. *British Journal of Social Psychology, 36,* 241-262.

Reid, F.J.M., Malinek, V., Stott, C., & Evans, J.S.B.T. (1996). The messaging threshold in computer-mediated communication. *Ergonomics, 39,* 1017-1037.

Russell, S. (1999). Clients who frequent Madam Barnett's Emporium. *The Writing Center Journal, 20,* 61-72.

Selfe, C.L. (1989). Redefining literacy: The multilayered grammars of computers. In G.E. Hawisher & C.L. Selfe (Eds.), *Critical perspectives on computers and composition instruction* (pp. 3-15). New York: Teacher's College Press.

Shadle, M. (2000). The spotted OWL: Online writing labs as sites of diversity, controversy, and identity. In J.A. Inman & D.N. Sewell (Eds.), *Taking flight with OWLs: Examining electronic writing center work* (pp. 3-15). Mahwah, NJ: Lawrence Erlbaum Associates.

Shewmake, J., & Lambert, J. (2000). The real(time) world: Synchronous communications in the online writing center. In J.A. Inman & D.N. Sewell (Eds.), *Taking flight with OWLs: Examining electronic writing center work* (pp. 161-170). Mahwah, NJ: Lawrence Erlbaum Associates.

Spooner, M. (1994). A dialogue on OWLing in the writing lab: Some thoughts about on-line writing labs. *The Writing Lab Newsletter, 18*(6), 6-8.

Tidwell, L.C., & Walther, J.B. (2002). Computer-mediated communication effects on disclosure, impressions, and interpersonal evaluations: Getting to know one another a bit at a time. *Human Communication Research, 28,* 317-348.

Walther, J.B., Anderson, J.F., & Park, D.W. (1994). Relational tone in computer-mediated communication: A meta-analysis of social and anti-social communication. *Communication Research, 21,* 460-487.

Chapter XI

Is This a Real Person?
A Tutor's Response to Navigating Identity in the Spaces of a Synchronous Electronic Writing Center

Amy Lee Locklear
Auburn University – Montgomery, USA and
Kaplan College Online, USA

Abstract

This chapter explores some of the theoretical and pedagogical issues that emerged from a study of identity, collaboration, and discourse methods in synchronous online writing center tutoring. Based on a newly introduced online component of an established university writing center, the premise of this study was to advance tutor training in the context of transferring traditional face-to-face (F2F) methodology to a synchronous terminal-to-terminal environment in a way that effectively preserved the integrity of dialogic collaboration. What emerged became a study of the rhetoric of face and space, in which an understanding of the complexities of online identity perception and projection becomes key to adapting existing F2F tutoring methods to online space in a way that promotes pedagogically sound discourse and learning.

....

Info: Please wait for a site operator to respond.

Info: You are now chatting with "Electronic Consultant."

Electronic Consultant: How may I help you today?

Visitor: Hello.

Electronic Consultant: Hello, welcome to Auburn University's online English Center. How may I assist you?

Visitor: Is this a real person?

....

This conversation is from an actual chat transcript generated by the Auburn University English Center's newest consulting tool—a synchronous online tutoring forum. This supplementary technology was designed to provide students with the same benefits offered by a face-to-face (F2F) tutoring session without the need to visit a physical office space. While the client's question may at first seem humorous, it also encapsulates the legitimacy of many of the concerns and needs of students (as well as tutors) as they navigate the relatively new realm of online space as a location for writing and learning. The student's quest to clarify the *identity* of this Electronic Consultant as "a real person" reflects both a need to establish a two-way conversation as well as a distrust of the medium. For the tutor, this transcript exchange foregrounds the need to establish and promote an online identity in order to effectively perform his or her collaborative duties and be accepted as a dialogic partner. It is also a revealing introduction into the question of how we communicate with others online and the ways in which this space can impact learning as well as teaching and tutoring. How *does* one consciously or unconsciously alter communication skills to traverse the "unreal" nature of this technological space, one which Reynolds (1998) has referred to as "transparent" (p. 14)? How *does* one collaborate online? What is sacrificed as untranslatable? How do we recognize that the faceless communication partner has misunderstood our last typed entry? If we accept Webster's definition of the term "identity" as the "distinguishing character or personality of an individual," how can that be reconciled to a medium in which many (if not all) distinguishing traits are stripped away, leaving only a text-presence? What seems to emerge from so much of the literature concerning online communication spaces and the authenticity of self is the idea of identity as self-definition/ perception in terms not of real-unreal but of absence or presence, overt or disguised. This condition, which some have termed a "facelessness" (Jackson, 2000; Hyde & Mitra, 2000), brings to mind Foucault's 1969 work entitled "What is an Author?" in which a name (an artificial sign-signifier with great associational power) becomes equated with character, persona, a face–in short, an identity. What is a collaborative partner to do if no *face* is provided and often not even a personal name? How does one function within a conversation without these familiar tenets of discourse?

All of these questions and more surfaced within the first month of activating the online consultant software (LivePerson), making it clear that the circumstances surrounding the participants were uniquely suited to investigate the interaction of identity and communication practices given both the purpose of the writing center and the impact an online environment can have upon the discourse partners. While these issues have been extensively explored in recent literature, some gaps still exist within a subject that must be seen in terms of layers of affect and effect. One such area concerns the question of how a theory of identity perception and projection might intersect with the application of synchronous online consulting in tutor training, or what Barbara Monroe (1998) calls "an effective online pedagogy" (p. 3). A large proportion of literature published in the last 20 years emphasizes a focus on the dynamics of the online medium, conversation, and collaboration. However, it seems that at the base of these is another layer that deserves careful and thoughtful scrutiny by tutors, teachers, and those who train them. At the root of the preceding questions is this: Is it enough for tutors to be versed in the "how to's" of technique and technology or should they be asked to look deeper into the very performance and motivation of their online tutoring—to train them to explore the "why's"? The EC presented a perfect opportunity to explore how such reflection can move beyond what Peter Carino (2001) refers to as the "theorizing [of the] Writing Center" (p. 124) into effective real-time application—with all its ups and downs, surprises and blind alleys, and more importantly, new questions and new discoveries. In the course of exploring the "how to's," it became clear that any effective training should ask the tutor to look much deeper than the words on the screen in order to discover how the identity created by those words has the potential to affect the learning process itself.

Given this opportunity to cull data and observations from actual tutoring session transcripts, it became clear that there were factors at work in a synchronous electronic consulting session that involved self-representation/perception concerns (identity) that required closer attention if our EC tutors were to remain effective and true to the vision of the writing center. Such exploration seemed especially conducive to recognizing and applying these "teachable moments" as a step toward training tutors to transfer their F2F skills and theory into an online synchronous communication environment. There are some, like Barber (1998), who insist there can be no crossover between F2F pedagogy and online pedagogy with "consistently positive results" (p. 254). However, it seems that such a transfer *can* take place as long as tutors are guided to examine and understand the impact of the medium on communication practices. Specifically, the implications of identity (trust, reliability, recognition) for communication skills in an online conference need to be explored by tutors (as well as teachers) if they are to successfully engage basic tutoring pedagogical issues such as dialogic or Socratic questioning and text ownership. Such training to be "reflective practitioners" has been promoted by Rickly (1998) as a way of "seeing ourselves clearly on and off the screen" in order to meet the needs of the student client (p. 44)—another reminder of the impact of identity upon tutor performance and function. As Rickly pointed out, if we as tutors reflect on our face, the space, and the mission, we can successfully alter our basic F2F practices to "fit a particular context" or medium (p. 45). The key is understanding how the medium reflects or projects the participants.

It should be noted here that this chapter is by no means intended to present a comprehensive examination of all the factors at play within the subject of technology and pedagogy. Rather, it is intended to examine a small slice of this pie, to offer a sampling of how one venue's introduction of technological tools and spaces raised issues which, while present to some degree in a traditional F2F learning environment, were magnified in both importance and visibility. Rather than revealing any potential shortcomings of an emerging extension to the learning environment, such magnification can serve to "teach the teachers" that the very things that matter in F2F encounters with students also matter in online synchronous conversations. The difference is that the same language, the same strategies used in F2F encounters have the same potential to succeed online. Just as the sound of a message travels one way in an air-based environment and another in an aqueous environment, the same basic principles remain at work. If the sender fails to anticipate and account for potential distortion that exists in the shift between mediums, the results can be counter-productive. However, if we ask the tutor/teacher to heighten his or her sensitivity to the effects this shift in environment can have upon communication dynamics and train them to adjust their techniques accordingly, such boundaries may be minimized. By examining the experiences of actual tutors engaged in this new environment, tutors who are using traditional pedagogical guidelines as a baseline for training, the conversation can move beyond the theoretical into the realm of application—a litmus test of sorts that gives us the opportunity to reflect on the viability of those methods and perceptions which we carry from one venue to the next.

Making a Case: A Brief Literature Review

Much has been written about the pros and cons of using online technology in writing centers (Blythe, 1996; Harris & Pemberton, 2001). While some have successfully established an online presence, many other centers have done so only as warehouses for supplementary material, not for dialogic interchange. Some come close with email exchanges (such as the Writing Center at the University of Minnesota and SUNY-Albany), but the drawbacks of such non-synchronous interchange—the most notable example of which is the delayed response time—has been documented by many (Carino, 2001; Harris & Pemberton, 2001; Hobson, 2001; Selfe & Selfe, 1994) and therefore will not be explored here. In the past, other writing centers have utilized MOO technology, but the daunting complexities of the software and technology required to navigate those spaces by both tutor and client proved to be a hindrance to many (Blythe, 1996; Reynolds, 1998; Selfe, 1999). Because the issue of access equality is one that is foremost in many discussions over the place of technology in the classroom and writing centers, any technological barrier imposed on the user or potential user is reason enough to pause at its implementation. Especially in the Freshman Composition classroom or the writing center, where the focus is on the writing process and not the tools, such roadblocks become one more reason for many to be suspicious of online technology as part of the learning environment.

In spite of such reticence, many in the realm of writing center and Composition pedagogy have optimistically forecast a place for an online presence in the modern university. Voices such as Muriel Harris, James Inman, Stuart Blythe, Donna Sewell, David Healy, and many others have engaged rather than shunned this option, contributing to an enormous (and still growing) body of literature on the subject. Perhaps the most valuable are those voices that approach the technology not as a flawless tool, but as a potential—one still fraught with areas for concern or caution yet still with enough potential to prove useful. As Cynthia Selfe (2001) so aptly expressed in her book *Technology and Literacy in the Twenty-First Century*, a primary responsibility of educators and scholars working with emerging technology is to recognize and act upon the "importance of paying attention" to both the risks *and* the advantages of the application (p. xix). This caution, then, as well as the work of other scholars of writing center theory and practice, provide the context for this examination of online synchronous tutor/student interaction in terms of the impact of identity on consulting, collaboration, and Composition pedagogy.

Background: Input and Output

In the fall of 2001, Auburn University's English Center launched its synchronous online writing lab (OWL), the Electronic Consultant (EC). Following months of research into various software and designs, the Center implemented one based on a real-time chat format in an effort to extend its services to off-site, online clients while retaining as much of an F2F methodology as possible. During the planning stages, the Center's coordinator, Dr. Isabelle Thompson, emphasized the need to make this online space mirror as much as possible the in-Center space in order to maintain a uniformity of theory and application for both consultants and clients. Because of its unique nature and potential contributions to the fields of writing centers, OWLs, and even Composition, Auburn's EC provided a unique, ongoing research opportunity in which to explore the ways the technological, pedagogical, theoretical, and practical aspects of synchronous Web spaces impact spaces of learning. More specifically, the EC at Auburn prompted an examination of the rhetorical possibilities that tutors must consider when all the same rules and guidelines of an F2F session still apply, but there is no "face" to face.

It is important to note here that the EC sessions represent only a small part of the Auburn Writing Center's tutoring. In operation, the great majority of Writing Center sessions take place face-to-face (either by appointment or walk-in). The center is staffed by both undergraduate peer tutors and graduate teaching assistants from the English department, all of whom receive extensive and ongoing training in F2F tutoring practices and theory, with the emphasis on keeping the student client in control of his/her work. Directed questioning, modeling behavior and techniques, and guided discussion were used to steer tutors (and clients) away from a more directive approach (i.e., tutor-centered) in order to reinforce the strategy-centered mission, working the writing process *with*, not *for* the student writer. "The Reference Guide for English Center Consultants" (2002) advised that "consultants [are trained to] focus their tutorial services toward...helping students [learn and apply] effective strategies for composing and comprehension" (p. 3). This pedagogical core remained the standard for online consulting techniques and training as well. With the opening of the EC, students would be given the option to access tutor help without ever setting foot in the door of the Center. Rather than access an email corridor or a drop-off service, as happens in many asynchronous online centers, student clients could now chat online using familiar IM technology to seek help with their writing from those very same tutors who, trained in F2F strategies, would now apply them to the online sessions. Prior to the entrance of our first EC client, in theory it seemed such transference would be merely a matter of duplication. However, when the first online client entered the platform, tutors began to discover that "we weren't in Kansas anymore."

Mirror, Mirror on the Wall—
Projections and Perceptions

Suddenly we were faced with unusual dynamics: dealing with an all-text session, lag times and overlap between typed exchanges, concerns over typographical errors in responses, comfort levels and familiarity with IM software, personal information revelation boundaries, typing thoughts rather than speaking, and of course the most important—no physical face with which to base our interaction. As tutors, we found we had to make certain mental and physical accommodations as we learned to approach the online sessions using the same methods as in our F2F sessions. In one case, one of our more experienced tutors expressed anxiety over the possibility of being perceived as inept (a definite challenge to the dynamics of the collaborative team) should she make typing errors in her responses to the online client—something she would never foreground as a concern during her sessions held face-to-face with a student client.

All of these issues seem to resonate from a question of identity perception or manifestation. Unlike its asynchronous email counterpart, the text-based nature of an ongoing synchronous exchange is more immediate and more interactive, more like conversation. However, the residues of this conversation—*text*—have the potential to be seen as a substitute for the flesh-and-blood face of the tutor, creating a text persona that must be read and interpreted. Because of the nature of this text-based mode of communication in the EC forum, the consultant and student identities essentially exist as both author and character (persona), representing themselves through their *written* word. In terms of an online presence, the *faceless* condition of participants in this space allows each to actively construct an online character at will. The degree to which the student or consultant invests a sense of authenticity into this act of representation may then influence the shape and quality of the interchange during a consulting session. Just as happens in an F2F session, a gregarious student who dominates the discussion with the consultant may result in a session markedly different from one in which the consultant, struggling to elicit responses from a timidly silent or resistant student, dominates the discussion. If a tutor is not critically aware of the nature of this text identity and how it can affect the tutor's reception, the risk is that the tutor will become more of a knowledge bank (from which the student expects to withdraw answers) and not a partner in conversation. In the case of tutors at Auburn, we received many requests for drop-off or email editing service or quick grammar questions ("Is this right?"), demonstrating that many students did not perceive the Electronic Consultant as a collaborative partner, but more like a file cabinet, like some other asynchronous online writing centers. In these cases, those of us conducting training seminars for tutors had to remind them that the same guidelines applied to tutoring online as did in F2F tutoring: Socratic questioning and modeling behaviors led to student ownership.

Wherefore Art Thou? The Impact of Space

This importance of space upon the dynamics of communication, and how communicators perceive their roles and position in the conversation, have also been central issues to the ongoing study of technology and the classroom of interest to both tutors and teachers. Given the close alliance of purpose between writing center tutors and Composition teachers, it is not hard to discern parallel interests as well as concerns with regard to the connection between this issue of online identity perception and effective student/tutor (teacher) interaction. In effect, the *space* where such communication and instruction takes place is *as* important as content and presentation, precisely because space exerts an unarguable and formative pressure on both. In the case of the EC, the sample transcript at the beginning of this chapter offers a fine illustration of this idea. As a default of the software program, when a tutor logs on for a shift, he or she signs on using a generic identification. In the case of this exchange, the tutor's presence is only identified using the non-descript moniker of "Electronic Consultant." It is not difficult to see why the client might question the vitality of this faceless and artificial persona, especially given the all-too-familiar existence of great numbers of automated online help sites that are in reality no more than a bank of preloaded questions and links. In her article in *College Composition and Communication*, Nedra Reynolds (1998) observed that "place does matter" to students as well as educators because our physical "surroundings do have an effect on learning or attitudes towards learning" (p. 20). More specifically, "*where* writing instruction takes place has everything to do with *how*" (p. 20). If students feel the online consultant is nothing more than an automated system, it is not surprising that they expect nothing more than a glorified grammar checker, demanding little to no input on their part.

While Reynolds' 1998 article was directed primarily towards those scholars in the writing classroom, her research also has meaning for the writing center, its tutors, and its clients, specifically as it pertains to *how* tutoring sessions take place. In the case of Auburn's EC, the online space into which students and tutor enter has, as Foucault said, the potential to "render visible those who are outside it" because it is has the ability to "transform individuals...to make it possible to know them, to alter them" (Turkle, 1995, p. 172). While Reynolds' concern is with what she refers to as the "transparent space" (p. 2) between student and teacher—or tutor—Foucault's observations raise the issue of how such online spaces have the ability and potential to reveal, mask, or transform its users. Nowhere did this seem more important than in the Auburn Writing Center, where one of the pivotal operating principles is that of dialogic interaction. Further, the implications of visibility/invisibility upon user identity are crucial to writing center theory on several rhetorical and practical levels, one of which is the ability of both the tutor and the student to focus on the writer's voice as authoritative. In the Auburn Center, these operating principles were the core of every F2F session and set the operational standards for using the EC for consulting sessions. However, while tutors had extensive training in dialogic interaction in an F2F environment, the nuances and complications of an online space demanded that certain theoretical considerations be highlighted in order to better equip the staff to successfully transfer their skills to the online client dialogue. These needs reflect many of the issues already raised by theorists writing of asynchronous communication or technology in the writing classroom (Barber, 2001; Carino, 2001; Hawisher & Selfe, 1991; Reynolds, 1998). The synchronous nature of the EC, however, takes these issues in a slightly different direction, one worth exploring within the operations of the Auburn EC experience.

"From Here to There, From There to Here...." (Dr. Seuss)

The concept of actual and perceived identity and persona in online spaces has become a significant area of concern for many in the fields of Computers and Writing, and Writing Centers—as illustrated by the nature and scope of the research and literature in these areas in just the past decade. Hobson (1998) proposed that there is a need for additional research related to this technology and its impact on the writing center's mission. One question in particular serves as a jumping-off point for this research. Hobson stressed the need for research to investigate "the dynamics of online talk in comparison to (F2F) conversation" (p. xxi). While there has since been additional literature published along this line, my intention for this project was to explore this issue on a subdermal level, if you will—how identity online (our "face") affected the dynamics of collaboration during actual documented EC conferences when compared to the F2F paradigm. Moreover, I wanted to discover what such an investigation might reveal about how we perceive and respond to a textual face when applying those collaborative techniques honed in F2F encounters. In essence, then, this study focuses on a "rhetoric of face" as it pertains to the ways in which an individual's communication strategies and self-representation are altered in online spaces and are subsequently manifested. As writing centers and classrooms move into an age in which the higher education students served are not always based in a physical campus environment, this information may prove valuable in the move to enhance tutor and teacher training as we navigate the issues relevant to the intersection of technology and academia.

Who Am I When I'm Online?

The term *identity* can carry a myriad of denotational implications, which may be based on such elements as gender, culture, or simple name-to-face connections. For the purposes of this study, *identity* in the online synchronous writing center is meant to be understood in terms of those means, whether physical or rhetorical, by which an individual places him or herself in a position of self-representation in order to function dialogically with others. It is also a means by which any interpersonal encounter establishes a basis of rapport—how can I know you, how can I refer to you, who are you in relation to the conversation and the power hierarchy? While this is still a very broad and potentially open definition, it does provide a useful basis upon which to ground this discussion. In her book *Life on the Screen*, Sherry Turkle (1995) asserted that in "the virtual reality [of the Internet], we self-fashion and self-create" (p. 180), meaning that individuals have the power to generate a projectable self-image based not on a communally shared and tangible experience of the Other, but essentially writing into existence as two- or three-dimensional an image as is useful for the creator. In other words, we present our identities and our online presence (*persona*) to an audience that must essentially accept them blindly, few or no questions asked. To be fair, it can be argued that even participants in real-time physical spaces such as classrooms and writing centers have at their disposal a variety of means to fashion and manifest identities, whether by vocal inflections, body language, attire, or facial expressions. However, unlike F2F encounters, identity online can be completely masked, empowering the user to reveal only as much or as little as desired, thanks to the medium's inherent separation from the typical discourse construction represented by Social Constructionist rhetorical theory. Such control over this self-image affects not only what is perceived by others, but also the environmental dynamics in which interaction with this individual takes place as well as *how* communication occurs. An abundance of current theoretical literature explores this issue from the perspective of how it frames or impacts questions of cultural frameworks and issues. However, given the real-time nature of the exchanges examined in this project, it seems important to focus on the element most basic to all of the other cultural issues—that of individual identity within what Cynthia Selfe refers to as the "ecosystem of writing centers" (as cited in Hobson, 1998, p. xiv). In the case of the EC, this ecosystem becomes a space for communication that can powerfully impact the perceived identity of the *Other*, thereby affecting the dynamics and efficacy of the very issue of collaboration on which all writing center pedagogy is based.

In the realm of synchronous online spaces, this communication of identity is confined to a textual presence. For precisely this reason, James Inman and Donna Sewell (2000) have cautioned that "individuals who tutor in online environs...have had to reinvent tutoring practices, rethinking their nature and values" (p. 8). In other words, because so much can be masked or missed, either voluntarily or as a result of the operating dynamics of the space itself, the writing center tutor (as well as the client) must engage in dialogue without the benefit of those physical, conversational cues and signals to which most are accustomed. What many take for granted in the course of "reading" the conversation and participants is dramatically absent in synchronous online space. This very issue emerged repeatedly in the Auburn Writing Center in terms of how to train tutors/ consultants to conduct sessions while retaining the effectiveness of those techniques found to be theoretically and pedagogically sound in F2F sessions (e.g., Socratic questioning). It is this difference in conversational dynamics which is the focus of this study, as well as how such knowledge can prove useful to both tutors and teachers as they learn to apply it in "practice...so that a student's or [tutor's] needs are better met" (Rickly, 2001, p. 45).

While a graduate student and writing center tutor, I was among the first to experience the nuances of the newly introduced online synchronous consulting sessions in Auburn's English Center. When I began to examine transcripts generated during the first months of operation of the EC, some of the more theoretical questions posed in the literature began to resonate and at times transform when put to the test of actual use. Foremost was the concern for how online consulting would transform, positively or negatively, the F2F methodology that forms the basis of most Writing Center operational theory. The very terminology used—"face-to-face"—carries special significance here. During conventional F2F consulting sessions, the tutor and student sit in relatively close physical proximity in a communication space that foregrounds each participant's physical presence and voice. Their dialogic interchange involves a myriad of visual and auditory interactions: eye contact, vocal inflections, hand gestures, body language, and the immediacy of conversational response. These same communication manifestations serve to establish and demonstrate identity and persona within the consultant/student relationship. In an online environment, however, such cues all but disappear, instead foregrounding communication via text and generating a text-based face. In the absence of a human face, the student may then question the reality or identity of the consultant, as demonstrated in the opening chat transcript. If we embrace the post-structuralist view that language constructs reality and that discourse reflects the community (or individual) which creates it, it stands to reason that the text-based environment of the EC relies on language to substitute for physical presence in an F2F interaction. This self-creation through text may be discussed in terms of online identity or, as Hyde and Mitra (2000) put it, a "text face" (p. 163). Rhetoric, according to Hyde and Mitra, "plays a crucial role in the construction of this [cyber]face" (p. 163), illustrating the importance of exploring this aspect of synchronous online consulting. In addition, Jackson's (2000) article "Interfacing the Faceless" provides a thorough and helpful exploration of ways in which the "facelessness" once thought to characterize online tutoring can in fact be given a "face" by adopting identity through the very writing being discussed and performed (p. 3).

This issue of online identity and persona—what Jackson (2000) calls "presence" (p. 4)—is best explored by dividing it into several areas that have proven to be of theoretical and practical concern for all online spaces, and especially the writing center. The questions raised during the course of this project seemed to fall into five areas, forming a general progression and plan of exploration for this project. These areas are: Boundaries and Intersections, Anonymity and Facelessness, Gender and Other Labels, Authority and Identity, and Identity and Communication Strategies. In each section, the theoretical perspectives of the current literature are balanced with an examination of how they played out in actual online EC sessions.

Text Identity and Discourse Analysis

Given the widely accepted modernist assessment that discourse constructs spaces (Reynolds, 1998, p. 13) and the individual self is socially constructed via language (Cooper, 1999, p. 144), it seems apparent that the impact of technology upon identity construction and manifestation via text in online spaces—whether it is the EC or a distance education classroom—are vital areas of study in the technologically savvy Composition classroom of the twenty-first century. The focus of this project, therefore, was on the nuances of self-creation through text in terms of online identity or a "rhetoric of face." In addition, this chapter is predicated on the assertion that only after first analyzing such online interaction in terms of the premises of F2F tutorial pedagogy and communication can tutors then improve services to online clients. While the specific contexts and tools of Auburn's EC may not be representative of all synchronous online spaces, the EC does provide a focal point for an exploration into the ways in which both implied and text-based manifestation of student and tutor identities demand attention in order to better equip tutors to most effectively utilize the potential of online space. In this study, permutations of and influences upon individual identity and persona are examined as a way to contribute to the ever-evolving theoretical groundwork for the purpose of reviewing and adapting existing F2F tutoring strategies and practices to work within this emerging technology.

Boundaries and Intersections—"Wide-Open Spaces?"

....

Electronic Consultant: Hello, welcome to Auburn University's online English Center. How may I assist you?

Visitor: thank you…I am writing my paper for my english 1100 comp class, and I was wondering how exactly do you help people requesting help?

Electronic Consultant: most people ask specific questions about grammar or sentence structure OR they cut and copy a sentence or two and ask questions. If you want more specific help, you can come into the center.

Visitor: I would come there, but my rough draft is due by 5 today, and I was just wondering how you helped online…is there anyway I could just send you or someone there my intro paragraph to see if it makes sense, or is that something I would need to do being at the center?...

Electronic Consultant: you can send me your intro. paragraph or thesis statement and I can tell you if you are on the right track.

Visitor: ok…fabulous…how would i do that?

Electronic Consultant: highlight it, hit copy and then put it on the screen and hit paste

....

This exchange vividly illustrates an acute awareness (on the part of the student) of entering a type of foreign land. Many students who visit a writing center for the first time ask such questions concerning the function of the tutoring experience. However, in this case, an additional complication exists due to the nature of the tutoring space. This complication requires that the tutor not only explain the general process of a tutor/client interchange but also walk the client through the technology itself. "How can you help me?" suddenly becomes combined with the question of "How do I make this work?"

Nedra Reynolds (1998) once observed that "place does matter; surroundings [including online] do have an effect on learning or attitudes towards learning, and material spaces have a political edge. In short, *where* writing instruction [or consulting] takes place has everything to do with *how*" (p. 20). Inman and Sewell's (2000) concern that online tutoring "may reach a different audience" than the one that typically frequents an F2F writing center speaks to the issue of *space* as well as *access* (p. 7). In terms of access, certainly those students most comfortable with the technology necessary to use the EC (i.e., computer and comfort with the IM-styled form of communication) are most likely to use the site. These two themes have a direct impact on our concept of the socially created self (identity) and its application (persona) within the sphere created by technology, in this case the EC space. Reynolds (1998) and Cooper (1999) also engage this issue of space as it affects the construction of discourse and self. Reynolds has observed that spaces effectively change the production of discourse, which in turn communicates information to each participant about the other's identity and role (or persona) in the discussion. A consultant who receives a lengthy excerpt of a student's paper may be tempted to assume an authoritative, answer-providing identity. As a result of the mere preponderance of text provided as commentary, it seems as if the tutor dominates the conversation, essentially turning the session into a "fix-it" encounter and thereby creating a passive conversational role for the student.

If we interpret Reynolds' remarks in terms of the EC rather than an online teaching environment, it becomes clear that the EC *should* be negotiated as material, not "transparent," space in terms of discursive practices and recognition of persona and identity issues. Just as student and tutor responses to certain physical or aural cues during conversation can vary according to the individual's sense of the Other (the audience), the demands of the space have a formative influence upon the textual cues and online personae created during a session. Just as onscreen text in a synchronous environment suggests dialogue, how that text is delivered helps to create a persona for the participant. Text suggests something more formal, more final, while a comment delivered verbally by a Center tutor carries with it the aura of informal, relaxed collaborative conversation. How each is *received* carries great significance for the integrity of the writing center mission. For example, Harris and Pemberton (2001) have pointed out that "onscreen text suggests delivered answers" (p. 538). Because the boundaries placed upon identity in the form of a text-presence occur in the absence of a verbal presence, it can be easy for a student to assume that the tutor's response via text is similar to a teacher's written comments on an essay— a terminal comment rather than an invitation to further discussion. Therefore, tutors must be even more vigilant with their online responses, and trained to remain cognizant of this appearance and authoritative *feel* of text. In addition, tutors should not assume that just because a student has *access* to the site that he or she is *fluent* in the variations of the IM dialect. While an IM forum seems to invite more informal communication style—incomplete sentences, emoticon use, clipped phrasing—the burden remains on the tutor to *model* correct writing behavior at every turn while maintaining the collaborative give and take of a Socratic interchange.

The final sections of this chapter represent other areas that affect and are affected by space. Examining each in turn illustrates a progressive interdependence between them, but at the base of it all remain the ideas of Space and Face.

Anonymity and Facelessness—A Rhetoric of Face

In one of our online consulting sessions, the tutor (a female) had signed on using her own name and was working with a student. After her shift ended, she left the center but forgot to sign off. When the next online session began, the next consultant on shift (a male) began chatting, never realizing that his screen persona was that of a woman until the student referred to him with that screen name. While such covert misidentification did not appear to have any tangible impact on the information exchanged or on the tutor's performance, it had the potential to affect the client's perception of his/her collaborative partner. In subsequent tutor practicum meetings, this episode was recalled with some humor; however, it also served as a potent reminder that in this communication venue or space, identity factors that we take for granted (subtle) seem, in their absence, to become surprisingly foregrounded—rather like a "loud silence."

In the transcript excerpt which introduced this chapter, a student writer asks, "Is this a real person?" The tutor then responds, "If you can call an English teacher a real person," offering the student a clue to her identity and promoting a persona drawing its form from a designation of function rather than name or gender. These sorts of generic identity crises led to many discussions during tutor training sessions over how we should identify ourselves to online clients within the limitations and complications of an online session—factors that included privacy issues for our female tutors as well as more mundane administrative points such as log in overlaps and forgotten screen names or passwords.

In these examples, and in scores of others found in the transcripts collected, the issue of non-identity/anonymity translates as a malleable presence, a sort of facelessness. As a byproduct of the space in which these online consultations take place, this component is an important one to both theory and application. The examples serve as an introduction to the impact of a visible face—as well as the cues it can provide to the direction and nature of discourse—on both the theoretical and practical levels of the online EC. The idea of a rhetoric of face seems to be a useful conceptualizing device with which to frame this study and discussion. Numerous scholars have approached the issue of "face" and anonymity online in terms of *voice*, implying identity and authenticity are to be seen together as a unique vehicle of personal representation. During the course of this study, the question arose as to *why* tutors need a physical face so much in order to have a legitimate, productive, and pedagogically sound tutoring session. In much of the literature exploring the viability of online writing centers, it seems that a face becomes equated with identity, identity with presence, presence with voice, and voice with legitimate discourse.

Hyde and Mitra (2000) investigated the issue of what they call "facework" and how the creation/perception of identity interacts with the factor of target audience in ways that impact their interaction. Just as Foucault asserted that space has the power to transform, Hyde and Mitra posited that an individual's perception of a dialogic counterpart emphasized the importance of the presence or absence of a discernable face during communication. One of the questions they explored in relation to this study of face was, "What misunderstandings, problems, and or contradictions arise in the setting that relate to facework?" (p. 170). These problems, as they put it, arose precisely because individuals who lack a physical visage in this communication space must then find a way to "get…across" their identity, or "how…interactants in a particular setting want to be seen or not want to be seen" (p. 170). With no bodies (or faces) around a table. and no definitive identity markers such as personal and gendered names, this anonymity factor essentially creates an empty space to be negotiated. Reynolds (1998) pointed out that because such spaces (and in turn the interactants) in which discourse takes place are constructed, the absence of physical presence to confirm or deny the reality of what is presented—in this case, identity—can be used to "mask material conditions" (p. 13), which is precisely what happened to our male tutor mentioned earlier. In terms of the EC, that means that the defining parameters of this space can also bury identity (as well as gender, race, ethnicity, or age), a potential which is discussed in the next section.

Because there is no eye contact or body language to supplement the text-persona of each participant, tutor and student must rely on a text language to both create and perceive a "face." This issue of identity online (or lack of same) has been a central point of criticism and caution for many scholars who find that such "facelessness" can not only remove authorial ownership and foreground text, it also detracts from the value of the interaction itself. Barbara Kossman (2001) has asserted that this environment "risks diminishing [the] intimacy" of F2F sessions and "inhibits an interactive partnership" (p. 3) based upon dynamics of conversation which she defined using such terms as "symbiotic" and "physicality" (p. 2). Kossman's definition of collaboration as "a give-and-take relationship between the student and consultant" (p. 3) based upon the dynamics of a face-to-face interaction is at the root of many scholars' concerns regarding OWLs. Kossman and others (e.g., Anson, 1999; Hawisher & Selfe, 1991) have expressed the reservation that the technology involved in online collaboration, rather than the writer/student, has the potential to become the focal point, as participants must learn new skills to navigate a communication environment devoid of accustomed physicalities.

The assumption inherent to this critique of online space is that only in the presence of a physical face can truly effective collaboration take place. The transparent space of an online consultation is then nothing more than an impersonal environment stripped of its primary collaborative property: conversation. Without the face-to-face environment, Kossman (2001) asserted that one of the greatest risks was the feeling of "detachment" (p. 3) or isolation fostered by the characteristics of a terminal-to-terminal interface, a concern shared by many others who have investigated the impact of technology and the classroom (Anson, 1999; Hawisher & Selfe, 1991; Reynolds, 1998; Selfe & Selfe, 1994). It should be noted, however, that the online interchange that is the subject of many of these concerns is one which is *asynchronous* rather than real-time synchronous, the focus of this chapter. Kossman (2001), in fact, was specifically referring to those OWLs that rely on email tutoring and information centers, or "grammar hotlines" (p. 3). In the case of the Auburn EC, the tutoring session takes on more of the immediate exchange common to F2F consulting, allowing the space to operate in a manner that is more of an extension of the Writing Center F2F operations. Numerous transcripts culled for this study display a sense of dialogue whenever the tutor applied the same tutoring principles as used for F2F consulting sessions. Not every tutor was as successful at this "transla-tion" as others, perhaps suggesting that many tutors still perceived their role on the EC as somewhat detached and distanced as a result of what seemed to be a text barrier rather than a text-face. Subsequent tutor training focused on the success stories of those tutors who took extra measures to establish and foreground a conversational "face" with which to interact with clients. Such steps included introducing themselves by name ("Hi, I'm Nancy, the Electronic Consultant.") early in the session, or by engaging in guided questioning, which also included supportive feedback ("I really like your choice of words in that sentence. How can you use that to remind readers of your thesis?"). These are examples of techniques that occur readily in F2F sessions and can be reinforced through training as a means of raising tutor awareness that a blank slate exists unless they take the initiative to paint a text persona to accompany their dialogue with a client.

The issue of collaborative intimacy in the absence of a "real person" is one which is crucial to any discussion of identity as it concerns the online tutoring session. Jackson (2000) explored this concern in terms of what he called a fear of writers becoming lost in the "facelessness" of online interchanges (p. 2). However, his assertion is one echoed by others such as Hyde and Mitra (2000): online tutoring *can* succeed using modified F2F cues and "gestures" (Jackson, 2000, p. 2) in order to locate a face for writer and tutor. Even though working with asynchro-nous (email) tutoring, Jackson's belief is that online is "anything but 'faceless'" (p. 3), that the space itself has forced the writer to "re-externalize" (Bruffee, 2001, p. 211) his thoughts into writing in the process of formulating questions or generating answers to the tutor's questions. That means that online students, by moving *away* from conversation and *toward* writing, must first work the process by analyzing the problem to put their ideas into written conversation. This process-oriented idea seems to address some of the criticism leveled against online tutoring as a mere "fix-it" exchange rather than dialogic collaboration because it demands a student critically analyze his or her own work in order to formulate the question (Jackson, 2000, p. 4). While there have certainly been a fair share of students who accessed the EC for such grammar hotline/fix-it questions, it would seem that even then the tutor and student must both be self-aware and self-analytical during the exchange. When such occasions arose, the online tutor would often refer the student to an online file or else suggest a visit to the Center itself.

A closely related issue to that of anonymity is the influence or affect of associational cues such as gender or ethnicity. These two factors play a greater role in discussions of online access and demographic equitability in the electronic classroom (Reynolds, 1998; Selfe, 1999), and are therefore included here primarily as a means of illustrating the point that identity creation, perception, and manifestation are affected by many forms of input.

Association: Gender and Other Labels— "He Said/She Said"

....

Nathan: Welcome to the Auburn University's Electronic Consultant, how may I help you today?

Visitor: is jane there

Nathan: no

Visitor: need appt w/her...

Nathan: Will you please call the Center to make your appt...?

Visitor: thnx man

....

The above transcript sample contains gender cues that are not present in every session. Typically in the Auburn EC, consultants sign in under the relatively neutral global identification of "Electronic Consultant." However, the option is available to sign in using personal names, thereby providing a more overt personal identification (a face, if you will) to sessions. In addition, the student's response of "thnx man" appears to acknowledge that gender identity. While none of the transcripts generated from over five months of EC operations appear to provide overt racial, ethnic, or age cues, it is very likely that such cues (whether revealed by choice or by textual clues) will appear at some point. Such factors in identity formation-perception are at the core of much discussion in literature focused on the effects of technology and electronic spaces, as well as the issue of access. Within the functional boundaries prescribed by the mission statement of the

Auburn English Center, it may be possible that the negative implications of such value-laden labels and the borders they suggest are minimized or blunted. However, the discussion remains an important context to consider when exploring the impact of the EC on the identities and personae of its participants, as well as another possible area for conscious reflexive consideration by both experienced and novice tutors in training.

Cynthia and Richard Selfe (1994) have written about the "Politics of the Interface" in terms of the "geopolitical borders" in our society that marginalize some while privileging others (p. 481). Their concern was that these cultural boundaries translate into spatial boundaries that determine accessibility in the realm of online technology. In terms of the EC, the concept of "discursive privilege" proposed by Selfe and Selfe takes on particular resonance due to the previously established connection between identity and text. If one's idea of self is "socially constructed in language" (Cooper, 1999, p. 144), then the text-based space of an online environment like the EC is certain to contribute to the manifestation of that self. The concern of Selfe and Selfe (1994)—as well as other writing center theorists—was that consultants viewed "computer inter-faces as non-innocent physical borders" between one computer and another (p. 405). In other words, the very gateway-type format of the EC, with its canned introductory phrases and indeterminate techno-label for all consultants, has the potential to lend an aura of borders that may create what some might refer to as an impersonal and techno-centered environment. As in the EC, in the online classroom the pedagogical emphasis is on decentering the learning space to enhance student participation in the act of learning. Just as the physical classroom might position the teacher as a core information provider, the online tools at the teacher's or tutor's disposal can either engage the student in decentered dialogue or create a dispensary atmosphere. For example, what type of collaborative partner is created when automated phrasing takes the place of dialogic interaction? Out of concern for this, in the case of the Auburn EC, stock responses were limited to such expressions as opening greetings and push-page links (predesigned forms and Web links stockpiled, much as paper handouts are made available to F2F clients). It seems prudent that every tutor be made aware that these tools possess an automated shortcut feel and should therefore always be accompanied by additional personalization.

In terms of ethnic or gender boundaries, the advantage of the online consultant is that those visual and auditory clues that have a tendency to reveal identities such as gender and race are largely absent (unless the writer chooses to provide lexical or overt cues—a choice that provides power over identity). Muriel Harris and Michael Pemberton (2001) proposed this as an almost utopian promise of "meeting onscreen...in a world where gender, ethnicity, and race are not immediately evident except through lexical and social cues" (p. 535).

On the other side of this discussion, Stuart Blythe (1996) has referred to this act of omission as a "masking [of] important non-verbal cues." Blythe discussed the belief by some that "we [should] be foregrounding (rather than masking) issues of gender, race, class" online in order to promote access. From yet another vantage point, Jackson (2000) even went so far as to remark that such lack of gender cues represents a type of "facelessness" that effectively empowers a student or tutor to create an online self that is recognized more for what he/she has to *say*. Moreover, by "decentering" the dialogue from a physical presence to a "faceless" one, the tutor has the ability to remove him or herself from a position of perceived authority to one that is more focused on what the *student writer* has to say (Jackson, 2000, p. 7), an important component of all tutorials whether online or F2F.

This issue of identity is also connected to issues of access in terms of technological literacy, a subject addressed by Selfe and Selfe (1994). This concern leads back to the issue of space and how it contributes to the creation of identity as well as discourse (Reynolds, 1998). The user data currently available for Auburn's EC does not at this time provide any comprehensive delineations for gender, race, etc. beyond what the student and tutor volunteer, suggesting a productive avenue for future research. While Blythe questioned the need for this avenue of concern given the current status of online consulting services as supplemental to, not replacements for, F2F writing centers, the issue is an important consideration for those who will be using and monitoring the EC environment as it evolves, especially because human identity is often patterned after or influenced by such gender or racial formative influences. Based on available transcripts, however, such identity markers do not seem to overtly affect communication online as such, while they certainly may be a component of demographic issues of access and literacy.

Authority and Identity— "Who's In Charge Here Anyway?"

Electronic Consultant: Welcome to Auburn University's Electronic Consultant, how may I help you today?

Visitor: hi can u help me with questions

Electronic Consultant: yes

Visitor: do u teach comp

Electronic Consultant: i am the online consultant

Visitor: i need help with comp

In a writing center, the operative concept is not directive but collaborative. Directive exchanges tend to place the consultant in the position of authority and dominance, usually resulting in a "fix-it" type of approach to the text, rather than one that "fix[es] students, not papers" (Crosland, 1998, p. 6). In the case of the EC, the text *is* the dialogic exchange, centering the focus on the persona of either the consultant as the final authority and voice or the writer as the owner of the text. If, as Cooper (1999) proposed, "power is a possession [which] validates established hierarchies" (p. 145), the risk in any writing center space (whether F2F or online) is that the consultant will be seen as the possessor and authority of rhetorical knowledge, resulting in casting the student's identity in a lesser role. Cooper (1999) cast this authoritarian structure in light of Foucault's idea that people construct power relationships between themselves by "the ways their actions impact others' actions" (p. 146). Essentially, these power roles affect identity and persona (the action) formation within a rhetorical relationship, as illustrated in the transcript example above. In the case of the writing center, this issue of authority and the way it manifests itself in the synchronous online exchanges of the EC must be examined in light of the influence of/perception of the text as dialogic interaction. In the above example, the student is in search of some assurance that she is dealing with someone whose identity is one that is an authoritative representative of the Composition field—a teacher.

Barbara Kossman (2001) emphasized the use of dialogue in F2F sessions to produce a collaborative atmosphere, one in which the tutor resists an authoritative dominance in the equation and instead operates on the premise of creating a "partnership" (p. 3). Kossman asserted that this sort of partnership is not possible in Writing Centers that use online technology, as it "shifts the collaborative focus to a consultant-dominated environment by altering the possibilities of conversation and intimacy" and positioning the consultant into a role of the "container of knowledge pouring into the spaces the student needs filled" (pp. 3-4). It is important to reiterate that Kossman's concerns were with *a*synchronous technologies rather than synchronous interchange based on textual dialogue. The Auburn EC is designed to avoid the very concerns Kossman raised by modeling the F2F strategies used by consultants in the non-virtual space. While EC sessions can still become glorified hotline sessions, tutors trained to create and maintain a dialogic environment can minimize this. Moreover, when it seems the limitations of the space have been reached and can no longer generate useful collaborative discussion, the consultant is encouraged to suggest the student take advantage of an F2F appointment. By doing so, the issue of passive student/authoritarian consultant can be attenuated.

The perception of authority is also at issue in the EC. If the issue is framed again according to a rhetoric of face, it may be helpful to consider the participants in terms of rhetor-audience: "A person's judgment of an audience plays a role in how they address, acknowledge, and persuade others" (Hyde & Mitra, 2000, p.

169). If "[c]omputer communication cuts the physical face out of the communication process" (Hyde & Mitra, 2000, p. 183) and results in what Hawisher and Moran (1993) refer to as losing "the sense of an audience" (p. 631), the result may be a loss of connection with/value for the Other (who is, in a real sense, one's audience in a rhetorical exchange). By so doing, the audience evaluation referred to by Hyde and Mitra (2000) can result in more directive "persuasive" strategies such as editing or directive remarks. In the case of email-based consulting, the isolation of the medium may create such an environment. On the other hand, the synchronous environment of the EC, if pursued as dialogic exchange-based, can create the opportunity to give a face (of sorts) to the audience members—student and tutor.

Identity and Communication Strategies— "Read My Lips"

....

Electronic Consultant: The first line is in Iambic Pentameter, it seems. You have five beats, with a U' beat. The first part is unemphasized, where as the second part is emphasized.

Visitor: is that like Shakespeare? Iambic pentameter?

Electronic Consultant: …Shakespeare has used it before…When read, it sounds like dadum dadum dadum dadum dadum. That's how the accents fall, anyway.

....

Stuart Blythe (1996) has asserted that "[n]ew media [such as the EC] may lead us…towards new, more beneficial ways of interacting with students. By providing new sets of cues (and, perhaps, by masking face-to-face cues), computer media may prompt people to interact in new ways with each other." Most OWLs typically rely on a non-synchronous relationship between consultant and student, providing reference materials and resources on issues germane to the writing process to download or print. Additionally, email consultations are another option at OWLs such as Purdue, in which a student client can email all or a portion of an essay to a consultant tutor for later response. In the case of the Auburn EC, however, this service is taken one step closer to the F2F model by allowing for real-time synchronous exchange. In the example transcript above, the consultant has translated what might occur in an F2F session into text. The immediacy of the interchange mimics what would normally occur verbally over a table in the physical Center, using text to translate a sound and rhythm to illustrate the consultant's point about form. This transcript provides a wonderful illustration of how effectively a consultant can use the synchronous chat technology to provide a collaborative atmosphere in an online space. The consultant has essentially taken a thought, imagined it as conversation, then "re-externalized" it in writing to take the place of conversation, accomplishing what Bruffee (2001) has referred to as "writing...[as] an act of conversational exchange" in discourse (p. 211). Such conscious adaptation of conversational cues for application in a text-based expression illustrates one of the subtle but vital areas of communication in synchronous online spaces which tutors and teachers must learn to tap into if their services are to "translate [in]to a quality of service" (Hobson, 1998, p. xviii) that supplements in a positive way the mission of the physical writing center or classroom.

Barbara Kossman (2001) emphasized the need for the collaborative element to carry over into the online realm in order to maintain a conversational, and therefore "symbiotic," relationship (p. 2). The sense of intimacy that results from the physical and conversational link between tutor and student in F2F sessions is, Kossman has asserted, diminished in those online consulting environments based on OWL models that function merely as "centers for information as opposed to labs of interaction" (p. 3). This model "shifts the collaborative focus to a consultant-dominated environment by altering the possibilities of conversation and intimacy...[because] the nature of the technology inhibits an interactive partnership" (p. 3). It is here where the EC succeeds, providing the type of interactive exchange that Kossman asserted encourages the student to identify him/herself as an active rather than passive participant. However, the immediacy of the exchange, while advantageous, still lacks a visual component; therefore, those communication strategies peculiar to an in-house F2F session must be modified to compensate for the lack of familiar visual clues so typical of the F2F forum.

Such an even transference of technique from one medium to the other is not without its skeptics. In reference to teaching online, John Barber (2000) advised that educators cannot expect those pedagogical theories and applications that are routinely applied in the physical classroom to function in exactly the same form when moved online (p. 254). It is reasonable to conclude that any communication moved to a synchronous online space demands critical adjustments, especially in a teacher/student relationship where, despite all modern pedagogical efforts, there is still a hierarchy of knowledge and communication lines. Gone are the tactile, visual, auditory components of dialogic interchange that provided cues between teacher and student. Gone too is the familiar component of space mediated by physical presence. These conditions exist in the tutor/student relationship online as well. However, the parallel is not precise. With training to become a "reflexive practitioner" (Rickly, 1998, p. 44), it seems that the nature and purpose of the one-to-one working relationship of tutor/ student more easily allows for writing center pedagogy and technique to successfully transfer between media. As long as the tutor is critically aware of how the tools at hand (including identity and persona) function, it seems quite possible to modify them in ways that still conform to the pedagogical directives that frame the act of learning that occurs in any F2F consultation. While it may seem as though the F2F pedagogy must be entirely "reconfigure[ed]" (Monroe, 1998, p. 23) for online use due to the text-based face it presents—essentially creating a completely different species—it should be pointed out that Monroe and many others (e.g., Barber, 2000) have expressed their concerns in the context of *asynchronous* learning exchanges, in which text becomes a rather static representation of the participants. The above transcript sample demonstrates how text can effectively imitate an F2F strategy of modeling a point and minimizing the limitations placed on dialogic interaction so essential to the tutor/ student roles.

In so doing, the persona of a participant is essentially constructed by the text itself. The idea that online conversations effectively create another type of discourse community can be taken one step further. If social context can be created through text, it is also possible that the discourse participants create and actualize an identity through text as well (Hawisher & Selfe, 1991, p. 57). By taking advantage of the text medium to create the necessary language, the consultant can, as Jackson (2000) stated, "appropriate many of the same gestures F2F tutorials employ when engaging writers" (p. 2) in order to fulfill his/ her function as consultant (persona) in a "true conversational interaction...played out onscreen" (Harris & Pemberton, 2001, p. 532). Coogan (2001) has concluded that such presence (as represented by textual dialogue based on the same strategies used in F2F sessions) "is everything. A student wears his paper like clothing...The paper doesn't communicate by itself—the person [identity] communicates. But an electronic text *announces itself* as communication" (p. 556). In so doing, the text becomes the concrete representative of the self as constructed in space, as illustrated in the previous transcript excerpt.

The architectural qualities of this space can also pose risks to the personae of consultant and student as they negotiate their roles through dialogic interchange. Just as it occurs in F2F sessions, the consultant must be aware of the potential for development of an instruction-like hierarchical relationship/interchange (consultant or authority centered) as opposed to a dialogic, writer-centered exchange. Here again, thorough tutor training in both F2F techniques as well as awareness of online dynamics—especially those that concern the impact of identity—is a valuable and necessary asset to successful synchronous online consultations.

Where Do We Go From Here?

Although the bulk of this chapter was concerned with implications for the synchronous online writing center tutor, the impact of such reflexive examination of identity and communication techniques can easily be extended to the realm of the online classroom and its teacher. In my experience as both an online tutor and a teacher in an online Composition classroom, the nuances of conversation in the absence of a "face-to-face" encounter take some getting used to. Perception and representation of identity become foregrounded whenever initial contacts are made. In the case of the classroom, the teacher has the "luxury" to develop her persona over the length of the academic calendar. This persona then becomes an instrumental component of the learning experience, as students and teacher alike learn to recognize and act upon the provided textual cues in dialogue. She also has the time to watch and learn the conversational habits of her students in order to "read" their identities in the process of determining their learning styles and habits as a means to maximizing assignments, interchanges, and feedback to enhance learning. In addition, no matter how decentered the classroom pedagogy, the fact is that the Composition classroom does have a teacher who must assign, respond to, and grade the written work of the students. The assignments offer an additional window through which the teacher may "read" her students and use to discern the level of learning going on.

For the writing center tutor, many of these "luxuries" are not part of the equation. The typical tutor consults with a student client for a limited amount of time, often on a one-time basis. As a result, there is no extended time to "get to know" a student based on the identity provided through the text medium. The tutor must engage the student and his writing only in terms of what the student chooses to provide in terms of both text and text-face. Despite these variations, however, the mission of both the tutor and the teacher are uniform in terms of their dependence on communication tools (whether F2F verbal or online text) to enhance the success of student performance or learning. The task ahead, then, is one from which both tutors and teachers stand to benefit and which must begin with a careful reassessment of the rhetoric of space and face. It seems possible, based on the experience in the EC, that online space need not be a foreign land requiring knowledge of a foreign tongue. Rather, teacher and tutor training should incorporate ways (like those explored here) to emphasize the shared strategic and theoretical bases between F2F and online discourse methods, and as a result recognize the underlying need to be conscious of the most basic components of any act of communication—the face on the other side.

Conclusion

While the question of synchronous online writing center tutoring is still in the early stages of exploration, the practical observations made during the study of Auburn's EC help make clear some important points that will certainly impact future development and use of this technological space. The primary conclusion is one that was never in question at the beginning of this study: Those communication strategies used in F2F sessions between tutor and student should remain a baseline standard for all consulting sessions, especially those online. As many of the transcripts from EC sessions so aptly illustrate, the Socratic method of dialogic questioning need not be limited to F2F verbal exchanges. With awareness, training, and practice, it proves just as critical and effective in synchronous online consultations. To this end, tutors must be made aware that while issues of identity and persona are more subtle (at times even invisible) in online spaces—suggesting *facelessness*—the manifestations and influence of these factors are present nonetheless.

Issues of online persona and identity—set in the context of a rhetoric of face—become especially significant in those environments in which student writers enter into dialogue with online writing tutors. Because of its synchronous nature, the EC is an emerging technology that holds great potential for the mission and scope of writing centers serving today's college students. The impact of this technology on individual identity and persona as perceived in terms of conversational roles is one which this chapter has only begun to explore as a means to enhancing tutor awareness and adaptability. As Eric Hobson (1998) observed, the combination "of computers and communication technology has created a new educational frontier" (p. ix), one which tutors and teachers alike must be prepared to enter with open eyes and minds. As these transcripts demonstrate, entry into this frontier need not require a complete refitting of existing strategies and methods. Rather it does require we "pay attention" (Selfe, 1999) to *how* the *"who"* functions in terms of communication strategies.

The unique communication style of the EC (i.e., part dialogic, part writing) presents great promise as well as rhetorical and ethical hurdles that must be addressed, as the nonverbal yet interactive medium is considered as an emerging option for writing centers in the twenty-first century. When filtered through this idea of identity's impact on collaborative methods, these first months spent working with tutors and clients in this new space revealed ways that tutors *could* apply F2F techniques to a synchronous online experience *only if preceded by careful reflexive examination*. Many scholars rightly point out that neither the online classroom nor the online tutoring session can safely be seen as "an electronic duplication" of its "traditional" counterpart (Barber, 1998, p. 254). The dynamics of online space demand that critical attention be given to how communication may be transformed in a synchronous text-based environment. While the usual identity markers (and their impact) may be absent from a synchronous tutoring session, the purpose and focus remain exactly the same. As long as the tutor is critically aware of how to modify the tools at hand to function in ways that conform to the pedagogical directives of the center, the EC can be a valuable *supplement to* (not replacement for) the traditional F2F sessions so vital to the Auburn Writing Center's function and Auburn's community of writers. As with any new tool, it is imperative that tutors take time to consider the dynamics of space and face in terms of their skills in order to make the EC an efficient and effective addition to the writing center in both theory and application. When tutors are trained to be, in Rickly's (1998) words, "reflexive practitioners" (p. 44), the synchronous online consulting tool can successfully extend the reach and potential of the center's ability to assist students by using available technology accessible from campus and home computers with nothing more than standard Internet capability—and an adequate supply of emoticons.

Acknowledgment

Many thanks to Dr. Isabelle Thompson and Dr. Mary Diamond, administrators of the Auburn University English Center, for their advice and tolerance during the course of my graduate student tenure as a tutor and practicum assistant. Thanks are due as well to the peer and graduate student tutors whose transcripted sessions provided the basis of this research. Finally, a special thanks go to Sarah Bowles, Nathan Meier, and Heather Vaughan for listening to me ramble on about identity, persona, and the EC.

References

Anson, C.M. (1999). Distant voices: Teaching and writing in a culture of technology. *College English, 61*(3), 261-278.

Barber, J. (2000). Effective teaching in the online classroom: Thoughts and recommendations. In S. Harrington, R. Rickly, & M. Day (Eds.), *The online writing classroom* (pp. 243-264). Cresskill, NJ: Hampton Press.

Blythe, S. (1996). Why OWLs? Value, risk, and evolution. *Kairos, 1*(1). Retrieved February 2, 2002, from: http://english.ttu.edu/kairos/1.1/index.html.

Bruffee, K.A. (2001). Peer tutoring and the "conversation of mankind." In R.W. Barnett & J.S. Blumner (Eds.), *The Allyn and Bacon guide to writing center theory and practice* (pp. 206-218). Boston: Allyn and Bacon.

Carino, P. (2001). Computers in the writing center: A cautionary history. In R.W. Barnett & J.S. Blumner (Eds.), *The Allyn and Bacon guide to writing center theory and practice* (pp. 494-520). Boston: Allyn and Bacon.

Coogan, D. (2001). Towards a rhetoric of online tutoring. In R.W. Barnett & J.S. Blumner (Eds.), *The Allyn and Bacon guide to writing center theory and practice* (pp. 555-560). Boston: Allyn and Bacon.

Cooper, M.M. (1999). Postmodern possibilities in electronic conversations. In G. Hawisher & C. Selfe (Eds.), *Passions, pedagogies, and 21st century technologies* (pp. 140-160). Logan, UT: Utah State University Press.

Crosland, A. (1998). Electronic mail and the writing center. *The Writing Lab Newsletter, 22*(8), 5-6.

English Center. (2002). *Reference guide for English Center consultants.* [Training Manual]. Auburn, AL: Auburn University Department of English.

Foucault, M. (1998). What is an author? In D. Richter (Ed.), *The critical tradition: Classic texts and contemporary trends* (2nd ed.) (pp. 890-900). Boston: Bedford Books.

Harris, M., & Pemberton, M. (2001). Online writing labs (OWLs): A taxonomy of options and issues. In R.W. Barnett & J.S. Blumner (Eds.), *The Allyn and Bacon guide to writing center theory and practice* (pp. 521-540). Boston: Allyn and Bacon.

Hawisher, G.E., & Moran, C. (1993). Electronic mail and the writing instructor. *College English 55*(6), 627-640.

Hawisher, G.E., & Selfe, C.L. (1991). The rhetoric of technology and the electronic writing class. *College Composition and Communication, 42*(1), 55-65.

Hobson, E. (Ed.). (1998). *Wiring the writing center.* Logan, UT: Utah State University Press.

Hyde, M.J., & Mitra, A. (2000). On the ethics of constructing a face in cyberspace: Images of a university. In V. Berdayes & J.W. Murphy (Eds.), *Computers, human interaction, and organizations: Critical issues* (pp. 161-185). Westport, CT: Praeger.

Inman, J.A., & Sewell, D.N. (Eds.). (2000). *Taking flight with OWLs: Research into technology use in writing centers.* Mahwah, NJ: Lawrence Erlbaum.

Inman, J.A., & Sewell, D.N. (2002). To build an OWL or not to build an OWL: Issues in conversation. *Southern Discourse, 5*(3), 7-9.

Jackson, J.A. (2000). Interfacing the faceless: Maximizing the advantages of online tutoring. *Writing Lab Newsletter* [Electronic Version], *25*(2). Retrieved February 2, 2002, from: http://owl.english.purdue.edu/lab/owl/tutoring/JacksonOnlineTutoring.html.

Kossman, B. (2001). Computers and the perception of the writing center. *The Writing Lab Newsletter, 25*(5), 1-6.

Leahy, R. (1998). The rhetoric of written response to student drafts. *The Writing Lab Newsletter, 22*(8), 1-4.

Monroe, B. (1998). The look and feel of the OWL conference. In E. Hobson (Ed.), *Wiring the writing center* (pp. 3-25). Logan, UT: Utah State University Press.

Reynolds, N. (1998). Composition's imagined geographies: The politics of space in the frontier, city, and cyberspace. *College Composition and Communication, 50*(1), 12-35.

Rickly, R. (1998). Reflection and responsibility in (cyber) tutor training: Seeing ourselves clearly on and off the screen. In E. Hobson (Ed.), *Wiring the writing center* (pp. 44-61). Logan, UT: Utah State University Press.

Selfe, C. (1999). *Technology and literacy in the twenty-first century: The importance of paying attention.* Carbondale, IL: Southern Illinois University Press.

Selfe, C.L., & Selfe, R.J. (1994). The politics of the interface: Power and its exercise in electronic contact zones. *College Composition and Communication, 45*(4), 480-501.

Stahlnecker, K.H. (1998). Virtually transforming the writing center: Online conversation, collaboration, and connection. *The Writing Lab Newsletter, 23*(2), 1-4.

Turkle, S. (1995). *Life on the screen: Identity in the age of the Internet.* New York: Simon and Schuster.

Section VI

Future Trends in Computer Use for Written Communication

Chapter XII

Telework:
A Guide to Professional Communication Practices

Nancy A. Wiencek
Monmouth University, USA

Abstract

This chapter discusses the emergence of telework or telecommuting and the need to rethink professional communication practices for this remote working arrangement. The chapter conceptualizes variations of telework and discusses distinctions within the telework arrangement in light of its impact on communication. Furthermore, the chapter lays the groundwork for effective employment of telework by discussing the importance of communication during design of the system, as well as the importance of communication while engaged in telework from both task-oriented and personal interactions perspectives. Case scenarios are used to illustrate key considerations and to begin a dialogue between teleworkers and those who manage them.

Introduction

According to a recent report published by the U.S. Census Bureau:

> "Efforts to describe the American economy over the last quarter century have generated terms such as post-industrial, service-oriented, information-based, and more recently, a plethora of e-terminology. These terms capture not only the technological advances, but also economic and social changes that have transformed our way of life—both at work and at home." (Kuenzl & Reschovsky, 2001, p. 1)

One manifestation of these changes has been the emergence of telecommuting or telework. While statistics can significantly vary depending upon how remote work arrangements are conceptualized, Telework America estimated that as many as 28 million Americans worked from home, in satellite offices or telecenters, from the road, or in some combination of these remote locations in 2001 (Davis & Polonko, 2001). Why the boom in alternate work arrangements? The traditional case for teleworking has always been relatively straightforward. For the organization, it has been promoted as a way to increase productivity, attract and retain qualified personnel, reduce absenteeism, reduce facility costs, address larger environmental issues such as air pollution and congestion among our roadways, and be more socially responsive to the needs and preferences of its workforce. For the employee, it has been a way to reduce commuting time, improve flexibility, have better control over work schedules, better meet dependent care needs, and reduce stress. And while these arguments for remote work arrangements remain valid, according to a recent study by AT&T, the real "business drivers" for telework in today's marketplace are "better technology, globalization, and cost pressures" (2003, p. 1).

With standard business practices so rapidly changing, the trend toward increased numbers of employees engaged in telework is expected to rise. While it is important to understand the motivating business forces behind the trend, and equally important to understand the current technologies that enable the arrangement, one must also take into consideration the importance and shifts in workplace communication. To address these concerns, this chapter will: 1) conceptualize the telework arrangement; 2) discuss distinctions within the telework arrangement in light of its impact on communication; and 3) lay the groundwork for an effective telework arrangement by discussing the importance of communication during design of the system, as well as the importance of communication from task-oriented and personal interactions perspectives.

Background–Telework Conceptualized

The globalization of the marketplace and advances in the technological environment have manifested themselves as radical changes in today's workplace. New
technologies have overcome traditional organizational boundaries such as regional and national borders, space and time limitations, and knowledge constraints. As research suggests, not only is the *way* we are working changing, but
where we are working is changing as well. In a recent white paper, AT&T notes,
"The expectation that everyone will be in the same office is fast being eroded by
actual business practices" (2003, p. 4). With advances in technology, global
sourcing arrangements, new training and educational capabilities, disaggregated
alliances, or networks of companies, teleworking has become commonplace.

Defining telework, however, can be somewhat ambiguous. In reviewing the
literature, commonly used terms to represent the phenomenon are home-based
work, flexiplace, off-site work, remote work, telework, and telecommuting.
Duxbury, Higgins, and Neufeld (1998) readily admit that these terms have been
used in the literature to refer to the same concept, but that "these terms should
not be used interchangeably…since they do not refer to the same phenomenon"
(p. 221). For example, the U.S. Census Bureau studies and defines "home-based
workers" as individuals who work exclusively from home, as well as "mixed
workers," those that report "working at home at least one full day in a typical
week" (Kuenzl & Reschovsky, 2001, p. 3). On the other hand, the U.S. General
Services Administration, on its telework/telecommuting website, uses the aforementioned terms interchangeably "to mean official work being conducted away
from an employee's official duty station, and at an alternate worksite, regardless
of whether it is a home office or telework center" (2003, p. 1). The American
Business Collaboration for Quality Dependent Care (ABC), a collaboration of
nine companies partnered to ensure quality employee programs and services,
recently issued a report examining "off-site" workers within which the ABC
delineates five specific types of arrangements:

> "'Regular tele-workers' work from home on a regular basis, an average
> of two days a week; 'ad hoc tele-workers' perform their work from
> home about two days a month; and 'remote workers' function full-time
> from a home location. 'Mobile workers,' as the name suggests, work
> from multiple locations including their car, their home, hotels, customer
> offices, and company offices. 'Customer site workers' are located in a
> customer office from which they do all or most of their work." (Richman,
> Noble, & Johnson, 2002, pp. 1-2)

In its simplest conceptualization, "telecommuting" has been traditionally used to describe work accomplished from an employee's home, whereas "telework" has become the more commonly used catch-all for any work accomplished away from the office. AT&T, for example, reinforces this notion when it defines telecommuting as "working from home one or more days a week during normal business hours" (AT&T, 2000), yet captures the essence of this relationship in its more broadly defined term:

> "Telework is an umbrella term for a wide range of alternative office arrangements including telecommuting, virtual/mobile offices, hoteling, satellite offices, and telework centers...Telework can mean a regular agreement where you work from home on specific days each week, or from a satellite office closer to home instead of commuting to a company location. It can also mean mobilizing your workplace while traveling or locating it temporarily—or permanently—in your customer's offices."
> (AT&T, 2000, *Definitions*)

So which definition works the best? The answer—it depends. It depends upon your organization and how telework is conceptualized and implemented. According to a recent study by the International Telework Association & Council (ITAC), a nonprofit organization dedicated to advancing the growth and success of work independent of location, 21.7% of American teleworkers work exclusively from home, 7.5% of teleworkers work exclusively at telework centers, 4.2% of teleworkers work at satellite offices, and 24.1% of teleworkers work solely on the road. More interesting to note, however, is the fact that 42.4% of American teleworkers use multiple forms of these telework arrangements as part of their regular work routine (ITAC Telework America, 2001). Thus, for the purposes of this discussion, the use of the phrases "telework" and "teleworker" will be broadly conceptualized and all encompassing to reflect a variety of remote work accommodations. As the ITAC explains, teleworkers are individuals "that work at home, at a telework center or satellite office, work on the road, or some combination of these" (Davis & Polonko, 2001, p. 1).

Issues Arising from the Telework Arrangement

While it is clear that there is no one universally accepted definition of telework in the literature or single conceptualization of remote work throughout industry, there are distinctions within the telework arrangement that impact workplace communication practices. McCloskey and Igbaria (1998) suggest that the most commonly discussed attributes of telework include technology, location, employment relationship, and structure. When considering *technology*, one looks at the technical tools necessary to accomplish his or her work from a remote location. From all accounts in today's technological environment, the tools are available. According to the ABC, "Most off-site workers have the staple range of technology: computer, printer, fax, copier, and multiple phone lines" (Richman et al., 2002, p. 3). Yet, with continued emerging connectivity such as broadband ("always-on" connectivity versus dialup online access), organizations such as the ITAC believe that remote work has "come of age." From its recent research report, the ITAC notes:

> "Rapidly evolving technology and telecommunications are enabling remote work. The personal computer began the transformation that makes it possible for individuals to work at any time from any place. The cell phone added mobility. But the Internet has had the most profound impact on transforming work. The Internet connects workers in a global information exchange and marketplace." (Pratt & Associates, 2003, p. 1)

According to AT&T, cost-effective networks and the increasing availability of connections with employees "is fostering more confidence in remote work" (p. 3). Furthermore, the same experts note that "while email and the telephone continue to be the primary communication vehicles, Web-based tools are helping virtual teams to work more efficiently through services such as file sharing, electronic messaging, and Web meetings" (AT&T, 2003, p. 3).

While careful consideration of the technological tools required of the job is critical to the telework arrangement, as is adequate technical support to complement the tools, the technology itself is not a barrier to remote work. Rather, the larger issue for this discussion is the human communication aspect associated with this technology: How does a manager effectively supervise a remote worker; how does the teleworker effectively communicate among team members, colleagues, and supervisors; and how are interpersonal relationships formed and maintained among a remote workforce?

The next attribute of telework that emerges is McCloskey and Igbaria's (1998) consideration of *location*. With a broadly conceptualized definition of telework, it has already been made abundantly clear that location simply means off-site. But from a communication aspect, one must clearly assess the individual teleworking arrangement. What are the expectations in terms of communication? Is an at-home worker expected to respond to instant messaging or does a flexible work schedule make this an unrealistic expectation? Do teleworkers engaged in heavy travel schedules, thus accessing a virtual office during the evening from a hotel room, receive after-hours technical support? Do mobile workers feel a sense of isolation and disconnectedness from the organization while on the road?

In terms of the *employment relationship,* McCloskey and Igbaria (1998) are raising the issue of a teleworker's full- or part-time status, and whether or not he or she is regularly or self-employed. These two points are critical with respect to supervision and overall expectations. In the context of this discussion, however, emphasis is placed on the regularly employed organizational member, with a particular emphasis on full-time status. The implication here is that employees will not only have a stake in the future of the organization, but in one's own advancement as well. Thus the issue arises, how does the teleworker effectively communicate remotely proposed initiatives, accomplishments, and aspirations? And for those that manage teleworkers, how does one go about imparting organizational culture, opportunities within the company, and everyday news about policy and personnel without the benefit of face-to-face communication?

Lastly, McCloskey and Igabaria (1998) look at *structure* and address issues related to chains of command, other team-based forms, workflow arrangements, and ongoing channels of communication. While reinforcing what has already been said, structure is important because work experiences and outcomes vary considerably depending on the telework arrangement. A useful term in this context is "telemanagement," used by Wigand, Picot, and Reichwald (1997) as a collective term to describe the responsibility of overseeing "all media-supported forms of dispersed coordination of tasks" (p. 330). Telemanagers, according to the authors, are charged with developing strategies that involve attention to both task-oriented activities (locomotion functions) as well as personal interactions (cohesion functions) for the employee engaged in a telework arrangement. Two questions that arise from the locomotion function of the management responsibility include: Who does one communicate with to accomplish one's job, and what are the expectations in terms of work completion? While these questions represent just the tip of the iceberg in terms of task functions, issues of trust, satisfaction, and personal accomplishment, and interpersonal relationships all relate directly to a manager's responsibility to attend to important cohesion functions.

Addressing the Issues

Telemanagement—Laying the Groundwork

The effective use and integration of new information technologies is a major challenge to organizations. Today's managers are no longer guiding productivity through close supervision of employees, but rather are charged with overseeing the progress of employees engaged in a complex set of arrangements. Of paramount importance is good communication, and while this communication begins with the organization, it more specifically rests with management.

In light of the telework arrangement, a significant amount of telemanagement will take place using Internet-based technologies. Thus an effective telemanager should begin by creating an inventory of task-oriented activities and assessing the necessary technological tools required to accomplish the job. While the teleworker and telemanager are both bound by the rules, norms, and expectations of the job, organization, and industry, they are open to the possibility of transcending those structures by designing a workplace free from traditional barriers. The specific forms in which the communication process takes place is specific to the situation, but generally requires establishing a good fit between available technological media and the requirements of the communication activities (Rice, 1987).

In assessing the needs of the telework arrangement, the communication process for teleworkers might begin with their inclusion in the original design of the system, both in the selection of appropriate technologies as well as social support systems. One survey found that teleworkers wanted to be included in the dynamics and flow of organizational operations (Hartman, Stoner, & Raj, 1992), thus including the teleworker in the design of their own arrangement may be an important first step. Once established, the telework arrangement should include

---

Sample Inventory of Task-Oriented Activities for a
Customer Sales Representative

Task	Technological Requirements
Place customer orders	☞ Wireless Internet access to corporate data network ☞ Secure Internet access to online inventory control ☞ Telephone to voice network
Consultation with technical support specialists	☞ Mobile voice and data network ☞ Internet access to e-mail
Coordination with management/sales team	☞ Networked access to sales team members

---

regular opportunities for continuous learning, possibly through on-site training activities, as well as feedback on performance and overall work progress through media channels such as telephone, fax, email, or other online network exchanges. With the potential for isolation a key concern among teleworkers, ensuring opportunities for regular communication of all kinds is key to the design. As arrangements evolve, managers should encourage experimentation and autonomy as appropriate, but should seek opportunities for direct, face-to-face communication whenever possible.

In light of this discussion, it is interesting to note is that organizations, such as Merrill Lynch, have moved to a formalized training of teleworkers to better manage their at-home workforce (Johnson, 1997). From a training perspective, Hamby and Sankar (1998) suggest training through the use of simulation, just as in the case of Merrill Lynch, thus enabling telework students to assume different functional roles, and providing the opportunity to visualize and experience different scenarios in a business environment. For example, if Internet access to your corporate data network failed during your marketing presentation or sales call, what would you do? If instructions regarding a new assignment were unclear, how would you communicate this with your telemanager? How can you provide a rapid response to a customer's question when the majority of the support team has a variety of flexible and different working schedules than you?

> **Consider the following scenario:** Your company, headquartered in New York State, has begun to market its specialized, high-end gardening tools across the West Coast. You are charged with hiring a team of five regional sales representatives for the new territory and have been given the flexibility to design a remote work arrangement. To minimize the sales reps' travel time, you plan to hire employees local to the region. The reps will be expected to perform portions of their work from their respective West Coast homes, from their customer locations, and perhaps from a regional telecenter yet to be determined. In designing this telework arrangement, you are expected to take into consideration necessary technological tools as well as social support systems. Where do you begin? Do you include your reps in the original design? What avenues do you use to train your reps and provide regular opportunities for continuous learning? What type of communication channels should be set up to provide feedback on performance and overall work progress? What do you propose to circumvent the potential for isolation among your teleworkers? How might you build-in opportunities for direct, face-to-face communication among and between the reps?

An additional benefit of in-depth training is that teleworkers are able to experience disasters that may never happen and see consequences of potential actions before they take place. While no one could have predicted the terrorist attacks that leveled the World Trade towers, it is conceivable that a natural disaster such as a blizzard or power outage could temporarily shut down a major corporate operating office. What types of contingency plans might be developed to provide ongoing communication from various remote locations that would provide spontaneous organizational contact and thus ultimately inspire customer confidence? What if travel was severely impeded due to war or a health epidemic, such as the recent outbreak of SARS? How might an organization plan to use the Internet or other means to remain in touch with important clients? While some of these questions impact all organizational employees, teleworkers based at home or other remote locations have been found to have as much, if not greater, need for training compared to workers located in corporate offices. According to Whalen and Wright (1998), "Training provides a formal means for employees to obtain the knowledge and skills that enable them to perform their jobs satisfactorily, and consequently, contributes to employee job satisfaction" (p. 88).

Telemanagement—Task-Oriented Activities

Coordinating the activities of remote workers represents a challenge for managers. Research suggests that in the telework situation, absence of direct feedback from supervisors increases errors and misdirection. Furthermore, many telemanagers perceive an actual loss of control and power as teleworkers may put other needs first (such as errands, families, and personal projects) (Ford & Butts, 1991). For these reasons, workflow-relevant knowledge of how work is performed, by whom, and with what means has become increasingly important.

Telemanagers have two primary responsibilities when it comes to task-oriented activities: The first is to advance organizational goals by managing the efficient and effective flow of work of one or more employees within a division, unit, or team; and the second is acting as organizational liaison for that same group of employees. In managing workflow, it is the telemanager's job to empower employees with the necessary information, skills, and technology to let them make their own decisions and recommendations, as long as it will ultimately move the entire organization toward some ultimate predetermined goal. Once a clear set of objectives are established, the telemanager and teleworkers can together assign responsibilities, agree upon workflow schedules and deadlines, and review necessary resources required to accomplish the job.

Ultimately, however, Katzer and Fletcher (1997) describe this process as a decisional role in which the telemanager serves an entrepreneurial function. Acting as disturbance handler, resource allocator, and negotiator, the telemanager sets organizational agendas, establishes networks, clarifies priorities, provides strategic planning support, and generally makes sense of the world for his or her employees. The communication process, then, becomes for the manager one of sense making in which an organizational agenda is set, priorities are clarified, and overall planning is strategically formulated and communicated with those central to achieving organizational success. Providing necessary direction, ongoing feedback, as well as establishing trust are vital to the success of the communi-

---

Consider the following scenario: You have recently taken a job as editor of a leading monthly health magazine. While you engaged the services of a number of freelance writers, one of your four regularly employed writers is a home-based teleworker. You have never managed a teleworker before and are unsure as how to do so. After holding the first editorial meeting under your leadership (the teleworker was absent—you never invited her), you assigned each of the in-house writers two stories. Unclear as how to manage the workflow of the at-home writer, you assign her only one story via a written email message and wait to see how it goes. You receive a reply to your message simply stating, "ASSIGNMENT RECEIVED." Periodic inquiries by you via email to the writer reap similar responses such as, "UNDER CONTROL" or "GOING WELL. WILL HAVE TO YOU BY THE DEADLINE." You try to call the teleworker, but always get the answering machine. You hear through the grapevine that the writer has two small children, and that leaves you feeling uneasy about the writer's commitment to the job. When the story is finally received in the editorial offices, you find that it has taken on a new direction. While the finished product is well written and well conceived, it is not what you had conceptualized within the larger theme of the issue. You finally speak to the writer by phone late one evening. While she clearly justifies the change in direction of the story, you ask why she didn't discuss the changes with you during the story's development. You feel a loss of control in managing the writer. The writer feels a lack of trust from you, her new editor. What issues are of concern here? What communication strategies might rectify this situation, both on the part of the editor and writer? If the first editorial meeting was Internet-based, such as a Web-based meeting, thus providing an opportunity for all writers to be involved, might the outcome have changed? At what point in time might a face-to-face meeting have been useful and how might it have ultimately smoothed ruffled communication?

cation process between the teleworker and his or her manager (Goodrich, 1990). According to one teleworker, "honest communication between a telecommuter and his or her supervisor is key: 'The telecommuter must be very accountable. Document everything you do to establish that trust relationship'" (Joslyn, 2002, p. 10).

As organizational liaison, the telemanager acts somewhat in an informational role in which the manager is a monitor within the larger environmental context, disseminator of critical information, and organizational spokesperson (Katzer & Fletcher, 1997). In the traditional office environment, this information is imparted through formal communication channels such as memos or monthly staff meetings, or simply through more informal means such as ad hoc discussions over lunch or at the water cooler. With the opportunities for face-to-face communication severely diminished, and informal email messages seemingly replacing both the formal and informal types of communication, the telemanager must take an active role in fulfilling and re-creating the role of information provider.

According to the ABC, "Getting in touch and staying informed is a problem for some [teleworkers]. Generally, workers see the grapevine as more dependable than formal communication mechanisms" (Richman et al., 2002, p. 2). An astute telemanager, conscientious of his or her informational role, will find ways to communicate with remote staff on an ongoing basis. First, the formal written memo should not be abandoned. In an effort to emphasize its importance, it should be sent via fax or as an attachment to email, but never in the content of the email itself. Less formal written means of communication might be provided through weekly updates distributed in a written, bulleted format that is easily read within the contents of an email message. E-newsletters, emerging as a popular communication tool, work well in mixing work-related issues as well as interpersonal news. Furthermore, weekly or monthly meetings are feasible and can still be inexpensively arranged, such as through a telephone conferencing system supplemented by visual presentations via the Internet. Larger meetings, sometimes called webinars, virtual meetings or seminars, or tele-seminars, should always be pre-arranged to accommodate travel and alternate work schedules, and supplemented prior to the actual date with the distribution of a written agenda or background briefing material.

Telemanagement—Personal Interactions

Just as training is important in equipping teleworkers and telemanagers with the skills necessary for successful task-oriented activities, it is equally important in build skills necessary for cohesive functions. According to Wigand, Picot, and Reichwald (1997), the use of computer-supported communication, such as email, is less useful in promoting social relationships between employees and managers. Researchers note that off-site employees will experience less social interaction with peers and supervisors which may lead to alienation from one's co-workers, as well as lack of identity to the organization's goals, values, and changes in its culture. Kraut (1989) suggests that because teleworkers are cut off from the integrated organizational structure and culture, they also become less valuable. Over time, these workers become less familiar with others' work and organizational goals, thus unable to take on new responsibilities easily. With lesser social interaction among peers, telework employees lose a source of identity, as well as a lack of team spirit and camaraderie. Furthermore, as noted earlier, isolation can become a problem for the teleworker, thus intensifying when regular organizational information is seemingly lacking.

Contrary to this belief, research by Knoll and Jarvenpaa (1998) suggests that some level of organizational socialization can be developed electronically. In this study, global virtual teams were simulated in 13 universities spanning nine countries and monitored for the development of socialization skills. Cohesive functions such as a sense of teamness and the development of group norms (including the emergence of task leaders and the learned ability to brainstorm online) were identified as being present during the study exercise. Of critical necessity to the process of socialization were communication skills, including overcoming language barriers and using good writing and listening skills. To help in this process, an astute telemanager might consider assigning a mentor to a new teleworker, someone who has successfully accomplished both task-related activities as well as maintained visibility within the organization. Professional mentors are not new in the realm of business, so why not employ the same strategy here.

Despite conflicting reports, most research on telework does suggest that some regular, face-to-face contact with the organization is still important. A real concern for many teleworkers is that a lack of "face-time" suggests an outcome that might limit one's visibility and potentially one's career advancement opportunities. While the evidence varies, it does underscore the importance of critical communication processes—both formal and informal. The benefits of personal contact may increase opportunities for organizational creativity and cohesiveness generated by meeting with colleagues, as well as minimize the isolation felt by many teleworkers (Goodrich, 1990). While certain telework arrangements may not be able to accommodate "face-time" on a regular basis, some suggest that it is vital for the teleworker to maintain other types of "visible" connections despite the distance. For example, one teleworker keeps in daily contact with her administrative assistant who is located in the office and relies on the assistant to provide not only a daily mail log, but also to keep her abreast of office news (Joslyn, 2002). Through this type of arrangement, the teleworker quickly hears about both organizational news such as personnel promotions or

> **Consider the following scenario:** For 10 years you have enjoyed working in a local brokerage office as a real-estate mortgage agent. However, you are now being forced to relocate due to your spouse's job transfer. Anxious to keep you, a knowledgeable worker with a proven track record for success, the brokerage firm offers you an opportunity to telecommute. You are delighted to accept and work diligently with your manager on the technological requirements of the job. While the arrangement seemed initially ideal, your manager of many years retired within six months of your acceptance of the telework arrangement. The new manager, formally a colleague now promoted to your supervisor, seems to take less interest in keeping you informed of organizational "news." The social exchanges between colleagues while getting morning coffee are gone, and the occasional luncheon invitation at a favorite local restaurant can no longer be accepted due to the distance. The occasional gossip sent to you via email has also dwindled with turnover in staff and mistrust for management. You feel isolated and have lost your sense of identity as one of this organization's best employees. If you were the telemanager in this case, what might you have done to head-off or rectify this situation? What means of communication might you employee to keep this employee "connected?" If you were the teleworker and could have recognized the warning signals for isolation and disconnect earlier in this scenario, what would you have done before the situation became irreversible?

changes in office procedure, as well as personal news such as marriages, children's graduations, or family vacations, and can create opportunities to reach out and make connections to organizational members at all levels, thus remaining "visible."

An additional issue to be considered within the scope of personal interactions is motivation. Praise, appreciation, and personal development have been identified as the most salient motivational factors for employees located outside the traditional organizational boundaries (Wigand et al., 1997, p. 323). Simple, to-the-point email messages can carry enormous weight when backed by sincere gratitude and sent within a timely manner. For example:

> Great job on the XYZ Account!
>
> Thanks for the extra effort on completing the project ahead
>
> of schedule...I recognize how much work that was.
>
> All of us at headquarters congratulate you on closing the deal.

While praise and appreciation of this kind recognizes accomplishment, can be saved as a piece of official organizational correspondence, and is well-received and easily sent in today's fast-paced organization, more personal and sometimes formal means of recognition should not be left to email. As with any message, the best method of delivery is an important consideration. Perhaps a personal phone call, a posting to an internal organizational bulletin board, or recognition as part of a formal memo that circulates weekly within the organization might be better received. Furthermore, as with any organization, appreciation can also be rewarded through employee perks or opportunities for personal development such as in the participation of a special industry-wide conference or convention. For the teleworker, opportunities to interact and connect with other organizational members or colleagues within the field may provide an additional sense of connectedness and pride in one's job beyond that of the traditional office-based employee.

Future Trends

With the growing interest in and rising number of documented telework arrangements, organizational structures and corporate management have had to become flexible in their approaches to handling information and in accommodating various types of workers. For the teleworker and others, values such as self-responsibility, autonomy, self-realization, and individual gain have again taken on new meaning in the organizational setting. As a result, organizations are being presented with new strategic opportunities as they reassess their operations and the way in which their work is getting done.

While the major challenge for management involved in coordinating the telework arrangement once was the availability of appropriate technological tools to effectively and efficiently carry out the telework arrangement, organizations will find that those tools are available now. Internet-based access to secure corporate data networks, mobile telephone and voice networks, and network support availability are all cost-effective options for most organizations. The issue that is paramount, however, is how to effectively communicate with those tools and equally understand when those tools may not be sufficient. The study of Internet-based communication tools must encompass a broader look at the human element in communication, isolation factors due to remote nature of the work, and the lack of face-to-face communication.

Conclusion

This chapter provided an overall conceptualization of the telework arrangement in today's business environment and discussed distinctions within the telework arrangement in light of its impact on communication. Furthermore, the importance of creating an effective framework for the telework arrangement was highlighted, including the importance of communication during design of the system. Lastly, the importance of communication from task-oriented and personal interactions perspectives was reviewed.

While this chapter does not provide concrete answers as to what the best uniform practices are in each unique telework situation, what it has hopefully accomplished is raising an important awareness of communication issues that should be addressed before engaging in the telework arrangement. The impact that Internet-based technologies have had on the ability to work from remote locations is phenomenal, yet some of the familiar communication issues in business remain, albeit in a new form and through new channels. An astute telemanager and educated teleworker will become familiar with these questions and begin to work through the issues early on, thus creating their own template for success.

References

AT&T. (2000). Introduction: Getting started. *Telework Webguide* [online]. Retrieved on June 10, 2004 from: www.att.com/telework/get_started/gs_definitions.html.

AT&T. (2003). Remote working in the net-centric organization. *Point of View*. Retrieved on July 14, 2003 from: www.business.att.com/content/whitepaper/remote_working_net-centric_org.pdf.

Davis, D.D., & Polonko, K.A. (2001, October). Telework America 2001 summary. *ITAC Telework America 2001.* International Telework Association & Council. Retrieved on January 10, 2002 from: www.working fromanywhere.org/telework/twa2001.html.

Duxbury, L., Higgins, C., & Neufeld, D. (1998). Telework and the balance between work and family: Is telework part of the problem or part of the solution? In M. Igbaria and M. Tan (Eds.), *The virtual workplace* (pp. 218-255). Hershey, PA: Idea Group Publishing.

Ford, R.C., & Butts, M.A. (1991). Is your organization ready for telecommuting? *SAM Advance Management Journal, 56*(4), 19-23, 33.

Goodrich, J.N. (1990). Telecommuting in America. *Business Horizons, 38*(7), 31-37.

Hamby, J.D., & Sankar. C.S. (1998). Adopting simulation models from military to academics and industry. In M. Igbaria and M. Tan (Eds.), *The virtual workplace* (pp. 177-186). Hershey, PA: Idea Group Publishing.

Hartman, R.I., Stoner, C.R., & Raj, A. (1992). Developing successful telecommuting arrangements: Worker perceptions and managerial prescriptions. *SAM Advanced Management Journal, 57*(3), 35-4.

Johnson, K. (1997, December 17). Limits on the work-at-home life; at Merrill Lynch, the office never seems so far away. *The New York Times on the Web*, Archives. Retrieved at: archives.nytimes.com/.

Joslyn, H. (2002). Charities find that telecommuting helps recruit and keep workers—despite glitches. *Chronicle of Philanthropy, 14*(9), 10-11.

Katzer, J., & Fletcher, P. (1997). The information environment of managers. In E. Auster & C.W. Choo (Eds.), *Managing information for the competitive edge* (pp. 217-252). New York: Neal-Schuman Publishers.

Knoll, K., & Jarvenpaa, S.L. (1998). Working together in global teams. In M. Igbaria and M. Tan (Eds.), *The virtual workplace* (pp. 2-23). Hershey, PA: Idea Group Publishing.

Kraut, R.E. (1989). Telecommuting: The trade-offs of home work. *Journal of Communication, 39*(3), 19-44.

Kuenzl, J.J., & Reschovsky, C.A. (2001, December). Home-based workers in the United States: 1997. *U.S. Census Bureau.* Washington, DC: U.S. Department of Commerce.

McCloskey, D.W., & Igbaria, M. (1998). A review of the empirical research on telecommuting and directions for future research. In M. Igbaria & M. Tan (Eds.), *The virtual workplace* (pp. 338-358). Hershey, PA: Idea Group Publishing.

Pratt, J.H. & Pratt Associaties (2003). Teleworking comes of age with broadband. Telework America Survey 2002. Silver Spring, MD: International Telework Association & Council. Retrieved on June 10, 2004 from: www.telecommute.org/pdf/TWA2003_Executive_Summary.pdf

Rice, R.E. (1987). Computer-mediated communication and organizational innovation. *Journal of Communication, 37(4)*, 65-94.

Richman, A., Noble, K., & Johnson, A. (2002). *When the workplace is many places: The extent and nature of off-site work today. Executive Summary.* Commission by the American Business Collaboration for Quality Dependent Care. Watertown, MA: WFD Consulting.

U.S. General Services Administration. (2003, May 15). *Interagency Telework/ Telecommuting Site.* Available online at: http://www.telework.gov/.

Whalen, T., & Wright. D. (1998). Distance training in the virtual workplace. In M. Igbaria & M. Tan (Eds.), *The virtual workplace* (pp. 87-107). Hershey, PA: Idea Group Publishing.

Wigand, R., Picot, A., & Reichwald, R. (1997). *Information, organization and management: Expanding markets and corporate boundaries.* New York: John Wiley & Sons.

Chapter XIII

An Open Source Primer

Brian Still
Texas Tech University, USA

Abstract

This chapter serves as an introductory overview of Open Source Software (OSS) and the Open Source movement. It is geared primarily for technical communicators. To provide a thorough overview, this chapter defines OSS, explains how OSS works in comparison to proprietary software, looks at the history of OSS, and examines OSS licensing types, applications in business, and overall strengths and weaknesses when compared to proprietary software. Lastly, it evaluates the practical potential of OSS as well as emerging and future trends relating to it. From this general but thorough overview the intended audience of technical communicators will gain the solid understanding needed to work successfully in an academic or professional environment where OSS continues to grow in popularity, spurring more organizations to rely on it or the Open Source ideas that have inspired and continue to drive its creation and growth.

Introduction

Eric Raymond, in his book *The Cathedral and the Bazaar* (1999), likens the key difference between proprietary and Open Source Software (OSS) development as similar to the relationship between building a cathedral and a bazaar. According to Raymond, OSS is not the product of a few "wizards or small bands of mages working in splendid isolation, with no beta to be released before its time" (p. 29). Instead, OSS development is like a "great babbling bazaar of differing agendas and approaches" (p. 30).

Facilitated by the Internet, hundreds if not thousands of developers working on OSS projects combine their talents to create software that addresses practical needs or solves problems. OSS projects are constantly reshaping themselves. A version of the software is produced and distributed, tested, debugged, and then improved upon and re-released. All of this process takes place in the open. Errors are not kept secret, nor are improvements. The software is made available to the developers and to anyone else who wants to access it. Moreover, the software is open for others to improve upon it. Depending on the OSS license, others can even release their improvements back to the public or sell them for a profit without needing the permission or authorization of the original programmer.

OSS development has literally exploded in popularity among consumers and software developers. For example, today the most popular Web server on the Internet is Apache, an Open Source, not proprietary, product.[1] Additionally, Linux, perhaps the software referred to most often as the perfect example of OSS, is challenging Microsoft Window's once unquestioned dominance of the operating system market. Still, OSS is not without its detractors. Just as there are those who would argue for it because of its little or no cost and flexibility, there are others that would argue that it is difficult to implement and its core developers are undependable hobbyists.

Despite these misgivings, businesses and even nations (Liu, 2003) in already lean economic times are increasingly relying on OSS as a cost-effective legitimate alternative to proprietary software. In some cases, larger companies have saved millions of dollars just by switching from Windows to Linux operating systems (Koch, 2003). As long as OSS proves more affordable and as (if not more) effective than proprietary software, organizations will continue to integrate OSS into their business infrastructure, using it to power their Internet services, operating systems, and other key software applications.

As a result, technical communicators in the workplace will—to some degree—become involved (if they are not already involved) with OSS or Open Source ideas. They may write end user documentation for Open Source software that their organization has acquired and then modified for its own purposes. They may manage or participate on project teams tasked with evaluating and adopting new software for a business. They may have to explain OSS and the intricacies of its licensing and development practices to decision makers who lack technical expertise. Because of these scenarios and others, technical communicators can benefit from a solid understanding of OSS and the role it plays in business.

The purpose of this chapter is to provide that solid, introductory overview of OSS. To accomplish this, the chapter presents the following information:

- a definition of OSS and a brief look at how it is used;
- an explanation of how OSS works in comparison to proprietary software;
- a history of OSS development;
- OSS licensing types;
- OSS applications in business;
- OSS strengths and weaknesses;
- an evaluation of the practical potential of OSS in the workplace;
- emerging and future trends in OSS; and
- online resources available to conduct further research on OSS.

Defining Open Source and Tracing Its Origins

OSS is currently used in a number of different roles. Linux, as already mentioned, powers computer operating systems for businesses offering services ranging from aerospace to telecommunications. OpenOffice (www.openoffice.org), although not nearly as popular as Linux, is an OSS alternative to Microsoft Office. OpenOffice offers word processing, spreadsheet, presentation management, and drawing tools. Other OSSs run certain key services, such as email and the Internet, that have become necessary staples many businesses consider critical to their core services. Sendmail, for example, is a free software program that handles a majority of all email. INN manages the collection and distribution of Usenet articles. Majordomo powers electronic mailing lists. BIND is also an OSS that enables the Internet's Domain Name System (DNS) to map connections between numeric and human-readable addresses. In other words, BIND makes it possible for users wanting to visit a website to type in an easy-to-use-and-remember address, like www.opensource.org, rather than a long string of numbers. Obviously, OSS is an integral part of today's business infrastructure.

The driving force behind OSS is the Open Source movement, which can best be understood by what it opposes (proprietary software) and what it also supports (open software development). OSS advocates believe in an open exchange of ideas, an open coordination if not merging of different software, and, at the most crucial and basic level, an open access to the source code of software. Bruce

Perens, creator of the Open Source definition, calls it a "bill of rights for the computer user" (1999, p.171). Perens helped found the Open Source Initiative (OSI) in 1999. OSI maintains the Open Source definition and its registered trademark, and it campaigns actively for the Open Source movement and strict adherence to its definition. Only those software licenses that adhere to the guidelines of the OSI Open Source definition can use the trademark.

The entire OSI Open Source definition can be viewed online at http://www.opensource.org/docs/definition.php. Its key tenets, however, can be summarized here: For a software license to be considered Open Source, users must have the right to make and even give away copies of the software for free. Additionally, and perhaps most importantly, users must have the right to view and, if they want, repair or modify the source code of the software (Perens, 1999).

Source Code

To better understand the significance of allowing users to view the software source code, we should take a brief look at what source code is. Source code is the wiring that makes software work the way it does. Put simply, programmers use a computer language to create source code or to script (write) commands that tell the software how to perform. In order to create new software, to fix or debug faulty software, or to modify existing software to meet a particular need, the programmer must have access to the source code. OSS allows for "open" access to this code. That is, individuals are free to modify/change software code at their desire and without needing approval from the original programmer who created the code.

An illustration of how source code works to instruct a computer to carry out a specific task is illustrated in the following example of a C++ computer programming language script (Figure 1).

Figure 1. Source code example

```
if (age < 16 )
   printf ("I'm sorry but you're too young to get a driver's license\n");
   else
   if (age = 16)
   printf ("Okay, you can get a license but I would suggest getting a learner's permit first\n");
   else
      printf ("It's about time—you could have gotten your license when you were 16!\n");
```

In this example the script prints a particular message depending on a set of conditions presented in the if/else commands written by the programmer. If the age entered is under 16, for example, the message returned is: "I'm sorry but you're too young to get a driver's license." The if/else conditions and "printf" commands of this program are the source code.

This source code, although useful to a programmer, cannot be read by the computer. It must be translated or compiled into object code or the binary 1s and 0s that computers can read and execute. This binary or object code is often referred to as "machine language" because it is written in numbers that can be easily understood by computers, or machines. Of course, what makes it easy to understand for computers makes it impractical for people to understand. Most proprietary software licensed for use comes in object code form only, which means that the computer running the software gets the numbers or machine language it needs to know what to do. However, users, such as programmers, do not get access to the source code or language needed to understand and if necessary modify the program. In other words, the source code is not open.

Assuming there are no problems with the object code or that no changes need to be made to the information the software is providing to the computer, access to the source code will not be needed for the proprietary software to run as it should on the computer. But what if changes are required? What if, for example, the legal age to get a driver's license in the state changes to 17? How would the software be changed to allow for this new wrinkle? If only the object code is available through the software, the programmer cannot make changes. Only access to the source code enables the if/else command to be modified so that it reflects the new legal driving age.

Proprietary software companies close access to the source code of their applications because they consider it intellectual property critical to their business infrastructure. If any user could change the source code of the software, there could be eventually many different versions of it not easily supported by computers. And if the user who purchased the software could change the source code, the user would not need to pay the software company to make the change. With unrestricted access to the source code, a user could even develop another version of the software and then distribute it at a lower cost or for free (Nadan, 2002).

The OSS model works differently, primarily because the profitability of the software in and of itself is not important. This is not to say that some OSS companies do not make money. Many do profit by providing service or support to users. RedHat (http://www.redhat.com) makes a decent profit packaging and distributing Linux to users. While any user can download and install Linux for free, RedHat has managed successfully to convince users that by paying a little extra to RedHat, they will get a guaranteed, ready-to-go version of Linux that comes with experienced support, such as training, manuals, or customer service (Young, 1999).

OSS source code is not the intellectual property of one company. Rather it is more like community property that belongs to every user. With barriers removed to who can access it and who cannot, the thinking behind this key Open Source tenet is, the more individuals who look at the source code, the better it will become. More bugs will be caught, more enhancements will be added, and the product will improve more quickly as the experience and talents of a large community of developers is put to work making it better (Raymond, 1999).

Such an approach to software development and distribution has successfully threatened proprietary software's hold over the market in recent years. Although it seems revolutionary, it is actually the way things are done, according to Alan Cox, "in almost all serious grown-up industry" (Cox, 2003, paragraph 11). In every field consumers can go elsewhere if vendors are not supportive. Cox uses the auto industry as an example: People can pick the car they want from the dealer they want, they can look for the best deal, and if they want save money fixing the car themselves. Because of OSS, software consumers now have that same sort of power. Instead of just one choice, one kind of license, and one price, consumers now have a choice of brand names, a chance to test multiple products for the right fit and buy, and ultimately the right to tinker with the software's source code on their own to make it work for their needs (Cox, 2003).

MIT, Hackers, and the Origins of OSS

If we trace the origins of OSS, we see that what now seems like such a novel business and philosophical approach to allow access to a software's source code is actually the way things were done long before consideration was given to turning a profit by selling software. In his book, *Hackers: Heroes of the Computer Revolution* (1994), Steven Levy examines the beginnings of computer programming that would lead to the development of, among other things, the personal computer and the Internet. Starting in the 1950s with groups such as the Tech Model Railroad Club at MIT and carrying through to the Homebrew Computer Club in the 1970s (Levy, 1994), the work of these early programmers was very much akin to scientific research and discovery. Since the only way computer scientists could then (and even now) learn from the work of others was to view that work, the source code of any hack or program was always available (DiBona, Ockman, & Stone, 1999). The idea was that another programmer might be able to improve upon the program, and once that improvement was made available to the group of programmers, improvements could be made on it (Levy, 1994).

The beliefs of these programmers parallel those of OSS developers now, and that is no coincidence. The same "hacker[2] ethics" that drove programmers at MIT and elsewhere are clearly principles that have been passed down to today:

- information, such as source code, should be freely accessible;
- nothing, not a person, a law, a government, or a business should stand in the way of programming;
- hackers or programmers should be judged by their skill;
- computers can always be improved and computers can improve life as we know it (Levy, 1994).

For early programmers, the potential profitability of a program was not the key element that motivated them to program. This is true as well for OSS developers. They want access to the source code because they want to tweak it and perhaps make it better. They are, according to the results of the Boston Consulting Group (BCG) 2002 Hacker Survey, primarily motivated by the challenge of programming. After that they want to improve their own skill and be recognized for that skill among their fellow programmers. Money, at least according to the BCG survey, is rarely a motivation for OSS developers.

Some critics look at such statistics and suggest that although that may be true now, OSS development does not have the steam to continue, precisely because OSS developers are primarily just hobbyists who are "hacking" for free. Developers, Robert Glass argues, like to be paid too much to continue doing anything free forever (2000). In truth, however, developers were hacking for fun and for the challenge long before they were doing it for money. And the same forces that drove many of the early programmers still drive OSS developers today: They want recognition for being good, and they want to make the software better so that they and others can do more positive things with it.

The Free Software Movement (FSF)

One of the recognized champions of this view is Richard Stallman, the founder of the Free Software Movement (FSF) and the creator of GNU, a free version of the Unix operating system. Disillusioned by the trend toward commercialization in software programming, Stallman founded FSF in 1984 on the belief that "source code is fundamental to the furthering of computer science, and freely available source code is truly necessary for innovation to continue" (DiBona et al., 1999, p. 2).

The FSF has been committed since its beginning to allowing users this freedom, serving as an alternative to the proprietary model. The "Free" in the Free Software Foundation does not refer to price, although many assume that it does. Actually, distributors of free software can charge for the copies they give out and the software will still be considered free. That is because the idea of "free" that Stallman is interested in refers to the "freedom to run the [software] program, for any purpose," and "freedom to modify the program" (1999, p. 56).

After creating the GNU operating system, Stallman drafted the General Public License (GPL), which was meant to govern the distribution and use of the GNU. Any software that wanted to be "free" according to Stallman and the FSF had to abide by the dictates of the GPL. One application that did was Linus Torvalds' Linux kernel, which when matched with GNU made it the robust, freely modifiable operating system commonly known as Linux today (Torvalds, 1999).

As successful as Linux has been as a free software application, other applications and other software companies have balked at the religious zeal of Stallman's FSF, and also the rigidity of its GPL. The GPL requires that any modifications made to software licensed under the GPL must be made public and freely accessible. Stallman calls this requirement *copyleft*. If a user, for example, downloads a piece of free software with a GPL license, and then that user makes modifications to the software, the user cannot take ownership over those changes, declare them to be intellectual property, and then sell them for profit. Any code derivative of any GPL software must abide by the same terms of the GPL to which the original software adheres. This prevents any programmer profiting from the use of free software source code. The notion of copyright, therefore, is turned upside down. No one owns the code; the GPL insures that it belongs to everyone. Copyleft means that it is free for everyone to use as long as they give back what they create by using it (Stallman, 1999).

Obviously, the GPL as well as FSF's overall intransigent position turns off many in the software industry. As much as they wish to contribute to the well-being of the community, they are most interested, as they have to be, in their bottom line. More than a few also regard the FSF as a political entity with an ideology that is very anti-business. Doug Palmer writes that because FSF is a political movement, "the aim is not to allow people to do as they will, but to force people to do as the movement decrees" (2003, *Free as in Speech,* paragraph 5).

Going Mainstream: The Beginnings of the Open Source Movement

Aware of these negative perceptions of free software, and sensing that some sort of positive effort had to be made at putting a more palatable face on the movement, a number of free software programmers, absent Stallman, met in 1997 to consider ways of re-branding free software. Their concern was that Stallman's all-or-nothing approach to free software was killing the growth of Linux in the business world. The use of the word "free" was also, they thought, too confusing, simply because the reaction of many, especially those in business, was that free meant no charge (Perens, 1999).

From this meeting and others, the Open Source movement was born (DiBona et al., 1999). The Open Source movement established the Open Source Initiative (OSI) to act as a clearinghouse and public relations vehicle for approving OSI-compliant software and forwarding the OSI definition. Based on the Debian Free Software Guidelines that Bruce Perens had written (Perens, 1999), the Open Source definition is more flexible and friendly to business than the GPL. It "allows greater liberties with licensing than the GPL does. In particular, the Open Source definition allows greater promiscuity when mixing proprietary and open-source software" (DiBona et al., 1999, p. 3). For example, one license that meets the Open Source definition's guidelines is the Berkeley System Distribution (BSD) license. Like the GPL, it lets developers view the source code of the original software and make a derivative version of it; unlike the GPL, however, the BSD allows the developers to make their changes private. In other words, the developers can make modifications and then distribute those modifications in object code form only, retaining intellectual property or ownership over the source code of their modifications.

OSS Licensing

As of January 2004, the OSI has approved more than 20 licenses, including the GPL and others, such as the BSD, MIT and X licenses, that offer developers more leeway than the GPL in controlling the derivative source code they create. In the past, the options for proprietary software licensing have been somewhat clear if only because they have been so limited. No access to source code means no ability to modify the software to do anything that might possibly violate a license agreement, aside perhaps from duplicating it and then distributing free copies to unlicensed users. However, the availability of open access to source code changes everything. What can be accessed? Can the software be modified? Must those modifications be made available publicly, or can the user who made them keep them private? Depending on the OSS license, the answer may vary. Here is a summary of the most commonly used OSS licenses:

- *General Public License (GPL).* The GPL is as much a manifesto as a license. If the developer wants the source code and any modifications to that source code by other developers to remain public, the GPL is the license to use (Perens, 1999).

- *Lesser GPL or LGPL.* This license, born from the GPL, allows OSS source code to be mixed with proprietary software. Specifically, software libraries, such as the C language library provided with Linux, can be used to build proprietary programs (Perens, 1999). Proprietary programs can also be used to "extend" the source code of the software under this license.

- *Berkeley Software Distribution or BSD.* The BSD allows the software licensed under it to be used for about anything (Perens, 1999). The X and Apache licenses are similar to the BSD. The BSD does require, however, that any advertising of the software licensed under the BSD must reference the University of California. For this reason, Bruce Perens encourages developers and organizations considering the BSD "to use the X license instead" (1999, p. 183).

- *Mozilla Public License or MPL.* Like the BSD and X licenses, the MPL allows OSS to be mixed with proprietary software and modifications made to source code to be privatized. But any derivative work of the original source code, although private, cannot claim patent rights (Wu & Lin, 2001). The MPL is an offshoot of the NPL or Netscape Public License, which was created specifically for Netscape when it made its source code publicly available.

- *MIT License.* This is perhaps the least restrictive Open Source license. Users of the source code licensed under the MIT can copy, modify, and redistribute without restriction the source code or derivatives of it. The only requirement is that the original copyright and terms of the license are retained.

For most users, the intricacies of OSS licensing are not that important. Software companies and technical communicators working for them should be aware, however, of the ins and outs of licensing. Of all the OSS licenses, the GPL presents the greatest worry, especially for small or startup software companies that "have not mastered the terms and conditions of the GPL" (Nadan, 2001, paragraph 9). According to Nadan, the infectious nature of the GPL is a danger, and if companies are not aware, the proprietary software they create could "become GPL if it merely shares data with the GPL code, even if the only such sharing occurs while the program is actually running" (Nadan, 2001, paragraph 9).

Ultimately, software companies have to make a choice. If they want anyone who uses their software to pay, then they should not use Open Source. If they want at least somebody to pay, perhaps for a commercially licensed, derivative work, then they can apply a license, like the MIT or X, that allows for that (Perens, 1999). Perens notes, however: "Most of the Open Source authors consider their programs to be contributions to the public good, and don't care if they are paid at all" (1999, p. 185).

Selling OSS to Business

Just as Open Source wants to contribute to the public good—a goal it shares with the FSF—it also wants to put a flexible, more practical face on free software. Faced with losing the war for the hearts and minds of software users, the Open Source movement sacrifices the religious zeal of copyleft for a software certifying system that enables more software companies to license their work as Open Source—i.e., leaving the source code of their applications available and modifiable. In other words, OSI does not see itself in an antagonistic relationship with the software industry as FSF does. Rather, "commercial software…[is] an ally to help spread the use of Open Source licensing" (Nadan, 2002, paragraph 5).

To facilitate this relationship, OSI argues that business has much to gain from OSS. Business can, for example, outsource work to OSS developers, and thus save money on in-house development. Additionally, a small business, even one with little capital, can quickly become the next Linux by interesting OSS developers in a project it has begun (Nadan, 2002). Almost overnight, scores of developers around the world, connected via the Internet, could be working for free to make the project a reality.

Open Source, therefore, is about the "true believers" in free software trying to convince individuals in the naturally cautious and skeptical business world to be believers too. Why do they want business to buy into OSS? Because innovation, research and development of software, once found primarily at big universities, is now carried out primarily in business. If business adopts OSS, its popularity will not only increase, but its quality will improve as more dollars and developers will be dedicated to improving it.

The OSI website goes out of its way to sell business on OSS by providing case studies, the full text of approved OSI licenses, and even example business models that employ OSS solutions. At the heart of this effective enterprise are the same ideals early hackers created with their work and Stallman continues to forward. Even though Stallman would probably argue that these original hacker ideals have been diluted if not abandoned, in actuality they have been re-cast. Some of the zeal has been replaced with pragmatism, but only so that OSS can remain a viable force in a software industry where the necessity of putting profits before community has been a fact for some time.

Comparing OSS to Proprietary Software

Despite the inroads OSS has made in operating systems and Web servers, many individuals in business are still standoffish toward it. Others, having heard positive and negative stories about OSS, are curious about what it can really do in comparison to proprietary software. By first taking a look at the strengths and weaknesses of OSS compared to proprietary software, we can establish the knowledge base needed to determine those specific situations where implementing OSS is the right decision.

OSS Strengths

Free Access to Source Code. Organizations, especially those with skilled developers, can take advantage of free access to source code. OSS code is always available for modification, enabling developers to tinker with it to make it better for all users or just to meet their own needs or those of their organizations.

Costs. A number of countries struggling economically, such as Taiwan and Brazil, have adopted OSS to save money (Liu, 2003). Many businesses faced with decreasing IT operating budgets but increasing software maintenance and licensing fees have also made the move toward OSS. Although there are indirect costs incurred using OSS, such as staff salary and training, proprietary software has these same costs. The fact that OSS starts free is a big plus in its favor.

Rapid Release Rate. In the proprietary software model, software is never released until it is ready. If there are changes that need to be made after that, these are not made and deployed as soon as possible, but instead are held back until it can be sure that all the bugs are fixed. But OSS works differently. As Raymond points out, updates to OSS are "released early and often," taking advantage of the large developer community working on the OSS to test, debug, and develop enhancements (1999, p. 39). All of this is done at the same time, and releases are sometimes done daily, not every six months, so the work is efficient and the improvement to the software is rapid.

Flexibility. Open access to the source code gives users flexibility because they can modify the software to meet their needs. The existence of OSS also gives users flexibility simply because they have a choice that might not have existed before. They do not have to use proprietary software if there is an OSS that works just as well. OSS provides further flexibility for those users that need to move to a new system. Rather than being stuck with "nonportable code and...forced to deal with whatever bugs" that come along with the software, they can use OSS that is "openly specified...[and] interchangeable" (Brase, 2003, paragraph 1).

Reliability. Because OSS is peer-reviewed and modifications are released quickly, any problems with the software are caught and corrected at a rate countless times faster than that offered by proprietary software. It is not an industry secret that Linux, for example, is much more reliable than Windows. Exposed to the prying eyes of literally thousands of developers, Linux and other OSSs are constantly being tested and tweaked to be made more crash proof. This tweaking also extends the life of the software, something which cannot be done with proprietary software unless users are willing to pay for upgrades. Many organizations have found themselves sitting on dated software and facing an expensive re-licensing fee to get the new version. OSS can be refitted by the organization if it is not already tweaked by the community of developers working on it. The software could be abandoned, and this has occurred before with OSS. But it has happened as well with proprietary software.

Developer Community. In the end, the developer community is the greatest strength of OSS and one that proprietary software companies cannot match. Not all developers working on any given OSS project actually write code. But literally thousands upon thousands working on larger projects test, debug, and provide constant feedback to maintain the quality of the OSS. They are not forced to do it. But they contribute because they are stimulated by the challenge and empowered by the opportunity to help build and improve software that provides users, including themselves, with a high-quality alternative to proprietary software.

OSS Weaknesses

Critics of OSS point out a number of deficiencies that make OSS too risky of a proposition to use in any sort of serious enterprise:

Loosely organized community of hobbyists. It is a very real possibility that an OSS project could lose its support base of developers, should they get bored, moving on to another project. Although many that work on OSS are paid programmers and IT professionals, they tend to work on OSS outside of normal business hours. Many in business feel that professional developers working for companies that care about the bottom line in a competitive software market will always produce better software. They will stick around to support it. And the company will put its name on the line and stand behind it.

In truth, the numbers of developers getting paid to work on OSS is increasing. Nearly one-third, in fact, are actually paid for their work. In 2001, IBM—now a strong supporter of OSS—had around 1,500 of its developers working on just one OSS application, Linux (Goth, 2001).

Forking Source Code. Source code is said to "fork" when another group of developers create a derivative version of the source code that is separate if not incompatible with the current road the source code's development is following. The result is source code that takes a different "fork in the road." Because anyone can access and modify OSS source code, forking has always been a danger that has been realized on occasions. The wide variety of operating systems that now exist based on the BSD operating system, such as FreeBSD, OpenBSD, and NetBSD, serves as one example (DiBona et al., 1999).

Raymond (1999) argues that it is a taboo of the Open Source culture to fork projects, and in only special circumstances does it happen. Linux has not really forked despite so many developers working on it. Carolyn Kenwood (2001) attributes this to its "accepted leadership structure, open membership, and long-term contribution potential" (p. xiv). The GPL license, which Linux uses, is also a major deterrent to forking because there is no financial incentive to break off since the forked code would have to be freely available under the terms of the license. Overall, however, forking is a legitimate potential weakness for OSS.

Lack of Technical Support. In *CIO* magazine's 2002 survey of IT executives, "52 percent said a lack of vendor support was Open Source's primary weakness" (Koch, 2003, p. 55). Very rarely is software ever installed without some kind of hitch. In smaller organizations the staff's depth of knowledge may not go deep enough to insure that support for the software can be taken care of internally. And because so many of the systems and applications organizations run these days operate in hybrid environments where different tools run together on different platforms, technical support is crucial. Proprietary companies argue that Open Source cannot provide the technical support business expects and needs. There is no central help desk, no 1-800 number, no gold or silver levels of support that organizations can rely on for assistance.

Recognizing that OSS must mirror at least the traditional technical support structure of proprietary models to address this perceived weakness, a number of "major vendors such as Dell, HP, IBM, Oracle, and Sun" are beginning to support OSS (Koch, 2003, p. 55).

Lack of Suitable Business Applications. Literally hundreds if not thousands of OSS applications can be downloaded for free off the Internet from sites like the Open Source Directory (http://www.osdir.com) or SourceForge (http://www.sourceforge.net). But a fair knock against OSS in the business world is that aside from Linux and a few others, most OSS lacks the quality, maturity, or popularity to make business want to switch from the proprietary products it currently uses. Some think this is because building a word processor just is not "sexy" enough for OSS developers (Moody, 1998).

Although it may be changing, the nature of OSS is that those projects developers choose to participate in are the ones that interest them, not necessarily those that others want done. If more companies begin to pay their developers to work on OSS, this may change. For now, however, OSS lacks the "killer app" for the desktop that matches Linux's impact on operating systems or Apache's on Web servers. OpenOffice, mentioned earlier, is an OSS alternative to Windows Office, but its user interface lacks the sophistication and ease-of-use of Office and so business has been slow to warm to it. Until it or another OSS desktop application comes along that can seriously challenge Windows' lock on the desktop, those in decision-making positions will still not see OSS "as a legitimate alternative to proprietary software" (Goth, 2001, p. 105).

Evaluating the Practical Potential of Using OSS

In what situations is OSS a legitimate alternative? How should OSS be evaluated to determine whether it is the right fit for an organization? Carolyn Kenwood (2001) proposes that a taxonomy be applied to costs, benefits, and other intangible factors to determine whether OSS or proprietary software is the best option. Each taxonomy has a list of attributes. For example, a taxonomy of benefits looks at, among other things, the availability, scalability, flexibility, performance, quality of support, and security of OSS compared to proprietary software. Using a scale from very weak to very strong, the organization can rank the attributes by comparing each one's "relative strength or weakness for OSS versus traditional COTS products" (Kenwood, 2001, p. xvii).

The specific organization affected by Kenwood's study is the United States Army (2001). But in practice any organization could use Kenwood's taxonomies to assist it in carrying out a more thorough and quantifiable analysis of the software options available for selection.

Huaiqing Wang and Chen Wang (2001) also outline a number of key technical and managerial requirements that should be considered when evaluating OSS:

- *Availability of technical support*. According to Wang and Wang, "commercial grade technical support" must be available and reasonably affordable (p. 91).

- *Upgrades*. The software should allow for upgrading so that it has an extended shelf-life and can be used by the organization long-term.

- *Customizable*. The OSS "must be flexible enough to be customized or integrated in widely different technical environments" (p. 91).

- *Reliability*. The best way to insure reliability is to use OSS that has been around for a few years and has a proven track record.

- *Budget*. OSS developers tend to cost more than other developers. This cost and others, such as ongoing technical support and maintenance, whether done internally or contracted, need to be considered.

- *In-house expertise*. If the organization does not have the staff to support the OSS, it needs to hire them. If it cannot do that, it should look at other software.

- *The long haul*. The organization should choose OSS that fits into its long-term plans and that has a status that indicates it will continue to be around and supported by Open Source developers (Wang & Wang, 2001).

Beyond these technical requirements are other equally important elements that must be looked at carefully. Just because an OSS application seems better than a proprietary choice does not mean it should be implemented. For example, organizational culture is a tremendously important factor. Small but brutal internal wars have devastated the morale of organizations that made top-down decisions to switch personnel to a different word processor. Staff tend to be loyal even to their Internet browser and resist changing it (let alone upgrading it). Ultimately, the bottom-line need for new technology rarely affects people in understandable ways unless it reaches into their paycheck.

Managers also tend to be leery of pronounced change outside of their areas of control because they have been burned so many times before by new initiatives. At the highest executive levels, anything associated with IT that sounds too good to be true is often just that. CEOs have become shell-shocked after sitting in too many meetings where IT people speak gibberish they do not understand and then ask for six-figure or higher budgets to implement new technology.

It can never be assumed that technology at any level is easy to understand, even for those that work in the field. The widespread opinions on OSS, many based on rumor more than fact, offer proof of this. For an organization to consider the practical implementation of OSS, therefore, it must understand OSS. This is where the technical communicator comes in.

The technical communicator can play a key role in educating the organization at all levels. Explaining the benefits, the cost reductions, the overall positive impact of adopting OSS is a key effort that must be made before it is ever actually adopted and put into use. Organizations should consider informational sessions, phased roll-outs of the software, and even beta testing groups made up of staff that start working with the software, eventually passing back to their colleagues their opinion on the performance and quality of the OSS. IT staff would be well-served before ever reaching this stage to convince reluctant decision makers by setting up OSS on an offline computer for demonstration purposes.

Even with these efforts, the push to adopt OSS, although gaining ground in large organizations, is still a hard sell to small organizations and home users. Brent Thompson is a Microsoft Certified Systems Engineer (MCSE) with a decade of experience in IT. He has investigated OSS for the mid-size organization (roughly 100 employees) he administers systems for right now. He is not happy with Microsoft's new licensing requirements, and he likes the robust performance of Linux. Still, he does not feel his organization is ready to go away from Microsoft.

The organization provides services, and it relies on Microsoft Word, PowerPoint, Excel, and Access to create, format, store, and present information to its clients. These same applications cannot run on Linux, and even though there may be alternative OSS applications that can, the organization's staff is too accustomed at this point with the Microsoft products to move away from them. "I personally would like to see, " Thompson says, "another five years of software developed for Linux, so the same applications that we use today have also been written for Linux. I don't feel the Open Source way is correct for us right now, but I do believe that it might be something to consider in the next 5 or 10 years" (personal communication, May 20, 2003).

Emerging and Future Technology Trends

OSS continues to grow in popularity around the world, increasingly offering a legitimate alternative to proprietary software. And the impact of the OSS movement is being felt even outside of the software community. According to Graham Lawton (2002), Open Source is "a political stand—one that values freedom of expression, mistrusts corporate power, and is uncomfortable with private ownership of knowledge" (p. 36). In other areas, therefore, the desire for the same openness that the Open Source movement has brought to software source code has been extended to other creative materials, such as publications and audio.

The Creative Commons (http://creativecommons.org) sponsors a number of licenses that allow authors and artists to share their work in a public forum while still retaining copyright of it. At present Creative Commons offers 11 licenses. Those organizations or individuals owning non-software, creative material can choose a license that prohibits or allows for their work to be modified or commercialized. Some licenses also allow the licensee to require that they receive some form of attribution should their work be used again or if a derivative version of it is created.

A number of organizations have used Creative Commons licenses to make their work openly accessible. The most prominent perhaps is MIT, which has made all of its course materials available through the Creative Commons Open Courseware License (http://ocw.mit.edu). Advocates are pushing that other educational institutions, especially those publicly funded, follow MIT's lead and make their coursework free and open to everyone (Newmarch, 2001). But the enthusiasm motivating such advocacy for more open access to information is matched equally by advocacy calling for the increasing protection of what many consider private, intellectual property.

The one trend, then, that can be safely predicted about Open Source is that the battle it has helped begin in the software industry and that has now carried over to other fields is only beginning. Regardless of laws or PR campaigns created to counter it, Open Source is, Raymond writes, "future proof" (1999, p. 171). This is all the more reason for technical communicators to make themselves aware of Open Source.

Online Resources Related to Open Source

http://www.opensource.org

The online home of the Open Source Initiative (OSI).

http://www.gnu.org

Home of the GNU operating system, a free alternative to Unix. Information can also be found here on the Free Software Foundation (FSF). The FSF's Internet home is located at http://www.fsf.org.

http://sourceforge.net

SourceForge provides free hosting for thousands of Open Source projects. Developers can correspond, exchange ideas, sign up for projects, and download applications on the site.

http://www.osdir.com

Another location for finding and downloading OS applications. An interesting feature on this site is the "blog" area where site users, such as OS developers, can comment on OS applications or other related issues.

http://www.osdn.com

The Open Source Development Network (OSDN) is geared for the manager as much as it is for the developer. It provides links to sites offering resources to developers of Open Source applications, or those interested in buying and managing Open Source applications.

http://www.mozilla.org

Open Source browser built and deployed after Netscape released its source code in 1998; Mozilla is now maintained in an Open Source environment by developers across the world.

http://www.linux.org

A good starting place for learning more about Linux; Linux-related downloads, documentation, and applications can also be accessed here.

References

The Boston Consulting Group. (2002, July 24). *Hacker survey*. Retrieved April 18, 2003, from: http://www.osdn.com/bcg.

Brase, R. (2003, March 19). *Open Source makes business sense*. Retrieved April 22, 2003, from: http://www.zdnet.com.au/newstech/os/story/0,2000048630,20272976,00.htm.

Cox, A. (2003). *The risks of closed source computing*. Retrieved April 22, 2003, from: http://www.osopinion.com/Opinions/AlanCox/AlanCox1.html.

DiBona, C., Ockman, S., & Stone, M. (1999). Introduction. In DiBona, Ockman, & Stone (Eds.), *Open sources: Voices of the Open Source revolution* (pp. 1-17). Sebastopol, CA: O'Reilly & Associates, Inc.

Glass, R. L. (2000). The sociology of Open Source: Of cults and cultures. *IEEE Software, 17*(3), 104-105.

Goth, G. (2001). The open market woos Open Source. *IEEE Software, 18*(2), 104-107.

Kenwood, C.A. (2001, July). *A business case study of Open Source Software.* Bedford, MA: The MITRE Corporation.

Koch, C. (2003). Open Source—Your Open Source plan. *CIO, 16*(11), 52-59.

Lawton, G. (2002). The great giveaway. *New Scientist, 173*(2328), 34-37.

Levy, S. (1994). *Hackers: Heroes of the computer revolution.* New York: Penguin Books.

Liu, E. (2002, June 10). *Governments embrace Open Source.* Retrieved May 27, 2003, from: http://www.osopinion.com.

Moody, G. (1998). The wild bunch. *New Scientist, 160*(2164), 42-46.

Nadan, C.H. (2002). Open Source licensing: Virus or virtue? [Electronic Version]. *Texas Intellectual Property Law, 10*(3), 349-377. Retrieved July 1, 2003, from WilsonSelectPlus, Article No. BILP02018629: http://firstsearch.oclc.org/FSIP?sici=1068-1000%28200221%2910%3A3%3C349%3AOSLVOV%3E&dbname=WilsonSelectPlus_FT.

Newmarch, J. (2001). Lessons from Open Source: Intellectual property and courseware. *First Monday*, 6(6), Retrieved May 3, 2003, from: http://firstmonday.org/issues/issue6_6/newmarch/index.html.

Palmer, D. (2003, February 15). *Why not use the GPL? Thoughts on free and Open Source software.* Retrieved May 26, 2003, from: http://www.charvolant.org/~doug/gpl/index.html.

Perens, B. (1999). The Open Source Definition. In DiBona, Ockman, & Stone (Eds.), *Open sources: Voices of the Open Source revolution* (pp. 171-188). Sebastopol, CA: O'Reilly & Associates, Inc.

Raymond, E.S. (1999). *The cathedral and the bazaar: Musings on Linux and Open Source by an accidental revolutionary.* Sebastopol, CA: O'Reilly & Associates, Inc.

Stallman, R. (1999). The GNU Operating System and the Free Software Movement. In DiBona, Ockman, & Stone (Eds.), *Open sources: Voices of the Open Source revolution* (pp. 53-70). Sebastopol, CA: O'Reilly & Associates, Inc.

Torvalds, L. (1999). The Linux edge. In DiBona, Ockman, & Stone (Eds.), *Open sources: Voices of the Open Source revolution* (pp. 101-111). Sebastopol, CA: O'Reilly & Associates, Inc.

Wang, H., & Wang, C. (2001l). Open Source Software adoption: A status report. *IEEE Software, 18*(2), 90-95.

Wu, M.-W., & Lin, Y.-D. (2001). Open Source Software development: An overview. *Computer, 34*(6), 33-38.

Endnotes

[1]   Netcraft, located at http://news.netcraft.com/archives/web_server_survey.html, keeps a constantly updated tally of Web server usage. As of May 2004, based on more than 50 million sites surveyed, Apache Web server powered more than 67% of all Internet sites. Microsoft's Information Internet Server (IIS) accounted for just above 21% of market share.

[2]   Although media coverage, movies, and other publicized incidents have created an image of the hacker as a trickster or law breaker up to no good, breaking into files and stealing credit cards or shutting down power grids, the original meaning of the word hacker was and in the OSS community still is positive. A hacker is someone who writes truly inventive, problem-solving programming, often referred to as a "hack," that other programmers admire for its skill.

Chapter XIV

Cut and Paste:
Remixing Composition Pedagogy for Online Workspaces

John Logie
University of Minnesota, USA

Abstract

This chapter posits a widening gap between workplace writing practices and traditional composition pedagogies. In particular, this chapter suggests that traditional composition pedagogies persist in foregrounding solitary, proprietary authors as model composers, despite the limited applicability of these models. The fields of technical and professional communication, by contrast, have long valued collaboration and modes of authorship that do not always imply the composer's ownership of a given text. These fields' biases are reinforced by the advent of digital media, and the Internet in particular. Digital technologies facilitate collaboration and promote a greater range of authorial stances than their print counterparts. The chapter concludes by offering pedagogical approaches directed at promoting composition pedagogies commensurate with the challenges faced by professional and technical writers working in digital composing spaces.

Introduction: Connections and Disconnections

The fields of professional and technical communication have never quite been reconciled with academia's policing of plagiarism and attendant composition pedagogies. Communicators in professional workplaces often depend upon inherited document templates, collaborative composing strategies, and source texts in which authorship is unstated or diffuse. The traditional academic focus on the proper forms of citation when summarizing, paraphrasing, and quoting does not always speak to the processes involved in generating a technical manual or an online help document. In such documents, questions of audience and content effectively trump questions of authorship and ownership.

Often professional and technical communicators are called upon to effectively "unlearn" the proprietary and individualistic approaches to writing that characterized much of 20th century composition pedagogy. This disjunction is exacerbated when the fluid intellectual property practices of many workplaces are linked to the similarly fluid understandings of intellectual property endemic to the Internet. For example, in an article documenting an early attempt at moving a technical communication class onto the World Wide Web, we find Robert Kramer and Stephen Bernhardt (1999) praising a student who "successfully copied a Web-based bitmapped image, pasted it into a Word document, cropped it into three separate images, made additions to those images, and then supplied contextual text to describe each phase of the solution" (p. 331). While this student clearly demonstrates a range of skills which most professors in any discipline would probably endorse, the foundational step in this student's work is "successful copying," a phrase that might well strike professors outside the fields of professional or technical communication as oxymoronic.

In the following pages, I illustrate the degree to which professional and technical communicators are routinely called upon to distance themselves from principles and practices maintained in traditional composition programs. Professional and technical communicators typically mobilize discursive strategies that both reject and critique traditional composition's focus on the cultivation and celebration of solitary intending agents. This suggests that scholars and practitioners of professional and technical communication should ally with those scholars and critics of composition pedagogy who recognize the potential of Internet technologies in promoting collaboration and enabling more complex modes of discursive agency. Also, because the solitary intending agent is maintained not only by traditional composition pedagogy, but also by current copyright laws, I argue here that professional and technical communicators bear a special obligation to study, critique, and, ultimately, change copyright laws, especially as they apply to the Internet. If professional and technical communicators fail to engage with both composition pedagogy and copyright policy, the likely result will be a radical circumscription of the Internet-based composing practices now commonplace in contemporary workplaces.

Background: Appropriation, Propriety, and Property

Consider the scene of a typical North American college-level technical communication classroom in the 2000s. The room is filled with students who are among the most technologically savvy people on their campus. Some students in the class have interned or worked in industries where they have had ready access to extremely powerful computers and software. When not working or completing assignments for class, these students use computers for self-expression, for socialization, and for entertainment, often downloading music, videos, movies, and electronic texts.

Among most college students, ready access to the World Wide Web has been a given for years. In many cases, this access has been fast and (at least for the students) cheap. They have learned how to create their own Web pages by "borrowing" HTML code from pages they liked, by parsing that code and by pasting their own words and images into spaces created by designers whose names are often unknown.[1] They have downloaded music from KaZaA, or any of the dozens of distributed computing systems allowing computer users to exchange files. They have, from time to time, simply cut and pasted quotes from online sources into the papers they're composing for their classes.

Many of the cultural artifacts these students value are currently available via the Internet. As of this writing, students at many universities are using their high-speed connections to download and watch full-length motion pictures at near-DVD quality. The speedy delivery of full-motion, full-screen video via the Internet will almost certainly be considered wholly unremarkable in a matter of months, as bandwidth expands, compression technologies improve, and the processing power of an affordable computer pushes toward two *billion* cycles per second (two gigahertz). To the extent that students can afford access to current technologies, they will be gaining access to an immense, chaotic library that has the potential to house not only the best that has been thought and said, but also most of the rest of what has been thought and said.

Now consider the following language, taken from the second edition of Killingsworth and Palmer's *Information in Action: A Guide to Technical Communication,* which was published in 1999:

> "[Y]ou will be guilty of *plagiarism*—intellectual theft—if you do not use citations to credit the source of your information, even when you are summarizing and paraphrasing instead of quoting directly. ...Always cite an author's ideas or interpretations, as well as any information that is not available in a general reference book, such as a dictionary or encyclopedia. Such common information is frequently reproduced without citation unless it involves illustrations, which are always strictly copyrighted." (p. 111)

This textbook, which is packaged with a CD-ROM linking the print content to hundreds of relevant sites on the World Wide Web, is to be credited for its anticipation of what it might mean to study and practice technical communication in networked environments, but the plagiarism policy I have excerpted is almost indistinguishable from the plagiarism policies that major research universities have been enforcing since the beginning of the twentieth century. In short, this passage reflects a print-directed, print-focused approach to the topic of plagiarism, and it manages to do so despite Killingsworth and Palmer's considerable attention of the power and potentialities of electronic media throughout their textbook. Killingsworth and Palmer's language, while accurately reflecting the tone and import of typical university plagiarism policies, does not speak to the day-to-day experiences of current technical communication students, or even of college-level students more generally.

For example, imagine a student preparing an assignment for a technical communication classroom in which she develops her own Web-based critical analysis of the communicative breakdowns leading to the disintegration of the space shuttle Columbia. As part of her research effort, the student surfs the Web, locates a brief video clip of CNN's coverage of the shuttle disaster, and incorporates it into the Web-based presentation of her Web-based "paper." In this video clip, the CNN logo is clearly visible (but tiny) in the lower right corner of the screen for the duration of the clip, and so the student decides that no additional information is needed in the "Works Cited" section of the "paper," reasoning that those wishing to verify the clip need only visit CNN's site and do a search on "Columbia." In short, this student does not "use citations to credit the source" of her information, instead relying on what she perceives to be an adequate citation within her borrowed material.

While the student's actions fall below the standards reasonably expected in most composition classrooms, she has not committed the kind of "intellectual theft" that plagiarism policies militate against. Whether the clip was downloaded directly from CNN or from another site wholly unrelated to CNN, the ultimate source of the video clip is arguably apparent. The student has not attempted to pass the clip off as her own original work, and readers have much (if not all) of the information they need to "verify" her "source material." Clearly the print-directed plagiarism policies of most universities do not address themselves to this kind of incomplete "citation." But technical communicators often depend upon similar, loosely cited uses of others' work. This fluidity is reflected in the current edition of *Reporting Technical Information* (2002), in which the authors distinguish between the partial in-text citations typical in journalism and the more formal requirements of academic citation to acknowledge that a range of citation practices can be traced across fields. This text also suggests that students creating websites should "locat[e] pages you would like to imitate or designs you would like to adapt" (p. 676). In a similar vein, Gurak and Lannon (2001) observe in *A Concise Guide to Technical Communication:* "Technical communicators rarely create every word, image, or sound from scratch. Often, just the right diagram, image, sound, or wording will be found in some other material" (p. 105). A professional technical communicator incorporating the same video clip into a PowerPoint presentation would probably not feel any special obligation to credit the source of the video. The student, by contrast, is forced to choose between the demands of her institutional setting and the common practices of her chosen profession. By Killingsworth and Palmer's print-inflected standards, this student is guilty of plagiarism, but by the more fluid standards common to many workplaces, the student has simply composed an effective multimedia document. This tension suggests that we are still struggling to come to terms with the advent of Internet and digital media technologies. I mean "terms" in both the sense of terminology and "terms of use"—the conditions and guidelines that establish reasonable interactions with particular tools.

Rough Cut: Composing Oneself

For two decades, scholars from a variety of disciplines have argued that computer-based discourse technologies are radically transforming both the creation and reception of textual materials. And for a decade, scholars in many disciplines have framed arguments that the Internet and its attendant genres effectively undermine existing understandings of literary and intellectual property. Nevertheless, the first year or two of a typical undergraduate education will, for most students, be marked by pedagogies designed to produce solitary, originary, proprietary *authors* of quasi-literary texts rather than interconnected, collaborative composers of complex documents. Even worse, the policies addressing the use and circulation of texts by students will serve to intimidate and, ultimately, stifle those who wish to model practices common in professional workplaces.

The advent of the Internet, and the increasing scholarly engagement of teachers of technical and professional communication are, after all, only the latest in a series of developments challenging the maintenance of traditional composition pedagogies. In *Standing in the Shadow of Giants: Plagiarists, Authors, and Collaborators,* Howard (1999) concludes, forcefully, that "the figure of the solitary author cannot and should not be sustained as the organizing principle of composition's representations of authorship" (p. 169). But Howard arrives at this conclusion only after documenting the degree to which the solitary author remains favored in composition studies. Howard cites Faigley's 1992 assessment that the rise of postmodern theories of text and production had done little to effect change in composition pedagogy:

> "Where composition studies has proven least receptive to postmodern theory is in surrendering its belief in the writer as an autonomous self, even at a time when extensive group collaboration is practiced in many writing classrooms. Since the beginning of composition teaching in the late nineteenth century, college writing teachers have been heavily invested in the stability of the self and the attendant beliefs that writing can be a means of self-discovery and self-realization." (p. 15)

The maintenance of the writer as an autonomous self within composition studies had, by the time of Faigley's writing, also withstood sharp criticism from successive waves of feminist critics, many of whom rightly pointed out the degree to which this presumed self was routinely situated in a highly gendered economy of literary competition.

Faigley viewed what he described as "the networked classroom" as offering a potentially viable counterweight to traditional composition pedagogies. Faigley describes how "vivid demonstration of the decentering of the subject in electronic discussions" as "unsettling for traditional writing teachers," adding that "it is…difficult for teachers to maintain a notion of students discovering their authentic selves through writing when writers try on and change identities in electronic discussions, even from one message to the next" (p. 191). But seven years later, Howard suggests that the ready availability of networked discursive spaces has done little to transform the teaching of writing in the academy. Howard argues that most contemporary pedagogies reinforce and stabilize definitions of plagiarism at odds with the modes of rhetorical invention common in workplaces and classrooms favoring collaborative pedagogies:

> "The plagiarist is the thief who is not original, but derivative; who works not in solitude, but in the company of others' texts; and who pirates from

these texts and represents the piracy as his or her own. For the representation of plagiarism, the most important property of authorship is that of morality. The property of morality is itself dependent on the belief that originality, proprietership, and autonomy are 'natural truths' about 'real' authorship rather than cultural arbitraries." (p. 100)

While Faigley suggested that networked discursive spaces could counter the maintenance of traditionalist pedagogies and their attendant policing of plagiarism, Howard suggests that even Internet-savvy students internalize the traditionalist presentation of the originary author as model:

"For students, the most powerful property of modern authorship may be the property of originality. …Overwhelmed by data that washes over them in ever-increasing waves—now reaching them through the burgeoning Internet—today's students hold quite a different view of authorship. Many will readily endorse the idea that originality is the hallmark of a 'true' writer *and* that the original ideas are all used up. They therefore believe that nothing is left to them but imitation. …Today's students' imitation is not the glorious affirmation of the medieval and early modern writers, but the sorry repetition of the disempowered. …Many of these student writers are haunted by college regulations against plagiarism that they suspect they regularly break, since they 'know' that nothing they write is or can be original and that they do not acknowledge every single source." (p. 100)

While Faigley posited that networked environments would effect a decentering of the self with largely positive resonances, Howard here suggests that the byproducts of the Internet have, instead, overwhelmed students, leaving them too inundated with others' words to take advantage of the manifold discursive opportunities afforded by new communicative media. For Howard, there is a strong note of tragedy in students concluding that "nothing is left to them but imitation." And indeed, when this depressing conclusion is set against the conventional claims of traditional composition pedagogies to create authentic, intending discursive agents, one is tempted to smash the machines in hopes of recovering a space in which students were free to discover (without interruption) just what it was they had to say. One cannot help but wonder, in this light, whether the Internet and its attendant critical architecture will ultimately take its place alongside feminist and postmodern critiques of traditional composition pedagogies as an arguably failed attempt to decenter concepts that ultimately prove central to how humans understand their creative processes.

But it is not necessarily the case that students who conclude that "nothing is left to them but imitation" have lost the opportunity to develop valuable discursive skills. Indeed, the fields of professional and technical communication often highly value composers who demonstrate particular strengths in reproducing the conventions and genres common in contemporary workplaces. And while imitation has indeed functioned as a marker of failure since the rise of the modern discipline of composition in the late nineteenth century, this is by no means reflective of the larger rhetorical tradition, in which pedagogies incorporating imitation were valorized for the better part of two millennia.

We do well to ask how it is that the relatively recent theoretical constructions of the composing process valorized within traditional composition pedagogy have come to dominate college-level instruction. After all, these pedagogies represent a sharp departure from the long-dominant rhetorical tradition, in which speakers are usually understood as inextricably tethered to their respective audiences. Here it should be noted that what I have referred to as "traditional composition" might also be understood as that strand of composition pedagogy marked, in the late nineteenth and early twentieth centuries as *English* Composition. A full accounting of the social pressures producing valorizations of specifically *English* language and literature is beyond the scope of this chapter. Briefly, I join with scholars like Andrea Lunsford and Kirt Wilson, who have observed that the movement away from rhetorical theory and toward a newly constructed Anglo-American canon served to perpetuate the marginalization of women and African-Americans, among others. A century later, I indulge in the potentially naïve hope that this exclusionary impulse no longer drives the bulk of the choices made in the development of contemporary composition pedagogies. Rather, my sense is that traditionalist composition pedagogies persist, to a large degree, because they reflect an entrenched understanding that coincides with favored modes of teaching literature within English departments, and this pedagogical tradition both informs and structures the thinking of those who set intellectual property and copyright policy in the United States.

In an article entitled "Visualizing English: Recognizing the Hybrid Literacy of Visual and Verbal Authorship on the Web," Craig Stroupe (2000) articulates how Internet composing spaces can appear strange to scholars with a primary commitment to English Studies:

"In an economy and culture increasingly mediated via Internet browsers, success in the 'new work paradigm' described by Web-design expert David Siegel depends less on the individual writer, or even collaborators, producing the well-wrought verbal text and more upon the coordination of a team whose members practice a variety of complementary technical, visual, verbal, and professional discourses. Among these, verbal literacy is not replaced or buried so much as layered *into* a more diverse accumulation of literacies. …As has long been the case in television production and print advertising, Web-based communication makes verbal expertise only one among many forms of literacy and professional/rhetorical authority, any one of which may provide the primary vision for the production as a whole." (p. 608)

Stroupe here highlights "breaks" with standard operating procedure within classes grounded in English studies that are all familiar to technical and professional communicators—team coordination; layered modes of discourse; a decentering of the verbal as necessarily favored discursive mode—all of these function as points of tension within an English Studies frame, but also as long-accepted dogma in technical and professional contexts. Stroupe's work creates an opportunity for dialogue, and indeed, articles like his are critical to promoting the kinds of exchanges needed to prevent technical and professional discourses from functioning as late-arriving participants in students' processes of framing of themselves as rhetorical agents. But Stroupe's article also suggests that those grounded in English-inflected composition pedagogy will prove especially resistant to recognizing communicative opportunities facilitated by the advent of Internet-based composing spaces. And this resistance is complemented by academia's century-old tradition of heavy-handed enforcement of plagiarism, a tradition that both creates and depends upon its legal counterpart: draconian enforcement of copyright. Traditional composition pedagogies have survived successive waves of critical interrogation precisely because these pedagogies coincide neatly with the preferences and positions implicit in United States copyright law.

Cutback: Copyrighting Authors

United States copyright law's individualistic orientation dates back to its inception. The Constitution specifies that among the enumerated powers of Congress is the power "to promote the Progress of Science and useful Arts, by securing for limited Times to Authors and Inventors the exclusive Right to their respective Writings and Discoveries" (Article 1, Section 8). In practice, U.S. intellectual property laws have, almost without exception, been developed around models which posit a single author or inventor generating a given writing or invention. As TyAnna Herrington (2001) observes:

"The term *author* is used regardless of the kind of work created and, in
the case of the legal fiction of corporate and university authorship in the
"work-for-hire" doctrine…regardless of the author's actual participation in creating the work." (p. 41)

The radiation of the author throughout copyright jurisprudence has the effect of
privileging the conventional narrative of literary creation, in which the solitary
author retires to a garret to await inspiration from the hand of a muse or a God,
or perhaps, Wordsworth's "spontaneous overflow of powerful
feelings…recollected in tranquility" (p. 151). Such models are, of course, clearly
at odds with the recursive and collaborative composing practices that have, for
many years, been considered characteristic of technical communication. More
generally, workplace communicators routinely find themselves depending on
laws like the "work-for-hire" standards, which are best understood as back-
formations premised on the laws developed for single authors. Indeed, work-for-
hire can be quickly summarized as a means of recharacterizing a corporate entity
as a solitary, proprietary author.

Throughout current U.S. copyright statutes, the single author is the default. And
this author is expected to generate novel textual material, notable chiefly for its
lack of dependency on existing texts. The principle of fair use, a relatively recent
(1976) addition to U.S. copyright laws, places considerable burdens on those who
wish to make use of others' texts, and ultimately, invites them to gamble. Both
courts and legal critics have long noted Congress' refusal to offer "bright line"
standards to those who are uncertain as to whether a particular "grey area" use
of another's work constitutes infringement. Congress has refused, suggesting
that each case of potential infringement is unique and merits its own evaluative
standard. Nevertheless, U.S. citizens demonstrably long for more definitive
standards, as suggested by the continuing circulation of the apocryphal "10%
rule," an oft-considered but never-adopted set of guidelines specifying a 10%
limit on the use of material from a given work.

Given the degree to which contemporary workplaces call upon writers to
incorporate and re-purpose existing works, the definitive nature of the "10%
rule" is superficially appealing. The uncertainty now attendant to the incorporation of a particularly lengthy passage or a particular media clip would conceivably
be replaced by recourse to simple math. The work is "X" long, and thus I am
entitled to 1/10th of X. But digital technologies offer a profound challenge to this
putatively simple standard.

For purposes of illustration, let's assume that I wished to include the Rolling
Stones' "You Can't Always Get What You Want" as the musical backdrop to
an electronic version of this chapter posted to the World Wide Web. If the "10%
rule" were in place, I could simply review the length of the song (seven minutes

and twenty-eight seconds) and determine that I was entitled to one-tenth of these seconds or 44.8 seconds, roughly enough to capture the chorus of the song, and far preferable to the 13.5 seconds I'd have at my disposal if I chose "Play With Fire" instead. But this is only one way to "slice" the song. Another approach might be to understand the full digital file as the whole, and to sample 10% of the data. Already the MP3 format offers massive compression, transforming large files into much smaller files amenable to file-sharing over even dial-up Internet connections. A low-quality MP3 that nevertheless provides a reasonable approximation of its CD quality parent might be only 10% as large as its parent file. And so, making a questionable interpretation of the apocryphal "10% rule," I determine to stream this compressed file along with my text. It's not quite as appealing as the CD from a sonic standpoint, but it gets the job done. As Jagger sings, "if you try sometimes you just might find, you get what you need."

But if I were to announce to university counsel my plans to post the electronic version of this chapter with the attached MP3 file to my departmental Web page, I am certain that I would be at least discouraged and very likely forbidden to post the MP3. The university's lawyers would rightly point out that my posting of the file, while arguably fair use and arguably falling within the 10% guidelines (even though they are not law), would nevertheless expose the university to *some* level of risk. They might even point out that Allen Klein, owner of the early Rolling Stones catalog, successfully sued the band The Verve for a very brief sample from an orchestral version of the Jagger-Richards song "The Last Time," used in the Verve song "Bittersweet Symphony." The band was forced to relinquish 100% of the royalties for the song and watch helplessly as Klein licensed the song to Nike for use in a commercial. University counsel would recognize that my use of the Rolling Stones song would expose me *and* the university to potentially devastating litigation.

Perhaps the most telling element of this example is the fact that the songwriters, Mick Jagger and Keith Richards, do not own these songs, and have little control over Klein's activities, having bargained away their rights early in their careers. Nevertheless, Anglo-American copyright law enforces Klein's claim as an "heir or assign," and does not treat him any differently than it would an aggrieved creator who had preserved her copyright ownership and objected to a parallel "infringing" appropriation.

Despite the advent of digital technologies that by their very nature transform the standards and techniques by which we achieve functional copies of existing works, U.S. copyright laws insistently perpetuate the single author as creator/ owner of a given work. As communicators in technical and professional fields learned long ago, there is no necessary relationship between one's personal investment of effort in a project and the level of one's legal claim to that project. Indeed, professional and technical communicators have, for years, occupied the margins of copyright law, at times valuing their distance from full accountability for their work products, at times mourning the anonymity with which they sometimes plied their trades.

Final Cut: Copyright in Technical and Professional Communication Classrooms

Instructors in twenty-first century technical and professional communication classrooms owe it to their students to foreground the degree to which their work intersects with intellectual property law. Two elements of U.S. law referenced earlier, "work-for-hire" and fair use, are critical for technical and professional communicators and should be addressed in textbooks and classroom exercises. While these are by no means the only aspects of intellectual property law worthy of discussion in the classroom, both are likely to arise early in the careers of students who go on to professional work. Further, the issues raised by interrogating "work-for-hire" and fair use will likely stimulate independent study and reflection about the reach and nature of U.S. intellectual property laws.

"Work-for-hire" is best understood as the legal substitution of the employer for the creator for purposes of copyright. The U.S. Copyright Act, as revised in 1976, specifies two classes of works as "works made for hire." The first class is works "prepared by an employee within the scope of his or her employment." The second class refers to a wide range of collaborative endeavors, including works: "specially ordered or commissioned for use as a contribution to a collective work, as a part of a motion picture or other audiovisual work, as a translation, as a supplementary work, as a compilation, as an instructional text, as a test, as answer material for a test, or as an atlas." While the first class of works is commonly understood to belong to the employer, the second class requires "express agreement in a written instrument" for the work in question to be considered a work made for hire. In short, it takes a contract.

There are many circumstances in which a work-for-hire agreement is entirely reasonable. For example, work-for-hire is appropriate in cases where a writer is asked to extend the narrative of an already existing character or set of characters. James Bond novels have been published fairly steadily since the death of Bond's creator, Ian Fleming, in 1964. And the James Bond film franchise long ago abandoned any connection to Fleming's novels and short stories. In both cases, the writers preparing contemporary James Bond novels and scripts do so under work-for-hire agreements. These agreements protect the owners of the Bond copyright from any dilution of their rights in this still valuable character. Work-for-hire is also appropriate in many professional contexts. Technical communicators preparing a manual as part of their daily employment have few of the investments of conventional literary authors. Their names commonly would not appear in their completed texts. Their work falls outside the literary business model. These writers have no expectation of royalties. Even so, students training to become technical communicators often feel a strong sense of personal investment in their work, and are sometimes surprised to discover that their legal rights to their work products are so sharply circumscribed.

One in-class exercise that is helpful in sensitizing students to the array of rights associated with their work is to invite them to review a sample work-for-hire contract. I typically frame this exercise by asking students to imagine that they have started work on a reasonably well-paying project as independent contractors, and that this is their first professional project after leaving the university. I then circulate a sample work-for-hire agreement (I'm partial to the example at Lloyd Jassin's Copylaw.com website, owing in large part to its brevity). I ask students to either return the signed form by the next class period if they find the terms acceptable, or to highlight any passages that concern them, and to begin the next class by discussing their concerns with me. Students typically have reservations, and I typically respond by applying some of the kinds of pressure that an employer or corporate counsel might apply. I suggest that the company rarely negotiates contracts, and almost never does so with beginning writers. I imply that the project may be held up or canceled if there is "a problem with the contract." And I implore the writers not to make waves, because it is not worth it for either side to get the lawyers involved. The goal is not to suggest to students that they must refuse any work-for-hire contracts they encounter, but rather to clarify the degree to which students feel a personal investment in their work, and to help them establish the circumstances under which they are willing to transfer their personal rights in their creative works.

Fair use is the second aspect of U.S. Copyright Law that I consider absolutely critical for contemporary technical and professional communicators. The digital workplace routinely involves incorporation and appropriation of existing work, ranging from quotations to clip art. Only *some* of the patterns of use common to technical and professional workplaces are assuredly legal. Unfortunately, the fair use doctrine is among the most difficult areas of intellectual property law, a body of law itself notorious for its complexity. I begin my treatment of fair use by ensuring that students are familiar with both the Constitutional basis for copyright and patent (limited monopoly rights granted to promote progress in "Science and Useful Arts") and the current duration of copyright, roughly "life of the creator plus seventy years" (but with a fixed 95-year term for works of corporate authorship). Lolly Gasaway's "When U.S. Works Pass into the Public Domain" is invaluable in this process, as her handout clearly illustrates the steady inflation in copyright terms during the twentieth century. Students routinely underestimate the duration of the copyright terms, and are rightly troubled when they learn that works from 1923 forward may be protected by copyright. They understand the value of the access to copyrighted works and typically reject the *de facto* public domain cut-off of 1922 as far too distant from the present. Once the scope and duration of copyright have been firmly established, students are especially interested in fair use, as it offers the promise of access even when works are still protected by copyright.

The fair use exception to copyright was codified in the 1976 revision of U.S. Copyright laws. Because the term of copyright was being extended dramatically, researchers, journalists, librarians, and educators lobbied for and won a specific provision in the law protecting reasonable access to texts. The 1976 act specifies "purposes such as criticism, comment, news reporting, teaching (including multiple copies for classroom use), scholarship, or research" as instances where an otherwise infringing use would generally not be subject to penalty. But this agreeably broad statement is undercut to a significant degree by a subsequent "four-point test," which is to be used to determine whether a particular use is infringing or not. The law reads as follows:

> "In determining whether the use made of a work in any particular case is a fair use, the factors to be considered shall include:
>
> 1. The purpose and character of the use, including whether such use is of a commercial nature or is for nonprofit educational purposes;
>
> 2. The nature of the copyrighted work;
>
> 3. The amount and substantiality of the portion used in relation to the copyrighted work as a whole; and
>
> 4. The effect of the use upon the potential market for or value of the copyrighted work."

The effect of these provisions has been considerable uncertainty over whether certain uses constitute infringements or not. Various bodies have petitioned Congress to offer a "bright line" standard in place of the four-point test, but have been rebuffed. Congress apparently prefers for judges to exercise discretion while applying each of the four factors in a dynamic fashion. The results have at times been startling.

One classroom exercise I use is a game entitled "Ought This Be Legal?" I encourage students to play the game with the four-point test in front of them, and

I articulate the facts of a particularly striking copyright ruling or incident. My presentation of a favorite exemplary case runs as follows:

"A noted literary critic is drafting a biography of a famously reclusive novelist. As part of his research, the critic contacts the novelist and asks for an interview. The novelist declines and states his wish that no biographies appear during his lifetime. Nevertheless, the critic continues and discovers that many of the novelist's unpublished letters to friends and professional colleagues have been donated to various university libraries by their original recipients. The critic includes material from the letters in a draft of the biography. The novelist objects and, as required by the law at that time, files registration notices for all of his unpublished letters with the U.S. copyright office. The critic responds by replacing all quoted material from the letters with close paraphrases. The novelist sues the publisher, and complains that the critic's paraphrases of his letters violate the novelist's copyrights in those letters."

After outlining the case, I ask whether the critic's biography ought to be legal under the fair use doctrine. There is typically some disagreement among students. Some argue for respecting the novelist's wishes. Others argue for maximizing scholarly access to texts. After students have an opportunity to determine where they stand, I acknowledge that the facts of the case are drawn from a noted copyright case, *Salinger vs. Random House*, in which Salinger prevailed in his attempt to block the publication of Ian Hamilton's biography as Hamilton had drafted it, with significant paraphrases from Salinger's letters. Hamilton abandoned the project.

This case is especially striking because it places the scholarly desire for access at odds with the creator's discretion over the use and circulation of copyrighted works. The arguments over what's proper sharpen students' sense of the interplay among the four factors critical for a fair use defense, and prepare them for subsequent examples of questionable appropriation and use of intellectual property in Web pages, multimedia projects, and electronic texts. Because students will, increasingly, be called upon to draft complex documents that depend on existing works, it is critical for students to be aware of the challenges that await them as they work in digital environments. A few rounds of "Ought This Be Legal?" serve to educate students to both the letter of the law and the silences within the law, which can only be addressed by informed judgment.

Paste: Remixing Academic and Professional Discourse

Scholars and students of professional and technical communication are particularly well-suited to the task of shaping future policies, both academic and legal, with respect to the use, appropriation, and circulation of digital texts. Committed members of these disciplines have developed both the communicative skills and the critical tools that are needed to offer constructive interventions in disputes over ownership and use. More importantly, their regular engagement with modes of discursive production that defy the expectations and biases of copyright law places them in a special position. The types of assignments common in technical and professional workplaces promote attentiveness to the complexity of textual ownership. This was true even before the advent of digital media, but it is especially true now that communicators in these fields are presented with increasingly ready access to one another's words, ideas, work products, and with the tools needed to expeditiously restructure and repurpose these materials. Principled interventions from scholars working in technical and professional fields could offer others the benefit of an altogether rare view of copyright. In technical and professional communication, questions of individual artistry are typically subsumed by the need for collective effort and by deference to a particular message. As a practical matter, this means professional and technical communicators need to make space for a regular engagement with legal matters, and to incorporate a measure of legal scholarship—and perhaps activism—into their work lives.

Action on this front should be complemented by efforts by professional and technical communicators to intensify their developing exchanges with scholars in composition. (And perhaps we should observe that several scholars would describe themselves as traveling comfortably across these perceived disciplinary boundaries.) If technical and professional communicators are bracketed by composition pedagogies that by and large valorize the solitary author on one hand, and copyright laws that do the same on the other, they must take steps to ensure that the particular understandings of authorship and textual ownership available to them become part of the ongoing discussions that will determine how and perhaps whether we will make use of one another's work in the 21st century. In particular, their discussions with composition scholars should highlight the degree to which their work experience involves discovering modes of discourse unanticipated by pedagogies grounded in authorial empowerment or urging discovery of an authentic inner voice. Professional and technical communicators bespeak a more layered position, reflecting the daily challenges of millions of working writers who create discursive power *without* necessarily assuming the mantle of authorship, and *without* necessarily entering into the economy of plagiarism fostered by the academy.

References

Bernhardt, S., & Kramer, R. (1999). Moving instruction to the Web: Writing as multi-tasking. *Technical Communication Quarterly,* 319-336.

Copyright Law of the United States of America, Title 17, Chapter 1, Section 101. Retrieved November 30, 2003, from: http://www.copyright.gov/title17/92chap1.html.

Faigley, L. (1992). *Fragments of rationality: Postmodernity and the subject of composition.* Pittsburgh, PA: University of Pittsburgh Press.

Gasaway, L. When works pass into the public domain. Retrieved on November 30, 2003, from: http://www.unc.edu/~unclng/public-d.htm.

Gurak, L., & Lannon., J.M. (2000). *A concise guide to technical communication.* New York: Addison Wesley Longman.

Herrington, T.K. (2001). *Controlling voices: Intellectual property, humanistic studies, and the Internet.* Carbondale, IL: Southern Illinois University Press.

Howard, R.M. (1999). *Standing in the shadow of giants: Plagiarists, authors, collaborators.* Stamford, CT: Ablex.

Houp, K.W., Pearsall, T.E., Tebeaux, E., & Dragga, S. (2002). *Reporting technical information* (10th ed.). New York: Oxford University Press.

Jassin, L.J. *Work-for-hire agreement (flat fee).* Retrieved November 30, 2003, from: http://www.copylaw.com/forms/Workhire.html.

Jerome D. Salinger a/k/a J. D. Salinger, Plaintiff-Appellant v. Random House, Inc. and Ian Hamilton, Defendants-Appellees. (1987). Retrieved November 30, 2003, from: http://www.bc.edu/bc_org/avp/cas/comm/free_speech/salinger.html.

Killingsworth, M.J., & Palmer, J. (1999). *Information in action* (2nd ed.). Boston, MA: Allyn & Bacon.

Stroupe, C. (2000). Visualizing English: Recognizing the hybrid literacy of visual and verbal authorship on the Web. *College English, 62*(5), 607-632.

Wordsworth, W. (1993). From preface to lyrical ballads. In M.H. Abrams (Ed.), *The Norton Anthology of English Literature* (6th ed., Volume 2, pp. 141-152). New York: W.W. Norton & Company.

Endnote

[1]   Online HTML tutorials routinely endorse "stealing" and revising HTML code from exemplary Web pages as one of the best ways to learn HTML coding techniques, and the major Web browsers have long enabled both the viewing and saving of HTML source code.

About the Editors

Kirk St.Amant is an Assistant Professor with the Department of English at Texas Tech University (USA), and he has a background in anthropology, international government, and technical communication. His research interests include intercultural communication with a focus on how online communication technologies affect cross-cultural interactions. He has taught online courses in intercultural communication for Mercer University and for James Madison University, and he has taught courses in e-commerce, distance education, and business communication in the Ukraine as a part of the USAID-sponsored Consortium for the Enhancement of Ukrainian Management Education (CEUME).

Pavel Zemliansky is an Assistant Professor of rhetoric and writing at James Madison University (USA) where he teaches courses in composition, computers and writing, and stylistics. Together with Wendy Bishop, he co-edited *The Subject is Research: Processes and Practices*, published by Boynton/Cook Heinemann in 2001. His collection, *Research Writing Revisited: A Sourcebook for Teachers,* also co-edited with Wendy Bishop, is forthcoming from Boynton/Cook Heinemann in the fall of 2004. He is the author of book chapters and articles on research writing pedagogy and computers and writing which have appeared in such journals as *Composition Forum*, *Kairos*, and *Virginia English Bulletin.*

About the Authors

Wendy Warren Austin, an Assistant Professor at Edinboro University of Pennsylvania (USA), teaches technical writing and first-year composition. She earned her Master's Degree in Rhetoric and Composition from Purdue University and her PhD from Indiana University of Pennsylvania. She has also published in *Kairos: A Journal of Rhetoric, Technology, and Pedagogy* and *Intercom*, a magazine published by the Society for Technical Communication. In the rare moments when she is unoccupied by work, she likes to watch movies and travel with her husband Dan, go snorkeling, and read mystery novels. She is currently working on a book about plagiarism.

David Blakesley is Associate Professor of English and Director of Professional Writing at Purdue University (USA), where he also co-directs of the Center for Digital Publishing. He is the author of *The Elements of Dramatism* (Longman, 2002) and the editor of *The Terministic Screen: Rhetorical Perspectives on Film* (SIU Press, 2003). He also co-edits *The Writing Instructor*, a networked journal and digital community. In 2003, he created Parlor Press, an independent scholarly publishing company. His forthcoming books include *FAQ: A Writer's Reference for the Digital Age* (Thomson/Wadsworth, 2004) and *Illuminating Rhetoric: A Guide to Seeing, Reading, and Writing* (Mayfield/McGraw-Hill, 2005).

Melody Bowdon is Assistant Professor of English at the University of Central Florida (USA), where she coordinates the Graduate Certificate in Professional Writing and teaches writing courses from the undergraduate to PhD levels. She is co-author with Blake Scott of *Service-Learning in Technical and Professional Communication*, part of the Allyn and Bacon series on technical communication, and her work has been published in journals such as *College English* and *Technical Communication Quarterly*. She is currently working on a new book project called *Professional Writing in the Nonprofit Sector*. She can be reached at mbowdon@mail.ucf.edu.

Stacey L. Connaughton, an Assistant Professor in the Department of Communication at Rutgers University, earned her PhD from the University of Texas at Austin in 2002. Her research interests include identity, identification, and leadership, particularly as they relate to virtual organizations and political parties. She teaches graduate and undergraduate courses in organizational communication theory, leadership, interviewing, and stakeholder groups. Dr. Connaughton is the Director of the Student Leadership Development Institute in the School of Communication, Information, and Library Studies at Rutgers University (USA). She has facilitated workshops and written guidebooks for corporate, governmental, educational administrative, and student groups in the areas of leadership, team-building, and work relationships.

Mark R. Freiermuth is an Associate Professor in the Center for Language Research at the University of Aizu in Japan, where he teaches EST/ESP to computer science students. Besides his research interests in Internet simulations, he is also involved in computer-mediated communication research, focusing primarily on the discourse features of Internet chat. His most recent publications and presentations have reflected these research interests.

Timothy D. Giles has been using computers to teach writing course for the past 15 years. He teaches with the Department of Writing and Linguistics at Georgia Southern University (USA). His other essays on computer-assisted composition have appeared in the *Journal of Developmental Education* and the *Journal of Technical Writing and Communication*. His other research interests include technical communication pedagogy, rhetoric of science, and Internet studies. He recently completed his PhD with the Department of Rhetoric, Scientific, and Technical Communication at the University of Minnesota, St. Paul.

Mark D. Hawthorne came to James Madison University (USA) in 1974. He taught in the English Department and published articles and books on Anglo-Irish and contemporary American literature and theory. Beginning in 1983, he wrote programs, gave conference papers, and published articles on computer-assisted literary research, theory, and bibliography. Between 1986 and 1989, he built and directing the English Department's first computer lab. During the 1990s, he began teaching courses on online research, computational literary statistics, and

Web design. In 1999, he joined the Institute of Technical and Scientific Communication, where he teaches online electronic publication, electronic graphic design, and document design.

Julia Lavid is a Professor at the Universidad Complutense of Madrid, Spain, where she teaches several courses on English Linguistics, Computational and Corpus Linguistics, and the contrastive analysis of English and Spanish. Her research expertise focuses on functional approaches to language and its computational applications, more specifically on language technologies such as Natural Language Generation, a field which she started to develop in 1990 as a Visiting Researcher at the Information Sciences Institute of the University of Southern California, Los Angeles, USA. She has participated as Team Leader and Site Manager of several EU-funded projects on language technologies, and has published extensively both at a national and at an international level in this interdisciplinary field.

Amy Lee Locklear received her BA in English Literature from the College of William and Mary in Virginia. Her MA in English from Auburn University, Alabama, included an emphasis on both Literature and Rhetoric/Composition, as reflected in her thesis, "Expressing the Inexpressible: An Alternative Rhetorical Approach to Reading Elie Wiesel's *Night.*" She currently teaches both traditional and online freshman composition courses at Auburn University–Montgomery and Kaplan College (online) (USA). Her research interests include composition theory and pedagogy, writing center theory and pedagogy, comparative literature, holocaust literature, and technology in the classroom. She can be reached at almlocklear@knology.net.

John Logie is an Assistant Professor of Rhetoric at the University of Minnesota (USA). His research focuses on rhetorical invention and textual ownership, with a particular focus on how these issues play out in digital environments. Logie's articles have appeared in *Rhetoric Society Quarterly, Rhetoric Review, First Monday, Computers and Composition,* and a number of edited volumes. He is currently working on a book-length project addressing the rhetorical features of the World Wide Web.

Jo Mackiewicz received her PhD in Applied Linguistics from Georgetown University, where she studied politeness strategies used in writing center tutoring interactions. Currently an Assistant Professor in the Composition Department and Linguistics Program at the University of Minnesota Duluth (USA), she teaches technical writing and linguistics. Her research interests include discourse analysis, technical writing, research methods, and website usability. She has published in *The Journal of Technical Writing and Communication, IEEE Transactions on Professional Communication, Technical Communication,* and *Business Communication Quarterly.* She is a co-investigator for the Study of Information Design and Processing at UMD. She can be reached at jmackiew@d.umn.edu.

Shawn McIntosh is co-author with John Pavlik of the textbook *Converging Media: An Introduction to Mass Communication* and the forthcoming *Newswriting for Television and Interactive Television* (with Peter Morello and Fred Shook). He is a Lecturer in Strategic Communications at Columbia University's School of Continuing Education and an Adjunct Faculty Member at Iona College, where he has taught online journalism, website publishing, and feature writing. He was a Co-Site Manager and Senior Producer at the online learning website Fathom.com. He also worked as an editor and freelance journalist for 10 years in Tokyo and London. He graduated from the Columbia University Graduate School of Journalism with a concentration in new media, and is a doctoral student in the journalism and mass communication department at Rutgers University (USA).

Jason Nolan is Scholar in Residence with the Knowledge Media Design Institute and Senior Fellow with the McLuhan Program in Culture and Technology at the University of Toronto (Canada), and a Lecturer in Early Childhood Education at Ryerson University. He has been running collaborative virtual environments for almost a decade, and has recently extended his interest to Blogs and Wikis. Present projects include co-editing the forthcoming *International Handbook of Virtual Learning Environments* and planning *The Encyclopedia of Learning Environments,* both with Kluwer Academic Publishers.

Rhonna J. Robbins-Sponaas currently teaches writing and literature with Florida State University (USA), particularly in the English Department's distance program. She holds a Master's of Arts in English (Creative Writing), and her doctoral dissertation is focused on the writings of two 19th-century American women writers. She serves as Executive Director for Project Achieve MOO, and continues to expand her studies of online teaching tools and pedagogies. Current projects include a book on Norway for elementary and junior-high school readers, and another about teaching writing online for higher education students.

Brent D. Ruben is a Distinguished Professor (PII) of Communication and

Organizational Psychology, and Executive Director of the Center for Organizational Development and Leadership at Rutgers University (USA). He is the author or editor of 40 books and 100 book chapters and journal articles on communication processes in individual, interpersonal, health, organizational, intercultural, and educational settings. Dr. Ruben received the 2003 National Association of College and University Business Officers (NACUBO), Professional Development and Scholarship Award. He also provides professional consultation to a variety of educational, corporate, healthcare, and governmental organizations.

Brian Still is an Information Technology Consultant and Lecturer teaching Technical Communications in the English Department at Texas Tech University (USA).

Nancy A. Wiencek is a graduate of Douglass College, Rutgers University, with a BA in Communication and Economics. She earned her MS at the University of Louisiana at Lafayette and is a PhD candidate at Rutgers University. She has more than 15 years of experience in strategic planning and management of public relations and fundraising initiatives, as well as extensive experience with executive-level communication initiatives. After a one-year appointment as Visiting Assistant Professor, Ms. Wiencek was appointed Assistant Professor of Communication at Monmouth University (USA) in the fall of 2001, where she specializes in public relations, research methods, and professional communication courses.

Index

software licensing fee 184
source code 184, 281
spatial metaphors 25
spatial politics 112
state of MOO 136
state of the art 211
statistical variation 4
student assessment 183
student satisfaction 72
student-centered approach 72
student-centered learning 160
"successful copying" 300
supplemental Web-based course 162
sustained dialogue 221
synchronous communication 71
synchronous communication environ-
    ment 233
synchronous/asynchronous dichotomy
    137

T

task-oriented activities 269
teacher assessment 183
teacher feedback 68
teaching communication 46
teaching methods 159
teaching of writing 27
teaching scenarios 159
team writing 194
technical communication 26, 30,
    90, 306, 308
technical communication classroom 88
technical communication instruction 35
technical communication instructors 25
technical communication students 302
technical communicators 300
technical documentation 121
technical writers 299
technical writing 25, 107
technical writing course 108
technological digression 133
technological literacy 250
technology trends 294
telecommuting 261
telemanagement 266, 267
telework 261

Telework America 262
telework arrangement 264, 267
Telnet-type client 141
text identity 242
text MOOs 134
text-based communication 47, 71
text-based MOOs 134
text-based multimedia environments
    130
text-based virtual environments 131
textual analysis computing tools (TACT)
    15
traditional composition pedagogies 299
traditional F2F learning environment
    234
traditional paradigm 43
trouble shooting 47
tutors' comments 222

U

U.S. Copyright Act 310
U.S. intellectual property laws 310

V

valuable collaborative environment 130
values-based learning 47
verbal abuse 71
virtual community 139
virtual environment 147
virtual learning environment 130
virtual networks 107
virtual teams/organizations 41
visual design principles 25
visual design theory 34

W

Web server 279
Web writing assignments 34, 24
Web-based communications 119
Web-based course 157, 160, 177
Web-based education 121
Web-based environment 177
Web-based information economy
    107, 119
Web-based learning 177

Copyright © 2005, Idea Group Inc. Copying or distributing in print or electronic forms without written permission of Idea Group Inc. is prohibited.

BROADEN YOUR IT COLLECTION
WITH IGP JOURNALS

Idea
Group
Publishing

is an innovative international publishing company, founded in 1987, specializing in information science, technology and management books, journals and teaching cases. As a leading academic/scholarly publisher, IGP is pleased to announce the introduction of 14 new technology-based research journals, in addition to its existing 11 journals published since 1987, which began with its renowned Information Resources Management Journal.

Free Sample Journal Copy

Should you be interested in receiving a **free sample copy** of any of IGP's existing or upcoming journals please mark the list below and provide your mailing information in the space provided, attach a business card, or email IGP at journals@idea-group.com.

Upcoming IGP Journals

January 2005

Int. Journal of Data Warehousing & Mining
Int. Journal of Business Data Comm. & Networking
International Journal of Cases on E-Commerce
International Journal of E-Business Research
International Journal of E-Collaboration
Int. Journal of Electronic Government Research
Int. Journal of Info. & Comm. Technology Education

Int. Journal of Enterprise Information Systems
Int. Journal of Intelligent Information Technologies
Int. Journal of Knowledge Management
Int. Journal of Mobile Computing & Commerce
Int. Journal of Technology & Human Interaction
Int. J. of Web-Based Learning & Teaching Tech.'s

Established IGP Journals

Annals of Cases on Information Technology
Information Management
Information Resources Management Journal
Information Technology Newsletter
Int. Journal of Distance Education Technologies
Int. Journal of IT Standards and Standardization Research

International Journal of Web Services Research
Journal of Database Management
Journal of Electronic Commerce in Organizations
Journal of Global Information Management
Journal of Organizational and End User Computing

Name:_____ Affiliation: _____

Address: _____

_____

E-mail:_____ Fax: _____

**Visit the IGI website for more information on
these journals at www.idea-group.com/journals/**

IDEA GROUP PUBLISHING

A company of Idea Group Inc.

701 East Chocolate Avenue, Hershey, PA 17033-1240, USA
Tel: 717-533-8845; 866-342-6657 • 717-533-8661 (fax)

Journals@idea-group.com   www.idea-group.com